Qualifying Times

SPORT AND SOCIETY

Series Editors
Randy Roberts
Aram Goudsouzian

Founding Editors
Benjamin G. Rader
Randy Roberts

A list of books in the series appears at the end of this book.

Qualifying Times

Points of Change
in U.S. Women's Sport

JAIME SCHULTZ

University of Illinois Press
URBANA, CHICAGO, AND SPRINGFIELD

Chapter 6 is adapted from Jaime Schultz, "Discipline and Push-Up:
Female Bodies, Femininity, and Sexuality in Popular Representations
of Sports Bras," *Sociology of Sport Journal* 21, no. 2 (2004): 185–205.

Library of Congress Cataloging-in-Publication Data
Schultz, Jaime.
Qualifying times : points of change in U.S. women's sport /
Jaime Schultz.
pages cm. — (Sport and society)
Includes bibliographical references and index.
ISBN 978-0-252-03816-7 (hardcover : alk. paper) —
ISBN 978-0-252-07974-0 (pbk. : alk. paper) —
ISBN 978-0-252-09596-2 (e-book)
1. Sports for women—United States—History. 2. Sports for women—
Social aspects—United States. 3. Women athletes—United States—
History. I. Title.
GV709.18.U6S38   2014
796.082—dc23   2013023555

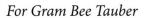

For Gram Bee Tauber

Contents

Acknowledgments

I would like to begin by acknowledging Willis G. Regier, director of the University of Illinois Press and the person who really made this book possible. I first met Bill at a North American Society for Sport History conference. More accurately, Melvin L. Adelman made sure we met, and for that (and a host of other reasons) I am indebted to Mel. Since that first encounter, Bill has been generous with his support, advice, editing skills, and thoughtfulness. I am lucky to know him.

Bill also had the influence and acumen to convince Patricia Vertinsky and Sarah Fields to review drafts of this manuscript. I cannot think of two scholars for whom I have more respect. I am grateful for the time, energy, and insight they devoted to helping me see this project to fruition.

In truth, I have had a lot of assistance along the way. A number of archivists and librarians took time out of their busy schedules to help me sift through and locate sources, including Jeffrey Monseau and Betty Mann at the Springfield College Archives; Troy Growen at the International Tennis Museum and Hall of Fame; William Finley, head of the Special Collections and College Archives at the University of North Carolina at Greensboro's Jackson Library; Jason Speck, assistant university archivist at the University of Maryland Libraries; and David Kelly, a former librarian at the Library of Congress. A grant from the Martha Blakeney Hodges Special Collections and University Archives allowed me to travel to the University of North Carolina at Greensboro, and the University of Maryland's General Research Board provided a summer stipend so that I could devote my time to writing.

Several people were kind enough to read drafts of individual chapters and provide important feedback. Thank you to Susan Cahn, Mark Dyreson, Katherine Jamieson, Kris Newhall, Catriona Parratt, and Alison Wrynn.

Thank you to Tad Ringo, senior editor at the University of Illinois Press, and Annette Wenda, copyeditor extraordinaire. Their careful and attentive edits were a tremendous help. There were also those who allowed me to interview them and advised me on ways to make this work stronger. To Martha Adams, Mildred Barnes, Bobbi Bennett, Jarnell Bonds, Della Durant, Joan Hult, Bev Johnson, Joan Johnson, Karen Johnson, Lucille Magnusson, Dorothy McKnight, Felecia Mulkey, Carole Oglesby, Roberta Park, Charlotte West, and Eula West, I express my most heartfelt appreciation.

Others have offered counsel, encouragement, and, most important, amity: Thomas Hunt, Maureen Smith, Rita Liberti, Chuck Korr, Russell Field, Malcolm Maclean, Gary Osmond, Murray Phillips, Dan Nathan, Sam Regalado, Doug Booth, Andy Doyle, Allen Guttmann, Wray Vamplew, Ronald Smith, Steve Gietschier, David Andrews, Damion Thomas, Pat Griffin, Jan Todd, Susan Brownell, Ellyn Barges, Karl Newell, and Scott Kretchmar. This list also includes my fellow graduate students at the University of Iowa who have remained friends over the years. I especially thank Shelley Lucas, Theresa Walton, Laura Chase, Bobbi Knapp, Jun-Nicole Matsushita, Penni Winberg, Kirsten Wolfe, Christina Johnson, and Amy Wilson.

It was at the University of Iowa, specifically in the Cultural Studies of Sport program (now part of the American Studies Department), that I really began to work on this project. There, I encountered wonderful mentors, including Dawn Stephens, Christine Grant, Bonnie Slatton, and Kathleen Janz, and my advisers, Susan Birrell and Catriona Parratt. I could not ask for better role models—both personally and professionally.

Since then, I have been fortunate to work with my own graduate students, and several played important roles in the writing of this book. Jennifer Collins's master's thesis on black elite female athletes and their hair was important for helping me think through my introductory chapter, and she was gracious enough to share her interview transcripts with me. Sarah Olson's research on competitive cheerleading was also invaluable. Sara Roser-Jones put in long hours helping me with the often-tedious work of digging up primary source material, and she did it with characteristic diligence and good humor. Andrew Linden helped me track down difficult resources and permissions in the final stages of this project, and I could not have finished without him.

I must acknowledge my family for its constant guidance, strength, and reassurance. Whether they like it or not, this includes the Heftys. Thank you for letting me be a part of your wonderful, wacky clan. As for my family who had no choice in the matter, well, if I could write as well as my grandmothers, Marcella Schultz and Bernice Tauber, this book would vastly improve. They were talented, smart, and inspiring women, and I am sorry I failed to finish sooner. I miss them dearly. To Gram Bee, I dedicate this book for reasons too numerous to recount. I love her muchly.

My little brothers, Rob and David Schultz, are smarter, funnier, and more accomplished than I will ever be. And I cannot imagine any child feeling more loved or supported than my parents, Robert and Deborah Schultz, have made me feel. I do not know what I have done to deserve so much goodness in my life, but I hope they never doubt how much I appreciate everything. Finally and above all, I thank Paul Hefty, my partner, my best friend, and Nella Bee's dad.

Abbreviations

AACCA	American Association of Cheerleading Coaches and Administrators
AAHPER	American Alliance for Health, Physical Education, and Recreation (before 1975: American Association for Health, Physical Education, and Recreation)
AAHPERD	American Alliance for Health, Physical Education, Recreation, and Dance
AAU	Amateur Athletic Union
ABP	Athlete Biological Passport
AIAW	Association of Intercollegiate Athletics for Women
AIBA	International Amateur Boxing Association
AMA	American Medical Association
APEA	American Physical Education Association
APER	American Physical Education Review
A&T	Acrobatics and Tumbling
ATA	American Tennis Association
CIAW	Commission on Intercollegiate Athletics for Women
CWA	Committee on Women's Athletics
DCC	Dallas Cowboy Cheerleaders
DGWS	Division for Girls and Women's Sports
ERA	Equal Rights Amendment
FIFA	Fédération Internationale de Football Association
HEW	Department of Health, Education, and Welfare
IAAF	International Association of Athletics Federation
IOC	International Olympic Committee
LPGA	Ladies Professional Golf Association
NAAF	National Amateur Athletic Federation
NAGWS	National Association of Girls & Women's Sports

NAIA	National Association of Intercollegiate Athletics
NAPECW	National Association of Physical Education for College Women
NCA	National Cheerleaders Association
NCAA	National Collegiate Athletic Association
NCATA	National Collegiate Acrobatics and Tumbling Association
NCSTA	National Competitive Stunts and Tumbling Association
nmol/L	nanomoles per liter
OCR	Office of Civil Rights
PEP	Performance Enhancing Polymorphism
PFCP	Primary Familial and Congenital Polycythemia
SPRINT	Sports Project Referral and Information Network (part of WEAL)
UCA	Universal Cheerleaders Association
USLTA	United States Lawn Tennis Association
USOC	United States Olympic Committee
WADA	World Anti-Doping Agency
WEAL	Women's Equity Action League
WNBA	Women's National Basketball Association
WPS	Women's Professional Soccer
WTA	Women's Tennis Association
WUSA	Women's United Soccer Association

Qualifying Times

Introduction

The Politics of the Ponytail

Consider the ponytail, that seemingly innocuous mass of hair bundled together on an individual's head. It might be worn loose or pulled tight, bound by a casual length of string or secured with a mass-produced elastic. It might be positioned at any number of spots: the nape of one's neck, the crown of one's skull, or the side of one's head should the fickle winds of fashion so dictate. Slicked backed, fringed with bangs, teased for volume, softened by tendrils, haphazardly fastened, or deliberately styled, it might sprout from the follicles of one who exists anywhere along the sexual, gendered, cultural, or historical continuum, though often with varying degrees of social acceptance.

Now consider the ponytail in the context of U.S. women's sport. Better yet, consider U.S. women's sport without its ponytailed participants. It is difficult, for the ubiquitous style has become a hallmark of female athleticism.[1] For confirmation, one need only visit the nearest court, field, gymnasium, track, or diamond where females congregate in athletic communion. Gaining popularity with American girls in the 1950s and 1960s, "especially among cheerleaders," writes Victoria Sherrow in *The Encyclopedia of Hair*, "women athletes have worn ponytails for practical reasons and to show their personal styles."[2] Over the years, it has become so synonymous with girls' and women's sports that administrators wedge the term into countless team names, league titles, and competitive events. Journalists and scholars use it as shorthand for female athletes. The finals of the 2009 National Collegiate Athletic Association (NCAA) Women's Basketball Tournament pitted perennial powerhouse Connecticut against a Louisville team described as "Rocky in ponytails." Ashley Martin, the first woman to play and score in a Division I football game became "the pony-tailed place kicker." Title IX's measure for proportionality has been (incorrectly) reduced to "counting ponytails."[3] Nearly every NCAA logo for women's sports shows the silhouette of an athlete with ponytail—trailing from beneath batting and ice hockey helmets, or swept back by the distinctive motions of field hockey, lacrosse, rowing, tennis, track and field, volleyball, soccer, golf, gymnastics, cross-country, and bowling. More than a cultural icon, the ponytail inspires a range of related merchandise. In the commercial sporting goods market, products abound to accommodate and adorn the style. There are hats, visors, helmets, headbands, "scrunchies," ribbons, hair clips, and pom-poms specifically marketed for the ponytailed (female) athlete.

For those who lack the requisite hair length or texture for the desired look, there are manufactured hairpieces available for purchase. Nowhere is the ersatz ponytail more common than in cheerleading, particularly those stylized Shirley Temple–ringlet curls that perpetually bounce along the sidelines or glow beneath the spotlight, be it in service to the competition of others or in contests of their own. The phony pony serves a dual purpose: it gives members of the squad the uniform look they strive to achieve while also signifying a bubbly, wholesome, and spirited persona that contributes to the emotional labor the female cheerleader performs—that overdetermined femininity executed for spectators (and, increasingly, for judges) that often masks the athleticism and physical demands required of her.

Gymnastics provides similar imagery, both in terms of athletes who disguise their efforts with a veneer of cheerful ease and in its preponderance of ponytailed participants. When the 2008 U.S. Olympic women's gymnastics team stood atop the podium to receive their silver medals, each squad member sported an identical taut and polished hairstyle. Throughout the Games, audiences watched as the gymnasts made their way to the floor in single file as their big red, embellishing bows bobbed in unison. Commenting on the spectacle, journalist Helen Anders wrote that "their lively ponytails aren't just functional; they also add an extra degree of technical cuteness."[4] What Anders articulates, perhaps inadvertently, is that the ponytail constructs and normalizes a particular version of femininity. There is a practicality to the ponytail, but it also communicates an aesthetic that contributes to cultural perceptions of female gymnasts.[5] It is more than a utilitarian hairdo; it is both product and producer of gendered ideologies. It is not just that the ponytail keeps a female athlete's hair out of her face. It conveys significant understandings and expectations about the girl or woman to whom it is attached and, by extension, to others who participate in sport and physical culture.

The ponytail's "cuteness" speaks to dimensions of gender and age in the context of women's sports, a message furthered by historian Bill Palmer's book on the rise of women's intercollegiate soccer, *Girls in Ponytails Chasing a Ball*. With just six words, the probably well-intentioned Palmer manages to infantalize, trivialize, and degrade several decades of toil and triumph in at least three significant ways. First, advocates of women's sports regularly criticize the use of "girls" to identify college-age athletes, arguing that the term "stresses the presumed immaturity and irresponsibility of women."[6] Second, young children, the unskilled, and the newly initiated chase the soccer ball. Elite-level athletes do not. Finally, the assumption that these "girls" who while away those forty-five-minute halves "chasing a ball" are all "in ponytails" overgeneralizes the appearance of female athletes and provides an inappropriate and hackneyed shorthand for a range of women who play the sport.

Women's soccer frequently intertwines with ponytail discourse and imagery. In an evidently newsworthy incident in 2009, University of New Mexico defender Elizabeth Lambert brought down her opponent (Brigham Young University's Kassidy Shumway) with a violent and flagrant yank of her ponytail. Video of the foul went viral and quickly made Lambert "an ignominious sensation on television, the Internet and talk radio."[7] Commentary often ignored the precipitating cheap shots and rough play, instigated by players from both teams, and pronounced the "hair-pulling" episode most remarkable. Lambert's actions inspired discussions of fair play, sexism, and the (d)evolution of women's sports and titillated those viewers who saw it as "sexy catfighting between two women."[8] As Lambert later told the *New York Times*, "I definitely feel because I am a female it did bring about a lot more attention than if a male were to do it." She was surprised by indications that "a lot of people think I have a lot of sexual aggression."[9] The ponytail effect significantly gendered and, consequently, sexualized the violence.

Ponytails seemed especially pronounced in relation to the U.S. women's national soccer team that won the 1999 World Cup, a group one television commentator repeatedly referred to as the "ponytail express."[10] *New York Times* reporter Jeré Longman noted that the team was composed of a "homogenous group of mostly white women in ponytails," and similar comments, according to communications scholar Helene A. Shugart, appeared throughout media coverage of the event. Shugart found that reports tended to emphasize the conventionally feminine attractiveness of players like Mia Hamm, whose "ponytail was noted in virtually every newspaper and magazine article that referenced her."[11] *Newsweek* identified Brandi Chastain, whose penalty kick clinched the victory for the U.S. team, as "a flamboyant, ponytailed blonde." And no less than the U.S. Women's National Soccer Team deemed their official fan club the "Ponytail Posse," explaining, "Yeah, yeah, so the whole ponytail thing . . . well, it's meant to convey the combination of femininity and athleticism that is inherent in putting your hair up in a ponytail."[12] In this case, the hairstyle serves as a signifier for the grammatical conjunction *and*—connecting *femininity* and *athleticism* to suggest that the two terms need something to mitigate their ostensible incongruity.[13]

In the world of women's sports, *femininity* often becomes a "code word for heterosexuality," and the ponytail serves as an accoutrement to one's feminine presentation of self.[14] Sociologist Annemarie Jutel argues that the "almost mandatory pony-tail" in women's sports is part of a "heterosexy demeanour" that athletes assert as a means to "visually identify themselves as straight." Juxtaposing the Brazilian and American women's soccer teams at the 2000 Olympic Games, critical scholar Judith (Jack) Halberstam speculates on both the hairstyle and the sexuality of the athletes: "The Brazilian team was clearly full of lesbians and had many, many women playing with extremely short hair, such that if you glanced at them, you wouldn't have been able to tell at first glance whether it was a male or a female player on the field. Now the [U.S.] women's team is so anxious to keep those ponytails, for display, so it's all very well for Brandi Chastain to have a very muscular upper body, but she's not shaving her head anytime soon."[15] To suggest that the ponytail is used "for display"—as a means to moderate the muscular and athletic female body and to disassociate that body from the continued presence of the lesbian stigma in sport—implies that there is a normative, perhaps compulsory, feminine aesthetic to which many women conform.

Jutel, Halberstam, and others allude to a shift in the concept of the "female apologetic," a term originally conceived in the 1970s to explain women's performance of emphasized femininity as compensation—as apology—for their presence in the traditionally male domain of sport.[16] The obvious styling of makeup, costume, jewelry, and hair, theorists proposed, helped to reconcile role conflict between conventionally feminine subject positions and the masculine qualities that sport required. Yet as scholar-activist Pat Griffin and others contend, with the increasing acceptance of women's place in sport, the "female apologetic" now translates into a lesbian apologetic.[17] Visual feminine markers like the ponytail are part of a distancing strategy that, while worn with neither circumspection nor by design, nevertheless creates symbolic space between perceived heterosexual and lesbian athletes.

During the 2011 Women's World Cup, viewers may have noticed several high-profile American athletes sporting short haircuts. Is this evidence of progress? Perhaps. Among them was Abby Wambach, the arguable star of that team, who subsequently inked several lucrative endorsement deals. So did the short-haired Megan Rapinoe who, approximately one year after the Cup, discussed her sexuality with *Out* magazine. She was not closeted and never dissembled. It was just, she explained, that the media never asked. "I think they were trying to be respectful and that it's my job to say, 'I'm gay.' Which I am. For the record: I am gay."[18]

Her affirmation inspired little commotion. Deadspin.com, a popular sports site, speculated the "news will likely be greeted with a yawn: an openly gay female athlete almost isn't news. A lesbian in the locker room conforms to a stereotype, just as a straight male athlete is a stereotype.... [W]e're no longer shocked when our muscular, short-haired female athletes announce they're gay."[19] So while we might interpret the lack of negative response to Rapinoe's acknowledgment as a sign of acceptance, Deadspin's take on the issue was to suggest that readers already assume lesbianism when it comes to athletic women, particularly those with short hair.

Adding to the conversation, Griffin cautions that the absence of backlash against Rapinoe does not mean "that everything is cool for lesbians in women's sports." She reminds readers of the often-unchecked heterosexism that manifests in overt discrimination, as well as in subtler acts: "Among softball players you might have noticed an increase in hair ribbons worn during games? There is a saying among women softball players, 'No bow? Lesbo.' One softball player told me about a straight teammate who freaked out when she realized that she forgot to bring her bow to an away game."[20] Implicit in the comment is that the bow typically adorns a ponytail, which, again, seems to signify heterosexuality in an athletic context.

Certainly, one might argue, today's girls and women no longer need to apologize or compensate for their presence in sport. At a time where they make up approximately 40 percent of all U.S. athletes, the notion that sporting participation is a social taboo seems a thing of the past. And surely, one might similarly contend, women who wear their hair in ponytails do not consciously set out to present themselves as necessarily "feminine" or heterosexual. I agree. My point is not to dispute the ponytail's utility and practicality, and, in the interest of disclosure, I wore one myself for at least thirty years, both in sport and outside of it. Instead, my intent is to consider how the ponytail, the most popular and prevalent hairstyle in U.S. women's sports, reflects and constructs the ways that the general public thinks about female athletes.

There is also a racial dimension to the ponytail that warrants acknowledgment. Women's sports advocate Donna Lopiano noted that when it came to coverage of the 1999 U.S. Women's Soccer Team, "the predominantly white media barely cover their racist inclination, embracing the ponytailed, cute All-American white girl soccer champions over the more muscular and diverse undefeated players who were relegated to background news."[21]

At the other end of the spectrum have been several high-profile incidents in which athletes of color found themselves the subjects of debasing comments for not wearing their hair "correctly" or for actively resisting racialized feminine standards. Perhaps most notorious among them was radio personality Don Imus's remarks regarding the 2007 Rutgers women's basketball team, in which he referred to the athletes as "nappy-headed hos." Before that, former Penn State basketball coach Rene Portland, who had a history of homophobic policies, allegedly demanded one of her African American players adopt a more "feminine" appearance and "stop wearing cornrows."[22] One presumes a ponytail would have better suited Portland's sensibilities. In 1997 the tennis world made much ado about the beaded braids of Venus and Serena Williams. The style became even more controversial after officials penalized the elder sister when, during the quarterfinals of the Australian Open, her beads scattered on the court and created a "disturbance."

Black athletes who wear their hair in ponytails are not immune from controversy. Neither, it should be noted, does criticism come only from white detractors. Gabrielle Douglas made history at the 2012 Olympic Games by becoming the first African American to win the individual all-around title. She also became the first American gymnast to earn gold medals in both the team and the individual competitions during the same Games. In the midst of such unprecedented success, it was her ponytail that inspired conversation on various social media platforms, especially on what one journalist referred to as "Black Twitter." Men and women of color criticized the sixteen-year-old's "gelled-up ponytail, hair clips and frizzy edges." They found it unkempt, calling it "a mess," and urged her to "fix" it, crying out that she was "representing for black women everywhere."[23] Others wished she would wear her hair "natural" and denounced what they felt to be her acquiescence to white feminine norms by chemically relaxing her hair and fashioning it like her white teammates.

Ebony columnist T. F. Charlton had a different take on the issue. "Reports of Black women hating on Gabby Douglas's hair have been greatly exaggerated." She argued that the mainstream media seized upon a few comments, treating "'trending topics' and viral posts as sources" to create a story: "as a result, the much more significant story of Black girls and women celebrating Gabby and pushing back on racism and sexism in the coverage of her has been lost." Her point is not, as has been argued elsewhere, that more people focused on Douglas's ponytail than on her remarkable performances; it is that the media hyped a handful of deprecatory comments about her hair, which overshadowed more important social critique. The distinction is important. "It's no coincidence that hair, one of the most visible markers and symbols of Black women's difference in a White-dominated culture, has become a focal point of Gabby's story. The media must forever make an issue of our difference, even in moments of triumph, but never in a way that engages with critical analysis of power and oppression." Charlton reads the controversy as another example in which "Black athletes at the top of their game are never allowed to simply be great."[24]

In spite of what may have been an overemphasis on a few petty comments, hair-related issues are of vital importance, as Jennifer Collins found in her interviews with black female elite athletes. Participants divulged that they yearned for "convenient hair" that they could simply "wash . . . and leave, like, that's convenient versus having to go through all that process to make sure you don't look crazy." As one woman expressed, "All the white girls' hair is like this long flowy ponytail that's like amazing and all they do is wash it and go." Collins found that women of color dealt with a range of related issues that, on the whole, white women do not—particularly the management and precautions involved with straightening or pressing one's hair in efforts to approximate culturally sanctioned styles. "Most of my teammates on my soccer teams were white; I was the token black girl. And I just always like, noticed that they could just put their hair in a ponytail and wear it down and go out in two seconds. And like, minimum an hour on my hair to get it to look the way that I wanted to, so I would be so envious and just want straight hair permanently."[25] The straightening process is an important step for many who wish to wear their hair in a ponytail, typically accomplished through the application of heat, chemicals, or a combination of the two. This comes with a range of complications, not least of which is the sweat one cannot avoid in the context of sport, which threatens to undo their efforts. These procedures also contribute to the relative fragility of black hair, adding concerns about further damage and breakage associated with fashioning some sort of pulled-back style. The time, effort, and money involved with doing one's hair may also serve as a barrier to exercise, as several studies have found.[26]

One African American female athlete in Collins's study related that she had to pull her hair back into a bun, lamenting that her ponytail "would just separate into two butt parts and it was horrible." The texture of her hair prevented the desirable effect, a problem others solved by affixing hair extensions or "tracks." Women shared stories about teammates who did not securely attach the pieces to their existing hair and suffered humiliation when they fell out during competition. Then there were those who successfully achieved what one woman referred to as the "power pony." Another remembered with pride "one time I straightened my hair and wore it in this like long pony . . . BEST EVER! . . . I wish I had done that every game every whatever. It just looked really sleek and like powerful."[27] Despite the labor involved in fashioning the hairstyle, it became a source of power and pleasure.

Points of Change in Women's Sport History

My aim in this introduction is to consider the ways that something as seemingly mundane as a ponytail is actually shot through with substantial and varied cultural significance. Unquestionably, the hairstyle provides a practical solution for dealing with longer hair (there is no doubt about it and there is absolutely nothing wrong with it), but what it comes to mean, how it is taken up in mediated discourse, the ways it becomes synonymous with female athletes, and its relationships to sexuality, age, race, nationality, and culture en-gender a normative, athletic femininity in the context of U.S. women's sports. At the same time, there are dynamics of power, pleasure, agency, and resistance involved with the everyday act of styling one's hair. That tidy coiffure is one messy bundle.

In successive chapters, I address several ostensibly banal elements of U.S. women's sport and physical activity—tennis fashions, tampons, competition, sex testing, aesthetic fitness, sports bras, and cheerleading—to consider their involvement in forging distinctly athletic, feminine subjectivities at different moments in history. As with the ponytail, we live in a time when it is difficult to imagine women's sport without these things, but I argue that it is precisely because they seem so commonsense and commonplace that they are powerfully connected to gendered ideologies.

Qualifying Times represents a partial history of U.S. women's sports according to seven "points of change." This approach is inspired by feminist historian Gerda Lerner who asks, as one of several "transforming questions" for research, "What are the *points of change* in women's historic experience by which we might periodize the history of women?"[28] I am not so bold to suggest that this work will reperiodize sport history, but I do hope it calls into question those eras by which we traditionally carve up the sporting past, as well as the traditionally masculinist approaches to chronological segmentation that revolve around Western politico-economic events (for example, combat, revolution, and financial booms and busts).[29] Although salient to the whole of history, these epochs and episodes did not influence women's and men's lives in the same way. The same is true with regard to other populations with historically differential access to material and symbolic resources.

Organizing a history of twentieth-century women's sport according to these points of change foregrounds specific attributes germane to women's active, clothed, menstruating, legislated, sexed, breasted, and commercialized bodies. These phenomena did not cause cultural transformation. While their introduction into the lives of American women facilitated participation in physical activity, they should not be dislocated from larger cultural currents. There is a mutually constitutive relationship between the debut of these elements and the historical contexts of which they are a part. Additionally, these points of change did not always induce or symbolize progress. They also initiated strife, backlash, and regression.

Presented in a loose chronology, each chapter addresses the genealogy of an element of women's physical culture, including the precursors and cultural conditions that encouraged its inception. Each aspect brought with it a unique set of controversies and evinced clashes between dominant, residual, and emergent ideologies about femininity and athleticism. These struggles played out among various arbiters of gender normativity, most notably the popular media, consumer culture, sports organizations, and the medical and physical education professions, before transitioning into a state of relative banality.

In chapter 1, I examine several high-profile moments in the early history of women's tennis fashions, accepting costume historian Anne Hollander's assertion that "changes in dress *are* social changes."[30] When upper-class women first took to the courts in the late nineteenth century, they did so clad in the constraining livery of their everyday lives. As the distaff game became more competitive, the need to shed the fetters of restrictive garb became ever more exigent. As a result, there emerged several conspicuous, controversial incidents when women appeared in increasingly abbreviated costumes, revealing their ankles and wrists, their arms and legs, and the shapes and forms of their bodies in the quest to free their sporting movements. Public reactions to these incidents indicate conflicts between conventionally genteel and athletic femininities and suggest changing perceptions toward women's bodies and their physical capabilities.

Chapter 2 concerns the commercial tampon, first available in the United States in 1936. The introduction of the mass-produced tampon marked a significant turning point in women's lives. It spoke to desires for physical freedom, changes in dress, and evolving viewpoints with regard to hygiene and the corporeal. Advertisers' use of the sportswoman in campaigns of the 1930s and 1940s was an important strategy for the product's viability.

Inside the pages of popular magazines, the tampon-advocating athlete at once represented modernity, encouraged physical activity, and contributed to a "culture of concealment" that perpetuated menstrual shame and stressed the need for secrecy and discretion.[31]

With physical freedoms brought about, in part, by new menstrual technologies and liberating styles of dress, women physical educators began to reevaluate their collective position against intercollegiate, commercial, and hypercompetitive sports for their students. In chapter 3, I focus on a series of National Institutes on Girls' Sports, jointly sponsored by the Division for Girls and Women's Sports (DGWS) and the United States Olympic Committee (USOC) that took place during the 1960s. At these clinics, educators, recreation leaders, and other interested parties learned the necessary tools to teach sport skills to their respective charges and to encourage them to engage in "the right kind of competition." An estimated 110,000 instructors attended the institutes, which, in turn, benefited millions of girls. The emergent groundswell of support was an important antecedent to the subsequent developments in women's sport.

At the same time educators held their National Institutes, leaders of several international athletic federations worked to quell anxieties about "manly" women competitors by instituting "sex-testing" policies to "verify" the femaleness of female athletes. Purporting to safeguard women's sport and its participants, the tests have too often disadvantaged women and served as a powerful form of social control that encouraged normative femininity in the context of sport, as I argue in chapter 4. Although most organizations have since declared an end to sex testing in their official policies, new forms of surveillance and detection continue to define who counts as a woman in the context of sport.

For better or worse, the introduction of the sex test signified that women's sports were on the rise, and in the 1970s American women went through what many felt was an athletic "revolution." A number of milestones peppered the era as women experienced unprecedented participation opportunities. But with that progress came the "backlash" of the 1980s, a reaction to women's athletic progress that particularly manifested in the aesthetic fitness movement. Within the context of the neoconservative "Reagan revolution," women flocked to all sorts of bodywork designed to sculpt their physiques in physically and sexually attractive ways and, in the process, forged a "new ideal of beauty." In chapter 5, I argue that this trend is indicative of what Naomi Wolf calls the "beauty myth," in which the accent on women's appearance detracts from their social, cultural, political, and economic status.[32]

One product that attested to the 1970s revolution in women's sport was the introduction of the commercial sports bra. Over the course of the previous century, active women struggled with how best to support their breasts. Critics charged that breasts, like menstruation, symbolized women's inferior biology and their unsuitability for sport, but the introduction of the "Jogbra" in 1977 proved a material and symbolic landmark. It also signified a niche market for the product, and its popularity grew throughout the 1980s and into the 1990s. Yet it was Brandi Chastain's 1999 celebration, in which she ripped off her uniform top following her game-winning goal in the Women's World Cup, that proved to be the garment's coming-out party. This marked an increase in visibility of both the sports bra and the sports bra–clad body and inspired cultural conversations about the changing feminine corporeal aesthetic. Chapter 6 explores those conversations and considers the liberatory potential of the sports bra, as well as related issues of body discipline, the sexualization of athletic bodies, and the trivialization of women's sport.

Chapter 7 takes on a similar analysis in the context of competitive cheerleading, an activity to which girls and women flocked at the turn of the twenty-first century. Over the past one hundred years, cheerleading has been noticeably gendered, regendered, sexualized, commercialized, and sportified. Recently, various organizations have worked hard to legitimize competitive cheer, though they have met resistance from women's sports advocates, members of the cheer industry, and residual perceptions of who a cheerleader is and what she does. In this final substantive chapter, I explore whether cheer's newest incarnations reconcile the persistent divide between athleticism and femininity or if it simply reasserts conventional schisms between them.

Qualifying *Qualifying Times*

Before moving on, I want to discuss some of the limitations of this work. It is always important to keep in mind questions of difference, that is, of sexual difference (between men and women) and, especially, of difference within the category of womanhood. In the case of the former, scholars have long argued for a move from women's history to gender history, one that accounts for the relationships of power between masculinities and femininities—between males and females "to understand the significance of the *sexes,* of gender groups in the historical past."[33] This book does not do that. Although I agree that an integrative, relational approach may yield robust understandings, I do not compare or incorporate men's and women's histories.

In the past three decades, historians of sport have produced empirically rich, theoretically insightful, and politically charged studies about women's physical activity. Sport history no longer "remains the history of man's involvement in sport," as Jack Berryman assessed in 1983; neither are women "neglected," as Steven Riess determined seven years later. In spite of this growth, however, females' sporting pasts often remain along the margins, "ghettoized" in stand-alone chapters on "gender," and within the minority of our collective scholarship. There is much work left to do. I fear that, at this point, to "mainstream" women's history into a broader "gender" or "human history," especially when it comes to sport, is to risk being sucked into a whirlpool of obscurity.[34] Perhaps I am just not sure how to do it. In any event, this is "women's sport history" that places women at its center and is devoted to considering women's athletic experiences on their own terms.[35]

Next there is the vital issue of difference among women. By now, it should go without saying that one must never treat *women* as a homogenous, undifferentiated category. Social class, race, ethnicity, religion, sexuality, marital status, age, familial structure, body shape and size, geography, (dis)ability, and historical location all intersect with sex in ways that asymmetrically influence women's lives.[36] The points of change analyzed in this book are not points of change for all women, and I do not mean to present them as such. Who had access to tennis courts and the latest fashions? Who could afford to buy tampons? To whom were the advertisements or the magazines in which they appeared targeted? Which women were affected by physical educators' philosophy toward competition and which women thwarted convention and dared to compete? Why are some women considered more "suspicious" than others when it comes to the history of sex testing? For whom was the 1970s a sporting "revolution"? What types of bodies do we see in sports-bra advertisements and competitive cheerleading? What types of bodies are marginalized and stigmatized in the process? These are just a handful of questions that vexed me throughout the process of researching and writing this book.

That vexation may not be immediately apparent to readers, for what develops in the subsequent pages has largely to do with white middle-class women with the means and opportunities to engage in organized physical activity. Whenever possible, I have tried to expand that narrow purview, but the ensuing analysis should not be the final word on the subject. Rather, I hope readers will consider it an invitation for further engagements with the intersections between athleticism, gender, and other imperative attendant categories.

With these caveats in mind, *Qualifying Times* is meant to tease out some of the complexities brought to bear by analyzing several elements in women's sport. Women's history, characterizes Honor R. Sachs, "brings the ordinary, the forgotten, the pedestrian, and the subtle realities of experience into sharper focus."[37] But before the ordinary, the forgotten, and the pedestrian *became* ordinary, forgotten, and pedestrian, they were extraordinary, conspicuous, and contentious. The banal has a history, and the advent of these elements into women's lives marked points of change in the development of sport and in cultural perceptions of physically active females. There is a persistent tension that pulls together the following analyses: tension between what it means to be a woman and what it means to be an athlete in U.S. society. Ultimately, each phenomenon examined in this book contributes to a complex matrix of gender differentiation, one that, throughout history, marks the female athletic body as different from—as less than—despite the advantages it may confer.

1. What Shall We Wear for Tennis?

After "vanquishing a young lady at lawn tennis, though in his judgment she was the better player," Major Wingfield, "the English gentleman who generally has the credit of being the inventor of Lawn Tennis," sought to understand why he emerged the victor. And so, following the 1881 match, he arranged for a comparative assessment of their respective costumes. "He therefore rolled up his flannel suit, lawn-tennis shoes, socks, cap, and belt. Five pounds and a quarter was the result." He requested the woman similarly weigh her ensemble, described as "a tweed tailor's made costume," the equivalent of which was tantamount to a man wearing "a railway rug strapped round his waist, tied in at his knees, and pinned up coquettishly behind." In all, the outfit tipped the scales at ten and three-quarters pounds. In this, Wingfield "saw clearly in this the cause of her losing and he strongly urges a lawn-tennis dress."[1]

Just what that dress might look like was a source of consternation for the moneyed elite. In response to the question "What shall we wear for tennis?" a writer identified only as "A Lady Tennis Player" recommended the following in an 1887 issue of *Godey's Lady's Book and Magazine*:

1. Flannel or silk combination garment (linen should never be worn).
2. Pair of loose flannel or serge drawers, gathered in at knee with elastic, or ordinary frilled garment.
3. Full petticoat (flannel or serge) to knees.
4. Pair of short riding corsets, either with elastic gussets at sides or laced with elastic. This latter way is a good plan.
5. Loose Norfolk blouse confined at waist by belt.

6. Loose full skirt of some not too heavy material, falling several inches below knees. Too light a fabric ought not to be chosen, as in windy weather
   great inconvenience will be caused.
7. Stockings to match dress; tennis shoes.[2]

The list envisioned an ensemble of equal parts propriety and comfort. Women
must wear corsets, as social codes dictated, but they should be constructed
with elastic, as opposed to more incapacitating stays made of metal, bone,
ivory, or wood. Skirts must remain long, but the fabric should be of a weight
that is neither too cumbersome nor too revealing. Women could thus move
about the court while maintaining gentility, refinement, and restraint. Consequently, they could participate in one of the few socially acceptable sports
available to them without ruffling the sensibilities of their peers.

From the moment women first picked up their rackets, their attire inspired
questions of decorum, social distinction, physicality, and femininity. From
the nexus of those considerations emerged several conspicuous and controversial fashion moments. By *controversial* I mean incidents when women
broke from convention to wear costumes that inspired extreme public and
media attention—occasions where Americans either revered or decried the
players' selections. And while women played tennis recreationally and in
physical education classes clad in a variety of clothing options, I am more
concerned with what fashion historian Patricia Campbell Warner terms
"sport dress—public dress" than I am with "gymnastic dress, or private dress."[3]
The cultural conversations about the public dress of American and the top
international players tell us something about the tensions between athleticism and femininity.

There are myriad contentious fashion moments in the history of women's
(and men's) tennis, but I concentrate primarily on the years between 1884,
when the Wimbledon tournament held its first "ladies" event, through 1960,
which tennis historian Angela Lumpkin marks as the end of the game's "modern era."[4] During this time, female athletes pushed customary boundaries
by purging their wardrobes of restrictive apparel, appropriating masculine
styles, and shortening their skirts to the eventual conclusion that their undergarments became more visible and, at times, strategically styled to entice
the public. Some of these sartorial points of change liberated female athletes,
permitting them to move and to strike the ball in new and increasingly
competitive ways. Other points of change demonstrate efforts to keep tennis
socially exclusive, bind women to feminine traditions, induce ballyhoo, and
titillate spectators.

"Almost universally," writes Warner, "sports historians ignore the significance of clothing as a factor in the development of women's involvement in

any athletic endeavor." She overstates her case, but it is true that fashion is an often overlooked and underestimated "social phenomena."[5] In the late 1800s and early 1900s, women adapted their standard apparel in order to play croquet, golf, field hockey and to ice skate, ski, ride horses, pilot planes, and race motorized vehicles, but no two activities were more intertwined with contemporary issues of dress reform than swimming and the "bicycle craze."[6] Bound up with issues of safety and sexuality, women's efforts to release themselves from the trammels of oppressive attire were also about their desires for corporeal emancipation, pleasure, and self-expression.

Tennis, according to scholar Allen Guttmann, "did more than any other sport to revolutionize the clothing worn by upper-class sports women." Perhaps in no other physical activity is fashion more important, not just in terms of athleticism, but especially for one's presentation of self. By 1929 sportswriter John Tunis felt that tennis tournaments had become "more like a display of mannequins at a fashion parade than a group of sportswomen engaging in the most strenuous competition open to the modern girl." Cultural studies scholar Toby Miller made a similar observation regarding today's game, remarking that "a coterie of present players have become icons of the *fashion* movement." Even the great Billie Jean King once maintained that styles of dress "contributed greatly to the popularity of women's tennis," making it "more interesting" than the men's game.[7]

At the turn of the twentieth century, argues textile historian Barbara Burman, athletic women "achieved a tangible physical freedom and unified bodily experience through their specialist clothing and by so doing they anticipated very significant changes in women's clothing generally, ascribed by some dress historians solely to the later effects of World War I." In other words, sportswomen who challenged the conventions of everyday dress presaged and sometimes precipitated broader sartorial trends. More than this, though, they presaged and sometimes precipitated broader *social* trends, for as costume historian Anne Hollander posits, "changes in dress *are* social changes."[8] Significant beyond the boundaries of the tennis court, the public dress of high-profile players speaks to broader cultural and historical issues.

Lawn Tennis Comes to America

In one form or another, people have played games similar to today's tennis since at least the medieval period. It was not until the 1870s that Americans took to the modern sport after socialite Mary Outerbridge, while vacationing in Bermuda, witnessed British officers playing the game. There are counternarratives regarding the origins of U.S. tennis, but most accounts generally

Figure 1.1: "A Representative Group of the Ladies' Club," Staten Island Ladies
Lawn Tennis Club, 1887, outing. Courtesy of the Library of Congress Prints and
Photographs Division, Washington, D.C.

agree that Outerbridge and her brothers introduced it to the Staten Island
Cricket and Baseball Club in New York, and the game quickly spread. Affluent
Americans found it attractive as they sought to assert their social distinction
by mimicking the pastimes and affectations of the English aristocracy.

Tennis required leisure time, a well-manicured lawn, and imported equipment that kept it sufficiently beyond the grasp of the hoi polloi in those early
years. Rallying on the grounds of private estates and within the confines of
exclusive athletic clubs insulated the game, as did a strict code of amateurism that followed the initiation of organized competitions. The costumes
deemed appropriate for play constituted another locus of class demarcation.
As conspicuous leisure, tennis was not necessarily a competitive sport but
rather another way to segregate the upper crust from the rest of the American
populace, as well as a site at which to perform a particular embodiment of
social class.

In the beginning, tennis was not a terribly strenuous pursuit. It was primarily a social activity rather than an athletic one, a characterization that
contributed to the acceptability of women's participation. In garden-party
finery, those content to pat the ball back and forth across the net with little

exertion showed minor concern for the practicality of their clothing—the fashion mattered most, for the tennis court was a place to see and be seen. This was true for men as well, though as historian Foster Rhea Dulles notes, "Women players suffered only the slightest handicap in having to hold up the trains of their long dragging skirts; they were not expected actually to run for the ball."[9]

The game grew increasingly competitive in certain circles of the tennis world. For that reason, a group of men banded together in 1881 to establish the United States Lawn Tennis Association (USLTA), now the United States Tennis Association (USTA), which hosted the first official American men's championships in Newport, Rhode Island, summer home to the superrich. The advent of prestigious tournaments intensified the visual display of athletes and spectators. On the grass courts of exclusive resorts, tennis matches became "a festival of the fashionable world," providing occasions for ostentatious displays of wealth, including the style of dress of participants and spectators alike.[10]

By 1883 there were approximately forty organized lawn tennis clubs in the United States, one-third of which admitted women as full or limited members. Yet as *Outing* magazine summarized: "None of the clubs that hold open tournaments admit ladies to membership, and perhaps it is owing to this fact that, with one exception, ladies have hitherto found no place in open competitions. That this should be the case, there is no adequate reason. Not alone the nature of the game, but also its popularity among ladies, has proved that it is a ladies' game, and in every locality where tennis is in vogue there are ladies who play as well as the gentlemen." Far from equal, women nevertheless enjoyed access to tennis more than any other sport at that time.[11]

In 1884 the All-England Lawn Tennis and Croquet Club added a "ladies" singles event to its Wimbledon tournament (established for men in 1877), though not without fierce resistance. Four years later, the USLTA invited women to compete in its prestigious national contest. By that time, most American athletic clubs sponsored women's competitions. These events, as reported in 1894, were "social functions of the highest class, and none enter their names but those of assured social position. As a matter of fact, all our first lady tennis players belong to the best families."[12] Tennis aficionados openly segregated their sport on the bases of social class, race, ethnicity, and religion, but less so on the grounds of sex.

England's Maud Watson triumphed over her younger sister Lilian in the finals of the first Wimbledon women's event, where the two evidently "revolutionized tennis dress by wearing separates, silk jersey blouses with long sleeves and low necks, and white wool skirts with a bustle." In the process, they set in motion "the basic principle of proper tennis dress is that *white is right.*" There are a number of explanations for the tradition of all-white tennis wear. First, it plays into the game's elitist character: "White clothes, hard to launder and keep pristine, were the prerogative of the rich," writes Warner.[13] To display immaculate clothing in the context of athletics was a way of asserting one's social rank.

White clothing also helped players stay cool in the heat and masked the rivets of perspiration that invariably bedewed even the daintiest contenders. "Victorian etiquette," explained acclaimed fashion designer Ted Tinling, decreed that women "must give an outward proof of cleanliness if they were likely to get warm." Visible signs of sweat and strain had significant class connotations. At the 1897 Ladies' Championship in Dublin, Ireland, the summer heat "brought to a head the problem of the coloured silk, or elaborate serge costumes, developing visible damp stains before spectators who might have in their midst some of the 'lower classes.'" As a solution, "All-white copies of their contemporarily high-fashion costumes were the miraculous Irish solution for those players who moved about enough to be called 'good' and who deliberately wished to demonstrate this fact in championship competition."[14] Whatever the rationale, the unwritten code of white clothing in tennis persisted with remarkable tenacity through the mid–twentieth century, to such a degree that flashes of color seemed garish and out of place.

In the late 1880s and 1890s, women began to navigate the court with a bit more latitude and adjusted their clothing accordingly. England's Charlotte (Lottie) Dod, who took the 1887 Wimbledon title at age fifteen, "broke with tradition advocating that ladies should run, and run hard, and not merely stride after tennis balls." In so doing, she "made women's tennis into a real sport."[15] Her skirt, cut four inches above the ankle (possibly part of her school uniform), allowed for her more vigorous style of play. Perhaps because of her youth, fans and journalists forgave her indiscretion. Still, most of her peers "remained safely and demurely at the baseline," where their hemlines safely and demurely brushed the ground.[16]

Dod chastened those who clad themselves in ponderous clothing, wondering, "How can they ever hope to play a sound game when their dresses impeded the free movement of every limb? In many cases their very breathing is rendered difficult." The women's game and its players remained repressed as long as they adhered to the dictates of everyday fashion. Dod concluded that a "suitable dress is sorely needed and hearty indeed would be the thanks of puzzled lady-players to the individual who invented the easy and pretty costume."[17]

Gradually, pundits and athletes alike began to heed Dod's plaint and question the conventions of tennis. At the end of the decade, *Outing* magazine marveled at the female player who "bravely struggles against the awful handicap imposed upon her, viz., much dress and little strength. . . . It is obvious that the wearing of a long and flowing skirt not only seriously interferes with quick movements from one part of the court to another, but, what is of still more importance, it prevents a woman from using her racquet and making a stroke in a correct manner, or, as it is more commonly called, in 'good form.'"[18] On the whole, clothes hindered women's ability to roam about the court, to breathe, and to strike the ball effectively.

The rules of the game further relegated women to second-class status. Until 1902 women, like men, competed in a best-of-five-sets series. That year the USLTA decreed that women would play the best of three sets, reflecting prevailing beliefs about their physical capabilities. The rules became the international standard and, in conjunction with women's fashions, kept the distaff game an inferior, feminized version of the male norm.

Of Wrists and Ankles

Like Lottie Dod, other female tennis players began to forge their own sartorial paths. Socialite Ava Willing Astor, for example, took the court in bloomers at a Newport match in 1893, much to the alarm of spectators.[19] First associated with the women's movement in the 1850s, the bloomer costume initially incited hostility and ridicule, but it held great value for working-class, agricultural, and frontier women (before they adopted trousers), as well as to swimmers and those who wore bloomer-style exercise uniforms in sanitariums, schools, and colleges.[20] By the latter decades of the nineteenth century, the bicycle craze inspired middle-class women to return to those "Turkish trousers" for matters of safety and comfort, and "Bloomer Girls" baseball teams barnstormed the country. The garment thus became associated with dress reform, practicality, emancipation, personal preference, and derision, for those who donned the bloomers, like Astor, publicly challenged gender norms, demonstrating clothing's powerful political symbolism.

Astor's bloomers did not inspire a fashion trend in tennis, though some women clearly began to rethink their costumes on the court in ways that suggest increased athleticism. In 1896 *Harper's Bazaar* bemoaned, "Girls who play for championship make everything subservient to the game, and apparently do not care how they look." Still, most women athletes endured the persistent encumbrance of their clothing during this time. One tennis player noted of the era, "No girl would appear unless upholstered with a corset, a starched petticoat, a starched skirt, heavily button-trimmed blouse, a starched shirtwaist with long sleeves and cuff links, a high collar and a four-in-hand necktie, a vest with silver buckle, and sneakers with large silk bows."[21] Another added that they were also required, by social if not official dictate, to wear a "long undershirt, pair of drawers . . . long white silk stockings, and a floppy hat. We were soaking wet when we finished a match." Clad in the vestments of upper-class life, the "one concession their costume might make to sport was an apron with a wide pocket to hold their tennis balls."[22]

As historian Nancy Rosoff argues, "Dressing in conventional clothing kept women from appearing too threatening while they engaged in their athletic activities."[23] Their bodies cloaked, their mobility restricted, and their game inhibited, women posed little challenge to the masculinist center of sport. At a time when critics worried about the "mannifying" effects of strenuous activity, proponents assured the American public that tennis was among the few acceptable athletic pursuits, provided women only "moderately indulged."[24]

Costume adjustments in the early 1900s were circumspect and generally fell along three lines: women tennis players freed their arms from the confines of long and often voluminous sleeves, they experimented with the material and style of their corsets, and they contracted the length and volume of their skirts, if only a little. Tennis fashion, like the game itself, was a matter of inches. This also allowed for the introduction of new strokes and styles of play. Forehand drives and overhead serves, for instance, were unimaginable in the circumscribed outfits of the Victorian era. Although subtle, these alterations point to larger changes in women's sports as well as women's desire for greater physicality within the context of the game and their own lives.

Initially, even exposing one's wrists was cause for alarm. In 1901 a writer for *Lawn Tennis Magazine* objected when one woman "made a distinction at Wimbledon of being the only lady player out of all the large entry who *turned up her sleeves* for play." The author went on to admonish, "It cannot possibly help the tennis, and it certainly does not improve the appearance." Three years later, tennis fans took notice when a young May Sutton similarly abbreviated her shirtsleeves, though she was a different sort of player. She brought "vigor and speed" to the sport, and although she "played predominantly from the baseline, she was not hesitant to move to the net to volley." Competing in the 1904 American championships at age sixteen, she "wore shorter skirts with fewer petticoats, eschewed high-collared skirtwaists, and rolled up her sleeves." Sutton therefore "helped pioneer women's emancipation from medieval sports attire."[25]

Sutton's youth excused her transgression. She also hailed from the West Coast of the United States, where fashion generally tended to be more casual

Figure 1.2: May Sutton, undated photo. Courtesy of the Bain News Service Collection, Library of Congress Prints and Photographs Division, Washington, D.C.

than it was in the East or in Great Britain. As one reporter commented, "In California the sunshine and absence of British tradition had long since made short sleeves, bare throats and forearms acceptable." Sutton became the first American woman to win the Wimbledon championship in 1905. She won it again in 1907. "Few women dress suitably for the tennis court," she remarked at the time. "It is a violent exercise and demands loose, simple garments, both for the sake of the game and one's health." Several years later, the press lauded Sutton for worrying more about her game than her fashion: "What did she care about clothes?" asked the *Chicago Daily Tribune.* "She knew how to play tennis."[26]

Sutton challenged traditional norms of corporeal femininity, for she "did not permit her gentility to interfere with her agility, or her garments with her respiration." She was, noted one newspaper in 1904, "a splendid specimen of modern athletic woman" who signified that the "summer girl of romance is gradually passing away, being obliged to make room for her more strenuous and athletically inclined modern sister, who gives much of her time today to fencing, tennis, golfing, bowling, and similar exhilarating sports, indulged in by the up to date young man all over the country."[27] Women seemed poised on the cusp of crafting a new, more active role for themselves, and their clothing was an important constituent.

On the question of corsets, Sutton allowed that they were "desirable for many reasons—I wear them myself and think that most players look infinitely better with them than without." Women cinched their waists for aesthetic reasons, but many also felt the constriction held salubrious benefits. As Sutton continued, "I have heard many doctors say that in running and jumping, corsets are an advantage, as they tend to keep the organs of the body in place during this kind of exercise."[28] Medical discourse often advocated the use of the accessory for lower-back, abdominal, and internal support.

Corsets had long plagued athletic women. They affected circulation, respiration, and locomotion. Feminist author Anngel Delaney writes that women competing in the 1887 Wimbledon tennis tournament had to retire to the dressing rooms between matches to "unhitch their bloody corsets. As they endeavored to twist, turn and lunge on the courts, the women were repeatedly stabbed by the metal and whale bone stays of the cumbersome garments."[29] Indeed, Elizabeth Ryan, a top player in the early 1900s, recalled a drying rack in the dressing rooms over which women hung their blood-soaked corsets.[30]

Manufacturers adapted their products to suit women's active lifestyles, changing the cut and fabric of the garment (see chapter 6). In 1898 the *New York Times* relayed that "a stiff corset would make playing almost impossible, but a little French corset, which is not much more than a band around the waist, gives perfect freedom." Nevertheless, just two years later *Harper's Bazaar* advised that it was "much wiser to play without corsets, if possible, although it must be admitted that few women do so."[31] The dictates of fashion proved a powerful form of social control for keeping women loyal to the constrictive item.

Sutton was not the only athlete to offer her opinion about appropriate attire for tennis in the first decades of the twentieth century. As the popularity of the women's game grew, its first stars penned advice about skill development, equipment, training, and clothing. In the main, they lobbied not for a radical reformulation of women's dress, but for slight accommodations. Simply designing skirts that fell several inches above the ankle and provided sufficient circumference to run, jump, and swing their racquets would suffice.

Helen (Homan) McLean, the 1906 national champion, and Edna Wildey, a runner-up in the 1913 doubles competition, coauthored an article titled

"Women's Apparel for the Court," for *American Lawn Tennis*. "The subject is one of great importance," the editor commented in the preamble: "In tournament play the contestants are on public view, and they must, or should be, sartorially perfect. The great players, or a very considerable majority of them, have always been most particular about their costumes, and as a result it is a distinct pleasure to watch them."[32] In this view, the significance of women's clothing is not about what it did for the athletes but, rather, how it enhanced spectators' experience.

McLean and Wildey recommended practical though pleasing white costumes—either a dress or shirt-and-skirt combination, free from frills and of sufficient weight to keep from exposing the player's underpinnings during a potentially cheeky gust of wind. Although they qualified that it was "impossible to prescribe a uniform dress for all, as there will always be a diversity of figure and a diversity in the size of the pocketbook," it was clear that suitable clothing was within the domain of the prosperous class. "To be satisfactory these dresses must, of course, be made to order, and that always entails more expense, time, and trouble." There were versions of apparel that one might purchase "at the stores which supply women's sporting clothes," undoubtedly shops that catered to affluent clientele. For the woman of "moderate means," they accommodated, "let her have one dress made at a good place perhaps, and the rest copied by a home dressmaker."[33] The various options presented to readers were out of reach for the average woman, thus maintaining the exclusivity of tennis and its fashions.

Other personalities did not concern themselves with financial details, but instead focused on practicability. In 1916 champion Molla Bjurstedt disparaged what she called "dressing for the tennis court and not for tennis" and advised women to "not put your clothes above your game." She recommended skirts that were "short enough and wide enough not to hamper any jump or stride you happen to make." Dorothea Lambert Chambers, then the topliner in women's tennis, similarly counseled that one's dress must not restrict motility. "It is essential to remember that you want, above everything else, free use of all your limbs; physical action must not be impeded in any way by your clothing. An overhead ball which may require your arm to be extended as far as it will go, a low volley at the net where you must bend down, a run across the court or up to the net—all these strokes you must be able to perform with freedom and facility."[34] Although they remained rooted in upper-class habitus, women's clothing concerns had shifted over the course of three decades: from striking an aristocratic visage to allowing for greater motility and competition on the court.

The Lenglen Effect

Officials suspended Wimbledon, the French Championships, and the Australasian Championships for the duration of the First World War. With the exception of 1917, the U.S. National Championships persisted, though the conflict cast a pall over the event. The war also necessitated a simplification in dress due to taxation and the shortage of labor and laundry work.[35] Clothing that required special care became impractical, and women and men began to shed their frivolous undergarments for more streamlined silhouettes. "In the immediate post-war era," wrote Tinling, "women everywhere were longing for some release from the restrictions of the Edwardian decade."[36] Although he refers specifically to tennis, women's release came in a number of forms—in newfound rights and liberties, in greater access to education and employment, in sexual mores, and in everyday livery.

When officials revived the Wimbledon tournament in 1919, the much-anticipated women's final pitted England's Dorothea Lambert Chambers, the forty-year-old, seven-time champion, against French phenom Suzanne Lenglen, who was half her opponent's age. The contest has since gone down in the annals of history as one of epic proportions. Sport sociologist Jennifer Hargreaves characterizes the contrast between the two competitors as "not a simple test of skill, but a symbolic battle between the old and the new—in terms of play, styles of dress and attitudes to the role of women. . . . Mrs. Chambers was reproducing a respectable image of femininity, whereas Suzanne Lenglen was actively redefining female sports and social skills."[37] The two were surprisingly well matched, with Chambers's tactical baseline proficiency set against Lenglen's balletic full-court flare. In a hard-fought battle that lasted more than two hours, Lenglen emerged triumphant (10-8, 4-6, 9-7). Her ascendancy signified a new age of women's athleticism and launched a new era in women's tennis. Perhaps the greatest champion of all times, she went on to win thirty-one Grand Slam titles before retiring in 1930.

Lenglen's rise also marked a transformation in clothing styles. When she met Chambers in 1919, her dress was similar to other Wimbledon contenders: "a mid-calf length white cotton skirt, a short-sleeved middy blouse, and a small wide-brimmed bonnet to protect her from the sun."[38] With her newfound fame came a costume change conceived by her couturier, the renowned Jean Patou. She replaced her long skirt with a shorter pleated version in a style similar to that worn by ballet dancers, which proved more comfortable and better suited the aesthetics of her game. She often appeared without an obscuring underskirt so that as she leaped about the court, the audience might catch a glimpse of her athletically graceful form beneath the gossamer

Figure 1.3: Suzanne Lenglen, Wimbledon, 1925. Courtesy of the Library of Congress Prints and Photographs Division Washington, D.C.

garment. Gone too was the traditional corset worn by her contemporaries, further revealing the contours of her natural shape.

Without the corset from which to secure her stockings, she was free to wear garters just above the knee, over which she often rolled her silk hose. And whereas bare wrists had once scandalized tennis patrons, she often eliminated sleeves altogether, exposing the length of her unclad arms.[39] Yet historian Larry Engelmann assesses that Lenglen's "clothes were not merely stylish, they were functional. . . . Suzanne was now much freer in her movement, less restricted, and literally less strait-laced than other women. She was free to leap and to dance and to whirl and to win." Although many considered her costumes indecorous, by 1924 most female players had adopted similar styles of dress.[40]

Lenglen's advice on the principles of tennis garb had less to do with sophistication than with pragmatism. Like her predecessors, she advocated that "a woman's first consideration necessarily must be comfort combined with perfect freedom of movement." At the same time, she cautioned, "it must not be forgotten that neatness and style are also essential, since a woman is never more under observation than when on a court, especially if, as during a tournament, there is a critical gallery."[41] Lenglen put this theory into practice, draping herself in accoutrements that secured her place in the public eye. She replaced the customary sunbonnet with her trademark bandeau—two yards of silk expertly wound about her head and secured with a diamond brooch. She further adorned herself with a gold cuff, worn above her left elbow, and ermine stoles. She appeared in full makeup at a time when most athletes did not, presenting herself as the height of glamour at all times. The French press dubbed her *La Divine*—the divine one, the goddess—both for her amazing talents and for her incomparable style.

Lenglen inspired great adulation from American audiences with her distinctive appearance during a 1921 U.S. tour. She was ideally situated for the 1920s "flapper" aesthetic. In the earlier era, middle- and upper-class women selected attire that forced their bodies into specific contours. "But in a period from 1919 onwards," write historians C. Willett and Phillis Cunnington, "it was the actual surface of the body which was to be exploited. A kind of 'skin worship' became almost a new religion." This trend represented "an aggressive spirit opposed to the symbols of class distinction in costume, and there is, after all, no more thoroughly democratic fabric than bare skin."[42] No one could accuse Lenglen of abating class distinction with her appearance—her finery was clearly beyond the purchase of the average woman. The principles of her grandeur nonetheless contributed to more general trends toward corporeal freedoms.

Along with a greater exhibition of skin, the "boyish" look predominated in the mid-1920s. Women engaged in slimming regimes of diet and exercise and, when necessary, availed themselves of breast and hip "minimizers" to attenuate their curves and approximate the androgyne silhouette. Hemlines rose and sleeve lengths retracted, making styles suitable for the era's vigorous dances, and Lenglen played an important role in popularizing the style.[43] "For the first time, then," writes Warner, "we see a sports figure influencing fashion in a complete, recognizable, and instantaneous way." The *New York Times* called it a "strange reversal. Nineteenth-century tennis had been played in the clothes of everyday life, but everyday life in the second decade of the twentieth century was lived in tennis clothes."[44]

The Emancipation of the Legs

By the end of the 1920s, fashion designers began to advocate lengthening women's hemlines, but "it was plainly absurd to reintroduce long skirts in what had now become a strenuous game," assesses fashion historian James Laver. The increased strenuosity encouraged not only shorter garments but also the liberation from stockings and, eventually, the donning of shorts.

"Emancipated legs," declared tennis champion Helen Wills in 1927, "mean better sports."[45]

At the time, Wills did not go so far as to recommend bare-legged play. She merely advised that silk stockings with lightweight wool feet were better than the heavier leggings so commonplace in the sport. The *New York Times* praised Wills's decorum, complimenting her "ample skirt and middie blouse with quarter sleeves" during the 1928 Wimbledon tournament. She set style trends of her own with her cerise cardigans and trademark eyeshade that made her "the very essence of conservatism." While her competitors forged ahead with more "immodest" costumes, Wills remained, one correspondent later assessed, "the antithesis of the sexy flapper."[46]

Wills's reserved style, welcomed by tennis's old guard, seemed outdated in the world of fashion. "Paris modistes say that her skirts are several inches too long, her blouse comes over her shoulders instead of being cut away in the great arm loops," wrote one journalist. When the other "scantily clad players swing their racquet every movement of their arms and shoulders is revealed. But when Miss Wills sends over one of her smashes the action is so curtained that it adds to the intriguing question of the girl's strength."[47] This suggests another reason women were encouraged to conceal their bodies on the court, for longer sleeves camouflaged their muscularity, thus maintaining a conventionally feminine facade.

Like the right to bare arms, unadorned legs also revealed the suntanned musculature of the female athlete. Thick, opaque stockings concealed those visible symbols of women's strength so that although they might exhibit extraordinary prowess on the court, their fashions tempered the continued antipathy toward their sporting involvement. The unveiling of limbs forced spectators to confront competitors' thewy athleticism in new ways.

Despite her earlier stance, by 1929 Wills was one of a handful of women who protested wearing hosiery at Wimbledon, declaring, "This stocking business is merely a question of comfort and greater freedom on the court." The "other Helen" of the era, Helen Hull Jacobs, testified that by 1931 most American players had "abandoned the ugly, white cotton stockings rolled above the knee that had once been a 'must.'" This did not mean that tennis officials approved. As Jacobs recalled, "When I attempted to play bare-legged that summer at Wimbledon, I ran into trouble." At the arrival of King George and Queen Mary, an umpire requested she wear a pair of stockings. She complied.[48]

Jacobs's "next step in my liberation from tradition," as she put it, was to don a pair of white shorts instead of the customary skirt: "They were cool and comfortable, and increased my mobility so much that I knew I would never want to play in dresses again."[49] Britain's Henry Wilfred "Bunny" Austin had set the precedent for tennis shorts, causing a mild stir at the 1931 U.S. National and the subsequent Wimbledon tournaments. "Why tennis players should fetter their legs in trousers," he reasoned, "when in every other strenuous sport the legs go free, I do not see."[50] Austin spoke only of male athletes. At the time, shorts, like trousers, were the decided apparel of boys and men. It was for this reason that many disapproved of them as women's wear.

Ted Tinling, who designed some of the game's most distinctive costumes, condemned shorts for women, lamenting that Jacobs had "crystallized the new trend towards masculinity." In fact, many disapproved of the garment, including Hazel Wightman, patroness of the Wightman Cup, and Helen Wills, who maintained that the "short pleated skirt is the only one for tennis." As officials debated whether to ban the garment at the Wimbledon tournament and elsewhere, the 1930s "battle of the shorts" became "the latest skirmish in the long fight that women have waged to be recognized as bipeds" as well as the most controversial phase in the evolution of women's tennis fashion.[51]

Through it all, Jacobs maintained her commitment to shorts, telling reporters at the 1933 U.S. National tournament at Forest Hills, "They're really a tremendous advantage. . . . Nothing but prejudice has prevented our wearing them for years. I know they improve my game and all the other girls say the same. I know I've lost many points through my racquet catching in my skirt. Not only that, but they are cooler and enable one to get around so much faster, particularly in the latter stages of a hard match." Jacobs later confessed that shorts also gave her a "psychological jump" on her opponents: "I thought, too, that I *should* play better without skirts flapping around my legs. I noticed another thing: my footwork was improving. This, I supposed, was because my legs were more conspicuous than usual, and when I made mistakes in footwork it was very apparent to me."[52] Her superior play and rationale for the garment struck a chord with other players.

In 1935 the *Chicago Daily Tribune* declared that, "in spite of the disapproving clicks and clacks from muscle and mind bound prudes, famous tennis stars, breathing a profound sigh of relief and hearty appreciation, wore [shorts] and started the emancipation of the legs." The next year, the magazine *Scholastic* estimated that about 30 percent of all women players wore the truncated trousers. It seemed "inevitable," speculated one journalist, "that skirts will no longer be worn on the courts within another year or two."[53] The prediction did not hold true, but it did speak to the popularity of shorts and their contribution to the increasing physicality of women's tennis.

There was at least one additional incentive behind the trend. As one player confided to a *New York Times* reporter, "I often hear players discussing whether to wear skirts or shorts. One more candid than the others will say 'nobody will look at you if you wear skirts.'"[54] Clearly, there were functional and decorative aspects to the garment. It offered facility of movement but also differentiated the wearer from her skirted peers. Women found that singularity, often more than performance, garnered headlines.

Opinions about shorts may also have been dependent upon who wore them and in what style. Jacobs explained that she designed the item herself, made from flannel and "of a Jamaica length that comes above the knee." She did not intend her shorts to titillate. One year earlier, at the 1931 Wimbledon tournament, Spain's Lili de Alvarez "set tongues to wagging and eyes popping when she appeared . . . in a tennis garb of her own creation featuring short trousers." When she arrived in culottes that grazed her knees, the *New York Times* declared, "Old ladies gasped and old gentlemen gurgled as the comely Spanish player pranced about in preliminary practice in her 'divided skirt' of cream crépe de chine, topped by a close fitting bodice." But the "tennis experts, turned stylists for the moment," the article continued, agreed that "the innovation in dress would be short lived." They were wrong. Alvarez sparked a trend that took hold both in and out of the sport, as the "world of Haute Couture invaded the courts, and the tennis style became all the rage."[55]

Figure 1.4: Helen Jacobs, National Tennis Championships at Forest Hills, Long Island, New York, 1934. Courtesy of the International Tennis Hall of Fame, Newport, Rhode Island.

Figure 1.5: Helen Jacobs, undated promotional photograph. Courtesy of the International Tennis Hall of Fame, Newport, Rhode Island.

Throughout the 1930s and 1940s, players and nonplayers alike adopted the divided garment—a hybrid of masculine trousers and feminine skirts.

The higher the hemlines, the greater the commotion. When California's Alice Marble won the Wimbledon singles, doubles, and mixed-double titles in 1939, *Life* commented that the tournament would "be remembered for two things: 1) Alice Marble's ascent into the ranks of tennis immortals, and 2) the most eye-filling collection of young ladies ever assembled for a world athletic championship." The "blonde, long-legged Marble girl," the author noticed, was especially attractive in shorts that "displayed a new high in grace and beauty."[56] Marble's look seemed less "masculine" than Jacobs's—rather than copying men's style of dress, many assumed she took her cues from physical education uniforms. By adopting a bifurcated item inspired by women's wear, she was not accused of approximating the men's style and remained within the realm of gender propriety, even as she bucked convention. The fact that many found her attractive certainly helped.

Outside the tennis world, Americans debated the appropriateness of women wearing shorts in public. Hollywood starlets began to sport them on-screen, which popularized the garment but apparently did little to certify their acceptability. In the summer of 1936, citizens of several states sought to ban shorts, though there was "some confusion as to whether the issue is moral or esthetic." Residents of Dover, New Jersey, decried the "demi-nudists" who invaded their town in the summer months, and police officers were ordered to "bring them in whenever you see them on the streets." The townspeople of Covington, Kentucky also objected to shorts on a moral basis. Said the head police matron, "Authorities have enough trouble protecting girls and young women without their flaunting themselves in the faces of men, dressed in such scanty costumes." In Yonkers, New York, there was concern for the "too fleshy bodies" parading about the street. Municipal leaders did not take the issue lightly and decreed that "anyone violating the ordinance against shorts in the streets of Yonkers is liable to a fine not exceeding $150 and a sojourn in jail of not more than thirty days."[57]

Although local governments eventually accepted the presence of women in shorts on their cities' streets, the garment remained controversial for several decades. Golf officials were steadfast in their opposition to shorts on the links, insisting they were too informal for the sport's character.[58] Park commissioners in Chicago issued a prohibition on girls and women wearing shorts on the city's public tennis courts.[59] Even within elite-level tennis, administrators tried desperately to resist the trend. Billie Jean King, for instance, often recalls her first tournament at the Los Angeles Tennis Club in the 1950s. Although officials permitted the eleven-year-old to play in shorts, they excluded her from the group photograph for her transgression.[60]

Putting Sin and Vulgarity into Tennis

A new "American look" emerged in 1930s fashion. This was due, in part, to the Depression era's limits on Parisian imports, restrictions placed on fabrics and findings, and the emergence of new American designers. The German army invaded Paris in 1940, effectively cutting off the fashion capital from the rest of the world and augmenting the Americanization of style. The Second World War also contributed to the Americanization of tennis. Officials suspended the French, English, and Australian championships for the duration of the war, though, as in World War I, the United States continued to hold its annual tournament at Forest Hills, which allowed American players to develop at a greater clip. It was also a time of democratization: public courts were built as part of President Roosevelt's New Deal policies, and mass production led to more affordable racquets. The advent of synthetic fabrics and ready-to-wear clothing additionally narrowed the chasm of class distinction, though tennis remained primarily within the province of society's upper strata.

The so-called American look, influenced and disseminated by sportswear designers and Hollywood films, was a simple, strong, clean, and somewhat masculine style that incorporated trousers, both long and short.[61] There was a comfort and a practicality to it, one equally suited for the thrall of athletics and the currents of everyday life. Ted Tinling, the tennis player–turned–tennis official–turned–tennis couturier referred to it as the "'manly look' of the late 'thirties" and loathed that it "carried over to the post-war years." He felt that, "by looking like modern-day Amazons, the sports girls were renouncing their birthright. . . . For this reason, in the beginning of 1947, I conducted a strong campaign for femininity in tennis."[62]

It began with a simple slash of color at the hemline of a dress designed for Joy Gannon. The following year, England's number-one player, Betty Hilton, requested a similar frock. Tinling complied with a wider colored band. This did not escape notice of Hazel Wightman, who requested that the Wimbledon Committee enforce the all-white convention, as she did in her annual cup. Tinling's greatest controversy, however, loomed on the horizon.

American Gertrude "Gussie" Moran, who typically played in shorts, asked the designer to make her "look more feminine" for the 1949 Wimbledon tournament.[63] Adhering to official requests, Tinling created an all-white dress trimmed in white satin. The length of her skirt was no different from that of other players of the era: "'kilt-length,' which is one inch from the floor when the wearer is kneeling down."[64] Moran did not own outfit-appropriate undergarments and implored Tinling to make her a pair of complementary knickers. After considering several prototypes, he trimmed the panties in coarse lace, "with a

Figure 1.6: Gertrude "Gorgeous Gussie" Moran and her scandalous panties, Wimbledon, June 22, 1949. Courtesy of AP Images.

bold design that would at least be visible from time to time in the stands when Gussy served. . . . So the notorious lace panties were born—not out of some erotic urge, but through some niggling attention to detail and a special insight into the ingredients required to project the character of the players I dressed."[65]

Moran first wore the "lace that launched a thousand excited ooh's" at the annual Hurlingham garden party, scheduled the day before the start of the Wimbledon tournament. Journalists, "tired with the drabness of women's tennis," went wild for her costume.[66] Photographers positioned themselves on the ground to capture up-skirt snapshots, and the world's major newspapers and magazines published the images and descriptions of Moran's ensemble so that audiences were agog even before the championship began.

Moran disappointed fans in her first round at Wimbledon when she first appeared in a shirt-and-shorts combination, somewhat orthodox by that time and no longer considered extraordinary. In the second round, though, she satisfied the expectant crowd. "The normal activity that goes with tennis was sufficient to flare her skirt and reveal to one and all the ballyhooed snuggies which she wore for the first time," recorded the *Washington Post*.[67] The "lace panties that showed in flashes around Gorgeous Gussie's shapely bottom produced just as many thrills" as did the top athletic performances—arguably more so.[68] It was enough to make her an instant celebrity, heralded as the latest international sex symbol. Newspaper editors made her underwear their lead story, and the *London Daily Express* carried photos of Moran on its front page for five days in a one-week period.

When Moran was eliminated in the third round (in a less controversial getup), the press bemoaned her absence and reported, "She left some sad faces among the newsmen and fans, who have found her the greatest personality since Suzanne Lenglen. . . . With her beauty and lace-trimmed panties she brought a spice to Wimbledon that had been lacking in the postwar years."[69] To focus on her appearance was to take away from her athleticism, as well as the accomplishments of her peers. No other woman received a fraction of the attention paid to Moran, and tennis played a subordinate role in her stardom. The press evermore referred to her as "Gorgeous Gussie"; *Colliers* described her as "a woman first and tennis player second." Commentators made much of her "lovely green eyes," "well-proportioned sun-tanned figure," and "36-inch bust" encased in her "snug T-shirt." She joined the ranks of other "sweater girls" of the era and incited comparisons to Hollywood starlet Lana Turner.[70]

In the days following her exit from the tournament, Moran was "called upon to visit hospitals, open fêtes, give her name to a race-horse and an aircraft, judge beauty contests, and become the central attraction of countless unlikely occasions."[71] The Marx Brothers invited her to join their act. The U.S. Fashion Academy voted her "Best Dressed Sports Woman." An underwear manufacturer "pleaded with her to endorse his version of the 'Gorgeous Gussy panties.'"[72] Through it all, Wimbledon officials were displeased but could not castigate her for her attire, for she had adhered to the directive of all-white clothing and had not technically violated any agreement.

Tinling, on the other hand, suffered for his creation, and members of the Wimbledon Committee reprimanded him for his impropriety, charging him with putting "sin and vulgarity into tennis." In the end, he resigned from his post as Wimbledon's master of ceremonies, a position he had held since 1927.[73] Though saddened by the disassociation, Tinling's design career skyrocketed after the introduction of Moran's panties. By 1955 he dressed "almost every important woman player—and about half of the men. . . . Mass-produced copies of his custom-designed Wimbledon costumes are also sold to more than 10,000 less well-known but equally ardent players in England and America."[74] He would go on to create outfits for nearly every top tennis star for the next several decades, including a stint as official designer for the women's Virginia Slims Circuit in the 1970s.

As for Moran, her post-panty career had even more to do with her appearance than with her athleticism. The press salivated with anticipation about what she might wear in the future. Although she won the Egyptian international tennis championship, the public was far more interested in the fact that she did so while wearing "eyebrow lifting black shorts" under her "conventional white costume."[75] Later that year, newspapers forewarned that "no added attractions will beautify her in the singles of the National Amateur Championships," to which officials worried the box office would "be swamped with irate patrons demanding their money back."[76] As she explained, "I know I will disappoint the crowd, but I can't concentrate on my game when people are staring at my panties."[77] She conceded that she might don something unconventional for the doubles competition, and legions of fans turned out to catch a glimpse.

By the 1950 Wimbledon event, media reports were consumed with the question of what Moran might wear. Journalists staked out Tinling's office, hoping to get a hint of what was to come. When Moran strode onto the court for first-round play, the crowd enthusiastically received her, clad as she was in a shirt-and-shorts ensemble constructed of white eyelet. The fabric exposed a diminutive though consistent pattern of her flesh across the entirety of the outfit, which correspondents christened the "Peek-a-Boo Suit." Department stores in the U.S. immediately requested the right to offer mass-produced versions to consumers.

Wimbledon officials were not amused and declared "no Bikini bathing dress" or similarly inappropriate attire would be allowed in 1951. Louis Greig, chairman of the All-England Club, fumed, "We don't like this business of running the thing into a dress show." Since Moran's initial spectacle, critics noticed that women began trying to "outdo" one another with their fashion. "There's a growing tendency among young players and little-known players of trying to get publicity with their costumes," Greig observed.[78]

A primary antagonist of Tinling, Greig may have been accurate in his assessment that long-shot contenders took their cues from Moran, for outrageous costumes would earn them publicity if their athletic talents could not. As *Time* documented in 1962:

> Every year the officials at sedate old Wimbledon endured more gaudy breeches of decorum. Shapely Tennis Player Karol Fageros, 28, took the gallery's eye off her serve with a pair of 24-carat gold-cloth panties that were later auctioned off for $70. Then Southern Belle Laura Lou Kunnen, 29, loyally stitched a Confederate flag to her undies. The living end was Brazil's Maria Bueno, 22, the 1959 and 1960 champion, who scandalized the crowd at this year's championships with a display of "shocking pink" briefs worn under a flapping "twist dress." No more, decreed the directors. From now on, it is "a condition of entry that all players will wear whites."[79]

Tactical underwear worked for a few players. A relatively unknown Jane Hopps made the papers for playing a tournament in Manchester, England, in "blue and white polka dot panties." Fans hoped for a matchup between Hopps and Fageros, the newly crowned "glamour girl" of tennis, who earned an eight-page spread in *Cosmopolitan* for her gold-lamé skivvies.[80]

Fageros later became one of just a handful of women, including Moran, to parlay their celebrity into a professional career. In 1950, at age twenty-six and never ranked higher than fourth in the United States, Moran signed a contract for seventy-five thousand dollars to go on tour under the management of Bobby Riggs. Like Lenglen before her, she was savvy to the lucrative possibilities associated with shedding the shackles of amateurism. "The difference," according to Tinling, "was that Suzanne's impact had resided in her supreme skill; Gussy's was dependent on other factors." The drawing card for her tour was not her athletic prowess, and she proved a poor match for her opponent, Pauline Betz, who allegedly had to tone down her game to keep the scores somewhat balanced. As the sheen of her costume choices began to tarnish, there seemed little to stimulate public interest in women's professional tennis.[81]

Racial Politics and Tennis Whites

A look at the press coverage of tennis during the late 1940s and 1950s shows that undershorts garnered greater attention than did talented players and relevant social issues—at least in the white press. The black press, however, devoted significant ink to more critical commentary, especially the push toward racial desegregation. For years representatives of the American Tennis Association (ATA), an African American institution (though they permitted participants of all races), pushed the USLTA to allow black players in their tournaments. Unlike golf, tennis officials never formally introduced a "Caucasian clause" into their bylaws; segregation was de facto, not de jure, but the understanding was just as powerful as one put into writing. In the post–World War II era, "gentlemen's agreements" barring black participation in major sports began to erode, first in professional football, then professional baseball, and finally professional basketball. Tennis, primarily an amateur game played at private clubs, stood stalwart against the prevailing tides.

African Americans began playing tennis shortly after their white compatriots. Around 1895, notes educator and historian Edwin B. Henderson, black players rallied at Tuskegee Institute and at interstate tournaments sponsored by Philadelphia's Chautauqua Club in 1898 and 1899.[82] Banned from white clubs and competitions, a number of African American tennis associations sprang up around the country, pointing to the need for a central organization. In response, a small, upper-class contingent of aficionados met in Washington, D.C., and formed the ATA in 1916. The next year, the group hosted its first national championships at Baltimore's Druid Hill Park.

The number of black tennis clubs grew over the subsequent decades, and ATA competitions, particularly the national tournaments, became important social events. The ATA held its first national championships in cities with significant African American populations. Within a short period of time, it moved the events to the campuses of historically black colleges, further cementing the sport's ties to elite circles. Like the USLTA, the ATA set certain measures in place to maintain the sport's privileged status. Officials insisted on proper attire and etiquette and enforced a strict code of amateurism that kept athletes from earning compensation for their play. In addition, it was "very necessary to belong to a club since in order to play in organized tennis you must belong to a club or association." The sport therefore required a fair bit of both cultural and economic capital; money was "the major problem of most tennis players," the *Chicago Defender* determined.[83] Costs for training, equipment, dress, travel, and contest entries kept it beyond the reach of most Americans of any race or ethnicity.

There is little in the black press (and nothing in the white papers) to suggest that tennis fans found African American women's costumes particularly noteworthy during the first half of the twentieth century. Photographs from the ATA's early days show competitors dressed in styles similar to white athletes (see figure 1.7). Players were habitually clad in white costumes, and hem lengths tended to coincide with trends witnessed in the USLTA. Early photographs of Ora Washington, winner of eight singles and twelve doubles ATA championships in the 1920s and 1930s, show a woman in a white, loose-fitting, calf-length ensemble, somewhat akin to that of the flapper, with her legs ensconced in heavy white stockings. A later image of Washington, taken in 1939, shows her standing with challenger Dorothy Morgan (see figure 1.8). Both women wear white skirts (Washington's appears to be bifurcated) that fall several inches above the knee. They are without stockings, wearing short socks and tennis shoes, while Morgan models a sunshade in the style of Helen Wills. The white champion Wills, it is worth noting, allegedly refused invitations to play Washington on the basis of race.[84]

Black competitors also began to don shorts at the same time as white players. At the annual grass-court meet in 1932, the *Chicago Defender* disclosed that "most of the women entrants . . . will wear shorts of the kind made famous during the recent tennis tournament held in Paris." Edgar G. Brown, president

Figure 1.7: Western Federation delegation from California, National Tournament, Wilberforce University, Ohio, 1940. Courtesy of Dale G. Caldwell and the Black Tennis Hall of Fame.

and founder of the black National Lawn Tennis Association, approved of the fashion, telling reporters, "Personally, both from an artistic and practical viewpoint, shorts seem to me proper attire for genuine devotees of the modern and scientific driving game. Brief, airy garments are certainly advantageous to fast tennis and play on grass. The officials of the association have therefore sanctioned the new fad as right and proper for those who find it in keeping with their own sense of individual propriety and aesthetic values."[85] While white authorities debated the merits of shorts at home and abroad, black authorities seemed to find little scandalous in the articles, at least based on what appears in published accounts. One journalist noted that "the glamour girl of tennis," Flora Lomax, who "refuse[d] to play in anything but shorts," earned some attention.[86] Her garments "were the center of attraction among the femmes' uniforms" on more than one occasion.[87] For the most part, however, commentary on women's attire was rare.

One interesting sartorial critique came in the form of a *Chicago Defender* editorial. The author censured an assemblage of male players he witnessed on the city's public courts clad in "trousers and BVDs [undershirts] . . . without a top shirt. . . . Some have spoken to them about it but say they follow after the

Penna. Open
July 24 -30, 1939.
Photo by - Mosley

Figure 1.8: Winner Ora Mae Washington (*right*) and Dorothy Morgan at the
Pennsylvania Open Tennis Tournament, Philadelphia, July 30, 1939. Courtesy of
the John W. Mosley Photograph Collection, Charles L. Blockson Afro-American
Collection, Temple University Libraries, Philadelphia.

Figure 1.9: American Tennis Association champion Flora Lomax, undated photograph, wearing what appears to be a short skirt, despite the comment that she "refused" to wear anything but shorts. Courtesy of Dale G. Caldwell and the Black Tennis Hall of Fame.

fashion of some whites. If the whites set a bad example, it is not the correct thing for us to follow." It was crucial that black tennis players held themselves to a high standard, the essay maintained: "The deportment displayed on the courts is watched, as all other races realize the better element take up tennis."[88] The comment alludes to the class-based foundation and aspirations of those who played, as well as disgust for the dregs who debased themselves and their race.

The editorial also suggested that African Americans appropriated white styles of dress. To sort out why blacks sought to emulate whites in manners of deportment and leisure that were so racially exclusionary is a complex undertaking. It is additionally complicated by the sport of tennis, for historian Mark Foster writes that in the early 1900s, "blacks shared whites' interest in sports such as baseball, albeit on separate diamonds. However, leisure sports with elitist or upper class overtones . . . appeared lily white, almost beyond reach." Sociologist E. Franklin Frazier critiques the "black bourgeoisie" for its concentration on materialism and status consciousness "copied from the wealthy upper white middle class."[89] He argues that the consumption-driven exclusivity drives a wedge between the classes and does little to advance the cause of civil rights.

In her autobiography, *I Always Wanted to Be Somebody,* the great Althea Gibson commented on the elitism of black tennis, epitomized by the Cosmopolitan Club in New York: "The Cosmopolitan members were the highest class of Harlem people and they had rigid ideas about what was socially acceptable behavior. They were undoubtedly more strict than white people of similar position, for the obvious reason that they felt they had to be doubly careful in order to overcome the prejudiced attitude that all Negroes lived eight to a room in dirty houses and drank gin all day and settled their arguments with knives." Members carefully cultivated and insisted upon a class-based performance of "respectability," the goal of which, according to historian Evelyn Brooks Higginbotham, "was to distance oneself as far as possible from images perpetuated by racist stereotypes."[90] Thus, the narrow dictates of propriety, though hierarchical and exclusionary, could also serve as a vehicle for racial progress.

African Americans attempted to cross tennis's color line throughout the twentieth century. In 1925 *Philadelphia Tribune* columnist Edgar Brown predicted that "in less than twenty years . . . a black man whose ancestors have withstood the burning suns of Africa and whose foreparents have withstood, bare-headed, the long seasons of backbending in American cotton fields will be crowned world's champion just as Jack Johnson earned that other crown on that hot afternoon in Reno." He was wrong on two counts: it took twenty-six years, and the first USLTA black tennis champion was not a man, but a woman—Althea Gibson.[91]

Gibson caught the notice of two physicians during the 1946 ATA National Tournament, where she finished second to the great Roumania Peters. Dr. Hubert Eaton of Wilmington, North Carolina, and Dr. Walter Johnson of Lynchburg, Virginia, were active ATA members. Assessing Gibson's need for formal training, they devised a plan. She would live with Eaton during the school year and practice on his backyard tennis court. In the summers, she would stay with Johnson, who would drive her around the country to compete on the ATA circuit. They would pay her living and tennis expenses, teach her the finer points of the game and, equally important, how to conduct herself with the decorum required in a sport like tennis. As part of their program of racial uplift, the doctors also insisted she finish high school in Wilmington and assisted with her matriculation at Florida A&M, a historically black college. Part of the "talented tenth" of African American society, Eaton and Johnson pushed for Gibson's self-improvement through education, etiquette, physicality, and dress. She adapted quickly, winning the ATA nationals in 1947 and in the nine successive years thereafter.

Gibson played her first USLTA-sanctioned events in 1950, winning the Eastern Indoor Tournament and finishing second in the National Indoor meet. The USLTA justified excluding her from the national outdoor tournament at Forest Hills by citing her lack of experience playing on grass courts. This was circuitous logic: to gain the necessary experience, she had to play on grass; to play on grass, she had to compete at the private clubs that hosted these contests and obstinately upheld their policies of racial segregation; without an invitation to play on the grass courts of private clubs, she could not gain enough experience to warrant an invitation from the USLTA.

ATA officials, the black press, and white supporters continued to lobby the elitist stronghold. Among her advocates was former USLTA champion Alice Marble, who penned a scathing editorial for *Lawn Tennis Magazine* that began, "For every individual who still cares whether Gussy has lace on her drawers, there are three who want to know if Althea Gibson will be permitted to play in the Nationals this year."[92] Marble excoriated those "sanctimonious hypocrites" who continued to ban black players. The magazine's editors endorsed her position and, in the face of such public shaming, along with the combined efforts of other activists, the USLTA relented. Officials invited Gibson as one of fifty-two women to compete in the 1950 U.S. Nationals.

In 1956 Gibson won the French singles event, the Wimbledon doubles title, and the championship at Forest Hills. She would go on to win the Wimbledon's singles and doubles titles the following year, as well at the U.S. Nationals, and repeated the same honors in 1958. She then retired from amateur competition, turning professional in order to eke out a living. Like others before her, a professional career did not provide the economic boon for which she had hoped, and she struggled financially for the remainder of her life.[93]

Playing amateur tennis, Gibson dressed in standard tennis whites—nothing that would give critics further reason to deprecate her presence. Historian Pamela Grundy writes that for players of color, "Refined manners, fashionable dress and conventionally feminine demeanor met community expectations, and also won acclaim as a challenge to racial stereotypes." Although journalists sniped about Gibson's "mannish" appearance and style of play, they could find no fault in her attire. Clothing could thus be a strategy women employed, a deliberate presentation of self designed to curry favor, assert the conventions of femininity, or generate media attention. Gibson alluded to this in her autobiography: "After a while I began to understand that you could walk out on the court like a lady, all dressed up in immaculate white, be polite to everybody, and still play like a tiger and beat the liver and lights out of the ball. I remember thinking it was kind of like a matador going into the bull ring, beautifully dressed, bowing in all directions, following the fancy rules to the letter, and all the time having nothing in mind except sticking that sword into the bull's guts and killing him dead as hell."[94] Her dress was an assertion of class- and gender-based propriety that made her incredible talents and racial subjectivity a bit more palatable for the otherwise critical audience.

Net Results

Between the 1880s and 1960, women's tennis fashions underwent tremendous change. So did women's tennis. From a staid and stationary pastime to an aggressively athletic sport, women's clothing transformed accordingly. Operating under the often tacit expectations that they were to comport themselves with appropriately feminine decorum, women adapted their costumes to improve their game. At the same time, liberating clothing meant exposing body parts previously shielded from public view—neck and décolletage, wrist and arm, ankle and calf, thigh and higher. What was once suitable only for private avail became incrementally staged for popular consumption, fetishizing and sexualizing the athletes' bodies even when their intention was merely to elevate their level of play.

Certainly, some athletes were complicit in this process, styling themselves with the understanding that unconventional getups grabbed tabloid headlines in ways that stellar play could not. Whatever their motivation, when athletes revealed their bodies, they risked sexualization. This is especially true for women, as well as in a sport like tennis, where class-based propriety and elitism reign supreme. These ideas dominated the collective consciousness of the tennis world, influencing even those most disenfranchised by the sport's character.

There are limitations to "reading" historical fashion trends. As Hollander cautions, "The social meaning can really only be adduced later and projected backward to account for a particular phenomena. And then, as with so much else, it is easy to interpret incorrectly from the standpoint of a different historical time, to miss something or add something."[95] Published commentaries about tennis clothing from witnesses and wearers do not provide direct access to the past, but they unquestionably point to elements of social change. Journalist Mildred Adams commented on this idea in 1934, proposing connections between women's rights, their contemporary style of dress, and their entry into sports:

> All this might seem to be making a mountain out of a molehill were it not for the close relationship which has always prevailed between sports and the modern freedom of women. There is division of opinion as to which was the cause and which concomitant, as to how impelling a part sport actually has played in the long process of emancipation, and how much of emancipation is due to weightier factors. But even the sternest economic determinist would not deny that the movement for the rights of women was accompanied by demands for the freedom of her ribs, her waist and her feet in playing.[96]

The historical relationships between sport, clothing, and women's enfranchisement are thoroughly intertwined with one another such that the seemingly pedestrian question "What shall we wear for tennis?" is not one to be taken lightly.

2. Commercial Tampons and the Sportswoman, 1936–52

Tennis underwent tremendous change after the 1960s. Television, corporate sponsorship, and the "open era" (bringing together amateur and professional players at Grand Slam events) all played important roles. Women continued to buck convention, bringing unprecedented strength and athleticism to the game, all of which contributed to a substantial "transformation in tennis clothing" during the postmodern age. Regardless of the time period, there is an attendant yet rarely acknowledged issue to consider when thinking about women's sport and fashion history: menstrual protection. Considering the often body-conscious clothing of the athlete, combined with her mobility in the context of sport, it is a topic that warrants contemplation. As feminist author and historian Susan Brownmiller frankly observes, "It is not easy to play the jock with a bloody cloth between one's legs."[1]

Discreet, reliable, comfortable menstrual protection is of vital importance to female athletes. For this reason, many expressed surprise when, in 1995, the financially struggling Women's Tennis Association (WTA) turned down a three-year cosponsorship deal worth more than ten million dollars from Tambrands, the company that manufactures Tampax tampons. Ann Person Worcester, the WTA's chief executive officer, told the press, "We think that at a critical time when we're trying to increase the popularity of the Tour, we did not believe Tampax sponsorship would be in our best interest." She justified the position by explaining, "Seventy-five percent of the insiders and experts we polled felt this would have a long-term negative impact." Tennis great Martina Navratilova initially voiced enthusiasm over the possible alliance affirming Tampax would provide "a sponsor whose product actually helped players perform 365 days a year." She later reversed her decision, conceding to the mentality that menstruation was a subject best left unacknowledged. As president of the WTA Players' Association, Navratilova disclosed, "We couldn't risk losing the local tournament sponsors. . . . [Menstruation] shouldn't be a stigma, but apparently it still is."[2]

It seems contradictory that a women's sporting organization should shun a product so important to women's physical activity. Addressing the decision to decline the sponsorship, Donna Lopiano, then executive director of the Women's Sports Foundation, lamented, "Tampax is a product that was designed for active women. It's a product that, for the first time, permitted girls and women to swim without concern." Others have similarly argued that without tampons, "the tennis tour would screech to a halt." "That's why it is so astonishing," wrote Leslie Baldacci of the *Chicago Sun Times*, "that the WTA, handed an opportunity to destigmatize women's biology, instead begged off, citing potential embarrassment."[3] Whereas tampon manufacturers considered sport a paramount venue to promote their products, the WTA's reticence to join with Tampax was merely one plot point in an enduring narrative of menstrual shame. From the beginning, the makers of commercial tampons struck advertising gold by featuring sport and athletic women, but because the tampon's primary selling point is that it conceals the social taboo of menstruation, real women athletes and their respective organizations often recoiled from the association.

The 1936 introduction of the commercial tampon was a significant point of change in the history of American women's lives, but it took until the early 1950s for the medical community and general population to agree upon its safety and acceptability. By then *Today's Health* told its readers that there is "absolutely no proof" that the use of tampons is harmful. *Good Housekeeping* also chimed in on the topic, announcing in 1952 that "the medical profession finds no objection to them."[4] The placement of advertisements in women's magazines provides a subtler indication of the product's approval. By the middle of the twentieth century, editors began to move tampon promotions from the back-page ghettos of their publications to more prominent forward sections. In *Good Housekeeping*, for example, Tampax ads began appearing with monthly regularity (!) on page 14 of after being relegated to the folio's stern since their debut.

Advertisements were crucial for the tampon's viability during this liminal period, and their composition proved a complex undertaking. Advertising executives faced the triple task of informing consumers that the product existed, that it was safe to use, and that it would improve their quality of life. They accomplished all three by deftly confronting women within the pages of their most beloved monthly magazines—*Good Housekeeping, Woman's*

Home Companion, McCall's, and *Ladies' Home Journal*—greeting them as friends and confidants, letting them in on the latest secret.[5] A survey of these publications reveals that at a time when marketing strategists rarely employed the sportswoman to hock their wares, she became a staple in tampon promotions. Caught in the unhampered exhilaration of her active lifestyle, the sportswoman told consumers that tampons "made life worth living" and that they too could get out and enjoy every day of the month.[6]

At the same time, these advertisements represented a narrow view of mid-century womanhood. Aimed at a white, middle-class or aspiring middle-class audience, the ads depicted activities such as golf, tennis, and especially swimming, all of which were class based, racially segregated, and "gender appropriate," as characterized by their elitism, movement aesthetics, and by the styles of clothing participants typically wore.[7] The often revealing costumes of these female athletes in advertisements were as important, if not more so, than their comfort or ease of motion, for the clothing emphasized the discretion this new form of internal protection afforded. Women no longer risked embarrassment from the telltale bulk of pads. The underlying message, therefore, perpetuated menstruation's traditional "culture of concealment," to use author Karen Houppert's phrase.[8] In other words, the tampon's main asset was that no matter what a woman might be doing, no one would ever know she had her period.

One cannot understand women's history and, specifically, women's sport history without attending to the medical and social prescriptions about menstruation.[9] In what follows, I trace some of the beliefs about menstruation, particularly as they relate to women's physical activity, before considering the advent of commercial tampons, the controversies they inspired, and the role of the sportswoman in product advertisements during the 1930s, 1940s, and early 1950s. Although tampons still inspire public apprehension, they are nonetheless banal in present-day society. Could they be, as one journalist assessed, the "product most responsible for liberating the female athlete"? Brownmiller once wrote that "menstruation asserts itself as a negative force to be overcome by the physically active woman."[10] Like a diminutive magic wand, if the tampon did not lift "the curse," it at least made things a bit more bearable.

Menstruation and the Question of Physical Culture

For centuries, even millennia, the question was not if tampons, pads, or other devices would facilitate women's sport and physical culture. Rather, it was whether women should even engage in physical activity—or any type of activity, for that matter—during their periods. This debate was part of a wider unease about what menstruation actually was and how it affected the female body. Even as late as 1907, renowned psychologist and educator G. Stanley Hall commented, "Precisely what menstruation is, is not very well known." It was not until the 1930s that physicians generally agreed upon its connection to ovulation.[11] Until that time, the list of menstrual theories grew long.

To delineate a catalog of historical conjectures associated with menstruation is well beyond the scope of this chapter.[12] Menstrual mythologies exist in myriad cultures, often deeply rooted in religious, folkloric, and medical beliefs. Many ancient legends connect menstruation to cycles of the moon or the rhythm of tides. Various collectives have conceived of catamenial discharge as a cure for a variety of ailments, a love charm, and an amulet against evil spirits. But it seems that injurious mythologies have had the greatest effect on women's lives. Few taboos, according to sport historian Patricia Vertinsky, have elicited such powerful and universal reactions.[13]

Many viewed menstruation as an outward symbol of women's inferiority, disability, impurity, and weakness. These beliefs, wrote Dr. Mary Chadwick in 1932, "were instituted primarily for the protection and safety of men, and secondarily for those of women."[14] It is an intriguing point. Many proscriptions are couched in the rhetoric of protecting and caring for menstruating women, but there is something to the notion that it was men who sought safeguard. Certain societies, for instance, segregated women from their larger communities, confining them to menstrual huts or other designated spaces during the duration of their periods for fear that they might contaminate water, crops, animals, or other humans.

There were a variety of theories about why women expressed blood with monthly regularity. Some felt that menstruation might be a symptom or cause of morbidity, the discharge resulting from a recurring internal wound. Others saw the process as a necessary purging of "bad blood" that might otherwise putrefy the body. Historian Lara Freidenfelds found that medical authorities, beginning with Hippocrates and continuing through the early twentieth century, advanced the "plethora" theory, or the idea that women's bodies produced excess blood that had to be expunged to restore humoral balance.[15]

Most "theories of menstrual disability" shared an element of scientific sexism, whereby women's biological differences were perceived as signs of their deficiency.[16] New hypotheses about menstruation quickly became incorporated into this standard trope of pathology. Those who argued that "biology is destiny" felt that regardless of how one explained catamenia, it was an indication that women were not as physically, mentally, or psychologically capable as men. It became a justification for restricting women's participation in everything from sport to education to politics.

During the Victorian era, vital energy theories held particular sway. The presumption was that women had a finite amount of corporeal power. To apply energy toward intellectual, social, or physical pursuits meant drawing it away from reproductive processes at a time when women's paramount duties were those of motherhood, domesticity, and wifehood. Physicians frequently advised that patients avoid mental and physical activity during their "periods of ill health," prescribing rest cures for middle- and upper-class women during which "ordinary occupations are to be suspended or modified."[17]

This concept received a great deal of traction from Dr. Edward Clarke's 1873 *Sex in Education; or, A Fair Chance for Girls,* in which he concluded that "during every fourth week, there should be a remission, and sometimes an intermission, of both study and exercise." He argued that a woman's body could not function properly while doing two things at once. Therefore, to direct one's energy toward physical or mental activity during menstruation would cause physiological peril and must be avoided. Clarke's work, reprinted seventeen times, proved wildly popular, and many agreed with his findings. But his work was not without detractors, including those who charged that *Sex in Education* was "utterly wrong in all its essential features."[18] Among Clarke's critics was Dr. Mary C. Putnam Jacobi, who determined that women received no physical benefits from menstrual respites, which had the additional drawback of cutting into working women's wages.[19]

Abstinence from movement and exertion was not a realistic option for most. It was a privilege of wealth. Rest was not for women working in agriculture, or factories, or taking care of the domestic chores. There was work to be done, money to be earned, households and children to be looked after. And although Dr. Jacobi considered the issue of social class in relation to menstrual rest, she failed to account for women of color, brusquely dismissing "negroes [*sic*], who for our purposes may be excluded from the reckoning."[20] The literature concerning menstruation during this era is virtually absent of racial and ethnic minority women, suggesting white physicians were either indifferent or perhaps unwilling to concede to them a commensurate level of humanity or femininity.

In 1926 the medical journal the *Lancet* declared that because of scientific advances and the need for women in the workforce during the First World War, Victorian attitudes toward menstruation had disappeared forever: "Everybody now knows that women are not necessarily 'unwell' once a month."[21] Although research about the effects of physical activity on menstruation (and vice versa) remained inconclusive, physicians began to change their collective opinion about menstrual rest.[22] It became fairly common for them to prescribe moderate exercise, especially to prevent or treat dysmenorrhea (painful menstruation), and doctors advocated strengthening one's abdominal muscles, improving one's posture, and developing one's overall strength to decrease afflictive and debilitating symptoms.[23] They also drew a decisive line between exercise and sport. The former was purposive, particularly with regard to women's roles as wives and mothers; the latter was foolhardy, for unnecessary strain in the context of sport jeopardized those very roles.

The medical admonition against sports competition provided a powerful justification for those who sought to keep women out of the Olympic Games and other elite events. In the 1920s and 1930s, women physical educators were among the most vocal opponents of varsity competition for girls and women, arguing instead for broad-based fitness opportunities for everyone (see chapter 3). Vertinsky explains that in the late nineteenth and early twentieth centuries, "the doctor and the gymnastics mistress were the main experts and controllers of the physical and mental aspects" in the lives of middle-class girls.[24] Together, these authorities concerned themselves with "strenuous exercise," which posed a "grave risk," especially during those days that women had their periods.[25] Uterine displacement figured acutely in such anxiety—a condition, doctors warned, that "may require an operation to prevent sterility."[26] Reproductive apprehensions lay at the heart of many denouncements against girls' and women's competitive sport.

As an indication of the strong connection between the fields of medicine and physical education, the editors of the *American Physical Education Review* extracted a section of an essay first published in the *Journal of American Medicine* in 1925. The result was a strong condemnation of sports participation during menstruation:

> Our young girls, in this age of feminine freedom, are also overdoing athletics. A girl should not be coddled because she is menstruating, but common sense . . . at such a period should be exercised. How many on a basketball team of girls, scheduled to compete with another team on a given day, are beginning or in the midst of this feminine function, in which the uterus is physiologically congested and temporarily abnormally heavy and hence, liable to displacement by the inexcusable strenuosity and roughness of this particular game? Why should girls try tests of vaulting? Is such prowess worth the price?[27]

Although one doctor confessed that "we can't actually put our finger on the harmful effect of too strenuous athletics on women," most agreed that uterine damage as well as "the tension and strain that come into competitive contests are apt to disturb the cycle."[28]

Perhaps the most vehement rebuke came in 1939 from Dr. Stephen Westmann, who conceptualized menstruation as a wound "in the most sensitive part of a woman's body" and declared that "no sports*man* would ever dream of competing with a wound in his vital organs!" He was unequivocal in his mandate "that *complete abstinence from activity in sport is absolutely imperative in the menstruating woman.*" Not only would women sacrifice their femininity and reproductive potential in their "ambition to win the laurel wreath of victory," but because of athletics, "typical female organs wither and that artificial monstrosity know as the virago comes about."[29]

Westmann's position seemed to be in the minority during the 1930s. For the most part, men and women in medicine and physical education promoted programs of moderate exercise that would develop women's reproductive and domestic capabilities.[30] They gradually began to temper their position with more liberal recommendations. For example, in 1935 Katherine Wells, a physical education instructor at Wellesley College, advised, "If a girl is over-strenuous during one of her periods she may suffer some discomfort for that period or even the following one, but there is no evidence that she will do herself any permanent injury or that she will 'pay for it later in life.' . . . On the whole the danger is in under rather than in over-exercising during the period." It is better, she suggested, to be too active than to be inactive.[31] Ultimately, many seemed to take the position that *exercise* (but not sport) during menstruation should be "decided individually."[32]

As physicians and educators debated what type of physical activity was best for women, new controversies about menstrual technologies entered the discourse. A commercially successful, disposable catamenial pad debuted in 1921, followed in 1936 by its Lilliputian cousin, the tampon. It was one thing for discussions about menstruation and menstrual management to go on in erudite circles, but to what extent did this knowledge filter to the rest of the population? Some girls and women gathered information from medical professionals or from adapted reports that appeared in popular magazines. Most, however, learned from other girls and women or by stumbling through a labyrinth of trial and error.

Middle-class girls typically learned about menarche and menstrual products from their mothers, provided they felt they could broach the subject. Many did not. Historian Joan Jacobs Brumberg found that working-class and ethnic minority mothers often "expected their girls to learn from their friends, older sisters, fellow workers, or even resident grandmothers or aunts."[33] Before (and even after) the advent of disposable pads, girls were likely to discover the cloths that their mothers or other relatives used and laundered. But there was a sense of shame and secrecy attached to menstruation, and the connection between menarche and sexuality exacerbated women's reticence to discuss the issue with newly initiated pubescents.

In the early twentieth century, the trend toward sex education in the schools provided another option for disseminating knowledge, though as late as 1959 it was reported that "menstrual education . . . is not permitted at all" in many school districts.[34] Unsure of where to place the topic in the wider curriculum—"in biology, physiology, physical education, or home economics classes"—instructors, physicians, and social workers consolidated their efforts to teach girls the facts of life, arguing that mothers too often failed to fulfill this duty.[35] The Girl Scouts of America also developed educational materials and, by 1921, earning the Health Winner Badge was dependent upon one's knowledge about menstruation.[36]

In the 1920s and 1930s, the burgeoning menstruation industry added to the educational materials used in homes and schools. Kimberly-Clark (manufacturer of Kotex pads) and Johnson & Johnson (maker of Modess pads and Meds tampons) produced leaflets on the subject, simultaneously promoting their brands and demystifying the biological process. The materials often addressed the issue of sport and physical activity. For instance, Kimberly-Clark's booklet *As One Girl to Another* included a two-page spread: one side devoted to "OK—go ahead!" the other to "No—Better wait!" (see figures 2.1 and 2.2). Among the six approved activities were "mild exercise and deep breathing" and dancing, provided girls "*sit down* now and then." They should also feel free to "bask on the beach. . . . But *don't* go in the water!" For the most part, only the gentlest forms of physicality were appropriate. Those "better-wait" endeavors bolster this position: Hiking was out, but "short walks are *good* for you." "Jumping and skipping jiggle you up! So *they're* taboo for a few days." Additionally, "Tennis, basketball, and other strenuous sports, should be *postponed*."[37]

By the 1940s and 1950s, the major corporations that produced menstrual products made terrific headway into the educational system. In one outreach program, Tampax, Inc., hired women with medical backgrounds to act as "trained menstrual educators" at schools, colleges, trade shows, and conventions.[38] The filmstrip also became a popular vehicle for delivering this type of information. It was "the ideal medium to impart sound information and develop a wholesome attitude toward [menstruation]," one reviewer assessed. "The film is impersonal. It is run in a darkened room which prevents embarrassment on the part of the students."[39]

Approximately ninety-three million American females saw *The Story of Menstruation,* coproduced by Walt Disney Productions and the Kimberly-Clark Corporation in 1946. The first half of the ten-minute feature offers a lesson in biology; the second half focuses on practical advice about hygiene, etiquette, and proper behavior. At one point, the narrator asks, "As for the old taboo against exercise? That's nonsense. Exercise is good for you during menstruation. Just use common sense. . . . It's going to *extremes* that's wrong,

OK — go ahead !

"Basin bathing" is *always* safe...if you hesitate to plunge in the tub.

Mild exercise and deep breathing are said by *many* to relieve cramps.

You can wash your hair if you dry it *quickly*—and stay out of draughts.

Warm showers are relaxing and beneficial . . . but *not* hot or cold!

If you dance—*sit down* now and then. You can always say your feet hurt!

Bask on the beach to your heart's content. But *don't* go in the water!

Figure 2.1: Kimberly-Clark, "As One Girl to Another" (1940). Courtesy of the Duke University Rare Book, Manuscript, and Special Collections Library, Durham, North Carolina.

no — Better wait!

Cold water gives your system a shock.
So diving is on the *don't do* list.

Jumping and skipping jiggle you
up! So *they're* taboo for a few days.

Tennis, basketball, and other strenuous sports, should be *postponed.*

Getting chilled may cause trouble.
So *don't* tumble about in the snow!

Hiking is on the "better wait" list.
But short walks are *good* for you.

Don't get your feet wet. Avoid
catching cold—at this time *especially!*

Figure 2.2: Kimberly-Clark, "As One Girl to Another" (1940). Courtesy of the Duke University Rare Book, Manuscript, and Special Collections Library, Durham, North Carolina.

and to be avoided." Personal Products' 1953 film *Molly Grows Up* similarly cautions that girls should avoid skating and horseback riding and that it is "not a very good idea to play fast games like volleyball and basketball or do strenuous dancing like square dancing or do anything that bounces you around a lot."[40] These types of materials filled two purposes. First, they offered education about menstruation, shedding light on a concern often shrouded in shame and secrecy. Second, they provided important advertising for the sponsor's product. Consumers were therefore plied with messages that they could continue their everyday routines, but only with the right menstrual technologies.

From Rags to Riches: A Brief History of the Tampon

When the first mass-produced menstrual tampon appeared in the United States in 1936, a significant proportion of the female population still relied on reusable clothes to absorb menstrual flow, despite the existence of several commercial options. Between 1854 and 1914, there were at least twenty different patents for sanitary napkins, catamenial sacks and supporters, menstrual receivers and receptacles, and monthly protectors.[41] By the 1880s, women could purchase mass-produced disposable napkins that they were instructed to burn after using, though they were cost prohibitive for most of society.[42]

Manufacturers tried selling their products in drugstores, in department stores, and through mail-order catalogs such as Montgomery Ward and Sears, Roebuck, Co. They advertised in magazines, including *Harper's Bazaar*, the *Delineator, Vogue*, and *Women's World* but had little success in selling their goods. The subject of menstruation and the products with which it was associated were anathema to contemporary sensibilities.

It was not until after World War I that American women began to embrace the idea of commercially made sanitary pads. In 1920 the Kimberly-Clark Company found itself with a surplus of the cellulose fiber produced for bandaging material during the war. Thinner and more absorbent than cotton, Red Cross nurses used it for menstrual protection. Upon learning this, executives developed a new disposable pad they called Kotex (for "cotton texture").[43] It was not an immediate success. Most magazines refused to advertise the product, drugstores and department stores would not stock them, and, consequently, sales were low by the end of 1921.

Executives decided to stick with it, and, in a few years, things began to turn around. The right advertising proved the key to success. In 1923 Kimberly-Clark hired the Lord and Thomas Agency, and "the ad copy became direct enough to spur sales, yet discreet enough to be accepted by the leading magazines. The delicate pen and ink drawings emphasized femininity and product quality," wrote Robert Spector in his history of the company. By the end of the decade, there were approximately three hundred menstrual pads on the market. Retailing at about ten cents per pad, "the benefits initially came primarily to middle and upper-class women but its long-run effect was revolutionary," according to historian Vern Bullough.[44]

By 1929 Kotex had become a nineteen-million-dollar business, primarily due to advertising campaigns that emphasized medical approval.[45] These campaigns worked well within the Progressive Era's emphasis on health and hygiene. World War I, the influenza epidemic, and the substantiation of germ theories heightened medico-scientific and public attention toward issues of sanitation. Referring to the commodities as "feminine hygiene products" and "sanitary napkins" reinforced their association with cleanliness and propriety and, consequently, with commercial success.

It would be a mistake to think that the concept of vaginal tampons originated in the 1930s. As one journalist wrote, "It goes back a bit. Tampons have probably existed in some form or other as long as women."[46] Egyptian women in the fifteenth century made use of soft papyrus to stanch menstrual flow; Roman women did the same with wool. In ancient Japan, women fashioned tampons out of paper, held them in place with a bandage, and changed them ten to twelve times a day.[47] For centuries Indonesians made similar devices from vegetable fiber, while traditional Hawaiian women used the furry part of a native fern. In 1776 a French physician reported the use of vaginal tampons to control hemorrhage and leucorrhea (discharge) using a piece of tightly wound linen cloth dipped in vinegar.[48] In 1872 a German Egyptologist discovered a document in the ancient capital of Thebes describing a medicated tampon used to prevent pregnancy. Women throughout the world still use grasses, mosses, and other plants during menstruation, but it was not until the mid- to late-nineteenth century that Western doctors advocated the use of tampons.[49]

It would also be a mistake to think that the advent of commercial tampons rendered obsolete the self-made varieties. A 1942 survey found that 37 percent of tampon users availed of homemade products.[50] This persistence was not necessarily due to conservatism, argue scholars Laura K. Kidd and Jane Farrell-Beck, but due rather to "other factors, such as cost, availability, personal embarrassment, and comfort." Some women bought natural sponges at art supply stores and cut them to size; others rolled strips of surgical cotton. Researchers found that physically active women, particularly ballet dancers, used homemade menstrual tampons long after they were available commercially. Nancy Friedman, author of *Everything You Must Know about Tampons*, wrote that women who made their own "belonged to an exclusive margin of society; they tended to be actresses, models, athletes or prostitutes—all dubious professions, in the eyes of 'respectable' women."[51]

There were several starts down the road to mass-manufactured tampons. In the early 1920s, John Williamson was an employee of Kimberly-Clark. Legend has it that he approached his father, a physician and medical consultant for the company, with a contraption in which he had "rigged up a condom, punctured it with holes and filled it with the creped wadding material that went into Kotex pads." It might have developed into the first commercial tampon, but Dr. Williamson summarily dismissed his son: "Never would I put any such strange article inside a woman!" he allegedly decried.[52] Historian Sharra Vostral found two patent applications in 1927 for "catamenial appliance" prototypes, though it appears that no commercial products resulted from them.[53]

A subsequent attempt came from Dr. Frederick S. Richardson, who patented his "Wix" brand of tampon in 1932.[54] Ten months later, Dr. Earle C. Haas received a patent for "a catamenial device" that he invented to alleviate the discomfort his wife experienced wearing sanitary napkins during her work as a nurse. Drawing on implements commonly used during surgery to absorb blood, he constructed the menstrual tampon out of compressed surgical cotton, which he augmented with a heavy waterproof cord and a two-part telescopic cardboard applicator. Calling it Tampax (for "tampon" and "vaginal pack"), Haas had difficulty selling it. Amid the Great Depression of the 1930s, few were willing or able to invest in such a controversial product.

Haas eventually sold his patent and trademark to a group led by businesswoman Gertrude Tenderich and manufacturing began.[55] As with sanitary pads, promoting Tampax proved a difficult task. Drugstore managers refused to openly display the products; others declined to include them in their inventory altogether, and so Tenderich joined forces with Ellery Mann, who became the founder and first president of Tampax, Inc. Mann employed high-profile advertising firms to engage marketing strategies that targeted consumers, pharmacists, and physicians through women's magazines and trade and professional publications such as *Drug Store Retailing* and the *Journal of the American Medical Association.*[56]

Tampax, Inc., launched its first advertising campaign in 1936. The inaugural ad was a full-page color promotion that appeared in the *American Weekly*, a Sunday supplement to several major U.S. newspapers. Inviting women to "welcome this new day for womanhood," it played on the notion that tampons facilitate active lifestyles while emphasizing the importance of discretion and "daintiness." Pictured throughout the text are several vignettes of women participating in various activities, including horseback riding, dancing, swimming, and tennis, along with the endorsement that Tampax will "stay in place through the most strenuous sports," though most physicians and physical educators reproved such endeavors in the 1930s and 1940s.[57]

These ads, like many of the era, also contained a mail-order form, sparing women the embarrassment of asking a pharmacist or salesclerk for "the most natural and the most hygienic method of sanitary protection." For thirty-five cents, purchasers would receive a box of ten tampons and an information booklet, all of which came wrapped in plain paper to ensure discretion. The price clearly locates the product within middle-class consumption. In fact, a box of tampons exceeded the hourly wage of twenty-eight cents earned by the women hired to run the Tampax production lines.[58]

Marketing executives had found their niche. Within a year, the product proved economically successful and inspired several imitators. In 1945 *Consumer Reports* informed readers that although "the percentage of tampon sales is still relatively small in terms of the sanitary napkin market, there can be no question about its rapid growth, as more women take advantage of the greater comfort of internally worn protection." By then there were nine brands of tampons on the market, including Lillettes, Meds, Pursettes, and Fibs.[59] The names are telling in that they emphasize that the products are feminine and diminutive, of medical origins, or allow women a "little white lie" that conceals menstruation.

There were several obstacles on the path to tampons' success. Clergymen denounced them, fearing they would aid in contraception, sexual pleasure, or both.[60] Physicians similarly cautioned that internal protection "brings about pelvic consciousness and undue handling, [which] may cause eroticism and masturbation." There were concerns that tampons would rupture the hymeneal membrane, making it difficult for a husband to confirm the virginity of his new bride. In the first study published on the subject, physicians advised women to exercise prudence when choosing menstrual products, warning, "Tampons are foreign bodies in the vagina." Throughout the 1930s and 1940s, medical opinions remained divided over their utility and safety.[61]

Illustrating this ambivalence was a 1943 issue of the *Western Journal of Surgery, Obstetrics, and Gynecology* that published two contiguous, contradictory articles on the topic. In the first, Drs. J. Milton Singleton and Herbert F. Vanorden declared that the majority of physicians were "definitely opposed" to tampons because they were unhygienic, easily lost in the body, and sabotaged virginity. Women, they admonished, were "absolutely unskilled" to "invade the vagina during menstruation" and blamed those who were "gullible to attractive advertising" for keeping what would otherwise be a fad from dying out. They did concede, however, that tampons were "of cosmetic value to dancers, actresses and during athletic competitions," but the value was merely aesthetic.[62]

In the second article, Dr. Karl John Karnaky disagreed with almost every one of his colleagues' findings. He reported that based on his five-year study of forty-two women, tampons were both safe and easy to use. "Unmarried women" (read: virgins), he determined, had no trouble using tampons. They overcame the "problem of menstrual odor," did not irritate vaginal tissue, and would not cause "cancer, erosion, or vaginitis." Similar studies corroborated his results and determined that as long as she was agreeable to using the device, the "average" woman could control "catamenial flow with safety, comfort, and complete protection."[63]

A 1945 study conducted by Dr. Robert Dickinson yielded similar conclusions. Dickinson surveyed more than 6,500 women as well as "19 sources in the literature, both medical and commercial," and found "satisfaction ranging around 90%, especially with younger women, educated groups and better incomes."[64] It is difficult to ascertain why certain populations were more amenable to tampons. Part of it may have had to do with the ways and places the products were advertised, for the targeted demographic was clearly the young, white, middle-class woman.

Another aspect probably had to do with price, for a box of ten to twelve tampons ranged anywhere from $0.20 to $1.60. In less affluent communities, women continued to use cloth pads well into the 1940s.[65] In addition, Brumberg argues, "When newly arrived ethnic immigrant women were presented with 'modern scientific' information about menstruation and personal hygiene, it was not always accepted or utilized," despite claims that this information "inevitably improved the quality of life and mitigated class differences."[66] Deep-seated culturally and religiously situated beliefs regarding menstruation, the body, and propriety surely influenced women's inclinations toward tampons and related products.

Then there were those groups that embraced the concept of internal menstrual protection from the beginning. Historian Heather Munro Prescott found that "working women and athletes in particular liked the product because it was less cumbersome and conspicuous than sanitary napkins."[67] Perhaps because these women already transgressed normative gender roles, they were more apt to experiment with different technologies. Then again, it may have been a case of simple pragmatics—with places to go and things to do, they could not afford to be inconvenienced by their periods.

The World on a String

Popular media forms, particularly women's magazines, were vital for disseminating information on menstruation and menstrual products, though few articles or editorials directly addressed the subject of tampons. Information primarily reached readers through advertising, which "stepped forward to fill one of the many vacuums of adequate communication and advice." As such, early campaigns for menstrual products, according to Brumberg, "constituted the first real public acknowledgment of menstruation."[68]

In 1946 an observer referred to advertisements as "humbler adjuncts" to periodical literature and predicted that they "may prove more valuable to the future historian than the editorial contents. In them we may trace our sociological history, the rise and fall of fads and crazes, changing interests and tastes, in foods, clothes, amusements and vices, a panorama of life as it was lived, more information than old diaries or crumbling tombstones." A half century later, sport historian Douglas Booth certified the importance of advertisements, arguing that they "are useful sources for the study of past attitudes to commodities and are excellent signifiers of cultural values." Communication theorist Marshall McLuhan went so far as to contend that "ads . . . are the richest and most faithful daily reflections that any society ever made of its entire range of activities."[69] That executives took particular care with promotions for controversial commodities like tampons tell us something about public attitudes toward menstruation. And the prominent connection they made between menstrual products and the sportswoman expressed something about the contemporary disposition toward athletic women. They offered an attractive version of womanhood. They were modern at a time when modernity moved products. Tampon advertisements employed imagery that advocated sport and active physicality even during "that time of the month," thereby assuaging some of the beliefs that held women as weak, frail, or mentally and physically inferior because of their menstrual cycles.

In the early twentieth century, determined historian Gregory Kent Stanley, "Advertisers frequently proclaimed themselves as missionaries of modernity, championing the new against anything which could be considered old-fashioned. . . . In that light, the image of the sportswoman appeared tailor-made." While she became a regular fixture in promotions for menstrual products, this was not her first foray into popular media. The bicycle craze of the late 1800s was stoked, in part, by a full-force advertising campaign that frequently featured women. Exemplifying the "new woman," the female cyclist pedaled her way into a variety of product promotions, for she at once thwarted convention and institutionalized a modern sensibility. Concurrently, the "Gibson girl," created by illustrator Charles Dana Gibson, replaced the voluptuous ideal that preceded her. A tall, thin figure of athletic carriage and aristocratic bearing, the Gibson girl "was identified with physical emancipation through sports, exercise, and dress."[70] She first appeared in *Life* in 1890, where she epitomized a new standard of beauty that proliferated in popular magazines, newspapers, and commercial advertisements through the start of the First World War.

At this time, notes historian Benjamin Rader, "advertisers, the popular press, and health and beauty authorities began to establish the modern linkage between physical activity and female beauty." Throughout the 1920s, admen used the female athlete not to sell a specific product, but rather to promote the lifestyle associated with the "modern" woman. By 1936, however, the "First Female Athletic Era" had ended, according to scholars Mary Boutilier and Lucinda SanGiovanni, to be supplanted by a "'Feminine' Reaction to the Athletic Era," a gendered backlash against the sportswoman of the previous generation.[71] The female athlete began to fade from mass-advertising campaigns with the exception, that is, of tampon promotions, where she continued to reign as the icon of modernity. It was not her sporting prowess consumers were compelled to envy, but her unencumbered joie de vivre—a spirit possible only with the correct consumer purchase.

Tampax set the tone for much of the menstrual industry's advertising. Initial campaigns relied on full-page color advertisements, which made them expensive and restricted their circulation. In 1937, under the new guidance of the McCann Erickson advertising agency, Tampax moved to narrow, one-column, black-and-white promotions. Other companies followed suit. This format, according to one executive, was "a money-saver and enabled us to advertise in a lot of magazines frequently." This meant that more women were likely to encounter the product. By 1941 Tampax promotions appeared in fifty-one different magazines with a total circulation of 49,575,450. Although a small company, Tampax, Inc., became one of the top one-hundred advertisers in the United States at the time, and executives estimated that women who read magazines would encounter approximately twelve ads per month, in addition to promotions from rival brands.[72]

Tampax, along with its main competitors, Fibs and Meds, leaned heavily on sportswomen in the 1930s and 1940s. Physically active females smiled on the golf course with banners reading "Tampax makes life worth living" and "As free as though you were ten years old" (see figure 2.3). A bowler urged consumers to "Keep going in Comfort!" "Why be a 'Sitter-Outer,'" the ad continued, "when Fibs (the Kotex tampon) permits you to keep going in

TAMPAX *makes* LIFE WORTH LIVING

NO BELTS
NO PINS
NO PADS
NO ODOR

THERE is no mystery about Tampax. It is simply a kind of monthly sanitary protection *worn internally.* Each individual Tampax is sealed in a hygienic container which allows you to insert the Tampax neatly and daintily.

Tampax was perfected by a doctor and more than 133,000,000 have already been sold. It brings new comfort and freedom to club women, office workers, athletes, students, housewives. It does away with chafing, odor and "bulking," providing a smooth costume-profile even in swim suits or sheer evening gowns. No belts or pins. You really forget you are wearing Tampax!

Made of pure, long-fibered surgical cotton, highly compressed. Tampax is extremely absorbent and efficient. No disposal problems. Sold at drug stores and notion counters. Two sizes: Regular Tampax and Junior Tampax. Introductory package, 20¢. An average month's supply, 35¢. As much as 25% saved by purchasing large economy package of 40.

Accepted for advertising by the Journal of the American Medical Association.

Today's SANITARY PROTECTION (FOR MONTHLY USE!)

TAMPAX

TAMPAX INCORPORATED
New Brunswick, N. J.   GH-79
☐ Send introductory box; 20¢ enclosed (stamps, coins). Size checked below.
☐ Regular Tampax ☐ Junior Tampax
☐ Send Tampax booklet with diagrams—free.
Name
Address

Which Tampon is best for you?

FIBS—THE KOTEX TAMPON— merits your confidence! Enables you to wear shorts or slacks any day you wish! Worn internally, Fibs provide *invisible* sanitary protection. Easy to use . . . no pins, pad or belt . . . no chafing, no disposal problem.

NOT 8
NOT 10
BUT 12

FULL DOZEN ONLY 20¢. Not 8 . . . not 10 . . . but 12 for 20¢. When you buy Fibs, you pay for no mechanical gadget to aid insertion . . . for none is needed! Fibs are quilted . . . easy to insert without artificial means. The quilting provides added comfort, and safety, too. Yet Fibs cost less!

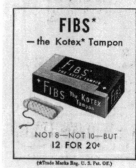

FIBS*
— the Kotex* Tampon

NOT 8—NOT 10—BUT
12 FOR 20¢

(*Trade Marks Reg. U. S. Pat. Off.)

comfort ever day . . . regardless of the calendar!" Others took to the tennis courts. Two women stood with rackets slung over their shoulders as one confided to the other, "Once it was a luxury, Dora—but now anybody can afford the modern, *inside* way." "Don't tell me," responded Dora, "I'd be sitting home today—if it weren't for Meds!" (see figure 2.5).[73] Implicit in these advertisements is an important change in menstrual convention: the new technology afforded opportunities that the old methods never could. The sportswoman symbolized this break with the past as one who had seized hold of these opportunities and embraced the progress and achievements of contemporary life.

Figure 2.5: Meds, "Now! New and Improved Internal Sanitary Protection . . . At Only 20¢!" *Good Housekeeping*, October 1940, 208.

A particular strategy of ad executives in the 1920s, 1930s, and 1940s, contends Roland Marchand in *Advertising and the American Dream,* was to juxtapose "the new against the old, the modern against the old-fashioned," a theme evident in contemporary tampon promotions. Comparing the seemingly archaic methods of menstrual management against the newest form of internal technology, the ads insinuated that product choice told a great deal about the consumer: "This wise, modern woman enjoys every day—convenience and freedom are hers—the Meds way." The tampon "liberates you from pin-and-belt nuisance" and from the shackles of yesteryear's primitive pads. Beneath the image of a woman in a two-piece bathing suit, the text chided, "Don't be so conservative! . . . Dress and act with more freedom."[74]

A 1938 Wix ad exemplified this type of comparison by apposing two women. The first is clad in a long skirt and shirt with a high collar and cuffs. Her hair is drawn back in an outdated bun as she sits in her rocking chair and stares wistfully out a lace-curtained window. The implication is that she would rather be active and outdoors, but menstrual customs forbid it. Superimposed across the image, in old-fashioned script, is the date, "1900" (see figure 2.6).

Ms. 1900 shares the ad with a second woman labeled in a modern font: "1938." Set on a mountainside golf course, she is caught up in the follow-through of her swing. With stylishly bobbed hairstyle and a smile on her face, she gazes, presumably, at the trajectory of her ball. Hers is not the longing look of a woman bound by tradition, but of one joyfully engaged in physical activity. A simple period cannot keep her from her pursuits. "Be modern!" the banner commands as smaller inset images depict women at work, lounging in bathing suits, and posing with tennis rackets in midvolley. Curiously, the text does not mention athletics. Instead, it tells consumers

Figure 2.6: Wix, "Be Modern!" *Good Housekeeping,* July 1938, 173.

that with Wix, there is "No Danger of Odors" and that the product is "Utterly Invisible" and "Always Comfortable."[75] It is the image of the sportswoman, not the sporting advantage that tampons provide, that is most important in these ads.

The "Be Modern" ad illustrates the two themes that appeared most prevalently in tampon promotions during this era. First, advertisers insisted that the device offered comfort, especially by comparison to homemade or commercial pads. This was no small accomplishment. Hampered by earlier products that required belts, pins, strings, harnesses, straps, girdles, or some combination of the like, pads caused chafing, irritation, and abrasion. Women likened them to wearing diapers, and the necessary thickness of the cloths and pads restricted the types of clothes they could wear as well as the types of activities in which they could engage.

"Be Modern," as did almost every midcentury tampon ad, also emphasizes the notion of discretion. Vostral conceptualizes menstrual hygiene products as "technologies of passing" that "allow women to present themselves as non-menstruants." With the use of tampons, advertisers insisted, no one would ever detect, in any way, a woman's monthlies. Accordingly, the relatively revealing clothing in these promotions accentuates the selling point of concealment. An ice skater's skirt flares out, skimming just below crotch level, a bicyclist rides astride in a diminutive pair of shorts: "Can You Trust Tampons?" they ask (see figure 2.7). Certainly: "with Fibs you can change to shorts, play suit or even a swim suit with nobody the wiser!"[76]

Of all the athletic endeavors depicted in tampon advertisements, swimming appeared most often.[77] At first glance, advertisers seem to have made a curious choice in this regard, for it was the one activity against which even the most liberal thinkers cautioned. Women should avoid the water not for their own safety, authorities advised, but for the well-being of their fellow swimmers. Menstruants were contaminants. At midcentury women were exhorted that they must not "pollute the water, even microscopically." Disdained Dr. Margaret Bell in a 1942 issue of *Hygeia,* "I should hate to get into a pool with a menstruating girl, who should be excluded from the pool—for purely esthetic reasons if for no other." But with the dawn of the commercial tampon, physicians and physical educators began to rethink their prohibitions. One instructor reported that, after much debate, her local athletic board decided "to allow the girls with parental permission to swim during their period if they used tampons" and that the "use of tampons makes it possible for many girls to enjoy without interruption of one of the most pleasant and beneficial sports—swimming."[78] In very real ways, then, the tampon directly encouraged physical opportunities in ways that other menstrual technologies did not.

Advertisements frequently promoted swimming as a way to authenticate the product's disavowal of biological processes. The appeal of the swimmer was not that she could stroke through the water at any time of the month, but that she could lounge by the side of the pool in revealing attire with no one the wiser. Although ads encouraged women to "swim to your heart's content," it was clearly more important that the tampon "does away with chafing, odor and 'bulking,' providing a smooth costume profile even in swim suits or sheer evening gowns." "Whether the [swim] suit is wet or dry," another ad explained, "Tampax remains invisible with no bulging, bunching or faintest line!" Women almost never appeared in the water in these promotions (for an exception, see figure 2.8). Thus, as Annemarie Jutel found in her analysis of Australian and New Zealand advertisements, "Modern, streamlined disposable products did not enhance women's sporting experience as much as they enhanced their ability to conceal a taboo process."[79]

Challenging the Curse

By the early 1940s, the sportswoman began to fade from tampon promotions, except for the persistent bathing beauty.[80] Instead, with the country embroiled in the Second World War, the product's primary selling point became the comfort and discretion it offered women in the workplace. Those laboring on assembly lines, typing behind office desks, or welding in the factories could continue the war effort and, whether dressed in sleek pencil skirts, trousers, or coveralls, their internal protection would not give them away. In advertisements they punched time clocks and carried lunch pails; military women held tire irons and knelt before disabled vehicles or crouched before an airplane, rivet gun in hand.[81]

Journalists reported that workplace truancies "because of menstrual cramps . . . became a war-production headache," and advertisers responded.[82] A promotion in the *American Journal of Nursing* recommended medical professionals push their patients to use Tampax in order to aid in the "reduction of absenteeism."

> Statistics show that women absent themselves from work much more often than men; indeed, such absenteeism is said to be 50 per cent higher among women.
> Though available data do not clearly assign the responsibility for this marked differential, obviously menstrual inconveniences account for a considerable proportion of the days lost. . . . Many physicians have discovered the contribution which *improved menstrual hygiene* (as with the intravaginal tampon Tampax). . . . Your patients should be grateful to you for recommending Tampax—and (in many cases) it may enable them to stay "on the job" where they are so vitally needed.[83]

Can You Trust Tampons?

—AND WHEN

A NAME YOU CAN TRUST...
Fibs are the *Kotex* Tampon and merit your confidence! And with Fibs you can change to shorts, play suit or even a swim suit with nobody the wiser! Worn internally, Fibs provide *invisible* sanitary protection . . . no pins, pads or belts . . . no chafing, no disposal problem. And only Fibs are *quilted* for greater comfort and safety. Easy to use, too!

NOT 8
NOT 10
BUT 12

FULL DOZEN ONLY 20¢. Not 8—not 10—but 12 Fibs for only 20¢ . . . you save the difference. That's because with Fibs you pay for no mechanical gadget to aid insertion, for none is needed. Next time buy Fibs, the tampon you can trust. You'll save money, too!

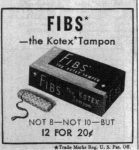

FIBS*
—the Kotex*Tampon

NOT 8—NOT 10—BUT
12 FOR 20¢

★Trade Marks Reg. U. S. Pat. Off.

Why I switched to Meds

—by a swimming teacher

I spend most of the summer in a bathing suit, and *internal* sanitary protection is practically a must! So when I heard that Modess had brought out Meds—a new and improved tampon —I tried them right away. Improved? Why, I've never known such glorious comfort! And such grand protection, too—for Meds are the *only* tampons with the "safety center." As for thrift, Meds cost only 20¢ a box of ten—an average month's supply. They're the *only* tampons in individual applicators that cost so little!

Figure 2.8: Meds, "Why I Switched to Meds," *Good Housekeeping,* August 1941, 146.

Figure 2.7: Fibs, "Can You Trust Tampons?— And When," *Ladies Home Journal,* March 1942, 62.

Traditional gender restrictions tend to ease in times of national crisis and necessity. Women's labor became central to the war effort and their vigor and stamina were encouraged as never before. Whereas social dictates once instructed they withdraw from activity during their catamenial weeks, by the 1940s medical literature and promotional campaigns advised them to remain active throughout the month.

As a result, women's work during the Second World War provided a boost to the tampon industry and sales soared. Bailey asserts that the "common ingredient in almost all of the changes in women's lives was physical activity. Here now were millions of active women of the kind Tampax long had targeted in its advertising campaigns. But instead of swimming or dancing as in the magazine ads, they were welding, marching or—like the mythical Rosie—riveting."[84] Postwar prosperity, along with the millions of women who relied on tampons in the early to mid-1940s, made the product an irreplaceable aspect of everyday American culture.

In subsequent decades, any admonishments against tampon use seemed antiquated and prudish, particularly within the budding sexual revolution and women's increasing demands for control over their own bodies. The 1980s toxic shock syndrome crisis rattled the tampon industry but could not fully dislodge women's loyalty to and reliance on the product. Once every so often, the sportswoman reappeared to endorse menstrual products, but most athletic celebrities and organizations, like the WTA, avoided public association.[85]

Fictional sportswomen, on the other hand, have historically been important figures in promoting menstrual products. Their movement and clothing emphasized the comfort and discretion the product affords women. And although these selling points prevailed over the actual physical activity in which women engaged, they contributed to the social acceptance of female athletes.[86] Communications scholar Alison Poe contends that "the image created by the advertising media may influence the American woman's attitudes and behavior toward activity. . . . [A]dvertising might be expected to reinforce the idea that sport is not only acceptable for women, but desirable and valuable for them."[87] Prominent representations of sportswomen certified a larger understanding that certain athletic endeavors were appropriate for women—on any day of the month.

These athletes, in turn, could feel confident to engage in physical activity without the shame or discomfiture of external forms of menstrual protection. Janet Phillips and Peter Phillips argue that "being able to carry on normal sporting activity made menstruation more normal and acceptable, less of a curse." In the 1930s, tampons emerged as a "liberating force," according to one physician, allowing "women to wear more revealing clothing, to participate in sports . . . and generally to act more freely during menstruation."[88]

By the mid–twentieth century, the sale and use of tampons no longer seemed controversial. Although firmly entrenched in the enduring "culture of concealment," those concerned with girls' and women's physical activity turned their attention to more pressing matters, including the question of elite and highly competitive sport. In particular, women physical educators, who had long advocated a democratic, circumscribed program of physical culture, faced unprecedented pressures from national agencies, the international athletic community, and a new generation of teachers and students who clamored for more strenuous, advanced-level sporting opportunities. Consequently, women physical educators were forced to examine their long-held beliefs about what constituted the "wrong kind" of competition.[89]

3. Rules, Rulers, and the "Right Kind" of Competition

For nearly a century, female physical educators provided athletic opportunities for girls and women. They offered programs for their students to learn about and experience physical activity in ways that contested residual beliefs about female frailty. At the same time, these leaders made sure students developed within gender-appropriate confines. A significant characteristic of the prevailing physical education philosophy, particularly between the 1920s and 1950s, was the denouncement of excessive, commercialized, exploitative sports for girls and women. Physical education leaders were not, as many interpret, "anticompetition." Rather, they advocated for a tempered approach that would not violate culturally sanctioned understandings of femininity.

By the mid-1900s, women physical educators began to alter their collective convictions in order to sponsor highly competitive, extramural (i.e., inter-institutional) sports. This new stance did not supplant their long-held tenet of "sport for all," but it did allow programs to develop in accordance with prevailing social mores. In so doing, they endorsed nothing short of a revolution in girls' and women's physical culture. This chapter concerns the ways in which women physical educators put their new theories about sport into practice through a series of National Institutes on Girls' Sports. At the time, these meetings may have constituted, as one physical educator estimated, the "greatest break through for girls in the history of sports."[1]

Sponsored by the Women's Board of the U.S. Olympic Development Committee and the Division for Girls and Women's Sports, there were five institutes held between 1963 and 1969 where physical educators, coaches, and recreation leaders learned to teach advanced sports skills. More than 1,000 attendees agreed to organize similar workshops in their home states, sharing the knowledge they gained from the larger conferences. More than 110,000 professionals, as well as an incalculable number of girls and women, reaped the benefits of these efforts.[2] One should not underestimate their influence, not just on elite athletes, coaches, and the millions of girls who profited from advanced guidance, but also for altering the national mind-set concerning females' physical, mental, and social capabilities.

Understanding the advent of these clinics requires an appreciation for at least three significant antecedents. First, to grasp the magnitude of these changes necessitates recognizing women physical educators' historic and prevailing antipathy toward elite extramural sport that lasted from approximately the 1920s through the 1950s. Second, World War II and the Cold War highlighted the need to readjust social perceptions of women's physical capabilities. During this time, anxieties about Americans' lack of physical fitness inspired governmental intervention in public and private programs, including those for girls and women. This coalesced with the increasingly symbolic importance of international sport and the desire to develop athletes into "cold warriors." The third dynamic therefore involves the push to improve American women's performances, principally at the Olympic level, in order to augment the country's medal count while simultaneously maintaining the fundamental belief in mass participation.

Women Physical Educators and the Issue of Competition, 1920s–1950s

Physical education for women first took hold in eastern women's colleges around the 1860s and 1870s and, by the end of the nineteenth century, had spread throughout the country. Governed almost exclusively by women and often cloistered from public view, programs varied from one school to the next. Educators initially promoted gymnastic and calisthenic exercises, and, as of 1890, college women engaged in at least fourteen different sports. By 1920 22 percent of colleges allowed some form of intercollegiate competition, typically between two rival schools in close proximity to one another, such as Smith and Vassar or Stanford and the University of California.[3]

Among these sports, basketball (or basket ball) proved especially popular. Invented in 1891 by James Naismith, Senda Berenson of Smith College quickly adapted the game's rules to accommodate the prevailing beliefs about females' limited capabilities. The Women's Basketball Committee, which operated under the auspices of the American Physical Education Association (APEA), standardized and enforced these regulations in 1899, initially splitting the court into three parts and restricting individuals' movement, ball possession, and interplayer contact. The Women's Basketball Committee eventually expanded to become the Committee on Women's Athletics (CWA), which organized scholastic basketball, hockey, swimming, track and field, and soccer. The CWA would eventually become the DGWS, functioning as a subsidiary to the American Association for Health, Physical Education, and Recreation (AAHPER, formerly the APEA). From the beginning, women's scholastic sports programs operated primarily under the control of physical educators.

Although the "new woman" of the early 1900s was decidedly more athletic than her older Victorian sister, she nevertheless remained constricted by the "myth of female frailty."[4] This was an ideology bound by race, ethnicity, social class, and geography. In the nineteenth and through much of the twentieth centuries, the majority of women in higher education came from white, upper-middle-class or wealthy families. Working-class women, women of color, agricultural laborers, factory workers, and domestic servants most often did not have the money, time, energy, means, or privilege of access required for educational and athletic opportunities. On the other hand, their necessary discordance with the predominant gendered ideals also eased their entry into competitive sport. Sweat, strain, and stamina were not anathema to their day-to-day lives—they were obligatory components.

Talented and ambitious women also found athletic opportunities outside the walls of academia. In the first several decades of the twentieth century, industrial leagues offered prospects, especially those devoted to bowling, softball, and basketball. Typically sponsored by companies or factories, teams competed against others of their ilk, established tournaments, and vied for national prominence at Amateur Athletic Union (AAU) championships. Others found competitive outlets in religious organizations and in those sponsored by municipal recreation agencies or local chambers of commerce. Around the country, high schools—particularly those situated in rural areas—also endorsed top-level competition for girls. Smaller schools often lacked a sufficient number of students for intramural play or substituted sports for physical education programs. Typically governed and coached by men, girls' sports thrived in areas of Georgia, Iowa, Kentucky, Ohio, Oklahoma, Pennsylvania, Tennessee, and Texas throughout the 1920s.[5]

At the collegiate level, women's physical education programs also became increasingly competitive during this time, much to the consternation of the profession's leaders. As a result, physical educators banded together and made a conscious, collective decision to curtail extramural elite-level contests for girls and women. This was a reaction to several contemporaneous problems in the world of sports, particularly found in men's programs or in women's opportunities that were controlled by men.

Unlike women's sport, men's collegiate programs developed outside their respective departments of physical education. By the end of the nineteenth century, men's sports, especially "King football," had grown into for-profit, spectator-oriented events rife with a number of "evils." Critics condemned the promotion of sport that seemed to come at the expense of education. They decried the building of ostentatious stadia in which thousands might gather to watch the athletic exploits of a few. The 1929 Carnegie Foundation's report exposed corruption in collegiate athletics, especially due to commercialization and an overemphasis on winning. Predicated on the "star system," from which only the most talented athletes would benefit, the college sports machine exploited so-called student-athletes who were often illegally recruited and financially compensated for their on-field talents. Physical educators took heed of the problems that plagued men's collegiate athletics with the mentality that they "should aid the women leaders in physical education in avoiding their chief mistakes."[6]

One way to ensure that girls' and women's athletics developed differently was to keep qualified women educators at the helm of their programs. These instructors not only would be in tune with the females' "unique" constitution, but would also foster an educational mission of sport for the greatest good. This would eliminate the type of unfettered competition that culminated in more "physical straining than physical training."[7] Reproductive concerns dictated much of the discourse—fears about what physical activity might do to women's menstrual cycles, sex organs, maternal potential, and spousal suitability.

In addition, overzealous competition might induce "emotional distress," "nerve fatigue," or cause participants to become "racked by hysterics" brought about by a "brittle state of taut excitement." The heat of athletic battle could lead to "scratches, blemishes and disfigurements of the face," or more generally destroy women's "feminine charms." Others worried about "the scantily draped feminine form" prancing before "hundreds of watching—and sometimes leering—eyes."[8] For the sake of girls' and women's physical and emotional health, appearance, and respectability, most professionals were of the opinion that they should not compete in extramural, commercial, public competition.

It was with these concerns in mind that the Women's Division of the National Amateur Athletic Federation (NAAF) developed in the 1920s. The U.S. war and navy secretaries established the NAAF after World War I revealed Americans' poor physical fitness levels. The organization also hoped to address problems with the ways the AAU and Olympic federations presided over high-level sport. NAAF organizers named Lou Henry Hoover, then president of the Girl Scouts of America and wife to future U.S. president Herbert Hoover, as one of its seven directors. Mrs. Hoover recommended separate sections for males and females within the NAAF and consequently became president of the Women's Division, an organization composed of politicians' wives and some of the most powerful leaders in women's physical education.[9]

At the Women's Division's first meeting in 1924, constituents adopted an official "platform" that articulated the group's philosophy and recommended standards for girls' and women's athletics (see table 3.1). Their aim was "to bring about a national realization that it is essential to develop the sport for the girl and not the girl of the sport, and has encouraged the direction of leadership of girls' and women's athletics by qualified women rather than men." They favored the "ideal of universal opportunity for participation in athletic activities" and a "play attitude" that would "protect girls' sports from commercialism and exploitation." Their guiding ideology focused on "sound constructive educational principles for women's and girls' athletics built on

Table 3.1. Platform of the Women's Division, National Amateur Athletic Federation

1. Promote such programs of athletic activities for all girls and women as shall meet their needs and as shall stimulate interest in activities that are suited to all ages and capacities.
2. Promote competition that stresses enjoyment of sport and development of good sportsmanship and character rather than those types that emphasize the making and breaking of records and the winning of championships for the enjoyment of spectators or for the athletic reputation or commercial advantage of institutions and organizations.
3. Promote interest in awards for athletic accomplishment that have little or no intrinsic value.
4. Promote educational publicity that places the emphasis upon sport and its values rather than upon the competitors.
5. Promote the use of suitable costumes for athletic activities.
6. Promote the provision of sanitary and adequate environment and facilities for athletic activities.
7. Promote the apportionment of adequate time allotment for a physical education program such as shall meet the needs of the various age groups for growth, development, and the maintenance of physical fitness.
8. Promote the training and employment of women administrators, leaders, and officials who are qualified to assume full responsibility for the physical education and recreation of girls and women.
9. Protect the health of girls and women through the promotion of medical examinations and medical "follow-up" as a basis for participation in athletic competition, and of a system of supervision that shall assure a reasonable and sane attitude toward participation in activities at times of temporary physical unfitness.
10. Protect the athletic activities of girls and women from the dangers attendant upon competition that involves travel, and from their commercialization by interest in gate receipts.
11. Promote the general adoption of approved rules for the conduct of athletics and games for girls and women.
12. Promote the study of the existing rules of all sports to the end that they may be changed to meet the specific needs of girls and women.

Reprinted in Sefton, *Women's Division*, 10–11.

the highest ideals of health, character, and citizenship."[10] Endorsed by influential groups such as the CWA, the Association of Directors of Physical Education for Women in Colleges and Universities, the American Association of
University Women, and the National Association of Deans of Women, these
precepts served as the foundation of women's physical education throughout
the successive decades.

Educators reportedly agreed on almost every issue outlined in the platform,
with one exception: competition. As such, the Women's Division developed
a separate document on the subject. They did not admonish all competition,
but warned that it must be of the kind "that brings joy to both the individual
and the group" and not of the "fatiguing and enervating" varieties.[11] One
should not construe contemporary women physical educators as endorsing
a wholesale campaign against competition. To the contrary, they believed
in it "wholeheartedly." Instead, they were against the "wrong kind" of competition.[12] They affirmed the standard that physical education should be of
the greatest benefit for the greatest number, not just the minority of girls or
women with superior athletic skills.[13]

When Dr. Harry Stewart, a physician and physical education instructor, announced he would organize a women's track and field team for the
1922 Women's World Games in Paris, female educators and their supporters demurred. Yet the quadrennial Games continued to grow in popularity,
"in spite of this opposition and of the added objection of practically every
other organization relating to women's athletics."[14] The AAU began offering
track and field events for women in 1924, and when Olympic organizers announced the addition of five women's track and field events (the 100-meter
and 800-meter races, the high jump, discus, and the 400-meter hurdles) to
the 1928 program, protests reached a fever pitch.

Until that time, female Olympians competed in ice skating, tennis, swimming, and gymnastics, but it was only when the AAU sanctioned track and
field that women physical educators expressed unified distress over the "sacrifice [of] our school girls on the altar of an Olympic spectacle." It appears as
though the perceived "masculine" and "masculinizing" sport of athletics was
the real issue at hand. Historian June A. Kennard intimates that educators'
strong stance against track and field also suggests racial and class biases, as
it seemed to be "the sport of black and working-class white women. Many
of the leaders of physical education were from exclusive women's colleges,
and they appeared disdainful of this low-status sport." At the time, physical
education seemed guided by doctrines that were "implicitly supportive of
class and ethnic divisions in American society," according to sport sociologist Jennifer Hargreaves.[15] Fundamental to their convictions were bourgeois,
nationalistic, and eugenic rationales.

The sensationalized accounts of the 1928 Olympic 800-meter race (described in chapter 4) confirmed physical educators' worst fears about the dangers of strenuous elite-level competition. In 1929 the Women's Division renounced women's participation in *all* events in the next Olympic Games, scheduled for 1932.

> *Whereas,* competition in the Olympic Games would among other things (1) entail the specialized training of the few, (2) offer opportunity for the exploitation of girls and women and (3) offer opportunity for possible overstrain in preparation for and during the games.
>
> *Resolved,* that the Women's Division of the National Amateur Athletic Federation go on record as disapproving competition for girls and women in the Olympic Games.[16]

Other powerful groups joined the Women's Division in their opposition to Olympic participation, including the CWA, the National Association of Physical Education for College Women (NAPECW), and national board of the Young Men's Christian Association. Most Olympic teams were, therefore, bereft of collegiate women throughout much of the twentieth century. In 1929 sportswriter John Tunis commented on this phenomenon: "Numerically, the college undergraduates form an inconsiderable proportion of the mass of girls all over the land who are interested in athletics to-day." Instead, he found that it was "mainly the girls" who worked for "the big industrial concerns, the big banks, the big insurance companies, and large corporations" who made up the women's Olympic teams.[17] It remained that way, particularly for white women, through the 1950s.

As an alternative, women physical educators promoted intramural programs, along with curricula devoted to health, hygiene, posture, games, play, gymnastics, and dance. By 1930 the "play day" became the standard variety of multischool contests for girls and women. In this format, two or more schools would convene for a day of activities. Organizers distributed "colors"—"pinnies" or "aprons"—so that participants from each school would be equally divided among the teams in a way that "fosters competition but discourages rivalry." Designed to encourage sociability, sports like basketball and volleyball soon dominated the agenda, though there were reports of schools sponsoring other activities, such as baseball, tennis, quoits, archery, swimming, horseback riding, horseshoes, Indian clubs, field hockey, marbles, track and field events, canoeing, stunts, tumbling, and croquet. When playtime ended, participants engaged in additional social niceties, often sharing tea or a meal before returning to their respective institutions. The aim of play days, explained Lou Henry Hoover, was "thoroughly American and democratic" and encouraged "an equal opportunity for health" and "an equal opportunity for joyous recreation . . . instead of overexertion for a few, bleacher seats for the many, and too strained intentness for all."[18]

Continued Intercollegiate Competition, 1920s–1950s

Contrary to popular belief, women's intercollegiate competition did not disappear during the 1930s and 1940s; instead, it manifested in alternate forms. Telegraphic meets, for example, allowed students at several schools to participate in a sport (typically bowling, archery, swimming, or riflery) on their own campuses, the results of which they telegraphed to a designated official or committee to determine the winner. Della Durant, a physical education professor at Penn State University, called the meets "murder. Kids would say, 'this was stupid.' You could lie about your times and they did, but not our kids." Play days quickly gave way to sports days, which permitted competitors to team up with their schoolmates. Student groups, primarily Women's Recreation Associations, sponsored the events.

"It was the students who changed things," recollected Martha Adams, a leader in women's sports and physical education. "They wanted sports days. They didn't want to have any of this play day stuff where you had punch, cookies, and you had to play with other people." Although organizers stressed the social aspects of sports days and attempted to minimize the element of competition between the schools, it was a "big, big deal" to beat a rival team, according to Lucille Magnusson, a contemporary advocate for women's sports. In addition, and against the expressed mandates of physical education organizations, surveys conducted in the 1930s and 1940s determined that approximately 16 percent to 17 percent of colleges offered varsity sports programs for women.[19]

Neither did all women physical educators fall into ideological lockstep with their profession. Gladys Palmer, head of Ohio State University's Women's Physical Education Department, organized a national intercollegiate golf championship in 1941. Martha Adams remembers that the powerful education organizations "condemned" Palmer: "It's a wonder she wasn't tarred and feathered." Yet at the inaugural meet, representatives from twenty-three schools participated in an "experiment in which there will be no paid admission and no commercialization, and in which certified health standards are being required of those skilled sportswomen who will take part." With the program discontinued during the Second World War, Palmer revived the tournament in 1946 and established a successful annual event. In addition to golf, 1940s college women competed in national tournaments for tennis and bowling, demonstrating the athletes' desires, the support of a handful of educators, and presaging important changes on the horizon.[20]

Sports also continued at some historically black institutions, even though, as one scholar noted in 1939, "in Negro colleges, little, if any, attention has been give to physical activities for women."[21] Where physical education and activity remained strong, educators typically upheld the same tempered stance as their white counterparts, especially at the more elite colleges and universities. Schools such as Hampton, Fisk, Morgan, and Howard, for example, followed the play-day path, de-emphasizing or eliminating their extramural programs.

At the same time, a handful of black colleges boasted some of the most impressive women's athletic teams in the history of sport. Cindy Himes Gissendanner argues that "racial segregation, relatively low-class status, and the ideal of a more active femininity predisposed African-American women as a group to reject the athletic model promoted by most white female physical educators." Sport studies scholar Rita Liberti demonstrates that programs across the southern United States authorized basketball during the 1920s and 1930s, though the number began to decline in the early 1940s. Tennis was also popular at schools such as Clark University and Tuskegee Institute, where sisters Margaret and Roumania Peters (both physical education majors) rallied during the 1930s and 1940s en route to fourteen ATA tournament doubles and two singles titles.[22]

At Tuskegee, tennis coach Cleveland Abbot taught the Peters sisters some of the game's finer points. He also coached football and men's and women's track and served as the school's director of physical education and athletics. At a time when almost no colleges, black or white, sent track and field teams to the women's AAU championships, Tuskegee and Tennessee State University rose to prominence. Tuskegee forged ahead first, establishing in 1929 what would quickly become a formidable team. During their "golden years," from 1937 to 1948, the Tigerettes won eleven out of twelve AAU outdoor championships.[23] Although the women faced racial discrimination and restricted opportunities, track and field was the singular sport in which they could test their mettle against white competitors.

Tuskegee's Louise Stokes and Tidye Pickett became the first African American women to make the U.S. Olympic track team in 1932, though for undisclosed reasons they "were unceremoniously discarded and replaced by two white girls" just before they were scheduled to run in Los Angeles. At the 1948 Games in London, Tuskegee's Alice Coachman, a basketball and track star, won the only individual medal for the American women's athletics team, taking first place in the high jump. She also became the first woman of color to medal for the United States. In Coachman's wake, female athletes from historically black colleges kept the U.S. women's track and field team afloat for the next three decades.[24]

Inspired by Tuskegee's success, Tennessee State University president Walter S. Davis began to develop a women's program, hiring Cleveland Abbot's daughter Jessie, a former Olympian and standout on her father's team, to serve as the Tigerbelles' first track coach. Successive coaches Tom Harris, Clyde Kincaid, and, eventually, the decorated Ed Temple began recruiting the top black athletes in the country, offering "work-aid grants" to assist with the financial burden of attending college. In exchange for working on campus, the school waived the student-athletes' tuition and fees.[25] Temple also established a monthlong summer program, based on Tuskegee's model, in which he invited high school girls to train on campus.

Either sheltered from or ignored by physical education's powerful leaders, the Tigerbelles engaged in rigorous year-round training. It paid off. In 1955, with a team of only six athletes, Tennessee State won its first national AAU championship. They defended their title every year from 1956 through 1968. When they lost the 1969 AAU meet by just one point, it was the first time in thirteen years that they did not emerge on top. Between 1948 and 1968, athletes from Tennessee State accounted for twenty-five of the forty Olympic medals the U.S. women won in track and field.[26] Over time, team members added twenty-four AAU titles and thirty Pan American Games medals, accomplishing it all on a shoestring budget and practicing on "a track that was one step above a cow pasture." As Coach Temple reflected in his autobiography, "Talk about Title IX? Shoot, we started at Title I."[27]

Yet for all their success and an abundance of Horatio Alger–type narratives ripe for the media's picking, no Tigerbelle ever made the cover of *Sports Illustrated*, or that of any other major sports magazine. Not even three-time gold-medal winner Wilma Rudolph (and one bronze that we tend to forget), whom the press revered as much for her athletic talent as for her great beauty, graced the front of the prominent magazine. For the most part, editors either dismissed women's track and field during the mid–twentieth century or offered derisive descriptions of the Eastern-bloc women who dominated the medal count.

Sports Illustrated provided two exceptions in the 1960s, both of which followed the "little girls and sweethearts" model of women's athletic media coverage.[28] The first highlighted two white "remarkable U.S. teen-age runners" on which much Olympic hope seemed pinned. The second introduced a team dubbed "Flamin' Mamie's Bouffant Belles." As reported, "The Texas

Figure 3.1: "Fast Steppers: Members of the U.S. women's 400-meter relay team, the Tennessee Tigerbelles, standing together in Rome after setting a world record. *Left to right:* Wilma Rudolph, Lucinda Williams, Barbara Jones, and Martha Hudson." Courtesy of the Library of Congress, United Press International Photo, New York World-Telegram, and the Sun Newspaper Photograph Collection.

Track Club is celebrated on two counts—its athletic achievements and the uncommon beauty of its girls, who compete in dazzling uniforms, elaborate makeup and majestic hairdos." It was a story about attractive women who happened to run, coached by a "beauty-minded Texan [who] pioneers a new glamorous look in women's track." Other stories published during this era advertised the sport for its beautifying benefits, informing readers about its "great influx of pretty young things" and that there was "a certain air of glamour in all this. For one thing, running does great things for the legs," one competitor commented. "It makes them shapelier."[29]

It should come as no surprise that those with a vested interest in seeing women's track develop in the United States utilized "apologetic" strategies that emphasized the attractive femininity of the sport's participants. Likewise, it should probably come as no surprise that they failed to implicate African American women in this rhetoric. Historian Susan Cahn contends that in order to improve the "image" of track and field at midcentury, "promoters could either incorporate black track women into approved concepts of athletic womanhood, or they could minimize the presence and contributions of black women in order to create a more respectable image of the sport."[30] It appears as though they opted for the latter, for in the mainstream press there was a distinct lack of acknowledgment of what black women had accomplished. For example, one read that the "Bouffant Belles" had "done more to promote women's track in the U.S. than if its members had, say, won the national AAU championships. (In fact, they finished 12th last year, with third-place finishes in the 440-yard relay and the 220-yard low hurdles and a sixth-place finish in the 220-yard dash.)"[31] The blatant disregard for those teams that actually and routinely won the AAU meets—Tuskegee and Tennessee State—is glaring.

World War II, the Cold War, and the Winds of Change

As women's physical education developed over the course of the twentieth century, the "same people who ran the sport programs conducted the teacher education programs and thus indoctrinated the teachers-to-be in the national philosophy," writes sport historian Ellen Gerber. "The result was a remarkable unanimity of opinion expressed in the literature and practices for several decades." For the most part, this uniformity advocated a philosophy of moderation and an aversion to elite extramural competition. There were, however, necessary changes in the curriculum as a consequence of World War II, the need for women's work in the war effort, and challenges to the profession as a whole. Accordingly, writes sport historian Joan S. Hult, the 1940s were "pivotal" for influencing changes in women's physical culture.[32]

Women educators devoted significant efforts to promoting physical activity during the war. Organizations passed resolutions that extended their work to civilian preparedness and national defense plans. They created physical training and recreation activities for women who served in the armed forces, some of whom engaged in competitive sport. They also scaled back on non-essential extracurricular activities, and, consequently, a 1943 survey found that most colleges had either abridged or eliminated their sports programs. Concurrently, as historian Nancy Bouchier contends, "female physical educators ... aimed to contribute to much more than simple war work. They hoped to create a postwar world that encouraged girls and women to step beyond gender constraints."[33] This included issues related to employment, higher education, exercise, and sport (though not varsity-type competition), while never compromising women's patriotic duties as wives and mothers.

Like the First World War, World War II revealed that a significant number of America's potential inductees were unfit for military service. The Korean War exposed the same deficiencies. Postwar affluence, technology, suburbanization, convenience, and more leisure time correlated with increasingly sedentary lifestyles, inciting condemnation of the "soft American." These fears were not only directed at adults; the results of the 1953 Kraus-Weber tests showed that American children were far less fit than their European peers.[34] From the 1940s through the 1960s, the U.S. government reacted with initiatives such as Hale America, Operation Fitness USA, and the President's Council on Physical Fitness, partnering with AAHPER, as well as other corporate, nonprofit, civic, and religious organizations to advance the importance of physical fitness as both an individual and a patriotic necessity for men, women, and children. As women physical educators would later advocate, increasing the physical activity of all Americans would be good for the nation; it would also broaden the base from which to pluck Olympic hopefuls.

The nationalism that permeated the midcentury fitness discourse intensified with comparisons to the Soviet Union. The rivalry between the United States and the USSR was comprehensive as the two countries vied for political, economic, social, cultural, scientific, and global dominance. In a sense, the competition yielded positive results. One athletic leader wrote that "Russia has been the nation which has prodded us to scientific achievement in the space age race and has called attention to the need for greater physical development of our people."[35] That antagonism was also good for women's sport, for it spurred unprecedented interest in encouraging their athletic involvement.

As sport became an important stage on which to act out Cold War politics, athletes became players in international diplomacy and global politics, utilized in contests such as the Olympic Games, the U.S.-USSR track meets, the Pan American Games, the World University Games, and goodwill tours. When the Soviet Union first competed in the 1952 Summer Games in Helsinki, it became clear that American athletic supremacy was in jeopardy. Although the United States came out on top of the medal count, the Eastern bloc was poised to take over, particularly due to the impressive performances of their female constituents. Indeed, the Soviet Union triumphed at the 1956 and 1960 Olympics. This put the United States and other Western countries in a quandary. Not only was promoting intense training for women anathema to convention, but there were also anxieties about what effects it might have on the athletes' femininity. Would it turn them into "big strapping gals, built along the lines of a 10-ton truck," or "big-limbed, hard-faced girls, with the legs and biceps of an all-American full back," as journalists described the Soviet women?[36] Conversely, refusing to evolve women's sports meant an unquestionable disadvantage when it came to international competition. As such, the 1950s marked a time of intense debate about whether and how to invigorate American women's sport.

Although the post–World War II era is often generalized as a time of gender conservatism, there was a strong undercurrent of social change that could not be ignored. The 1950s were "a decade of frustration for women," and their dissatisfaction with the status quo began to foster change in successive decades.[37] Betty Friedan's 1963 *The Feminine Mystique* publicized the "problem that has no name"—that women in the 1950s were unhappy and unfulfilled in their roles of mothers and housewives. Three years after the book's publication, Friedan became a founding member and the first president of the National Organization for Women. In the early 1960s, President Kennedy signed the Equal Pay Act and the Civil Rights Act, which included Title VII, banning discrimination in employment on the basis of sex, race, color, religion, or national origin. More women entered college than ever before. Everything, including sport and physical activity, converged at midcentury to destabilize traditional American gender roles.

In addition to government and civic-sponsored fitness campaigns, girls and women found other forms of encouragement to pursue sports. Educators proclaimed that women "have never withdrawn from their new position in society. Thus the barriers of what are considered *appropriate* pursuits for women have largely disappeared, and the presence of a woman on the assembly line or on an athletic field is no longer considered an oddity." Photographers regularly captured Jacqueline Kennedy, "the most athletic wife of a president in memory," riding horses, water-skiing, and swimming.[38] The influence of the iconic first lady was profound, and her athleticism made such pursuits more palatable to the public.

In 1964 a report from the American Medical Association declared that girls and women needed to be more physically active than conventions allowed. "Whether from culturally imposed restrictions, untenable physiological taboos or from disproportionate allotment of time, facilities, and leadership, many are not receiving the desired experiences from suitable and regular physical recreation. It is *imperative* that all girls be reached and involved."[39] Medical knowledge had long informed the discipline of physical education, and this was no exception, though women disagreed on the best way to implement the pronouncement.

By midcentury, surveys showed that Americans were beginning to more favorably view competition for girls and women. Colleges such as Waylon

Baptist, Immaculata, and West Chester successfully established varsity programs. A 1954 study found that at 63 percent of colleges, women competed in sport outside the purview of their physical education or recreation departments (or "activities sponsored by non-college groups").[40] It was clear that if schools did not provide athletic opportunities for their female students, they would go elsewhere to compete. If these options developed without the control and supervision of physical educators, there was no telling what types of calamity might befall the coeds.

Educators thus began to implement changes within their collective philosophy toward extramural competition, changes that seemed to come at both a glacial pace and, somehow, all at once. A site at which to discern this evolution is in the DGWS's regularly published position, "Desirable Practices in Athletics for Girls & Women." In the early 1940s under the heading "Types of Competition," they listed just two: intramural ("between teams made up within the school, recreational group, club or organization. Team divisions should be formed from the natural units within the group, such as: classes, homerooms, sororities, dormitories, business girls, married women, and other units") and extramural (either play days, sports days, or telegraphic meets). In 1949 they added another category under the "extramural" heading: "Informal Extramural Competition: Occasional games played toward the end of the intramural season." This suggests that both students and teachers were more amenable to the possibilities of competitive athletics.

In 1957 two additional options appeared under the "extramural" heading. The first was "Invitational Events—Such as a symposium, jamboree, game, or match other than a league game." The second involved "Interscholastic or Intercollegiate Games" in which "selected groups trained and coached to play a series of scheduled games and tournaments with similar teams from other schools, playgrounds, cities, or institutions within a limited geographical area. To be offered only as a supplement to adequate intramural and extramural programs."[41] In less than a decade, the DGWS began to endorse forms of competition that contradicted their long-held position.

These changes did not come without careful study and consideration. In the summer of 1958, the NAPECW and the DGWS held the National Conference on Social Changes and Implications for Physical Education and Sports Programs. There, representatives conceded that "life will never again be as it was before the last great war." One of the many transformations in the postwar era was the understanding that "every woman will work at some time during her life; the dependence of our economy on the working woman is unlikely to decrease."[42] Girls and women needed physical education more than ever—for their own health, the health of the economy, and the health of the nation. Conference attendees also recognized that their current sport programs were not "conducted on a level of skill sufficiently to meet the sport interests and needs" of all girls and women.[43] In their mission to provide athletics for the greatest good, they had ignored the development of highly skilled athletes and, therefore, fallen short in providing "sport for all."

By 1956 Ohio State University could no longer shoulder the financial burden of sponsoring the national golf tournament. In response, representatives from the DGWS, NAPECW, and the Athletic and Recreation Federation of College Women, a student group, joined forces to form the Tripartite Committee, designed "to study the larger implications of extramural sports for college women." Their task was specific to the golf championships, and members determined the event should continue under DGWS sponsorship, a recommendation accepted by their parent organizations. Executives of the NAPECW, however, maintained that the issue needed further study, which led to the creation of the National Joint Committee on Extramural Sports for College Women (NJCESCW—a physical educator once commented, "We are a group of women who have a strong attachment to the alphabet").[44] The Joint Committee expanded its purview to establish guidelines for competition and sanction intercollegiate tournaments for several sports. It was a watershed event when women physical education leaders authorized and assumed direct control over women's intercollegiate competition.

Contemporaneously, the U.S. Olympic Committee (USOC) began to address the necessity of improving the country's overall showing at the Games. They needed top performances from both men and women in order to compete with the world's athletic superpowers. After the American team lost to the Soviets at the 1956 Summer Games, the USOC Executive Board established a Development Committee, and, shortly thereafter, executives solicited assistance from the DGWS to advance its distaff program. The outcome was the Women's Advisory Board for the U.S. Olympic Development Committee, eventually known as the "Women's Board."[45] At a 1961 meeting, members of the USOC articulated the reasons for establishing its latest subsidiary.

> [T]hat possibly with the exception of swimming, women's sports in the United States have not achieved the caliber of performance nor acceptance that they have in Europe, notably Russia, and that if we are to maintain our Olympic prominence this situation must be rectified.
>
> It is felt that the major, and most basic, hindrance to the increase of competitive women's sports in this country is the existing cultural concept that such physical activity is unfeminine, e.g., "mannish." Therefore there is a definite reluctance on the part of physical educators to encourage and conduct sports programs for women on a "league" basis.

Representatives developed a two-pronged approach. First, they must improve the image of sport to make it more attractive to girls and women. They hoped to accomplish this by designing more "feminine" Olympic uniforms and creating a series of promotional films (with the help of the Wheaties Sports Foundation) to show "the most feminine women athletes who competed" in the Games.[46]

The second strategy the committee devised was to "obtain and develop people with sufficient knowledge and training" to instruct female athletes. Because so many women physical educators had "no time to specialize" in individual sports skills, the board proposed a series of clinics to assist their training.[47] The Olympic Development Committee received a boon from philanthropist Doris Duke Cromwell, who in 1960 donated five hundred thousand dollars to bolster women's sports programs. A portion of that money would be used to establish the National Institutes on Girls' Sports.

The National Institutes on Girls' Sports

"Dear Mabel," wrote DGWS consultant Rachel Bryant to longtime physical education leader Mabel Lee in a letter dated December 4, 1957, "I think, maybe, we are in the Olympic business." After decades of fighting against the USOC, women physical educators had secured an arrangement to work on behalf of female athletes through the establishment of the Women's Advisory Board of the U.S. Olympic Development Committee. The agreement was important for both sides. In order to advance women's performances in the Games, the Olympic committee needed the approval and assistance of the DGWS. Retired rear admiral Thomas J. Hamilton explained, "As chairman of the Olympic Development Committee, I was seeking some way for the United States to promote proper development of women athletes. I sought advice from many knowledgeable people; and the substance of their suggestions was—if acceptance of girls sports could be gained in schools and colleges from the women physical education leaders, a proper program might be evolved."[48] Without endorsement and active participation from educators, the Olympic committee feared it might never succeed in developing girls' and women's sport.

In turn, the DGWS could make sure that the program would progress under its watch and not come at the expense of its democratic ideals. The purpose of the Women's Board, then, was about more than identifying potential Olympic champions. It would protect women's sports so that they remained compatible with "the philosophy and standards of the DGWS." It would also "improve the fitness of all girls, as well as increase the numbers for recruitment of future teachers and leaders in physical education and recreation."[49] It was an admirable though thorny position to take—to advance a system for elite female athletes while simultaneously staying true to their traditional adages of "The game is for the good of those who play," "Play for play's sake," and "A sport for every girl and a girl in every sport."

Members of the Women's Advisory Board, headed by Sara Staff Jernigan (then vice president of AAHPER and chair of the DGWS), must have balked at the insinuation that they were acting only in an consultative capacity, for in a 1961 letter to board members, Hamilton wrote to "dispel a misunderstanding that the word 'Advisory' in the title of your Board does not mean the USOC is looking for only advice from you. You are it; we expect you ladies to give us leadership in the field of women's sports and to accept responsibility in getting the job done." They received Hamilton's charge with vigor and, as a cornerstone of their proposals, recommended the establishment of a series of National Institutes to train educators so that they would be equipped to teach elite-level skills to their pupils.[50]

The Women's Board insisted that the purpose of the institutes was "to increase the depth and breadth of women's sports throughout the nation." In this way, organizers worked to "provide a sound operational plan for the 'greatest good to the greatest number,'" aligning their mission with the more traditional women's physical education philosophy (see table 3.2). Nevertheless, individuals from DGWS, AAHPER, and the NAPECW criticized their partnership with the Olympic Development Committee, a reasonable position considering the long-held opposition to women's Olympic participation. "They believe," wrote physical education leader Katherine Ley to Jernigan, "and I agree, that we must continue to emphasize the total program as a taking off point prior to discussing the problems of the highly skilled girl. . . . If we suggest that we are now concerned particularly about the highly skilled girl we will have people who will rush to that end of the scale. I'm merely saying that although we admit our inadequacy in programs for the highly skilled girl, we must be sure that people retain the philosophy of a program for all girls."[51] The Women's Board thus found itself trying to appease both camps—developing Olympic champions while promoting fitness for all.

The Women's Board and the DGWS held the first National Institute at the University of Oklahoma in 1963. Preparation began early that year, and the Planning Committee determined to schedule the event "at the earliest date in the fall so that maximum results could be accomplished within the present school year." In addition to sessions devoted to philosophical, medical, and social concerns regarding girls' competition, organizers focused on two sports: track and field and gymnastics. The rationale for beginning with these pursuits, Jernigan explained, was because "track skills are so basic to

Table 3.2.   Philosophy of the National Institutes on Girls' Sports

1. To improve communications and interpretation of competition in women's sports.
2. To help the American public, and specifically American teachers, to better understand the role of competition in our culture and society, and in our nation's interrelations with other countries the world over.
3. To effect a greater recognition and acceptance by women physical education teachers of the need for properly organized and administered sports experiences for girls and women.
4. To encourage and provide information for women physical education teachers and recreation leaders to organize and administer appropriate competitive experiences for girls and women.
5. To improve the competence of women physical educators in teaching and coaching sports skills.

In Smith, "First National Institute," 58.

many other sport skills; track is easier to include in physical education school programs because of the nominal financial cost . . . and girls want to learn gymnastics today because it denotes a feminine self-image and is a graceful activity comparable to dance." It was sound justification, but the U.S. Olympic Development Committee had also identified these as two sports at which women needed significant improvement.[52]

For the first three institutes, the steering committees accepted nominations from regional organizations and agencies, inviting the top three candidates from each state and Puerto Rico to join them for "a week of concentrated study and work." For the final two institutes, "a special committee" selected applicants "on the basis of specific qualifications, including experience as a player, rated official, and coach, and present coaching and teaching responsibilities."[53] Regardless of the formula, it seems that organizers endeavored to recruit women who worked with athletes at the high school, collegiate, and recreational levels.

They also attempted to increase racial diversity. There was at least one African American woman, Dr. Nell Jackson (a former standout on the Tuskegee track team and one-time Olympian), on the steering committee. Executives relied on Jackson for advice when they worried that "not too many Negro women will be suggested [for participation in the institutes]. So—how do we go about involving some?"[54] Organizers increased the number of participants they accepted from certain southern states with the hope of drawing women from historically black colleges. Existing photographs from the institutes show an overwhelming number of white faces, though there were a handful of representatives of color who attended.

Organizers also included men in the first few institutes "because of the inadequate supply of qualified women leaders in these activities," one

Figure 3.2: Fourth National Institute on Girls' Sports, 1966. Courtesy of the Springfield College Archives.

Planning Committee member explained. It was clear from the beginning, though, that coordinators continued to champion the understanding that "girls' sports should be controlled and directed by competent and qualified women physical education leaders . . . and all men's organizations must merely cooperate and help as much as possible." Phebe Scott, a leader in women's sport and physical education, reasoned that "while this point may seem to smack of militant feminism, actually this is not the case." Instead, she reasoned, girls "must actually see good girl performers and women doing the jobs that in the past have been done by men." By the fourth institute in 1966, first on the list of "minimum criteria" for participation was that the individual "must be a woman."[55]

The National Institutes brought together women from diverse backgrounds. Most had been invited because they specialized in particular sports, but others came as administrators, representatives from groups like the DGWS, or as physical education "generalists." There was also a wide range of athletic experiences and talents. Many attendees had grown up and attended schools without opportunities to play competitive sports. Karen Johnson, who coached basketball and volleyball at California State University, Los Angeles, in the 1960s, "loved the girls and the sport, but I didn't really know how to coach. You know, when you haven't been brought up with a sport it's difficult to figure out how to coach it." At the fifth institute, she continued, "I learned so much about coaching and of course a lot of the instructors were coaches who had been coaching AAU teams, so the difference between us and them was night and day, they were far superior. It was an opportunity to really upgrade my coaching. . . . So many of my contemporaries were learning by the seat of their pants."[56]

Charlotte West, on the other hand, grew up playing industrial league basketball in Florida. The then head basketball coach at Southern Illinois University (SIU) recalled, "When we got to the institute, it was very evident to me that we knew a lot more than most of the teachers we brought in, because they were P.E. [physical education] people who had maybe been on the sports committee or written articles about the sport, so we knew a lot more. But the wonderful thing I remember is that it was a sharing of information. . . . It was very much a sharing experience." Attendees helped each other and fostered an environment of support in ways that many had never encountered. Dorothy McKnight, who coached basketball at the University of Maryland and also came from a competitive sport background, thought the discrepancies in experience was important: "I think that it opened some people's eyes who weren't as lucky as I to come from the same situation that I grew up in to understand about excellence and about how it can be achieved and the importance of coaching people to win—young women to win."[57]

It was also an opportunity to network with other coaches. At the fourth institute at Indiana University, Coach West was introduced to Billie Moore, "a high school teacher from Kansas who I had never met before. She was not only an excellent player, but she was also one of the few women at that time who had a jump shot. . . . We buddied up, and I convinced her that week to come to SIU and be my graduate assistant for the next year because I thought she had so much to give." That year West took her team to the first women's national basketball championship, hosted by West Chester University in 1969. "I think I praised [Moore] too loudly because that summer, . . . [California State University at] Fullerton called and asked her to be their coach." Moore went on to lead Fullerton to a national championship in 1970, a title she won again as the head of UCLA's program in 1978. In 1976 Moore became the first women's Olympic basketball coach.

Although the organizers "tapped every national resource, including the Federal government, and every state organization for assistance," most women paid their own expenses because, the proceedings applauded, they believed "so deeply in the need for extending sport opportunities for girls and women in the nation."[58] By attending the institutes, participants also agreed to "an age-old pattern—'Each one teach one'—the initiation of a chain reaction of teaching and learning through the institutes which you will sponsor on your return."[59] In other words, they assented to become "master teachers" and hold similar trainings at the state and local levels upon completion of the program. In this way, the institutes' influence might "reverberate on and on like ripples in a pool."[60]

Years later, many women remembered the sense of commitment they felt to fulfill this duty. "They encouraged us that this was an obligation to go back to your community and teach," recalled Charlotte West, who put on at least five local workshops. "So it was a massive grassroots effort, and all of a sudden people are caring more about women in sport." Dr. Carole Oglesby, who attended the fourth institute as a physical educator and accomplished athlete, estimated that "90 to 95 percent of the people followed through on their commitment, because that's just the way the women were at that time. They followed through on their promise, and so these skills that I learned that were kind of brand new to the mainstream in volleyball, they were everywhere in five years."[61]

By all accounts, the institutes were a success. At the first meeting in 1963, there were more than two hundred attendees from across the country, providing an occasion for like-minded educators to come together and discuss women's sports in a supportive environment. As Phebe Scott told the audience, "Those of us who for years have felt like one small voice crying in the wilderness to promote these activities for girls, will, I think, live to see these programs grow in schools all over the country and will be justified in knowing that efforts have borne fruit." It was a sentiment with which many women agreed. Dorothy McKnight, for instance, attended two meetings. When asked to reflect on her experience fifty years later, she replied, "I don't remember a lot. I just remember a feeling. It was just exciting." The excitement, she explained, came from being able to meet with like-minded individuals who wanted to advance girls' and women's sports. Oglesby concurred, recalling that the instructors "were just so knowledgeable." Although a woman had coached Oglesby's world-class softball team in the early 1960s, it had been a "singular experience. Now I was looking at cadres of women who were that accomplished in the leadership, and the people that were the participants like myself were very, very competitive, very dedicated. . . . Everything went from being a singular, personal thing to actually this kind of 'marching millions' kind of thing. That was big. It was really transformative." As a consequence of the inaugural meeting, the Executive Committee proudly reported that participants subsequently held 234 state workshops, training an estimated 25,350 teachers in teaching gymnastics and track and field.[62]

Successive institutes concentrated on canoeing and kayaking, fencing, diving, skiing, figure skating, basketball, volleyball, and officiating (see table 3.3).

Table 3.3. The National Institutes on Girls' Sports

Year	Site	Sports focus	Estimated participants
1963	University of Oklahoma, Norman	Gymnastics and track & field	200
1965	Michigan State University, East Lansing	Gymnastics, track & field, canoeing & kayaking, fencing, and diving	220
1966	Salt Lake City, Utah	Skiing and figure skating	140
1966	Indiana University, Bloomington	Basketball and volleyball	204
1969	University of Illinois, Champaign	Advanced coaching in track & field and basketball; officiating in basketball, gymnastics, track & field	400

Consorts learned methods for skill development, training techniques, conditioning, rules and regulations, officiating, offensive and defensive strategies, and how to organize programs and conduct competitions. Supplementing their concentration on specific sports were sessions devoted to injury prevention and treatment, the latest advances in girls' and women's sports, and those designed to address lingering doubts about female suitability for strenuous competition. The conferences were also "characterized by *participation* rather than *observation.*" Attendees were advised to bring specific equipment and workout wear and to make sure they turned up in good physical condition. As organizers instructed, "It is altogether appropriate for each prospective participant to engage in a minimum preconditioning program so that she will be able to keep pace in a week that is, of necessity, crammed and jammed with activity ranging from the quite light through the moderate to the extremely strenuous."[63] The workshops "were arduous and people were sore," remembered Oglesby.

Proceedings also show the vestiges of physical educators' perceived role as gatekeepers of feminine virtue. Presenters cautioned against approximating the "male model" of sport: "In all our efforts we have stressed the importance of avoiding the mere imitation of existing programs for boys and men. What we want are programs designed specifically for women—which is easier said than done." Those addressing the conference-goers admonished that they must avoid the hubbub associated with men's sports. There was no need, for example, to provide a locker room for visiting teams; one communal room would suffice and stimulate a spirit of collegiality. They should not seek out media attention or publicity. There were other ways to avoid the "frills commonly associated with varsity play in men's programs. . . . Leave the bands, the majorettes, the cheerleaders out of the picture." Although the nature of women's sport was changing, it was vital that the emphasis remain on its educational and not entertainment value, for "sports should be for the participants, not the hot-dog buying public."[64]

By shunning the commercial trappings of men's sport, organizers emphasized what they believed were the fundamental differences between the sexes. When skeptics raised fears about "masculinization," they were reminded, "Sports for women must help them retain their feminine identity, not destroy it." For this reason, "the DGWS has for years promoted and fostered the use of women teacher-coaches, women officials and women administrators as appropriate personnel form women's sports."[65] They approached the question of women's suitability for sport from medical, physiological, biomechanical, psychological, sociological, anthropological, and philosophical perspectives, addressing incessant beliefs about the ways that athletics would affect reproduction, gender, and psychology.

Clothing provided another concern relative to gender and sexuality. *Sports Illustrated,* for instance, lauded the institutes, particularly in light of women's "bad-to-worse American showing in international competition." Convinced that the plan would encourage participation and improve coaching techniques, the unnamed author continued, "The institute would do well, too, to put a stop to those feeble jokes about girl broad jumpers, to make those outfits more attractive and to find a stylish Miss America who high-hurdles." Yet conference attendees were advised to the contrary: "We need not dress our women in satin uniforms which resemble bikinis—for there is absolutely no correlation between fancy outfits and the number of goals scored. . . . In short, costumes should be utilitarian in design rather than suitable for go-go girls. The feminine image must be consciously preserved."[66] They may very well have had women's tennis costumes in mind.

While members of the Women's Board were constant in their reminders that the foundational premise was gender-appropriate mass participation, presenters clearly stressed the importance of raising the level of prestige of women's sports, especially in international competition. The United States had been "unpleasantly jolted during the 50's by the emergence of Russia as a strong and threatening contender." As of the 1960s, "Sport and sports competition have become a major factor in international prestige. The Federal government and the State Department regard excellence in sports as an essential weapon in the cold war." Subsequently, Ley proposed, physical educators "must do two things: train the best we have to perform to the best of their ability and at the same time promote all sports for all girls and women so that eventually we will have many more prospects from which to choose the best."[67] With the Olympic Development Committee as their primary benefactor, one might assume that the women felt a certain obligation to advance the Olympic cause.

"So where will we get women Olympic participants?" speaker Evalyn Gendel asked attendees of the fifth institute. "They will come from this group of conditioned youngsters. The gifted athletes and those inspired by the programs will appear as a matter of course. Of paramount importance, however, is that *all* women will benefit in their roles as women—athletes or not!" Once again, organizers kept a foot firmly planted in each camp: fitness for all and grooming the "highly skilled girl" for elite sport. "By bridging the gap between the beginner and the top level performer," reasoned Scott, "we can supply a talent pool of women for international competition."[68]

Those representing the U.S. Olympic Committee dispensed with more overt gestures toward the egalitarianism of physical education to emphasize the relevance of women to their mission: "Just how important your women athletes are to our Olympic efforts is emphasized by the fact that the International Olympic Committee now permits women to participate in 14 of a total of 28 Olympic sports." Others highlighted the political ramifications of enhancing women's sports, as "our athletic showing has great significance in the cold war," as Hamilton remarked at the first meeting in Oklahoma City. "Our responsibility, then, is to properly cultivate and marshal the tremendous power and resources of the United States and not only present our strongest teams but also use our coaching talent and know-how to gain friends in other nations. Our greatest chance to improve in the Olympics lies in women's sports."[69]

Attendees remember that the rhetoric of "participation for all" remained strong at the meetings, though it was clear that the true emphasis was on developing women's sports by training women coaches. As Karen Johnson observed, "Assembling all these individuals together really elevated the competency of girls' and women's sport in the country. . . . We were really poised to take our place and really be able to coach. . . . [W]hen you're trying to enhance competition, it tends to take away from physical education." It was not a conscious decision to increase the distance between athletics and physical fitness, but an unavoidable consequence. Dorothy McKnight recalled an almost palpable "philosophy of excellence. . . . It was a pleasure to be surrounded by an atmosphere of excellence—wanting excellence—and teaching us to be as excellent as we could be. And from the unabashed idea that you were coaching." By encouraging superior training for coaches and, by extension, their athletes, organizers clearly headed down a path toward elite extramural competition for girls and women.

In 1970, with all the institutes completed, Sara Staff Jernigan reported on the magnitude of their efforts. "As a result of the national Institutes thousands of teachers and coaches have had the opportunity to become master instructors in the following sports: gymnastics, track and field, kayaking, fencing, diving, skiing, figure skating, basketball, and volleyball. Since more than 110,000 instructors have attended these Olympic Sports Institutes or state workshops, more than 3,000,000 school girls and college women have benefited through the accelerated school and community athletic programmes."[70] As attendees and organizers looked toward the future, it is difficult to imagine that they might have predicted the current state of girls' and women's sports in the United States.

Progress and Consequences

As of 1963, the DGWS officially adapted its stance on competition, advocating for the first time "a sound, carefully planned, and well-directed program of extramural sports" for those girls and women "who seek and need additional challenges in competition and skill." This was meant to augment, but by no means to replace, inclusive educational intramural programs. It was a controversial move but one that seemed inevitable in the contemporary climate. In 1964, at the request of women leaders, the NCAA added a "men-only" clause to their bylaws that would keep women's sport under the purview of distaff organizations. Although the NCAA complied, it continued to make overtures toward sponsoring women's sports in successive decades, motivated, it seemed, by its decades-long struggle against the AAU for control of amateur sport.[71]

In 1965 the DGWS held a Study Conference on Competition for Girls and Women in order to recommend strategies for developing athletic programs. A result of this meeting was the *Guidelines for Conducting Interscholastic and Intercollegiate Competition,* a monumental step toward establishing the Commission on Intercollegiate Athletics for Women (CIAW).[72] Operating under the DGWS, the CIAW was an outgrowth of the Joint Committee and assumed responsibility for designing, sponsoring, and sanctioning women's collegiate sports and championships. "Members of DGWS believe that creation of national championships will give talented young women something more to strive for and will give them greater incentive for continuing to develop their athletic skills. The championships and the naming of national annual champions in different sports should motivate less talented girls to learn sports skills and to enjoy them on their own. In other words, sports activity will become more desirable as an area of endeavor for women."[73]

The first sanctioned tournaments took place in 1969, and by 1972 women competed in national championships for golf, tennis, track and field, gymnastics, swimming and diving, basketball, and badminton. That same year, at the direction of the DGWS and the NAPECW, the CIAW formally ceded control to the Association for Intercollegiate Athletics for Women (AIAW), a membership organization better equipped to handle the demands of governing women's college sport.

These efforts, in concert with the National Institutes, led to revolutionary change in women's sports. But revolutions tend to carry within them seeds of their own destruction. There were a number of negative, unintended consequences that came with the unprecedented growth of women's sports that began in the 1950s and 1960s. First, expanding opportunities for all women heralded the decline of historically black college programs. With the advent of the AIAW and Title IX implementation, schools equipped with superior resources added athletic opportunities for women. Despite its superlative record of AAU national championships, Tennessee State never won a title sanctioned by the AIAW or NCAA, and 1968 marked the last time that the Tigerbelles had any significant presence on an Olympic track team. Although Title IX had a tremendous influence on white women athletes, by 1978 one researcher found that "it appears at present that there exists an extremely low rate of participation by Black females, at least at the intercollegiate level."[74] Even today, sports participation rates for girls and women of color lag behind their white counterparts.

A second repercussion was that the specialization required to advance women's sports made it difficult for those trained in physical education to reconcile the divide. Karen Johnson recalled, "With the AIAW emerging, many had to make choices whether to coach or to teach, and we lost a lot of great women from coaching. . . . The initial cadre of the women who established the institutes believed that we could maintain our physical education–coaching dual roles. As it emerged and things became more competitive, many women had to choose. I chose to be a physical educator. The intent was great and results were great, but eventually and especially with the loss of AIAW we lost control." Johnson's comment points to a third reaction to the growth of women's sports: the eventual end to women's dominion over female programs.

Women physical educators' separatist philosophy could not withstand larger political and economic forces. In 1972, the same year the AIAW came into existence, the NCAA's Executive Committee approved a recommendation to remove their male-only policy for intercollegiate sports. The men's organization continually pressured the AIAW to relinquish control to, affiliate with, or become a subsidiary of the NCAA. Women leaders resisted, committed to their educational, female-centered agenda, but the NCAA found chinks in their armor. Separate simply cannot be equal in the same way that equality and difference cannot escape hierarchy. As discussed in chapter 5, the AIAW collapsed after the NCAA voted to sponsor women's sports in 1981. As men's and women's athletic departments merged, women were relegated to secondary positions or drummed out of the profession entirely.

Finally, one might consider the decline in physical education programs as an effect of the emphasis on competitive sports. The precarious state of the field today is connected to, though not caused by, the increasing importance placed on institutionally sanctioned sports for girls and women, boys and men. There has been a tremendous divide between athletic and physical education programs. Currently, intramural programs are practically nonexistent in many areas of the country, and so, in the end, the move toward competitive sports for girls and women did detract from more inclusive programs, despite intentions to the contrary.

But girls' and women's sports could not have advanced to its current status without the contributions of midcentury physical education leaders who recognized the undeniable, irrevocable social trend. Girls and women wanted more and better athletic opportunities, and if schools were unwilling to provide them, they would look elsewhere. Educators' efforts opened up a world of possibilities that many girls had never considered, namely, that sport was something approved, appropriate, and available.

More than anything, assessed Martha Adams, who attended three institutes and twice served as program chair, the clinics "got people thinking." Dorothy McKnight adds that we must appreciate the risks that these leaders took: "When women's sport turned the corner, it turned the corner because of some women who took a chance, because there wasn't a great hew and cry asking everybody to back women's sports. . . . Women who took that chance and realized, you know, for some, it might have been a career bust . . . they took a chance on something administratively that people weren't supportive of." It was a gamble for women steeped in the discipline of physical education to dispute the positions of their foremothers. This was another consequence of the push for progress and one that deserves respect.

In the mid- to late 1960s, the National Institutes on Girls' Sports were indicative of rapidly expanding athletic opportunities. This was not confined to the United States, for it was the performances of women from other countries, especially the Soviet Union and Eastern Europe, that provoked the need to develop women's talents. If the United States was to assert its politico-athletic dominance on an international stage, it could no longer afford to repress women's sport, though an aversion to transgressing conventional ideals of femininity prevailed. These antagonistic propositions played out in another point of change, one that emerged around the same time as the institutes: the sex test for elite female athletes. Like the National Institutes, the tests signified the need to take women's sports seriously and, simultaneously, reflected anxieties about preserving and ensuring conventional femininity in the process.

4. Women's Sport and Questionable Sex

I do not know why Santhi Soundarajan attempted suicide in September 2007, though many speculate it had something to do with the "sex test" she was forced to take at the 2006 Asian Games. Following the Indian athlete's second-place finish in the 800-meter race, officials compelled Soundarajan to face a medical panel responsible for determining her sex. Her birth certificate indicates femaleness. Her parents raised her as such. She grew up, competed in sport, and lived her life in accordance. Yet media outlets soon reported that the Indian Olympic Association determined that she "did not possess the sexual characteristics of a woman." They stripped her of her silver medal for a "Games rule violation," and Soundarajan left the event in a cloud of humiliation and controversy. Nine months later, she allegedly ingested enough of a veterinary drug to end her life.[1]

Santhi Soundarajan is just one of countless women affected by these tests. Although procedures designed to identify women of questionable sex have changed over time, all are premised on and emanate from the tensions between athleticism and femininity. They speak to persistent anxieties—not just in the United States, but around the world—over how women should appear and perform in the sporting realm. The examinations, therefore, muddle the distinction between sex and gender, an issue exacerbated by the use of alternative terms such as *femininity control* and *gender verification*. Sociologist Dayna Daniels finds the latter particularly "oxymoronic": "To verify something is to confirm the truth or reality of that thing. Since gender is a constructed, social practice that changes over time, the ability to verify gender is indeed a challenge." The same can be said for sex, a protean concept with historically and culturally contingent meanings.[2] Perhaps nowhere is this more evident than in sex testing's procedural points of change.

An analysis of sex testing in elite women's sports provides a starting place to engage in a "critical attack on sex" as well as a "historicization and deconstruction of the terms of sexual difference."[3] As part of this process, I discuss several women who, like Soundarajan, found themselves casualties of sex-testing policies. I hope to do so in a way that does not perpetuate the often contemptible manner in which they have been treated over the years. Though paternalistically purporting to "protect" female athletes, create "equal opportunity," ensure "purity," and uphold "dignity and integrity" in women's sports, the various iterations of sex testing are designed to disadvantage women who, for one reason or another, do not align with the established social, biological, or genetic parameters of femaleness.[4]

Women Athletes and Manly Sport

Most accounts note that regular, systematic sex testing in athletics began in the 1960s, but in his second-century *Description of Greece,* Pausanias gave this account of the ancient Olympics: "It is a law of Elis to cast down [Mount Typaeum] any women who are caught present at the Olympic games. . . . However, they say that no woman has been caught, except Callipateira." Callipateira, the mother of the athlete Peisirodus, "disguised herself exactly like a [male] gymnastic trainer, and brought her son to compete at Olympia." Upon her son's triumph, Callipateira reportedly "jump[ed] over the enclosure in which they keep the trainers" and "bared her person." She escaped the capital punishment typically dealt to women who sneaked into the Games "out of respect for her father, her brothers and her son, all of whom had been victorious at Olympia. But a law was passed that for the future trainers should strip before entering the arena."[5] A visual inspection of the nude participants provided sufficient evidence for Olympic officials and apparently prevented further incident.

If Pierre de Coubertin, the so-called father of the modern Olympic Games, had his way, the ban on women might have continued well past the ancient era. Largely responsible for reviving the Games in 1896, Coubertin was a staunch opponent of women's Olympic competition, believing that their "participation should be absolutely prohibited" and that their only role at the Games should be to provide "male athleticism . . . with the applause of women as a reward."[6] Coubertin based this logic on the pervasive belief that "real" women were physically incapable of handling the rigors of sport and competition. If they were capable, then they were not "real" women.

Should women prove themselves both capable and "real," what would that mean for men?

Sports have always been a proving ground for masculinity; if women entered that "male preserve" and succeeded, they might disrupt the gendered binary upon which so many social relations are based. It is no coincidence that the rise of the modern Olympic Games corresponded with the late-nineteen- and early-twentieth centuries' "crisis of masculinity." In the United States, sport was an important technology to assuage the destabilization of white masculine dominance brought about by an increase in immigration, changes in the nature of labor, campaigns for women's rights, and the perceived feminization of society.[7]

Much to Coubertin's chagrin, women slowly gained entry into organized sport. In the first decades of the twentieth century, the International Olympic Committee (IOC) reluctantly added golf, archery, tennis, fencing, skating, and aquatic contests for women, but women's athletics remained anathema to officials. Indeed, "Track and field events for women have faced the most ardent opposition throughout America's sporting history."[8] Lingering Victorian beliefs in vital energy theories—that women possessed a finite amount of corporeal power and to apply energy toward intellectual, political, or physical pursuits meant drawing it away from reproductive processes—constrained the activities in which females could engage. This discourse, couched in the hegemony of heteronormative, patriarchal familial relations, induced women to shun competitive sport for the sake of their progeny and the welfare of the nation.

Closely adjoined to reproductive concerns was the notion that sport would masculinize women. Not only would they be unable to bear children, but they would also fail to draw male attention and affection or, perhaps worse, would not care to do so. These concerns were particularly prominent in reference to athletics. Weighing the possibilities of "Olympics for Girls" in 1929, Dr. Frederick Rand Rogers argued that track and field events were "profoundly unnatural" for women and were "essentially masculine in nature" and that women would "develop wholly masculine physiques and behavior traits" if they participated. A few years later, the editor of *Sportsman* ranted that women "are ineffective and unpleasing on the track," and involvement causes their "charms [to] shrink to something less than zero."[9] Athletics might lead to the atrophy or displacement of the uterus, unseemly musculature, unattractive facial strain, flattened chests, psychological role conflict, lesbianism, and so on, all of which served as stigmas that kept many women out of organized sport.

Against such resistance, some of the most talented and ambitious women found competitive outlets in industrial leagues, faith-based organizations, and company-sponsored teams. In 1921 Alice Milliat founded the Fédération Sportive Féminine Internationale, which sponsored the first Women's World Games the following year. The popularity of this quadrennial event, in terms of both participation (though the *New York Times* reported they were "not proper women") and spectatorship, eventually persuaded the IOC to add five women's track and field events to the 1928 Olympics Games, to which, reported *Time*, "the minute portion of U.S. womanhood which is diligently muscular looks forward."[10]

Many critics believed that women were simply too delicate to withstand the rigorous demands of these competitions, and the sensationalized, exaggerated accounts that followed the 1928 women's 800-meter run only confirmed their suspicions. Popular sportswriter John Tunis reported that at the race's end, along the track lay "eleven wretched women, five of whom dropped out before the finish, while five collapsed after reaching the tape." There were only nine women in the race, and existing footage provides evidence to refute his description, but the damage had been done. The distance made "too great a call on feminine strength," lamented the *New York Times*.[11] In response, the IOC cut back on the number of women's track and field events, and the 800-meter race remained absent from the program until 1960.[12]

There were, without question, dimensions of race, ethnicity, class, and nationality that exacerbated the ideology that track and field events were distinctly "unfeminine." By midcentury, emphasized femininity proscribed excessive strain and noticeable musculature, thereby marginalizing women who engaged in physical labor. Such exclusion, however, sometimes freed those from lower socioeconomic strata to enjoy the corporeal exhilaration and liberatory potential of athletic involvement. As historian Susan Cayleff contends, "Working-class female athletes were judged by a more lenient set of standards although they too had clearly demarcated lines they were not to transgress." So-called Amazons and "muscle molls," like Mildred "Babe" Didrikson Zaharias, inspired "a sporting universe revolving around women from modest social origins [that] began to flourish in the 1920s and 1930s."[13] It remained, however, that track and field was viewed as a particularly masculine and masculinizing sport.

During this time, officials may have instituted the first sex tests for female Olympians, though reports vary. At the 1936 Games in Berlin, IOC member Avery Brundage, according to *Time*, "roundly recommended that all women athletes entered in the Olympics be subjected to a thorough physical examination to make sure they were really 100% female. Reason: two athletes who recently competed in European track events as women were later transformed into men by sex operations." At those same Olympics, Polish officials allegedly demanded American runner Helen Stephens prove her sex after beating Poland's Stella Walsh in the 100-meter race. In her biography of Stephens, Sharon Kinney Hanson writes that the athlete's response to such charges was that reporters could "check the facts with the Olympic committee physician who sex-tested all athletes prior to competition."[14]

If all athletes were in fact tested, they might have picked up on what is, to date, the only noted case of a man impersonating a woman in elite competition: Heinrich (or Hermann) Ratjen, who took fourth place in the high-jump event while competing under the name Dora. Although scholar Vanessa Heggie argues that Ratjen may have been unfairly inducted into the "cannon of gender frauds," his story routinely appears in the history of sex testing. In 1957 Ratjen purportedly revealed the deception, explaining its perpetration under the mandate of Adolph Hitler "for the sake of the honor and glory of Germany. For three years I lived the life of a girl," said Ratjen. "It was most dull."[15]

At least one additional incident demonstrates that Olympic women underwent some type of check prior to the modern era of sex testing.[16] In 1949 Foekje Dillema was poised to rival the great Fanny Blankers-Koen as the Netherlands' latest track star. The next year, the Royal Dutch Athletics Federation issued a lifetime ban against Dillema and erased her national record in the 200-meter event. Some accounts explain that she refused to take a sex test; others say that the results of the exam, "based solely on physical examination," ruled her ineligible.[17] In any case, she was done with sport. This and other incidents may have been what the authors of a 1966 *Journal of the American Medical Association* editorial had in mind when they wrote that "certain 'lady' contestants in track and field have, over the years, turned out to be men." Such stories contributed to already rampant suspicions about the "femininity" of female athletes.[18]

During the Cold War era, these stereotypes were intensified by the success of African American and Soviet female athletes, seen by the white Western gaze as "two symbols of mannishness," according to historian Susan Cahn.[19] These sentiments became especially pronounced in the 1952 Olympic Games when, to the consternation of many Americans, the U.S. women's track and field team made an "anemic" showing, scoring only eleven points to the Soviet Union's seventy.[20] In response, the American and British media published stories that ridiculed the prowess and physiques of Soviet women. Leading into the 1956 Games, for example, *Life* printed a photographic spread that seems a clear attempt to demonstrate what editors viewed as Russians' perversion of the gender order. Captions to the photographs described the female athletes as "determined," "muscular," and "hefty" and showed one broad jumper "lift[ing] her doctor husband 25 times" into the air. The men, on the other hand, were "clumsy," "awkward but effective," and "working on weakness," while a male weight lifter "hoist[ed] his 2-year old daughter."[21]

It is important to consider sociocultural factors involved with conceiving of successful female athletes as male, masculine, or otherwise deviant by Western norms. In one of many telling examples, the New York Times reported that competitors "from Communist countries" were "of questionable femininity."[22] But it may have been that female athletes, particularly those from Eastern European countries and perhaps not bound by the Western "feminine mystique," were among the first to unapologetically apply new sciences to their athletic training regimes. It should also be acknowledged that part of the technological advancements in training—for both men and women—included the use of anabolic steroids, before governing bodies banned the substances or conclusive evidence existed about the harm they cause.[23]

The Second X

The International Association of Athletics Federations (IAAF), track and field's international governing body, formally initiated sex tests at the 1966 European Athletics Championships, "because," related Life, "there had been persistent speculation through the years about women who turn in manly performances." The IAAF ordered all female athletes to submit to visual inspections or "nude parades" before a panel of three female physicians. As Time reported, "The examination, as it turned out, was perfunctory. Lined up in single file, the 234 female athletes paraded past three female gynecologists. 'They let you walk by,' said one competitor afterward. 'Then they asked you to turn and face them, and that was it.'" Of the athletes who consented to the tests, all were determined to be women; however, there were five record holders who opted not to attend the event. Maria Vittoria Tria, an Italian broad jumper, believed the test was an affront to her religious beliefs: "I have been raised a Catholic and I refuse to undress in front of unknown people," she told the press.[24]

The other athletes, one from Romania and three from Russia, including Tamara Press and Irena Press, did not give reasons for their unexpected absences. In the 1950s and 1960s, the Press sisters dominated international track and field competitions, winning a combined five Olympic gold medals and one silver in the shot put, discus, hurdles, and heptathlon events. But the women, derisively referred to in the media as the "Press brothers" and "squat troglodytes," opted not to attend the competition that introduced sex testing.[25] Their subsequent retirements fueled speculations that they had something "male" to hide.[26]

In the first year of testing, officials experimented with the protocol used to determine athletes' sex. Competitors at the 1967 Pan-American Games were required to expose themselves upon facing a medical panel—baring their bodies for approval. As American shot-putter Maren Seldler remembered, "They lined us up outside a room where there were three doctors sitting in a row behind desks. You had to go in and pull up your shirt and push down your pants. Then they just looked while you waited for them to confer and decide if you were O.K. . . . [I]t was hideous. I was just sixteen at the time and though I wasn't really afraid of not passing, I just felt that it was humiliating."[27]

Even more invasive were the tests at the 1966 Commonwealth Games in Kingston, Jamaica, where female athletes were subjected to a gynecologist's manual examination. Lined up outside an examining room, the women had not been given "a hint about what kind of procedure we might expect," wrote Mary Peters, who later won an Olympic gold medal in the 1972 pentathlon. In her autobiography, Peters continues:

> I went into a bare room which contained two women doctors, one examination couch and one large enamel bowl containing some white, cloudy antiseptic in which the doctors apparently washed they hands after each examination. What occurred next I can only describe as the most crude and degrading experience I have even known in my life. I was ordered to lie on the couch and pull my knees up. The doctors then proceeded to undertake an examination which, in modern parlance, amounted to a grope. Presumably they were searching for hidden testes. They found none and I left. Like everyone else who had fled that detestable room I said nothing to anyone still waiting in the corridor and made my way, shaken, back to my room.[28]

IAAF officials next turned to a "simpler, objective and more dignified" laboratory-based chromosome assessment for the 1967 European track and field championships.[29] At what was dubbed the "Sex-Check Track Meet," there was clearly some uncertainty about exactly what the tests would determine. According to the *New York Times*, for instance, "the three Russians would not have passed because they had been taking male hormones to increase their strength."[30] The tests did nothing to assess the presence of "male hormones," an issue that would become increasingly problematic as rumors of doping surged throughout the athletic community. The *Times*'s comment, however, speaks to the difficult task of determining what criteria would and should be used to place athletes in the "male" or "female" category.

Olympic officials experimented with the same chromosome test at the 1968 Winter Games in Grenoble, France, and officially adopted it for all female (but no male) participants in the 1968 Mexico City Summer Games. Defending the new policy, the IOC's Monique Berlioux asserted, "The chromosome formula indicates quite definitely the sex of a person and, so years ago, it was discovered that a simple saliva test will reveal its composition."[31] Technicians then analyzed these cells for the presence of a second, inactive X, chromosome, or Barr body.[32]

In brief, human cells typically possess forty-six chromosomes that determine genetic constitution. Technicians usually attain those cells by swabbing the inside of patients' cheeks, harvesting hair follicles, or through a blood test. They then arrange the chromosomes in pairs, sorted according to size. A karyotype typically shows twenty-three pairs of chromosomes from an individual cell. Of these twenty-three pairs, twenty-two are numbered autosomal chromosomes; the last pairing constitutes sex chromosomes, or those that determine whether a person is classified as male (XY) or female (XX). A "normal" male karyotype is 46, XY; a "normal" female karyotype is 46, XX. The second X (or Barr body) in the female array is "inactive," and its appearance affirmed a "positive" sex-test result.[33] Those athletes who exhibited the 46, XX, pattern effectively passed their examinations. Administrators then presented them with cards, otherwise known as "sex passports" or "certificates of femininity"—small laminated licenses that they were required to carry with them to all competitions and submit as proof of their sexual legitimacy.[34]

But it gets a bit tricky. Some individuals are born with more than forty-six chromosomes. Klinefelter's Syndrome, for example, carries a 47, XXY, karyotype. Some people are born with fewer than forty-six chromosomes. This is the case for those with Turner Syndrome, which encompasses several chromosomal variations, the most common of which is 45, X. Under the provisions of the Barr-body test, the lack of the second X would have made a woman with Turner's ineligible to compete. In addition, as renowned geneticist Albert de la Chappelle notes, "Structural abnormalities of the X chromosome and various mosaic conditions may result in X chromatin findings that are difficult to interpret."[35] Based on sporting organizations' definitions, athletes displaying these genetic arrangements would be ineligible to compete as women, although they may have no athletic advantage.

Polish sprinter Ewa Klobukowska, who passed the visual inspection at the 1966 European championships, had the debasing distinction of being the first woman to "flunk" her chromosomal sex test. After submitting to the exam for the 1967 European championships, a six-man medical commission determined that Klobukowska had "one chromosome too many" and ruled her ineligible.[36] She did not intentionally set out to perpetrate any fraud; however, as one member of the commission put it, "A lady can not be a lady and not know it." The IAAF nullified all of her victories, records, and medals, including the gold and bronze from the 1964 Olympics. At twenty-one years old, Klobukowska could no longer compete at the international level. "It's a dirty and stupid thing to do to me," she said at the time. "I know what I am and how I feel."[37]

Polish athletic representatives disputed the ruling: "We do not agree with the officials," remarked one spokesperson. "It is not sufficient to say that there is a dividing line, that this is a girl and this is not. . . . You must allow for those persons who are complicated to be able to take part in sport."[38] This phrasing, "that there is a dividing line, that this is a girl and this is not," is an excellent summation of what the test sets out to do. Whereas men's sports may be open to a whole host of participants with wide-ranging genetic variations, the "woman" in women's sport is narrowly defined.

An individual whose tests result in the 46, XX, karyotype may also have certain conditions that confer athletic advantages.[39] Marfan syndrome, for instance, causes individuals to be unusually tall, which can assist in sports like basketball and volleyball. This was the case for the great Flo Hyman. One of Finland's most decorated athletes, cross-country skier Eero Mäntyranta, has primary familial and congenital polycythemia, which causes his body to produce 25 percent to 50 percent more red blood cells than the average human—a decided advantage in endurance sports. Additional genetic predispositions can augment endurance, blood flow, metabolic efficiency, muscle mass, bone structure, pain threshold, and respiratory and cardiac functions. Researchers now assess that there are at least two hundred autosomal performance-enhancing polymorphisms (PEPs), or variations in one's DNA sequence, that can enhance athletic performance.[40] As Dr. John S. Fox, an honorary medical adviser to the British Amateur Athletic Board, points out, "One has only to look at the enormous variation in physique in both sexes to appreciate that 'unfairness' is more often attributable to autosomal genetic variation, irrespective of the sex chromosome complement." There are a host of biological issues (not to mention the use of steroids or the access to training, coaches, facilities, and competition associated with higher socioeconomic status or cultural and geographical context) that will give women advantages in athletic competitions that the sex test would not detect.[41]

Then there are instances like that of María José Martínez-Patiño. At the 1983 IAAF World Championships in Athletics (Helsinki, Finland), Martínez-Patiño passed her sex test and received her "certificate of femininity." She neglected to bring her documentation to the 1985 World University Games in Japan and submitted to a buccal (cheek) smear, the results of which officials found problematic. They informed her that her results required a more sophisticated analysis and that it would be best if she faked an injury, dropped out of the race, and awaited their verdict. She complied. Two months later, she received a letter that read: "Karyotype is decided 46, XY."[42] Genetically speaking, and much to her astonishment, they classified Martínez-Patiño as male.

Until that moment, Martínez-Patiño had no reason to doubt her femaleness because she also has (unknown at the time) androgen insensitivity syndrome (AIS), a condition that affects an estimated one in five hundred athletes and because of which "several women are unjustly excluded at each games."[43] With AIS, cells do not form normal androgen receptors and, consequently, cannot respond to the "male hormone" testosterone. These women appear to be genetically male but do not develop strength and musculature associated with testosterone; neither can they benefit from the use of anabolic steroids.[44] As one track and field expert stated in reference to Martínez-Patiño, "She was disqualified for having an advantage that she didn't have."[45] The tests blindly invalidated women with a Y chromosome even when that genetic makeup did not bestow any benefit.[46]

This might be a bit confusing because our generally agreed-upon bimorphic categories of sexual difference are neither discrete nor mutually exclusive—they are messy, fluid, and fraught with inconsistencies. And somewhere along the way, someone has to decide who *counts as* a man or a woman, who gets labeled as "normal" or "abnormal," and, accordingly, who does and does not get to compete in certain sporting events. This is just the tip of the classificatory iceberg. Up until now, my focus has been on the use of chromosomes to conclude sexual identity, and the "fundamental failure of sex chromatin screening of female athletes is that it determines the least relevant parameter of sex in this contest, ie, chromosomal sex," according to Dr. Albert de la Chapelle, a geneticist and leading expert on sex testing.[47] This does not begin to address gonads, genitals, hormones, secondary sex characteristics, psychological identity, or trans-issues. And what about considerations such as socialization, the (dis)advantages associated with being raised male or female, or those that stem from social class, or geography, or race, or how this affects our understandings of sexuality? Personally, it makes my microscopic XX chromosomes spin. Well, I assume they are XX—they have never been "verified," which brings us back to María José Martínez-Patiño.

Despite the results of her karyotype, Martínez-Patiño planned to enter the 60-meter hurdles in the 1986 Spanish national championships. The Real Federación Española de Atletismo informed her that she could either withdraw from the race quietly or face public castigation if she opted to compete. She competed. She won. The Spanish press went on attack. As she recounted: "I was expelled from our athletes' residence, my sports scholarship was erased from my country's athletics records. I felt ashamed and embarrassed. I lost friends, my fiancé, hope and energy. But I knew I was a woman, and that my genetic difference gave me no unfair physical advantage. I could hardly pretend to be a man; I have breasts and a vagina. I never cheated. I fought my disqualification."[48]

The IOC formed a working group to examine the issue, and at the first meeting in 1988 Dr. de la Chappelle, an outspoken critic of the tests, championed Martínez-Patiño's cause. It was the first time a disqualified athlete publicly challenged her disqualification, and three months later the medical chairman of the IAAF restored her license to compete. But the next Olympics were not until 1992 and Martínez-Patiño failed to qualify by ten hundredths of a second.

There are two additional instances that warrant analysis here, for they illustrate further violence done by the practices of sexual designation. The first concerns the murder of Stella Walsh. During a 1980 robbery, assailants shot Walsh, who won five gold and four silver medals for Poland in the 1932 and 1936 Olympics (where her loss to Helen Stephens incited questions about the American's sex). Although both her birth and death certificates indicate that she was female, two television stations in her adopted hometown of Cleveland, Ohio, reported that police were investigating rumors Walsh had both male and female genitalia. The coroner ordered an autopsy and determined that she did possess "tiny," "incomplete," nonfunctioning male sex organs. Additionally, she had a condition known as mosaicism, which meant she possessed both male chromosomes and incomplete chromosomes bearing male and female characteristics: "The majority of her cells examined had a normal X and Y chromosome, and a minority of her cells contained a single X chromosome and no Y chromosome."[49] Popular and scholarly pundits have interpreted this diagnosis in a particular way—that the "autopsy revealed that Stella Walsh was a man."[50] It is an unfair assessment and one that demonstrates the narrow parameters for the definition of woman.

Stella Walsh's posthumous scandal brings up a number of considerations, not least of which is a person's right to privacy. Many Clevelanders expressed outrage at the media's coverage of the story, particularly the television stations that instigated the investigation. In order to gain access to the coroner's report, lawyers for one station petitioned the state appeals court, arguing that the findings were public information: "Now had this been somebody else," said the station's president, "I don't think the sex angle meant a thing, but in this case it does."[51] His statement was not explained in the article, but it seems likely that he referred to the relevance of the "sex angle" in women's sports. In what other sphere are females put through such rigorous paces to convince authorities that they are "truly" women?

A decade after international track and field introduced the exams, American women's tennis did the same. But whereas the IOC, IAAF, and other sporting organizations ostensibly initiated genetic testing to keep out any number of sexual interlopers, the United States Tennis Association adopted the procedure to keep out one person in particular: Renee Richards. Faced with an application from Richards for the 1976 U.S. Open, the USTA announced that the chromosome test would be required for all potential participants. The test effectively barred her entrance because Richards, a male-to-female transsexual, was born Richard Raskind.

As a man, Raskind enjoyed moderate achievement on the men's amateur tennis circuit. As a woman, Richards successfully applied to compete in the Tennis Week Open after the tournament director received a "gynecological affirmation that she is a woman." Twenty-five participants withdrew in protest. The *New York Times* reported that they "argued that Dr. Richards's presence was unfair, that despite her operation and resulting feminine appearance, she still retained the muscular advantages of a male and genetically remained a male." As Susan Birrell and C. L. Cole point out, however, Richards's advantages were not necessarily biological, but were instead about the social "advantages of Raskind's life of white male privilege, including attendance at a boys' prep school, graduation from Yale, completion of medical school, a successful surgical practice, the thrill of being approached by a scout from the New York Yankees, and access to highly competitive tennis which s/he took as his/her natural right as a male." In other words, the sociocultural entitlements that Richards amassed from her Raskind life outweighed those uncovered by genetic scrutiny—the type of scrutiny that determined she had "failed" her sex test.[52]

Richards fought her disqualification, and her case advanced to the U.S. Supreme Court, where the justices ruled that the sex test was "grossly unfair, discriminatory and inequitable, and violative of her rights." In fact, based on her analysis of Olympic sex testing, legal scholar Pamela Fastiff found that the policy potentially infringes on U.S. citizens' constitutional Fourth Amendment right to privacy. It also breaches individuals' entitlement to equal protection, as the IOC is unable to demonstrate that the exam "serves an important governmental interest." Because the results of sex tests are not released to the public, the IOC cannot legally justify that they are necessary.[53] Then again, the organization is a global body and not beholden to a particular country's rules, allowing it a nearly unrestrained scope when it comes to governing sport.

Table 4.1.   Results of Genetic Testing for Gender Verification at Various Olympic Games

Olympic Games	Number of athletes tested	Number ineligible (%)	Frequency
Munich, 1972	1,280	3 (0.23)	1 in 426
Montreal, 1976	1,800	4 (0.22)	1 in 450
Los Angeles, 1984	2,500	6 (0.24)	1 in 416
Barcelona, 1992	2,406	6 (0.25)	1 in 401
Atlanta, 1996	3,387	8 (0.24)	1 in 423
TOTAL	11,373	27 (0.25)	1 in 421

Elsas et al., "Gender Verification of Female Athletes," 252; Malcolm A. Ferguson-Smith, "Gender Verification and the Place of XY Females in Sport," 355–56.

There is no telling how many women these preclusions might have affected over the years, though several scholars have approximated the figures (see table 4.1). Drs. Malcolm Ferguson-Smith and Elizabeth Ferris appraised that one in five- to six-hundred women have been excluded based on the results of sex testing. Dr. Eduardo Hay, the IOC's former chief of testing, estimated that "one or two [women] have been banned at each Olympic Games, except for one since 1968." Although these numbers seem small, there are other factors to consider. An athlete might "fail" a test implemented by a local, regional, or national organization and never make it to the international stage. "They give you the test . . . in your own country," said Jane Frederick, a former Olympic pentathlete, "so that if you don't turn up with the right number of Xs they can take you aside and ask you if you'd like to have an 'injury.'" Although women who do not pass their sex test can appeal the results and submit to further scrutiny, most do not. Instead, coaches or physicians may instruct them to withdraw from competition under the pretense of injury or illness rather face the humiliation of additional analyses.[54]

Women are understandably loath to discuss their experiences, even those who successfully received their "fem cards." Following the humiliation suffered by Ewa Klobukowska, IOC regulations stipulated that the results of the examinations "will not be made public out of deference to the human rights of the individual." The chairman of the IOC's Medical Commission reiterated the position in 1984: "The whole procedure will be conducted in absolute secret. We must avoid pointing a finger at someone who has a problem of this nature."[55] Perhaps a more accurate assessment would be that "we must avoid pointing a finger at someone who has a problem of this *culture*," for natural and normative sexed bodies are ideal constructs produced by the discourse that attempts to define them. It is only a "problem of this nature" because highly regulatory practices render it so.

A Question of Y

There has never been a simple divide between the sponsorship of sex testing from sports officials and opposition from athletes. To the contrary, many competitors support the use of the tests and express that ensuring the sex of participants creates an equitable playing field. Five-time Olympic champion Willye White, for instance, believed that the woman who broke her 1964 long-jump record "was a man. . . . Had it not been a man, I would have been a record holder." Mary Peters likewise wrote that it "is satisfying to know . . . that when you've been beaten you've been beaten by a genuine woman. That wasn't always the case in my career before the introduction of sex tests." At the 1996 Olympic Games, researchers distributed questionnaires to all 3,387 female athletes; of the 928 who responded, 82 percent expressed their support for the continuation of sex tests.[56]

It should also be noted that, from the beginning, many members of the international medical community found the use of sex testing "grossly unfair."[57] As early as 1969, specialists refused to administer the procedures, arguing that they were scientifically and ethically objectionable.[58] Leading geneticists and physicians condemned the sex chromatin test on the grounds that it identifies only chromosomal and genetic sex and that the tests were discarded as a common diagnostic tool in the 1970s.[59] In the 1972 "Memorandum on the Use of Sex Chromatin Investigation of Competitors in Women's Divisions of the Olympic Games," five Danish researchers maintained that "the International Olympic Committee has made its own definition of sex" and proposed that "the use of the test should be cancelled." Opposition to the tests usually fell along three lines: they are unreliable and easily misinterpreted, there was a possibility that "men with a female sex chromatin pattern" would pass the tests, and the tests were useless for considering anatomical, psychological, or social status.[60]

In response to these arguments, the IAAF convened workshops in 1990 and 1992. The participants, including experts in medical genetics, gynecology, pediatrics, biochemistry, psychiatry, endocrinology, pathology, psychology, and sports medicine, as well as female athletes and representatives from women's sporting events, discussed the issue of gender verification. Collectively, the group recommended the discontinuation of laboratory-based methods for determining the sex of athletic competitors and that "only masquerading males (individuals reared and living as men) should be excluded" from women's events. Instead, a "medical examination for the health and well-being of all athletes (men and women) . . . would be to ensure satisfactory physical status for competition and would, of course, include simple inspection of the external genitalia."[61] The tightness of contemporary sports clothing and the close observation athletes undergo while submitting to urinalyses for drug testing make it virtually impossible to disguise external sexual organs.

The IAAF accepted these decisions and declared that, as of May 1992, "We have no femininity list—the file is closed."[62] In its official "Policy on Gender Verification," the IAAF Medical and Anti-Doping Commission qualified that "a search has continued for an acceptable and equitable solution in order to be able to address the occasional anomalies that do surface." If, as specified in the document, "another athlete or team" were to "challenge" the sex of a competitor, or there is "'suspicion' raised as to an athlete's gender as witnessed during an antidoping control specimen collection," or an athlete seeks advice or clarification about her sexual status, then that athlete "is referred to the investigating authority in confidence." From there a "verdict" would be passed as to whether the athlete would retain her eligibility to compete in women's events sanctioned by the IAAF.[63]

In the years that followed the IAAF's initial decision to end comprehensive testing, the IOC remained "wedded to the notion that gender testing was necessary to prevent masquerading males from infiltrating female-only events."[64] At the 1992 Winter Olympics in Albertville, France, the IOC replaced the Barr-body test with one based on gene amplification through polymerase-chain-reaction technology, arguing that was "more reliable."[65] Whereas the previous procedure looked for the presence of the second, inactive X, chromosome (or Barr body), this test first looked for the presence of Y chromosomal material. Any resultant positive samples were then reanalyzed for the presence of a specific gene (*SRY*, or sex-determining region Y), believed to lead to embryonic testicular development and determine an individual's sex.

Implicit in this decision is that sex is not, as commonly understood, as simple as women = XX and men = XY. By searching for the *SRY* gene in female competitors, the IOC tacitly admits that women can exhibit evidence of a Y chromosome. The new procedure did little to quell critics. Just prior to the Games, twenty-two French geneticists signed a letter to the IOC demanding all genetic tests be discontinued, and the ethics commission of the French medical association threatened disciplinary action against any doctors who administered the test.[66]

Stronger pressure began to mount in the 1990s. Doctors called sex testing "morally destitute" and a "futile exercise causing embarrassment, anguish and expense."[67] Athletic and genetic groups in Canada and Australia condemned the tests. A prominent Spanish geneticist refused to participate in sex testing during the 1992 Barcelona Olympics.[68] The Norwegian medical community declined to assist the IOC with the exams at the 1994 Games in Lillehammer, and in 1996 Norway's parliament ruled gender verification illegal. By then, nearly all major medical societies in the United States had passed resolutions that called for the end to sex testing, although the Atlanta Committee for the 1996 Olympic Games agreed to the IOC contract that stipulated a requirement for on-site screening and the issuing of gender-verification cards.

At the 1999 IOC World Conference on Women in Sport, constituents called for a resolution that would end comprehensive sex testing. This was followed by the IOC's Athletes' Commission's unanimous decision to abandon widespread examinations, a conclusion facilitated by the work of Dr. Arne Ljungqvist, member and chair of the IOC's Medical Commission.[69] The IOC's executive board accepted this recommendation and decided to suspend the tests on a trial basis for the 2000 Games in Sydney. Still, the new mandate left officials the option to evaluate individual athletes if they seemed "suspicious." This policy continued at the 2008 Beijing Olympics, inspiring a revivification of protest against the exams.

The End of (Sex Testing) History?

The most recent changes in sex-testing protocol came in the wake of what is, to date, the most publicly contentious incident involving a female athlete. At the 2009 IAAF World Championships in Athletics (Berlin, Germany) a South African woman named Caster Semenya won the 800-meter race and clocked the thirteenth-fastest time in the history of the event. During live televised coverage of the championships, sportscasters read from an official IAAF statement confirming "concerns that she does not meet the requirements to compete as a woman."[70] Never clarifying what those requirements were, the IAAF requested Semenya abstain from competition. She obliged for eleven months while a panel composed of a gynecologist, endocrinologist, psychologist, internal medicine specialist, and a "gender expert" worked to determine her sex.

As she waited, Semenya experienced unprecedented publicity. Competitors, critics, and the popular media mocked and excoriated her, leaning heavily on accusations of "too": she was too fast, too muscular, her chest too flat, jaw line too square, voice too deep, hips too narrow. She improved too much too quickly. She was too good for a woman.[71] It was an extension of the narrative, set in place decades before, that made gendered expectations the grounds for questioning one's sex. She also received unparalleled support from the public, fellow athletes, physicians, politicians, and legal counsel. As a result, and unlike other disqualified women who preceded her, Semenya did not fade from collective consciousness but remained at the fore as the experts deliberated.

On July 6, 2010, nearly a full year since her last race, officials issued a brief release stipulating that the IAAF "accepts the conclusion of a panel of medical experts that she can compete with immediate effect."[72] Many speculate that, in the interim, Semenya underwent some type of hormonal or surgical intervention (or both) designed to diminish an endogenous and potentially advantageous condition. She later qualified for the 2012 London Olympics, where she finished second in the 800-meter race. Predictably, pundits rehashed debates about her sex and speculated that she might have a biological edge over other women. Never again will she be judged solely on the basis of her performance.

The IOC and IAAF do not reference the beleaguered athlete in their newest procedures, but it was clear they hoped "to avoid any repeat of the controversy that surrounded South African runner Caster Semenya." After eighteen months of deliberation, an IAAF-appointed panel of experts, working closely with the IOC's Medical Commission, publicized its resolution. In a twenty-eight-page document, the IAAF announced official regulations for women with "hyperandrogenism" or "the excessive production of androgenic hormones (Testosterone)." These standards, the document reads, "replace the IAAF's previous Gender Verification Policy and the IAAF has now abandoned all reference to the terminology 'gender verification' and 'gender policy' in its Rules."[73] This is merely an issue of semantics. Sporting organizations continue to pursue "suspicious" women, but instead of searching for genital or chromosomal indicators, they are now on the hunt for hormonal markers.

The new guidelines, also adopted by the IOC before the London Games, are based on testosterone levels in serum: the "normal" reference range for men is 10–35 nanomoles per liter; for women, the range is much narrower and lower, at 0.35–2.0 nmol/L. The IAAF and IOC stipulate that eligibility to compete in women's events (for those who can legally demonstrate femaleness) requires serum testosterone levels less than 10 nmol/L.[74] Those above the established threshold—potentially hyperandrogenic females—come to the attention of medical commissions in several ways. An athlete who has been diagnosed with hyperandrogenism or is in the process of such a diagnosis must notify the sporting organization of her condition. Under other circumstances, including analytical results from routine antidoping tests or concerns raised by a medical official at a competition, the IAAF medical manager or the chairman of the IOC Medical Commission (or those in similar positions in other organizations) can initiate further investigation. Those athletes determined to have benefited from hyperandrogenism (women with AIS are cleared to compete) must submit to "prescribed medical treatment" designed to "correct" any "Disorders of Sexual Development" or "Intersex Disorders." The language here is telling, for it pathologizes naturally occurring, randomly selected variations in human constitutions—at least when it comes to women.

Treatment occurs in one of six approved specialists centers around the world. There, it is possible that any procedures an athlete might undergo could negatively affect her health and athletic performance. And the new policies provide no provision to pay for the treatment. It is unlikely that an athlete's own organization or government will foot the bill, so her socioeconomic status compounds the situation in which she finds herself.

Moreover, there is no definitive connection between hyperandrogenism and athletic ability.[75] Members of the IAAF and IOC working groups that established the new policy say there is enough evidence to suggest testosterone is associated with qualities beneficial to physical performance.[76] Karkazis and colleagues, on the other hand, argue that "the link between athleticism and androgens in general or testosterone in particular has not been proven."[77] And even if hyperandrogenism does confer some type of advantage, according to one expert, it "should not be considered more unfair than any genetic giftedness of any other athlete."[78] To single out those conditions that affect a woman's testosterone levels and show little to no concern for detecting other potentially advantageous endogenous conditions seems both arbitrary and sexist.

Hyperandrogenic females who consent to treatment must be reexamined to determine their eligibility. They remain banned from competition until their test results satisfy the experts. Those who refuse to comply with the additional investigation or decline prescribed treatment are disqualified from all future women's competitions.[79] The guidelines are "imperfect," according to Dr. Eric Vilain, a medical geneticist and the director of the Institute for Society and Genetics at UCLA who served on the IOC's advisory board. But, he continued, "you have to draw a line in the sand somewhere."[80] His turn of phrase is apt, for it implies an arbitrary, impermanent division imposed on the infinite, shifting grains of human biology, one that demarcates an ideal type of femaleness and renders everything else out of bounds.

As in the past, the organizations justified the need for some type of detection by asserting the need to "guarantee the fairness and integrity of female competitions for all female athletes." The "condition" or "deviation" of female hyperandrogenism brought with it a new justification: "to protect the health of the athlete."[81] Presumably, this is only an issue about which women must worry, for male athletes are not subjected to similar scrutiny. A man with elevated levels of endogenous androgens is endowed with a genetic gift. A woman with the same condition is a freak; her affliction must be corrected.

Fair and Foul

The logic that undergirds the history of sex testing is such that gendered expectations become sexed imperatives: what women's bodies *should* look like and how they *should* perform in sport becomes how they *must* look on the macro- and microscopic levels. As a result, social concerns are exercised on the material body of the female athlete. The sex test—in all its myriad forms—is at once a diagnostic, prescriptive, and proscriptive assessment that produces sex as it attempts to determine it.

Despite the assertion that sex, like gender, lies on a continuum, there remains a distinct unease about opening the gates of women's sports to any and all competitors who care to call themselves women. It is a challenge: to say that sexual status is relevant only in the cultural meanings assigned to men and women is one thing, but to break down the barriers that separate men's and women's sports is quite another. At the elite level of sport, men and women generally differ in physical characteristics such as height, musculature, strength, and speed, despite arguments about the closing "muscle gap."[82] Moreover, the frequently meager monetary and promotional rewards in women's sports force athletes to struggle over limited resources. Any hint of "unfair" advantage is likely to leave competitors calling "foul."

There are no easy answers to whether and what kind of sex testing should go on in sports. Initiated under historically specific circumstances that stigmatized strength, strain, and stamina as distinctly unfeminine, the tests have unjustly disqualified a number of women while allowing unrestricted biological variations within men's sport. Although critical scholar Judith Butler argues that sport "allows the category of 'woman' to become a limit to be surpassed," sex testing ensures the category is continually hemmed in at the edges.[83] As athletic women challenge and redraw definitional boundaries, the surveillance and biopower to which their bodies are submitted renders nonnormative sex and gender performances suspect, abject, and too often censored.

5. From "Women in Sports" to the "New Ideal of Beauty"

The advent of sex testing and the National Institutes in the 1960s were attempts to control gender normativity in the face of an undeniable and impending explosion in women's sport participation. Both were important precursors to what many felt was an athletic "revolution" in the 1970s, an era replete with points of change. Symbolic of this transformation, editors devoted the June 26, 1978, cover of *Time,* a weekly publication that rarely featured sportswomen (or any women, for that matter), to "women in sports" (see figure 5.1).[1]

The simple title, in stark yellow font, appears as a banner across the figures of two intercollegiate lacrosse players caught in the throes of competition. The focus is on one woman from Penn State University. The photographer has captured her with stick raised and in midstride. Between the top of her knee-high sock and the hem of her pleated skirt peeks the muscular thigh of an athlete. Nothing about her gaze or body position suggests an awareness of the camera's presence. It is an action shot as opposed to the "poised and pretty" image that historically predominates the coverage of sportswomen.[2]

The corresponding story, "Comes the Revolution," is one of athletic achievement and autonomy: "Spurred by the fitness craze, fired up by the feminist movement and buttressed by court rulings and legislative mandates, women have been moving from miniskirted cheerleading on the sidelines for the boys to playing, and playing hard, for themselves. . . . They have come a long, long way."[3]

A second cover story, published four years later, concurred: "You've come a long way, sister." But in language that conspicuously paralleled the earlier piece, its message took on a decidedly different cast. "The sports for which

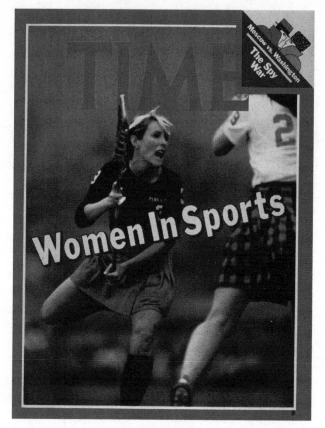

Figure 5.1: "Women In Sports," *Time,* June 26, 1978. Courtesy of PARS International Corp.

you were once only a cheerleader now serve as your after-work recreation and, thanks to Title IX, part of your school-age daughter's curriculum. Spurred by feminism's promise of physical, domestic and economic freedom, you have done what few generations of women have dared or chosen to do. You have made muscles—a body of them—and it shows. And you look great."[4] The emphasis is on, as the title of the cover story articulates, "the new ideal of beauty." The accompanying cover illustration shows a model clad in a red, faintly transparent leotard and matching thigh-high leg warmers (see figure 5.2). Despite the article's praise of female muscularity, she exhibits almost none. With windswept hair, she stands provocatively, arms akimbo, legs apart, and looks levelly—suggestively—into the camera. She is, as the caption asserts, "coming on strong."

Figure 5.2: "Coming on Strong," *Time*, August 30, 1982.
Courtesy of PARS International Corp.

Generally speaking, the covers of *Time* "serve as benchmarks to history," and, taken together, the two covers described in this chapter suggest important points of change in women's physical culture. Specifically, they express what Naomi Wolf calls the "beauty myth," a "backlash against feminism that uses images of female beauty as a political weapon against women's advancement."[5] The complementary articles go further. In 1978 *Time* reported that the female athlete is "acquiring a new sense of self, and of self-confidence in her physical abilities and her potential. She is leading a revolution that is one of the most exciting and one of the most important in the history of sport." Readers learn that girls' and women's participation had virtually erupted since the early 1970s, by nearly 600 percent at the high school level and, at the time of publication, more than one hundred thousand women competed in intercollegiate sports. "Such statistics are impressive," writes the unnamed author, "but they merely reinforce the most significant aspect of the explosive growth of women's sport: the new, refreshingly unapologetic pride of the female athlete." The piece celebrates the changing landscape of U.S. sport and the physical, psychological, and social benefits that female athletes were beginning to reap.

In contrast, the 1982 cover story fetes sport and physical culture for altering women's bodies and the ideal feminine form: "As a comely byproduct of the fitness phenomenon women have begun literally to reshape themselves, and with themselves, the American notion of female beauty." Muscles and the "fit look" are in vogue, readers learn. "The new body is here, and men may decide it is sexy for one basic reason: it can enhance sex." Physical activity becomes a means to a heterosexy end and not, as presented in 1978, an end to itself. By converting women's quest for physical equality into a quest for physical perfection, public culture of the early and mid-1980s effectively diffused the forward momentum of women in sport.[6]

The beauty-myth recoil against women's movements in sport and society was part of a more encompassing "backlash," as Susan Faludi characterizes it, that "coincided with signs that women were believed to be on the verge of a breakthrough." It was not so much a direct attack against the consolidation of feminist entitlement, but rather a "preemptive strike that stops women long before they reach the finish line." The reaction affected every aspect of American culture and struck brutal blows—both overt and subtle—against women's work to increase their power and status. Faludi writes that this backlash was neither a "conspiracy" nor an "organized movement," but a dispersed, powerful aggregation of antifeminist rhetoric, representation, and actions, particularly manifested in popular culture, the media, and contemporary politics.[7] Symptoms of the 1980s backlash could be found in everything from the film *Fatal Attraction*, to distorted "trend stories" reporting that career women were less likely, to find husbands to the tragic defeat of the Equal Rights Amendment. The overarching message was that women were bound to suffer when they endeavored to disrupt the prevailing gender order.

Another look at the 1982 cover reveals an interesting element: President Ronald Reagan literally peers over the model's left shoulder. The 1980 election of Reagan, "the great American synecdoche" of the era, ushered in a neoconservative political agenda that permeated every social facet. His inauguration was more a symptom of the times than its source, and his occupation of the presidency and unparalleled public approval spoke to and galvanized an important cultural shift. Although the Reagan era "cannot be reduced to a simple tale of the triumph of the right and the demise of feminism," the regime struck significant blows against women's advancements.[8] The backlash was about more than women's power and the perceived threat to masculinity; it was also a response to the country's apparent erosion of international status, its economic "stagflation," and a reaction to New Deal and Great Society liberalism. As part of cuts to federally funded social programs, Reaganite politicians dismantled, stymied, or stalled progressive legislation that protected issues such as reproductive freedom, affirmative action, financial assistance, equal rights, and equal opportunity.

These assaults affected girls' and women's sports, both contextually and by direct application. The early-1980s trend toward cosmetic exercise was not a knee-jerk reaction to the burgeoning progress in women's sports, though there were plenty of overt forms of aggression on this front. Instead, with women on the cusp of a sporting revolution in the mid- to late 1970s, feminist retrenchment in the subsequent decade meant a cultural recalibration that directed attention toward aesthetic fitness, and especially aerobic dance, at the expense of women's athletics.

The Revolution in Women's Sports

In reading both popular and scholarly accounts of women's sports in the 1970s, it is hard to ignore the number of times writers use the word *revolution* to characterize the transformations that occurred. The 1978 *Time* piece, for example, is both titled by and riddled with the descriptor. Scholars note that the "revolution" really began to gather steam in the 1960s and flourished the following decade. Others imagined that "when Title IX became law in 1972, the leaders of women's intercollegiate athletics started dreaming of a revolution." In the end, as one *Chicago Tribune* writer declared, "Athletic opportunities for women exploded in the 1970s, scholarships were offered and spending increased. It was nothing short of a revolution."[9] The term overgeneralizes the issue. Girls and women of color or from working-class backgrounds did not experience the same "revolution" in sports participation as their white, middle-class peers. Oftentimes, the revolution was geographically discrete or offered a limited (and limiting) program of sports.

There were also a fair number of stumbles and setbacks during this time. *Sports Illustrated*, which historically treated women's sport as an afterthought, declared in a May 28, 1973, cover story, "Women are getting a raw deal." The first in a three-part series began

> There may be worse (more socially serious) forms of prejudice in the United States, but there is no sharper example of discrimination today than that which operates against girls and women who take part in competitive sports, wish to

take part, or might wish to if society did not scorn such endeavors. No matter what her age, education, race, talent, residence or riches, the female's right to play is severely restricted. The funds, facilities, coaching, rewards and honors allotted women are grossly inferior to those granted men. In many places absolutely no support is given to women's athletics, and females are barred by law, regulation, tradition or the hostility of males from sharing athletic resources and pleasures.[10]

The articles went on to detail the myriad ways in which the sports world excluded, discouraged, and disadvantaged girls and women. That such an influential publication addressed women's sports, and in such a high-profile way, provides clear affirmation that, notwithstanding persistent inequities, women's sport was on the move. "If in 1972 opportunities for women were terrible," conceded one advocate in 1976, "now they've improved to bad— and that's certainly progress." And so, reported the *Washington Post*, "The revolution inches resolutely forward."[11]

Change happened, in the words of historian Mary Jo Festle, as "two trends— greater support for women's rights and greater interest in physical well-being— came together to make the mid-seventies a very promising period for women's sports."[12] In fact, there were a number of monumental events that punctuated the era. Accumulated and set along a time line, the milestones that emerged at the amateur, Olympic, professional, and organizational levels do seem almost revolutionary. For example:

- 1971: the DGWS forms the Association of Intercollegiate Athletics for Women; in its first year of operation (1972–73) membership included 386 institutions and offered national championships in eight sports[13]
- 1972: President Nixon signs Title IX (a "revolutionary piece of legislation")[14] into law
- 1972: the AAU sanctions the marathon race for women
- 1972: *Sports Illustrated* names Billie Jean King its first "Sportswoman of the Year"
- 1972: Bernice Gera wins her discrimination suit against the National Association of Baseball Leagues and becomes the first woman to umpire a professional baseball game
- 1973: eleven students and three teachers from Florida colleges file a lawsuit to challenge the AIAW's prohibition of athletic scholarships; the AIAW concedes, and women begin earning tuition dollars based on their sporting talents
- 1974: with the help of the National Organization for Women, girls successfully lobby to play Little League Baseball; Little League Softball is also established, and nearly thirty thousand girls sign up in the first year
- 1974: the Women's Equity Action League (WEAL) files suit against the federal government for failing to enforce Title IX; in 1977 a court order

requires the Office of Civil Rights (OCR) to respond to Title IX complaints within specified time frames

- *Sports Illustrated* names 1974 "The Year of the Woman in Sport"
- 1974: Billie Jean King establishes the Women's Sports Foundation; Donna de Verona is the organization's first president
- 1975: WEAL forms the Sports Project Referral and Information Network (SPRINT) to collect and distribute materials about women and girls in sport
- 1975: the AAU sanctions women's power lifting
- 1975: Dennis Murphy, Billie Jean King, Jim Jorgenson, and Joan Joyce co-found the International Women's Professional Softball Association
- 1975: the State of Nevada grants Caroline Svendsen the first documented boxing license for a woman in the United States; in 1978 Cathy Davis, Jackie Tonawanda, and Marian Trimiar win their lawsuit to become licensed professional boxers in New York
- 1976: the IOC adds women's basketball, rowing, and handball to the Olympic program
- 1977: Janet Guthrie becomes the first woman to qualify for the Indianapolis 500; Shirley Muldowney sets a drag-racing speed record
- 1978: the AIAW boasts 659 member institutions and sixty thousand intercollegiate athletes[15]
- 1978: the Women's Professional Basketball League is established
- 1978: the first Avon International Marathon (Atlanta, Georgia) takes place
- 1979: the American College of Sports Medicine publishes its "Opinion Statement on the Female Athlete in Long-Distance Running," recommending that "females be allowed to compete at the national and international level in the same distances in which their male counterparts compete"[16]
- 1980: the AIAW has 971 members; more than ninety-two thousand women participate in intercollegiate sport[17]

And "Tennis!" exclaimed Boutilier and SanGiovanni. "Who could possibly write about the female sporting revolution without mentioning tennis?" Journalist Marianne Taylor agreed, contending that "the changes in the tennis world cleared the way for a revolution that reached from professional sports down to junior high schools across the country." It began in 1970 when nine players, fed up with the egregious inequalities between men's and women's purses, broke from the USLTA to form their own separate tour. After their first invitational, journalist Grace Lichtenstein decreed that "the New Feminism in tennis was born."[18] Gradually, more women joined what became the Virginia Slims Circuit. They risked their livelihood by parting from the USLTA but, in the process, won greater earnings, exposure, and respect for their sport.

The year 1973 witnessed a number of groundbreaking moments in women's tennis. As the fledgling organization gained traction, Billie Jean King convinced the sixty-three members to unionize, forming the Women's Tennis Association. Shortly thereafter, the WTA merged with the USLTA, and, for the first time, women competing in the U.S. Open earned prize money equal to the men. It was also the year that King played Bobby Riggs in the "Battle of the Sexes" match. More than thirty thousand people gathered in the Houston Astrodome, while another ninety million television viewers in more than forty different countries tuned in to see King wallop Riggs in three straight sets. In the end, the match "legitimized women's tennis," wrote King. "It was the culmination of an era, the noisy conclusion to the noisiest three years in the history of the women's game."[19]

The King-Riggs match provided the seed capital for the champion to launch the magazine *womenSports* the following year. As King's then husband remembers, she had been thumbing through an issue of *Sports Illustrated*, condemning the lack of women in its coverage. He suggested she start her own magazine, to which she replied, "Let's do it."[20] Women were also beginning to make headway in the media's traditionally male bastions. After a year of struggle, the National Hockey League allowed postgame locker-room access to journalists Robin Herman and Marcel St. Cyr. "It was at the height of the women's movement," Herman later said. "It was important to be bold. It was a matter of equity."[21] During that time, *Sports Illustrated* reporter Melissa Ludtke and her employer, Time, Inc., successfully sued Major League Baseball and its commissioner, Bowie Kuhn, in order to gain access to locker-room interviews for all journalists, regardless of sex.

Women continued to chisel out additional, albeit limited, toeholds in the world of print media. Lesley Visser became the *Boston Globe*'s first woman National Football League (NFL) beat reporter in 1974; Le Anne Shreiber, once editor in chief for *womenSports,* became the first female sports editor at any major newspaper when she joined the staff of the illustrious *New York Times*. Television was also caught in the social currents. Lamented one *Chicago Tribune* critic, "If the sight of a woman sportscaster makes you choke on your suds, you're in for some rough times . . . because the Sex Revolution has arrived in the TV sports business."[22] Women might not belong in sports or sports broadcasting, the writer suggests, but there was little men could do to stop their invasion.

One might chalk up some of these landmarks to "tokenism" that led to few "substantial gains," but there is no denying the larger transformations at hand.[23] The most dramatic changes happened with regard to girls' and women's athletic participation. In 1971 approximately 294,000 girls played interscholastic sport; by 1979 the number grew to more than 2 million.[24] At the intercollegiate level, there were around 16,000 women athletes in 1967, a number that grew to about 100,000 by 1980. At that time, a poll determined that 62 percent of *Glamour* readers had become more involved in sports in recent years.[25] The benefits of participation were more than physical, as studies found that athletic experiences augmented girls' self-confidence, self-actualization, and leadership abilities. Researchers determined that "sports are a training ground for female assertiveness and defiance of sex-role restrictions" and that "competition brings about a sense of mastery and accomplishment that has a profound impact on the rest of their lives."[26] By competing in sport, women could "inherit the essential source of human self-confidence—pride in and control over a finely tuned body. That alone would be a revolution." All together, these trends constituted "a full-fledged phenomenon. . . . [I]t isn't a single victory engineered by one organization, but rather a thousand stories happening everywhere at once—on the playgrounds and courts, in national magazines and on coast-to-coast TV, in backyards and on college campuses. Women athletes are making their mark."[27]

But by the early 1980s, many mourned that the women's sports revolution was "over." Instead, a new revolution had taken hold of the country—the "Reagan Revolution"—characterized by the president's aims to cut taxes, bolster military defense, and reduce government intervention in private, public, and business affairs. Reagan "did not 'cause' the revolution" argues critical scholar Susan Jeffords, "rather the circumstances made it possible for him to stand at the head of a changing social and political situation."[28] Nevertheless, he epitomized the prevailing tide of right-wing conservativism that washed over the country, which included, among other significant issues, attacks on women's rights and affirmative action programs.

The Backlash against Women's Sports

Assaults on Title IX during the early 1980s are illustrative of the more pervasive retaliations against women's social progress. Title IX, often considered the most important point of change in women's sport history, passed in 1972 with no mention of sport or physical education. Within a year, women began filing complaints over the lack of athletic opportunities. By 1975 the Department of Health, Education, and Welfare (HEW) drafted its final regulations specific to athletics, which President Ford subsequently signed into law, giving elementary and high schools one year to bring their programs into compliance, while granting colleges a three-year grace period.

Finally, on December 6, 1978, HEW secretary Joseph Califano announced the policy interpretations "aimed at clarifying, for the colleges and universities that must comply with Title IX, what they must do with their athletic programs in order to obey the law."[29] If a school received any type of federal funding, whether through direct aid or through students who benefited from federal tuition moneys, it must adhere to Title IX in all its academic and athletic programs. Prior to the policy announcement, HEW had not enforced Title IX, although its mere existence induced many schools to add athletic opportunities for girls and women. As such, the law "had no direct legal impact on sport during the 1970s," writes Sarah K. Fields, "but it did have an immediate social impact." Donna Lopiano, then women's athletic director at the University of Texas, likened Title IX to "a guillotine in a courtyard. People were afraid of it. For a while, people did things because they felt they had to. But when the Reagan Administration came in and showed it was not interested in minorities, the Office of Civil Rights stopped enforcing Title IX at all."[30]

During the early years of Title IX, politicians and men's sports enthusiasts protested the legislation. Their party line was not that they were against women in sport, but that those opportunities would come at the expense of men's sport. Congress considered and rejected several bills and amendments that would exempt athletics in general and, specifically, football and men's basketball from Title IX compliance. The NCAA, which, at the time, governed only men's intercollegiate sport, supported many of these motions, and NCAA executive director Walter Byers urged his constituents to back lobbying efforts to eliminate athletics from the purview of the law. The NCAA sued HEW on the basis that it had overstepped its authority with regards to athletics, though in 1980 the U.S. Court of Appeals ruled that the NCAA did not have standing to take legal action.[31]

Title IX opponents often framed the law as federal interference, arguing that the government had no business encroaching on the ways schools ran their sport programs. Fred Davison, director of athletics at the University of Georgia, criticized Title IX, arguing that the "incursion of the Federal government into college athletics can only lead to the destruction of sports programs as we know them and result in a loss of opportunity and enjoyment for both men and women." Thomas C. Hansen, assistant executive director of the NCAA, similarly reviled that the "federal government has overextended its authority." William E. Davis, president of the University of New Mexico, offered a football analogy, charging the federal government with "trying to become the fifth man in the Notre Dame backfield."[32] Commentary from these and other high-ranking officials fitted nicely with Reagan's agenda to scale back governmental enforcement of social programs.

As a presidential candidate in 1980, Reagan told voters, "We must not allow the noble concept of equal opportunity to be distorted into federal guidelines or quotas which require race, ethnicity, or sex rather than ability and qualifications to be the principal factor in hiring or education." Sheryl Sklorman, who worked with the SPRINT program on equal opportunity in sport (which folded in 1983 due to lack of funding), warned about the way this disposition might affect Title IX: "Despite the steady rise in the numbers of girl athletes, girls' participation in sports may still encounter new hurdles ahead. The Reagan administration and the new, more conservative Congress would like to limit the federal government's power to 'intrude' into the problems of state and local governments." In one of the first initiatives of his administration, Reagan established the Presidential Task Force on Regulatory Relief, charged with finding ways to scale back federal involvement. Chairman of the committee, Vice President George Herbert Walker Bush, announced there were more than thirty "burdensome" policies and regulations that his task force would review, with the prospect of modification or elimination. Title IX was on that list.[33]

By then HEW had "failed to close even one case having to do with sex bias in intercollegiate athletics."[34] The biggest blow came in 1984, when the Supreme Court ruled 6–3 in favor of Grove City College (Pennsylvania), supporting the school's contention that because the athletic department did not receive direct federal funding, that particular program should not be beholden to the law. The ruling effectively excused athletic departments from complying with Title IX. Almost immediately, the OCR scaled back its investigations, including those pending and already in progress. As historian Hugh Davis recounts, "Within weeks of the Supreme Court's February 28, 1984, decision on Grove City College, the Reagan administration began closing civil rights investigations under the program-specific statutes. The Department of Education, citing lack of jurisdiction, closed investigations of sex discrimination complaints against athletic programs at the universities of Maryland, Penn State, Alabama, Auburn, Duke, Idaho State, and Washington, among others, and also against the New York City public schools."[35] The ruling, in effect, struck the death knell for Title IX's application to athletics.

That women's sports were still under threat from the NCAA in the early 1980s compounded the adversity. As historian Mary Jo Festle describes it, "The NCAA seemed to arrive at a two-pronged policy: it would lobby hard to stop the government from mandating equal opportunity in athletics, but in case that failed it would keep the possibility alive of taking over women's sports." Beginning in 1966, the organization made overtures toward governing women's programs and championships. They pushed that separate was not equal and that the different philosophies of the AIAW and NCAA meant female athletes did not receive equivalent intercollegiate experiences. Detractors charged that the NCAA's motivation was either based on a desire to protect itself from allegations of discrimination or a "purely financial move" to monopolize college sports.[36] The AIAW repeatedly refused offers to merge with or become a subsidiary of the NCAA, arguing that it was in the best interest of women's sport to maintain autonomy and operate from their uniquely educational philosophy.[37]

These maneuvers came to a head at the NCAA's 1981 convention, where constituents voted to offer Division I national championships for women's intercollegiate sport, essentially usurping control from the AIAW.[38] The NCAA offered member institutions a litany of perks that the AIAW could not: a significantly larger operating budget, greater television exposure, less restrictive recruiting standards, and free membership. With the NCAA's decision, the AIAW lost a considerable number of affiliates and, with them, their association dues. It also lost guarantees for televised coverage of the national championships and the money associated with broadcast rights, all of which put the organization in dire financial straits.

With little recourse, the AIAW's Executive Board filed an injunction against the NCAA, which became an expedited antitrust trial. The district and appellate courts ruled in favor of the NCAA, effectively sentencing the AIAW to extinction. Women's governance over women's intercollegiate sports had ended, and although the NCAA promised women 25 percent of the leadership roles in the organization, their collective power had been destroyed. Adding insult to injury, the NCAA would now represent women's interests in the event of congressional hearings on the issue of Title IX—a law that the NCAA never fully supported.

The gut-wrenching loss of the AIAW contributed to the dramatic decline in the number of women in key functionary positions. In 1972 women coached more than 90 percent of all women's intercollegiate athletic teams. This makes sense. Growing out of women's physical education and its separatist philosophy, combined with the dearth of participation opportunities at the collegiate level, it stands to reason that women should be overrepresented in these positions. But as schools added sports for women, the percentage of female coaches trended inversely. By 1978, the year of mandatory Title IX compliance, women coaches had already dropped to 58.2 percent for women's intercollegiate teams. By 1985 that percentage was down to 50.7 percent. There was a similar pattern for women administrators. In 1972 they governed more than 90 percent of all women's college athletic programs. By 1984 they constituted an abysmal 17 percent—a trend exacerbated by the NCAA's seizure of control.[39]

Thus, while opportunities to participate in athletics expanded for female athletes, it was men, and not women, who increasingly governed their sports. "The revolution is over, the battle won," asserted *Sports Illustrated*. "Women athletes have long since taken their positions on playing fields across America. The power structure for women's sports is in place, a perfect pyramid, broad at the base, thanks to Title IX, visible from great distances, thanks to the spotlights trained on individual athletes. Yet who sits astride this pyramid? Who has the power to build, to change, to pick up a telephone and say, 'Do it now'? Men, that's who." In 1983 *Educational Digest* likewise reported that the "women's sports revolution in schools and colleges is currently in remission. . . . The AIAW is in the mothballs. . . . Leadership for women in governance has been reduced from over 1,000 positions in the AIAW to under 500 positions in the NCAA and NAIA [National Association of Intercollegiate Athletes] combined." Festle referred to the trend as "backsliding"; Ellen Vargyas, an attorney for the National Women's Law Center, characterized it as "'backtracking,' a slow elimination of the gains that were made more than a decade ago." In 1982 researchers cautioned that "political backlash could effectively decrease the recent acceleration over the last ten years of women's sport and athletic participation."[40] *Remission, backslide, backtrack,* or *backlash*—all terms connote a sense of recession, of diminishment, of loss.

The Beauty Myth in Public Culture

The beauty-myth backlash against women's sports was subtler, though every bit as pernicious as the outright assaults on the gains of the previous decades. Some manifestations of the beauty myth seem innocuous. Others might be chalked up to the fickle whims of fashion. Aggregated, though, these changes were part of a broader public culture in which 1980s counterattacks blunted 1970s breakthroughs for women, evident in everything from political debates to governmental policies, legal decisions, popular media, advertising, and fashion trends.

There are countless examples of the beauty myth in early-1980s culture. Take, for example, advertising campaigns for Charlie perfume. When Revlon introduced the product in 1973, it quickly became the nation's best-selling fragrance, inspiring a host of other companies to jump on the bandwagon with their own products that advocated spirited, independent images of womanhood. In these campaigns, notes Faludi, "superathletes abounded, from Coty's ice-skating champion, Smitty, to Fabergé's roller-skating dynamo, Babe ('the fragrance for the fabulous new woman you're becoming')—in homage to Olympian Babe Didrikson Zaharias."[41] Suddenly, in 1982, Revlon executives "phased out" the "single, independent working woman" who starred in Charlie ads and replaced her with "a new campaign that substituted a woman who was seeking marriage and a family." Executives just "sensed" it was time, according to Revlon's executive vice president. "There's a need now for a woman to be less striving. . . . [S]he doesn't have to be so assertive anymore. She can be more womanly."[42] The implication is that idealized femininity precludes ambition and, by extension, participation in sports.

Children's commercial culture also shied away from sports iconography during this time. In 1975 Mattel marketed "Gold Medal Barbie," an Olympic athlete who competed in downhill skiing, figure skating, and gymnastics. Accessories (sold separately, of course) included "Barbie's Olympic Ski Village," authorized by the U.S. Olympic Committee. Executives undoubtedly wanted to cash in on Olympic fervor in 1976 but, curiously, did not attempt the same strategy in 1984, even though the Games took place in Los Angeles. Instead, that year Mattel came out with "Great Shape Barbie," an aerobics instructor outfitted in spandex leotard, leg warmers, and ballet slippers. Consumers could buy a doll-size workout center, along with dumbbells, a ballet bar, an exercise bike, a workout bench, and a mirror to complete the experience. These added trimmings at once insinuate an individualized program of corporeal betterment and the "epidemic consumerism" of the eighties.[43] Barbie's "great shape" also provided an unrealistic corporeal model to which girls might aspire but could never come close to approximating.

Other toys marketed for girls accentuated the early-1980s exercise craze and the importance of one's "shape" at the expense of athletic role models. As one advertising executive explained, "Fitness products for kids are going to follow what's happening to adults."[44] For those not content to put Barbie through her paces, Hasbro offered "Get in Shape, Girl!"—a series of workout kits that included gear, instructional posters, and cassette tapes with "popular music and verbal cues" to which girls could follow along. "Get in Shape, Girl!" also came with an array of fashion accessories, including a pink visor, athletic socks, a "sporty tote bag," and wristbands. The "Workout Plus" kit was "ideal for the fashion-conscious little lady," explained the advertising copy. In addition to two lightweight dumbbells, the package contained a terry-cloth headband and leg warmers. The fitness lifestyle, in this case as in others, relied on consumer choices—on buying the correct accoutrements to assert oneself as a workout devotee.[45]

The product sold extremely well, joining the ranks of the magazine *Toy and Hobby World*'s Toy Hit Parade.[46] By 1985 girls could choose between several different versions of "Get in Shape, Girl!" For $24.99 they could own "The Ultimate Workout" set, consisting of a soft vinyl mat for floor exercises, jump rope, and logbook. Additionally, "Pump 'n' Run" allowed users to adjust the heft of hand weights by adding water, "Twist 'n' Twirl" offered four batons, and "Feet Beat" endorsed jumping rope. Hasbro did include one sport in the series: "Rhythm and Ribbons," the least expensive option at $5.99, which encouraged users to "get in on the latest sports rage of rhythmic gymnastics, as demonstrated in the 1984 Olympics." Of all the sports on the IOC's program, rhythmic gymnastics was an interesting choice in light of gold-medal performances from the likes of Mary Lou Retton, Joan Benoit, Jackie Joyner-Kersee, and Tracy Caulkins. Further, the mandate that girls "get in shape" played upon both fitness and corporeal ideals, a common trend in 1980s fitness discourse that promoted the aesthetic benefits of physical activity.

womenSports also went the way of the beauty myth. Debuting the magazine in 1974, publisher Billie Jean King intended for it to be a vehicle "to let young women know . . . that their desire to compete and excel wasn't abnormal." Espousing an explicitly feminist agenda, *womenSports* featured athletes on its cover, an entire issue devoted to the Equal Rights Amendment, offered tools like a Title IX "Action Manual," and urged its readers to challenge sport's status quo and demand equity. Editorials lambasted the AAU and the NCAA, and those in charge took pains to make sure that its content reflected their agenda. As then editor Rosalie Wright proclaimed, "We object to sexist descriptions of athletes and we don't give you 12 different recipes for hamburger," thereby distinguishing it from other sports magazines as well as those that catered to "women's" issues.[47]

But in the succeeding years, the publication underwent radical changes before succumbing to the prevailing spirit of the times. Following financial decline and reorganization, the magazine became "the membership publication of the Women's Sports Foundation" and changed its title to *Women's Sports* in 1979. The new editor clarified that "*Women's Sports* will continue to be first and foremost a *sports* magazine. We are, however, broadening our editorial policy to include more material that will benefit all active women—those who are primarily interested in recreational athletics as well as those whose main concern is organized competition."[48] Once King was no longer at the helm, it lost much of its activist thrust. In 1984, again in financial jeopardy, the magazine underwent yet another transformation, becoming *Women's Sports & Fitness*. As the latest editor explained, "With this issue we're making a modest change in our logo to better reflect the contents of the publication. *Women's Sports & Fitness* is what we're all about."

It was about a bit more than that. Boutilier and SanGiovanni argue that editorial changes to *womenSports* constituted "a giant step back for women."

It caters to conventional stereotypes of both women and women in sport; it fails
to challenge traditional definitions of femininity; it preys on the homophobic
fears among women; it maintains the insidious demands that all women conform to elitist, sexist images of women's proper involvement in sport. In sum
. . . it signals the demise of a magazine that could have been a forum for reconstructing women's roles and their relations to sport as an institution. Instead,
we have a magazine that flirts with liberal feminism, but leaves intact the sexist
underpinnings of society's vision of both women and sport.[49]

Less like a serious publication for women in sport and more like the contemporaneous *Self* and *Shape*, *Women's Sports & Fitness* appropriated feminist
rhetoric of empowerment that contradictorily endorsed oppressive messages of bodily perfection often inimical to health. Discourse that seemed to
encourage exercise as part of one's freedom of choice, personal acceptance,
aseizing mastery over one's life and control over one's body, researchers argued, instead kept women in a perpetual state of body anxiety and insecurity
to ensure they continued to buy the magazines and the content advertised
between their covers.[50]

Whereas *womenSports* prided itself on promoting athletes—professional,
amateur, celebrity, and lay—on its early covers, *Women Sports & Fitness*
increasingly relied on fashion models as the face of its publication. Between
1975 and 1979, one study determined that 25 percent of all covers depicted
"recreational activities"; the other 75 percent portrayed female athletes. Beginning in 1985, however, "non-athletes outnumbered athletes on the covers,"
a trend that increased in subsequent years.[51] Following the change in name,
vision, and mission, the magazine's content progressively emphasized the
beauty myth and downplayed serious sport involvement. Publishers did not
make these adjustments with caprice. They were business decisions designed
to maximize profits. Consequently, changes to the magazine were based on
the dictates and desires of corporate advertisers and consumers and tapped
into the cultural mores of the era.[52]

The cover of *Women Sports & Fitness*'s December 1984 issue featured
fitness champion Cindy March, deemed to have "the perfect body for the
1980s." It was quite a mantle, considering the eighties were the "decade of
the body." By 1981 "a record 70 million Americans—almost half the adult
population—[practiced] some form of corporeal betterment." The physical
capital of a toned, taut, disciplined body translated into statements about
one's economic and social status. As scholar Nicolaus Mills observes, "The
1980s were not only the decade of the power lunch and the power tie, but the
power physique."[53] The body as a visual symbol of power represented internal
mastery over one's life. More than ever, women were encouraged to cultivate

their bodies at home, at work, or in the gym because the fit aesthetic made a public statement about their self-mastery and intrinsic worth.

The Aerobic Dance Phenomenon

Men similarly found themselves swept up in the "bodicon" (body conscious) zeitgeist. After all, the "Reagan era was an era of bodies."[54] But men's athletic opportunities had been secure from the start. They were not in jeopardy. Women, on the other hand, faced repeated threats to the modest though impressive progress they made during the preceding years. The trend toward aesthetic fitness was one of many reactions to the opportunities for which women sought to compete in sport.

As women populated the "once-masculine province of exercise," public culture framed the movement as one that met the needs and desires of the modern female who could finally admit that the sports revolution had been unsatisfactory. One reporter noted that "despite the growth of feminism and the invention of the jogging bra, many women continued to perceive running and other aerobic workouts as activities meant mainly for men." Other journalists conveyed that aesthetic fitness provided a feminine alternative to the feminist agenda: "In the past decade, as liberated women took up sports, some followed the male example. . . . But," the article continues, "a shift has begun in the last few years." As women entered the workforce in increasing numbers, they found "a new sense of identity. With self-fulfillment and success on the job, they don't need to satisfy their competitive drives through sport. . . . [T]he increasingly popular answer is a combination of exercise and recreation, rather than strenuous competition."[55]

Competitive sport is not for everyone, yet the insinuation from these comments seems to be that sports are the stuff of men, that is, endeavors that instill and fortify masculine characteristics in participants and, therefore, are of little interest or use to most women. The "athletic feminism of the seventies" had championed sport as "part of a larger movement for female physical autonomy, a movement in which efforts to gain control over pregnancy, birth, family size, and individual safety figure prominently." Conversely, in the subsequent decade, Americans were bombarded by a different message: a "highly toned body" gives women a "feeling of power . . . a physical and emotional independence that many translate into a social freedom."[56] Hence, empowerment comes not from physical autonomy and competency, but from approximating a culturally sanctioned standard of physical beauty.

Women (and men) could participate in myriad forms of bodywork in the 1980s, including slimnastics, figure conditioning, yoga, dance, jogging, weight lifting, and sport. Yet among these many options, there was a clear victor: "If there's one activity that exemplifies the fitness movement of the '80s, it's aerobic dancing." Sporting goods experts declared it to be "the hottest thing in the industry. . . . It's fun to do, and it's mostly women."[57] Indeed, by 1986 the American College of Obstetricians and Gynecologists speculated that women accounted for at least 90 percent of the estimated twenty-five million people who participated in aerobics programs.[58]

Scholars are conflicted in their assessments about what aerobics mean and whether women are subjects or objects of the exercise discipline. Critics maintain that the aerobic dance movement is one that reasserts passive femininity, emphasizes oppressive heteronormativity, and advocates a body ideal that contradicts the principles of health and physical autonomy.[59] Sport sociologist Jennifer Hargreaves, for instance, contends that "aerobics has been successfully packaged to persuade women, specifically, to participate in order to lose weight and improve their sex-appeal, rather than for reasons of fitness and enjoyment or competition."[60]

Others argue that the aerobics phenomenon is liberating: "For women the very practice of strenuous exercise—smelly, sweaty, uncontrolled—was subversive. Far more important than an improved appearance was the empowerment—the improved bodily function and confidence—that could be achieved through aerobics."[61] Providing a physical culture alternative to what some perceived to be the elitist, hypercompetitive "jockocracy" of sport opens a range of possibilities for women of various body types, fitness levels, and abilities.

Then there are those researchers who ascertain that aerobics' adherents find their participation contradictory and may engage oppositional or resistant strategies in the face of a potentially coercive practice.[62] One should not discount women's agency, the pleasure or health benefits they derive from exercise, or the camaraderie many experience during a fitness class. Ultimately, the false binary of oppressive-liberating is unproductive when it comes to analyzing aerobics in the 1980s. It was and could be both; it was and could be neither.

What appears more clearly and prevalently throughout the public culture of this time was that aerobics became "linked explicitly with a changing aesthetic of the female form." More specifically, it was responsible for "creating a new esthetic for women of the '80s" in which women were "actually actively reshaping their bodies so their muscles are delineated." This new ideal, asserts sociologist Barry Glassner, pulled together "several cultural antitheses: strength with beauty, muscularity with thinness, and hardness with curvaceousness."[63] The work required to achieve and maintain this ambivalent look was substantial, and women were encouraged to chase this standard rather than pursue fitness for its salubrious or emancipatory benefits.

As a result, public culture endorsed working out for its cosmetic benefits, "perfecting" one's body by identifying one's flaws and improving one's "trouble spots."[64] The correct external physique was indicative of the correct internal discipline. In this manner, writes feminist philosopher Susan Bordo, "the firm, developed body has become a symbol of correct *attitude;* it means that one 'cares' about oneself and how one appears to others, suggesting willpower, energy, control over infantile impulse, the ability to 'shape your life.'" The converse of this line of thinking is that those who do not realize the "best" feminine form have somehow failed. Hence, the "onus is shifted firmly onto women's shoulders: their bodies are their responsibility—if they do not (try to) conform, then they have only themselves to blame, they are deficient in their womanly duties."[65] Success is defined by one's appearance as achieved through working out, getting fit, and staying in shape.

1980s Aerobics Culture

The term *aerobics* (meaning "with oxygen") entered the American vernacular with Dr. Kenneth Cooper's 1968 book. In *Aerobics*, Cooper, the former surgeon general of the U.S. Air Force, advocated an exercise program that would elevate and sustain one's heart rate to improve the "body's capacity to bring in oxygen and deliver it to the tissue cells." Aerobic exercise, Cooper asserted, was the best method for improving "overall health."[66]

The wife of an air force officer, Jacki Sorensen drew inspiration from Cooper's fitness tests and training methods. Although there were earlier exercise entrepreneurs who set coordinated moves to music, Sorensen (along with Judi Sheppard Missett, who invented Jazzercise in 1969) was a pioneer in popularizing aerobic dance. When military officials asked her to host a television exercise program for an air force base in 1969, Sorensen came up with dance-inspired fitness routines based on aerobics principles. Her program "drew favorable response," inspiring her to develop a twelve-week aerobic dancing program. She offered her first public class in a church recreation room in South Orange, New Jersey, in 1971. The fitness trend exploded, and, by 1979, Aerobic Dancing, Inc., boasted tens of thousands of students and had expanded into every U.S. state, spawning a host of imitators and innovators in the process.[67] Devotees soon dropped the "dance" descriptor, and "aerobics" became most popularly known as a style of rhythmic exercise set to music that usually incorporates elements of body conditioning and flexibility.

By the early 1980s, "-cize" mattered: people could aerobicize, Jazzercise, Dancercise (with Carol Hansel), Powercise (at Elaine Powers's figure salons), Nutricize (sponsored by Nutri/System weight-loss clinics), sexercise, Mousercize to an album produced by Disney, or Texercise to the country-western stylings of Irlene Mandrell. Women were, as the suffix suggests, in a constant state of becoming—always caught in the process of body cultivation and perfection—of getting in shape, of staying fit, of working out toward ever-elusive goals.

In the sphere of 1980s aesthetic fitness, actress, political activist, and exercise entrepreneur Jane Fonda and her "Workout" series reigned supreme. In fact, aerobics "did not take off as a mass movement" until she entered the scene.[68] Predated by proselytizers like Jack LaLanne and Richard Simmons, she "undertook the task of 'womanizing' exercise."[69] Although Fonda was not the first to make an aerobics workout tape, as scholars Elizabeth Kagan and Margaret Morse argue, "her videos—*Jane Fonda's Workout* (1982), *Pregnancy, Birth and Recovery* (1983), *Workout Challenge* (1984), *Prime Time Workout* (1984, retitled *Easy Going Workout* as part of Jane Fonda's Video Fitness Library in 1987), *New Workout* (1985), *Low Impact Aerobic Workout* (1986), *Sports Aid* (1987) on sports medicine, and *Workout with Weights* (1987)—which followed her workout studio, *Workout* book, and audiotape, were the first to be video bestsellers and to establish a lucrative market in made-for-video productions."[70]

Extended by Fonda's empire, the fitness trend seeped into nearly every aspect of commercial media. Aerobic dance albums helped reinvigorate the "sagging record business." Said one distributor, "It's unbelievable. The music industry's new hope is—I don't even know what to call it—sweat music?"[71] Sales of audiocassette tapes soon eclipsed their vinyl predecessors in the early eighties, which made the recordings less fragile and more portable. Aerobics also infiltrated text-based media. But the trend seemed tailor-made for the visuality of postmodern culture, for the "worked-out" body was not only about individual achievement, it was about a form of embodiment that was meant to be seen. Fit female bodies, often clad in workout wear, cropped up everywhere: in film and advertising, on fashion runways, on the newly initiated MTV (Music Television) and other cable and network television channels, on the streets, and in the gym. The availability of home videocassette players offered yet another medium through which the public could apprehend the idealized female form, along with instructions on how to approximate it.

The burgeoning videocassette industry also helped democratize the aerobics trend. Those with inflexible work or family schedules, those shy about exercising in public, could follow along to albums, books, or videos in the privacy of their own homes. These options also provided alternatives to pricey fitness club or health spa memberships. Local recreation centers offered more affordable options. Even so, read the 1984 edition of *Our Bodies Ourselves,* "Many women cannot afford the money to join a club or a Y, or the time away from work. Accessibility, too, is a problem." As one teenage girl commented, "My mother walks for exercise. There has never been a dime available for her to go to an evening group of any kind. I try to run around a lot and have fun in gym class because the way everything is getting cut, after-school sports may get dumped."[72] The Reagan administration's efforts to privatize the state's social welfare programs relocated women's sports and fitness from a federal responsibility to a corporate initiative, and government-sponsored programs for physical activity diminished during this time.

Everyone, in theory, had access to the aesthetic fitness movement. *Time* reported that although "the fitness craze is still mostly a middle-and upper-middle-class phenomenon, the fit look has nothing elitist about it. It represents an attainable ideal for all ages, races, walks of life." It is worth noting that the excerpt articulates the "fitness craze" not with any health benefits it might provide, but with the "fit look"—a cosmetic ideal to which anyone could (should?) aspire. And although many women found it difficult to find the time, money, energy, or social support to exercise, the "obstacles that confront us all are much more formidable for women of color," qualified *Our Bodies Ourselves.* Furthermore, these women did not find themselves represented in the ubiquity of related media representations: "You can scan hundreds of product catalogs, mail- order brochures, fitness magazines, books and videos and see nothing but attractive lily-white faces," reported *Sports Illustrated* in 1984.[73]

The "fit look" was also about the ways that women clad and accessorized their bodies, and fashion played a significant role in promoting aerobics culture. The aerobics visage of the 1980s evolved from dance wear, and early entrepreneurs, such as Gilda Marx, appropriated its leotards, tights, leg warmers, and sweatbands, adding unique designs and an array of colors to the mix. In 1984 the sales of fitness apparel grew by 35 percent, with profits estimated at $500 million.[74] Leotards alone accounted for $231 million worth of sales that year as Americans bought approximately twenty-one million bodysuits at an average price of $10.90.[75] Reebok tapped into the market in 1982 with its "Freestyle," a shoe specifically designed for aerobic dance. Retailing at around $50, by 1984 Freestyle made up more that 50 percent of Reebok's sales and became a fashion icon of the era.

In 1983 the *New York Times* offered readers "a good example of someone's being decked out for a workout": "She was wearing a satiny red leotard cut high on the thighs and low in the back, a white headband, shimmery white tights, black wool leg warmers, a thin black belt around her waist and a gold Egyptian necklace. 'I work out every day of the week,' the 32-year-old graphic designer explained, 'and when I look good, I work harder.'" Looking good evidently meant distinguishing oneself from the female athlete. As another woman explained, "We don't want to be wearing men's sweatshirts and sweatpants. We want to bring our femininity to it. We don't want to be considered unfeminine jocks."[76] The to-be-looked-at aesthetic seems a reaction to the preceding sports revolution and the presumed masculine connotations of athletic female bodies.

Emphasized femininity, as manifested in aerobics culture, almost immediately gave way to its hypersexualized counterpart. This was, perhaps, most apparent in a look that journalist Blair Sabol dubbed the "high-intensity crotch (HIC)." She determined its emergence first evident in the swimwear of 1979 that provocatively elevated the apex of one's thighs while simultaneously narrowing the coverage of one's nether regions. The "sweat couture" of the early 1980s followed a similarly dramatic trend, as the cuts of leotards continued to ascend and contract. In particular, the "thong-style brief or leotard with high French-cut legs in front and a G-string tailored back" was "much in demand."[77] Fashionably worn over a pair of tights (and often accompanied by complementary leg warmers and sweatbands), the leotards became a staple in the intersecting worlds of fitness and fashion.

HIC was everywhere in the public culture of the early 1980s. If clothing did not sufficiently draw one's gaze to exercisers' genitals, the popular media made sure to emphasize them. MTV proved to be an auspicious outlet for HIC dissemination. There was, for example, Diana Ross's 1982 video for *Work That Body*. Set to the eight count of an aerobics instructor's chant, Ross appears alone throughout its duration. Shots alternate between her undulating leotard-clad body and her sexually (often orgasmically) suggestive facial expressions as she jumps and twists to the music before performing supine on a weight bench, the camera suspended above her.

Olivia Newton John's chart-topping *Let's Get Physical* similarly veils sex in exercise idiom: "There's nothing left to talk about," she sings, "unless it's horizontally." The bizarrely plotted three-and-a-half-minute video opens with a series of male crotch shots emphasized by their bikini-brief swimsuits. When John enters the gym in an HIC leotard, the men morph into out-of-shape, beer-gutted schlubs. She puts them through a workout before retiring to the locker room for a sexy solo shower scene. When she returns to the gym, now clad in HIC badminton wear, she finds the men transformed back into the bulging (in every sense) hunks. Alas, their desire to "get physical" is not with John, but with each other, and the men exit the scene hand in hand.

The movie *Perfect* also presents a gender-equitable proclivity to accentuate one's genitals in a fitness setting. In the 1985 film, *Rolling Stone* reporter Adam Lawrence (John Travolta) interviews and woos Jessie (Jamie Lee Curtis), a popular aerobics instructor, for his exposé on health clubs as the "singles bar" of the 1980s. While Adam deals with the more serious, ethical dilemmas of investigative journalism, the film lingers over the bodies of the clubs' members, particularly Jessie's, which is, one assumes, positioned as "perfect."

Roundly panned by critics who found *Perfect* vapid and undeveloped, reviewers routinely commented on Curtis's physique ("she of the fantastic body"; "her astonishing body looks incredible") that filmmakers emphasized in "no less than five major and two minor exercise scenes in the film, her leotards ranging from the merely revealing to the nearly transparent."[78] The most remarkable of these episodes is a five-minute vignette in which Jessie leads her aerobics class, including Adam, through an astonishing routine. It would be a significant challenge to find any film, outside the pornography industry, with a more conspicuously HIC scenario. If she is mistress of "slimnastics," then he is surely master of the cods. The session comes to a climax when the two trade a series of punctuated pelvic thrusts and rolls, their sweaty bodies moving in unison from across the room. As they phantom-boink through the workout, the two maintain intense eye contact—even if Jessie has to look in the mirror to see her lover behind her. It was, as one reviewer dubbed it, "aerobisex," and viewers were made voyeurs of their simulated copulation.[79]

Female body-centric films such as *Perfect, Flashdance* (1983), and *Heavenly Bodies* (1984) substantiate "the myth that women are made to be looked at and that men do the looking. Such a myth encourages women to view their looks as a source of power and to predicate their self-esteem on their ability to attract the male gaze." Even movies purportedly about women's athletics, such as *Personal Best* (1982) and *Pumping Iron II: The Women* (1985), emphasize the body-for-sex at the expense of the body-for-sport. In her analysis of *Getting Physical* (1984), a made-for-television special about female bodybuilding, Laurie Jane Schulze observes that, for women in the 1980s, "the normative mode of being physical has seemingly shifted from the 'passive' to the 'active.'" This does not, she continues, "necessarily [indicate] that there has been a weakening of patriarchal control. . . . The female athlete can be conceptualized as the consummate (hetero) sexual athlete. Popular discourse repeatedly emphasizes that athletics for women also enables them to 'work out' sexually. This neutralizes the potentially threatening elements of the physically powerful female by redefining that physicality in terms cut to the measure of male desire." Scholars have extended this critique to the aerobics discipline, arguing that it perpetuates the "sexualization of physical activity" and provides "another arena for women to compete for male attention."[80] Potentially liberating exercise thus becomes subordinated to heterosexual attraction—its purpose to pique the desire of men. The aerobics-cultivated body is valued for its ability to offer aesthetic and sexual pleasure.

This concept played out in a number of articles advising women that aerobics could enhance their sex lives. As one woman tells Adam in the movie *Perfect*, working out "makes sex so much better. The better your body looks, the more you want to take off your clothes." In a *Mademoiselle* piece titled "Exercise for Lovemaking," women are counseled, "If your body is in great shape—limber, firm and flexible—your mind is free to relax and really enjoy the experience." The implication is that an aerobicized physique can placate a woman's body anxieties and enrich her experience in bed. These types of messages appeared in publications outside the usual suspects that regularly titillate readers with risqué, albeit important, coital information. Magazines like *McCall's* also offered articles on "sexual fitness" and "X-rated exercises" for a "more pleasurable sex life." It went both ways: "Try sex as an exercise," suggested *Today's Health,* "and exercising for sex."[81] It is not enough to work out for the sake of fitness. Its purpose is perpetually redirected toward heterosexual attractiveness, desire, and performance.

A Matter of Time

By 1984 the aerobics craze had reached its peak. Although it remains a popular exercise discipline today, in the mid-1980s there were signs of change and perhaps even decline. Between 1984 and 1985, for instance, bodywear sales plunged by 18 percent. Many who zealously dedicated themselves to the cult of aerobics became plagued by a host of overuse injuries. Health advocacy groups began to promote "low-impact" aerobics after "thousands" suffered from the high-impact, "feel-the-burn" variety. The relentless pounding on hard floors left aerobicizers with damage to their feet, backs, and knees. They suffered heel spurs, shin splints, fractures to bones in their legs and pelvis, and permanent impairment to their ligaments, cartilage, and tendons.[82] Americans were beginning to grow weary of the no-pain-no-gain mentality, and the 1984 heart attack and subsequent death of running advocate Jim Fixx at age fifty-two pushed exercise buffs to rethink their devotion to strenuosity.

It may also have been that people were not as fanatical about working out as public culture would have us believe. Despite the pervasiveness of workout discourse, the U.S. population remained largely sedentary during this time. A 1987 University of Michigan study determined that only 18 percent of Americans between the ages of eighteen and sixty-five exercised more than twice a week, while 47 percent did not exercise at all.[83]

At the same time, aerobic dance underwent a process of sportification in the mid-1980s that illustrated an altered mentality toward the pursuit. Aerobicizers could compete in events like the National Aerobic Championship, established to "provide fitness instructors, trainers and enthusiasts with a platform for the recognition of their skill and accomplishment." As one woman explained, "I think basically what it is, is a forum for people who have been training in aerobics to show what they're in training for."[84] Backed by corporate sponsors including Crystal Light, Coppertone, and *Shape* magazine and broadcast by ESPN, the format took off. The AAU sanctioned a Team Aerobic Dance program, and there were motions to add it to the Olympic program. Jazzercise instructors performed during the opening ceremonies of the 1984 Games in Los Angeles, and the discipline's originator, Judi Sheppard Missett, ran in the torch relay. At a global venue designed to showcase American culture, the inclusion of aesthetic fitness was significant.

And so the nature of the beast showed signs of change by the mid-1980s. During its heyday, as *Women's Sports & Fitness* determined, "aerobic dancing exploded from organized calisthenics to a national craze to a way of life." But it, like all trends, had a shelf life. There were other "body-molding regimes" on the horizon—new ways of shaping a "modality of embodiment that is peculiarly feminine."[85] And it would be a mistake to think that women's sport completely stalled during this time. Participation opportunities increased, albeit slowly, at high school and intercollegiate levels, although the NCAA affirmed that all sports, for both men and women, were in the midst of financial crisis. The IOC added new women's events, including field hockey, shooting and cycling events, synchronized swimming, rhythmic gymnastics, and distance running. The predominant pattern, however, counteracted much of the hard-fought progress women tenuously secured in the preceding years.

The beauty myth continues to lurk behind every corner when it comes to women's sports. In the early 1980s, public culture emphasized the aspirational body culture of aerobics, often at the expense of serious women's sports. This marked an element of a more general backlash against the social, political, and economic gains women made in the preceding decades. By the end of the 1980s, it seemed as if the pendulum had begun to swing the other way. After the 1984 Grove City verdict, members of Congress worked to overturn the decision. Each time the Reagan administration opposed the bill that came to be known as the Civil Rights Restoration Act. In 1988 the Senate and the House voted to override President Reagan's veto, and, "as a result, only sixteen years after Title IX was enacted, it finally, clearly, applied to athletic departments."[86] Four years later, the NCAA published its first *Gender Equity Report*. With this, the public learned that women made up only about 30 percent of all varsity athletes and received only 30 percent of scholarship budgets, 17 percent of recruiting funds, and 23 percent of total operating budgets.[87] That same year, the NCAA established its Gender Equity Task Force to address the enduring inequities in college sports.

As the first generation of "Title IX babies" came of age in the 1990s, women's sports experienced a second-wave revolution.[88] In spite of this, following the "Women in Sports" cover of 1978, *Time* continued to ignore female athletes. In fact, another sportswoman remained absent from the magazine's cover for a full decade, despite immense progress, superlative performances, and unmatched accomplishments in the interim. Readers finally saw skater Debi Thomas, billed as "America's sweetheart," on the front of the publication in 1988, followed later that year by trackster Jackie Joyner-Kersee and her quest "to be the best." Gymnast Kim Zmeskal, described as leading her "American team in search of Barcelona gold," posed on the balance beam in 1992 and Tonya Harding's "strange plot to cripple Nancy Kerrigan" made headlines two years later. The first non-Olympic coverage of women's sports did not appear until 1999, as the exuberant U.S. women's soccer team celebrated their World Cup win: "What a Kick!" it read across the photo of those athletic bodies embraced in the thralls of victory.[89] But it was only a matter of time until the beauty myth again reared its ugly head.

6. A Cultural History of the Sports Bra

The U.S. women's victory in the 1999 World Cup certainly was "a kick," as *Time* described it.[1] After 120 minutes of spectacular scoreless action, the championship match between the United States and China came down to a penalty shoot-out. One after the other, ten athletes—five from each squad—traded shots. A key save by American goalkeeper Briana Scurry evened the score at 4–4, opening up the possibility for her team's success. In the tenth and final spot was Brandi Chastain, who stepped up, drove the ball into the top corner of the net, and clinched the win for the U.S. In her book, *It's Not about the Bra,* Chastain recounted the now-famous moments that immediately followed.

> If you're lucky, a moment like this happens once in your lifetime, and when it does, your response can only be uncalculated. So while forty million watched on television and in front of over ninety thousand people (including the President of the United States) at the Rose Bowl, I took my shirt off. It was spontaneous. It made me notorious. It was not the sort of thing anybody expected a woman athlete to do. . . . But in the end, it was just a moment, a celebration. At that instant, as I lifted my shirt, it was as if I'd shed the weight of the entire tournament and replaced it with the thrill of victory and fulfillment at the same time.[2]

The media blitz that ensued, however, was indeed (with all due respect to Chastain and her teammates) all "about the bra." Featured on the front pages of newspapers and the covers of major magazines, discussed at water coolers, parodied by comedians, debated on chat sites, and the focus of questions for contestants in the Junior Miss America pageant and on *Who Wants to Be a Millionaire?* attention to Chastain's celebration reduced one of the most significant moments in sport history to one that gave the world "that girl in the sports bra."[3]

The moment came at the end of a decade that witnessed both the rise of women's sports and the increasing visibility of sports bras. Worn as foundational athletic equipment, as a stand-alone top, or as a costume statement by the likes of pop singers Britney Spears and Sporty Spice, sports bras are more than utilitarian. In the context of physical culture, fashion, and marketing campaigns, they contribute to the ways in which women relate to their bodies—bodies that are at once externally bound and internally managed by the bra. The public spectacle of women in their sports bras also contributes to redefinitions of feminine aesthetics and the body beautiful, as well as to the continued trivialization of female athleticism.

These themes were especially pronounced in the popular media's reactions to Chastain's celebration and in 1990s sports-bra advertising, both of which generated consideration of physically active and breasted forms of female embodiment. Yet there was a critical undercurrent beneath what seemed to be celebratory images, for they drew attention to notions of women's sexual difference and positioned their bodies as sexualized objects. They reinscribed a distinctly feminized subjectivity while concomitantly espousing themes of empowerment and autonomy. What emerged was a depoliticized sports-bra feminism that underscored the importance of the best-possible breasted presentation of self and ultimately diminished the liberatory potential of sport and physical culture.

A Historic Foundation

Breasts, notes Collette Dowling, have been considered "standard symbols of women's frailty through the ages." As with menstruation, women's biological and physiological differences have often served to justify their exclusion from serious sport. In 1895, for instance, the *New York Times* published an article in which doctors argued that women would never become proficient swimmers even though they "love to flounder" in the water. Whereas men have "muscles across the chest," in women, "the bosom takes the place of these sinews." But our thinking has advanced since then, right? Maybe not. Consider what golf commentator Ben Wright said a full century later: "Women are handicapped by having boobs," he told a reporter. "Their boobs get in the way."[4]

To say that breasts "handicap" women is one thing, but to acknowledge that they can be something of a nuisance during sport is quite another. Biomechanists note that "the minimal intrinsic structural breast support" makes it difficult to reduce "breast displacement associated with exercise." Others find that breasts may cause "discomfort and inconvenience . . . in activities requiring extensive running, jumping, landing and rotational activities."[5] Because of this, women have devised all sorts of methods to discipline their breasts during physical activity.

Legend has it that the Amazons of ancient Greece cut off their right breasts to facilitate archery.[6] In modern history, Frenchwoman Violette Gouriand-Morris, an accomplished athlete in multiple sports, elected to have a double mastectomy upon "finding that her heavy breasts impeded her control of the steering wheel of her Donnet racing car." As *Time* reported in 1929, "Because Nature had not shaped her conveniently for the accomplishment of her athletic ambitions, she last week horrified Paris by having a surgeon remove both her breasts. Said she: 'Sport is all my life.'"[7]

In less extreme measures, women invented ways to stabilize their breasts during activity. Some bound their chests with strips of cloth or leather. Women in ancient Greece and Rome wore "breast bands" to minimize the jounce.[8] Among the fourth-century mosaics in Sicily's Villa Romana del Casale is a depiction of ten women engaged in a variety of athletic pursuits: running, jumping, throwing the discus, and lifting weights. The "Bikini Girls from Piazza Armerina," as they have come to be known, wear a "fairly wide band which is worn high under the arms, and appeared designed to strap down the breasts for vigorous activity."[9] A fifth-century kylix shows Atalanta, perhaps the most accomplished female athlete in Greek mythology, in a similar top, complemented by shoulder straps that may have provided additional breast support.

The history of undergarments is vast and varied and reveals quite a lot about women's social standings at different moments in time. Used to mold, support, protect, reshape, insulate, and swaddle human bodies, underclothes have been modified in accordance with changing fashions, hygienic concepts, textile production, manufacturing techniques, and commercial distribution. They have also become increasingly important in everyday life.

Women's forays into sport have influenced the history of underclothes. Corsets, for example, helped women compress or bolster their bosoms (as well as their torsos, hips, and thighs) according to the era's prevailing ideal body type. But as women's participation in physical culture changed, so too did the garment. Nineteenth-century English equestriennes wore special corsets for riding.[10] Designers later incorporated elastic for those who played tennis, as mentioned in chapter 1. Manufacturers followed with a "Callisthenic Corset" and a "sports corset" in 1911. The 1914 tango craze inspired a "dancing corset," and one specifically suited for skating debuted the next year.[11] Although women remained bound to (and by) their corsets, the introduction of specialized styles indicates burgeoning physical opportunities.

Inventors started designing protobrassieres as the dress-reform leaders of the late 1800s called for more "rational" undergarments. By the 1920s, American women began to favor the brassiere over the corset, though many found the cost prohibitive. Prices ranged between twenty-nine cents and one dollar, and an even less expensive version, "as shown in the catalogs of Sears, Roebuck and Montgomery Ward, was a luxury to unskilled laborers, most farm women, and those supporting families on small incomes," write Jane Farrell-Beck and Colleen Gau, authors of *Uplift: The Bra in America.*[12]

Designers quickly adapted brassieres (or "bras," as they were called by 1937) to suit the active woman's lifestyle, including the 1906 "bust supporter" for "acrobatic dancing and other theatrical use."[13] In 1925 competitive runner Sophie Eliott-Lynn wrote that the "bust bodice" was "essential for all women athletes."[14] But it was not until several decades later that a bra specially designed for the sporting woman achieved popular acceptance and commercial success. What did women do before the introduction of commercial sports bras? Some made do with their everyday brassieres. Others bound their breasts with cloth. When Roberta (Bobbi) Gibb "unofficially" ran the Boston Marathon in 1966 (the event did not allow women to race until 1972), she was forced to improvise: "They didn't have jog bras," she told a reporter. "I wore a tank top bathing suit."[15]

The 1970s "revolution" in women's sports and the concurrent "fitness boom" created the need for specialized equipment. Women's increased purchasing power during this time helped as well. Among the era's many points of change discussed in the previous chapter, companies also began to manufacture gear, apparel, footwear, and, eventually, underwear specifically designed with the female athlete in mind.

In 1977 runners Hinda Miller and Lisa Lindhal created a prototype for the modern sports bra. Inspiration for the garment came when the two women considered the utility of jockstraps for male athletes. "We said," recalled Miller, "what we really need to do is what men have been doing: pull everything close to the body."[16] They created their original "Jockbra" by sewing together two athletic supporters—the oval pouches of which became the bra's front panels; the waistband reconfigured into the bra's wide, torso-encircling elastic; the leg straps became the over-the-shoulder straps; and the "Jockbra" became the "Jogbra."[17]

Initially available only by mail order, promotions that appeared in magazines such as *womenSports* and *Runner's World* were vitally important. Jogbra's first advertisement adopted a woman-centered, practical approach, advancing that "no man-made sporting bra can touch it" (see figure 6.1).

Jogbra.
No man-made sporting bra
can touch it.

Invented by two women runners.

Jogbra is not the product of a fancy lingerie firm or an aggressive marketing group. Two women athletes invented Jogbra.

Lisa Lindahl runs thirty miles a week. Hinda Schreiber runs fifteen. They learned that bouncing breasts can be painful and medically dangerous. And that ordinary bras chafe, slip around and fall down.

"We went looking for a sporting bra and what we found were regular bras with sporting labels."

They decided to create their own jogging bra. Rather than look to other bras for inspiration, they studied the jockstrap. Says Lisa, "We cut two in half, sewed them together, and they kept us from bouncing."

As a result, the Jogbra looks like no other sporting bra on the market. It is not a modification of a normal bra. It's a totally original piece of athletic equipment.

The only sporting bra with an inside-out design.

All Jogbra's seams and other construction are on the outside, away from the body, to prevent irritation. And there's no hardware to dig into your skin.

Jogbra's fabric is an ideal blend: cotton for softness and absorption of sweat, Lycra® for stretch and control. Jogbra's unique design holds breasts close to the body without binding.

Wide rib band keeps Jogbra firmly and comfortably in place. All elastic is perspiration resistant. Straps cross in back and cannot fall.

You'll want to be seen wearing Jogbra.

The Jogbra is also a halter top that looks as good as it feels.

This spring Jogbra is coming out not only in basic white, but in two new sporting colors: blue with white trim and green with white trim. Even the label on these colorful Jogbras is functional. It doubles as a pocket to hold a key and emergency money. We call it our Pocketlabel.

Treat your breasts as well as you treat your feet.

You know cheap footwear can ruin active feet. A less than professional bra can do just as much damage.

Jogbra may be the most expensive sporting bra on the market. For good reason. Lisa and Hinda left no seam unturned, no fold unexplored, to make Jogbra the best athletic supporter a woman ever had.

Mail this coupon today!

Jogbra/SLS Inc. (802) 863-3548
P.O. Box 661 Burlington, Vt., 05402
Charge my ☐ Visa ☐ Mastercharge
Card # _____
Expiration date _____
Signature _____
☐ Enclosed is my check or money order made out to SLS, Inc.

Name _____
Address _____
City _____ State _____ Zip _____
Size Guide: S: 32-34; M: 34-36; L: 36-38

JOGBRA	SIZE	QUANTITY	PRICE
white			$14.95
blue			$16.95
green			$16.95
VT residents add 3% sales tax		TOTAL	

(Prices include shipping & handling.)
SATISFACTION GUARANTEED
or your money back.
4-6 Weeks Delivery

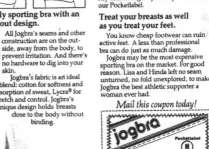

Lisa Lindahl and Hinda Schreiber of Jogbra.

Figure 6.1: Jogbra, "No Man-Made Bra Can Touch It," *womenSports*, March 1979, 21.

With a blend of humor and matter-of-fact commentary, the ad concluded by declaring the Jogbra "the best athletic supporter a woman ever had." In the first year of production, women purchased around twenty-five thousand sports bras.[18] Soon, they were able to buy them in stores and through mail-order catalogs, and there was no turning back. Researchers found "greater comfort and better performance among women wearing the sports bra," while the lack of proper support could lead to "refusal to exercise, breast discomfort, and the irreversible breakdown of breast tissue."[19] In the 1980s, experts deemed it "probably the single most essential item for female athletes," and at century's end some considered it to be "as important to the growth of women's sports as the passage of Title IX."[20] By that time, sports bras accounted for 6.1 percent of the $4.5 billion bra market.[21] Yet even in the face of such widespread promotion and popularity, one could argue it was the 1999 World Cup that served as the sports bra's coming-out party.

Women's Sports Bust Out

That Chastain's celebration came when it did provided a fitting exclamation point on the end of a decade fraught with ambivalence. On one side, there were significant gains in women's sport, celebrated in the popular media with exuberant proclamations. The 1994 Winter Olympics were the "Games of the Woman." Two years later, the Centennial Olympics became the the "Women's Games," following historic performances in soccer, softball, basketball, tennis, swimming, track and field, synchronized swimming, and gymnastics.[22] It was "the Year of the Female Athlete," and advertising campaigns exalted, "The Women Have Arrived!"[23]

The Women's National Basketball Association (WNBA), one of a handful of newly formed leagues offering professional opportunities for women, marketed its product with the slogan "We Got Next."[24] In 1998 the U.S. hockey team took home the gold medal in the Winter Olympics and, along with their Summer Games peers in softball, soccer, and basketball, did so with a full roster of "Title IX babies," the first generation of women to benefit from the legislation during their elementary school, high school, and college years.[25] Individual sport athletes such as Lindsay Davenport, Jennifer Capriati, Venus Williams, and Serena Williams in tennis and figure skating's Michelle Kwan, Tara Lipinski, Kristi Yamaguchi, Nancy Kerrigan, and Tonya Harding garnered unprecedented media attention and lucrative endorsement deals. "Girls Rule!" hailed the cover of *Newsweek* following the 1999 World Cup victory, and, according to Harvey Araton of the *New York Times Magazine*, there had never been a "better time for women and girls to get in the game."[26]

Araton may have been correct. In 1996 2.4 million girls participated in high school athletics, representing an eightfold increase since 1971. As Title IX celebrated its twenty-fifth anniversary, the number of women in intercollegiate sport had grown by 400 percent, but participation rates still lagged behind males. Girls made up 39 percent of high school athletes, and women constituted 37 percent of collegiate athletes.[27] Additional discrepancies contest the typically progressive narrative that recounts the fin de siècle history of women's sport.[28] Evidence suggests that girls and women of color have not benefited from Title IX to the same extent as white females.[29] There has also been an inversely proportional relationship between women's gains in participation and their roles as key functionaries. In the early 1970s, women made up more than 90 percent of coaches and 90 percent of athletic directors; by 2000 those proportions dropped to all-time lows of 45.6 percent and 17.8 percent, respectively.[30]

Relative to men, women continued to suffer from lack of opportunity, compensation, and exposure in the sports-media-commercial complex.[31] A record number of women competed at the 2000 Olympic Games, for instance, yet they only constituted 30 percent of all athletes. Members of the 1999 World Cup team each took home $12,500 for their victory; had the U.S. men's team won the 1998 World Cup, every teammate would have earned $388,000.[32] Several women's professional leagues did not survive the decade, and participants earned significantly less than men in parallel sports. During the 1997–98 season, the average National Basketball Association (NBA) salary was $2.6 million, nearly ten times as much as the WNBA's $30,000.[33] Between 1991 and 1995, the Ladies Professional Golf Association (LPGA), the oldest ongoing professional league for women, increased its annual prize money to a record $24.4 million and doubled its media coverage. At the same time, the Professional Golfers' Association (PGA) (where awards totaled $60 million) and the men's Senior Tour ($30 million) eclipsed the women's organization in both financial compensation and the number of televised tournaments.[34]

In all, women received less than 10 percent of all U.S. print and electronic sports media attention. Sociologist Michael A. Messner agues that this "actually *overstates* the extent to which women's sports were given fair and respectful coverage," for in much of that underrepresented treatment are themes that perpetuate the marginalization and trivialization of female athletes.[35] Scholars have found that journalists more often refer to women by their first names and downplay their skill, hard work, agency, and autonomy while granting greater consideration to "gender appropriate" sports, selectively incorporating standout athletes and emphasizing women's appearance and (hetero-)sex appeal.[36]

Sporting officials colluded in the sexualization of female athletes. As Jim Fushe, the WTA's director of player promotions, once commented, "We're never going to stop selling sex."[37] The International Volleyball Federation, taking cues from the increasingly popular beach version, ruled that for the indoor game, women's shirts "must follow the body line" and their shorts "must be tight in waist and length," with a maximum inseam of five centimeters and "cut in at least a 30° angle toward the top of the leg." Fédération Internationale de Football Association (FIFA) president Sepp Blatter notoriously suggested that women's soccer adopt a new strategy: "Let the women play in more feminine clothes like they do in volleyball. They could, for example, have tighter shorts."[38] Officials employed these tactics for two reasons. First, they believed that sexualizing the athletes would draw a larger (arguably male) audience. The second, often implicit, strategy behind these campaigns was to quell the homophobia that remains so pervasive in women's sports.

The LPGA is one organization that enacted policies to counteract what some call an "image problem" or a "whisper campaign" concerning lesbians on the tour. In the early 1990s, LPGA commissioner Charles Mechem hired an "'official image and fashion consultant' available to counsel players on how to dress for success as well as provide skin care, makeup and hair advice." Before the work of the consultant, one golfer commented, "There were a lot of rough-looking" women on the tour; the arrival of this "beautician," assessed another athlete, "softened" many golfers' looks.[39] Tour publications focused on "players with families, with fashion spreads of some members and stories of husbands who caddy for their wives," reported the *Washington Post*.[40] By emphasizing conventional femininity and heterosexuality, LPGA officials not only trivialized the talents of its athletes but, in the process, exacerbated the already rampant and dangerous heterosexism in sport and society.

Female athletes were neither passive dupes nor uniformly resistant to the contemporary "sport-sex *Geist*."[41] To be sure, many actively embraced and celebrated their (hetero-)sex appeal with aplomb. Swimmer Amanda Beard, volleyball player Gabrielle Reece, and high jumper Amy Acuff are just a few of those who have appeared nude or seminude in men's magazines, sustaining an industry based on the soft porn of hard bodies. The once incongruous image of the strong, muscular female body and overt sex appeal now abounds in popular culture.

Olympic swimmer Jenny Thompson's Wonder Woman–esque pictorial for *Sports Illustrated* epitomized this trend. Standing resolute in stars-and-stripes swimtrunks, she is unapologetically muscular and unabashedly topless as she conceals her breasts behind clenched fists.[42] Although some chastised Thompson's choice, she defended the image: "My stance in the picture was one of strength and power and *girls rule!* It's nothing sexual. . . . It's pretty cool," she continued. "I've started a new feminism." Exactly what this new feminism entails is difficult to pin down, though many have claimed its mantle, advocating a corporeal confidence that finds comfort at the intersection forged between sex object and athletic subject. Conversely, there are those who argue that such "cheesecake photos are part of an active backlash against women's successes on and off the playing field"—a means to subvert female strength, power, and autonomy into eroticized attractiveness.[43] That women athletes appear in provocative spreads may indicate that the general public has not fully embraced the female athlete qua athlete.

What Lies Beneath

Brandi Chastain also staked a claim in this so-called new feminism. Just before the 1999 Cup, she posed for the men's magazine *Gear* in nothing save her cleats and strategically placed soccer balls.[44] She called it "a picture of a confident, strong woman," but many juxtaposed it with her World Cup jubilation in ways that undermined both her athletic accomplishment and the sincerity of her revelry.[45]

Reactions to Chastain's celebration of her team's 1999 World Cup victory provide salient examples of the tensions between achievements in women's sports and the simultaneous "recuperative strategies" that keep those advancements in check.[46] In reporting the incident, journalists alternatively framed Chastain as a triumphant athlete, a poster girl for the success of Title IX, a paragon of changing feminine ideals, a corporate shill, and a scheming opportunist.[47] Despite these competing interpretations, discourse consistently turned to what it meant for her to take off her shirt and how the public did, or should, understand the display of a woman in her bra.

That male athletes seem to have set the precedent for this type of performance further complicates the "Brandi bra moment."[48] Andre Agassi, Pete Sampras, and Goran Ivanisevic have all "yank[ed] off" their sweat-drenched shirts and flung them into the stands following tennis matches.[49] Dennis Rodman and Paul Pierce did the same in professional basketball, but the practice is most widespread in soccer: "Men do it all the time," said the editor of the magazine *Women's Soccer World*. "It wasn't as though [Chastain] didn't have a bra on. It certainly would be discriminating to suggest a woman can't do it if a man does."[50]

Yet the resulting discrimination is based not upon whether female athletes should have the same public disrobing rights as male athletes, but, rather, what is made of those athletes once their tops come off. As the *New Yorker*'s Rebecca Mead gauged, "Girl Takes Top Off . . . is freighted with an entirely different symbolic weight" than "Sports Figure Takes Top

Off."[51] She's right. Many described the Chastain incident as a "striptease," a "peeldown," a "provocative gesture," a "half Monty," and "the most brazen bra display this side of Madonna," suggesting she acted with the deliberate intention of titillating onlookers.[52]

Public readings of the moment were additionally complicated because the sports bra is, at once, considered lingerie, sports equipment, and a statement of style. During the 1990s, it became increasingly acceptable to don it as a stand-alone piece of outerwear. The Sporting Goods Manufacturers Association's Mike May said that Chastain "made it OK for women to wear sports bras without anything else on top." A 2000 article in *Women's Sports & Fitness* asked, "When is a sports bra really an athletic top?" The answer: "Whenever the hell *you* want it to be."[53] The picture accompanying the article was, unsurprisingly, of Chastain. Bra-bearing activity thus became a sign of agency—a disavowal of traditional prudery that consigned the brassiere to underwear and a public declaration of one's corporeal pride and identity as a "workout woman."[54]

Literary scholar Susan Willis writes that women who wear workout clothes outside of an athletic setting "unabashedly define themselves as workout women. In making a public body statement, a woman affirms herself as someone who has seized control over the making and shaping of her body." Fitness-related fashions frequently expose the flesh or contour of women's bodies, rendering visible their physiques, as well the requisite discipline those physiques suggest. Thus, the "'properly shaped' female body is taken as evidence of achievement and self-worth," making the worked-out body a symbol of regimentation and self-governance.[55]

The (presumed) athleticism of the bra bearer mitigated the taboo of the bare bra in public, a trend that coincided with the rise of the "bare-midriff fashion" of the mid- to late 1990s.[56] Both styles expose a woman's stomach, a site of excess or restraint—the paunch of gluttony or the six-pack of discipline. This is another aspect of the aesthetic-fitness industry that dissects the female body into distinct, separable, and trainable entities that gave us, as examples, the once popular *Buns, Legs, Arms, Thighs,* and *Abs of Steel* workouts designed to sculpt those body parts whose ideal shape and size shift according to the fickle whims of emphasized femininity. In this vein, the sports-bra-as-athletic-top in popular culture contributes to a distinct form of breasted embodiment that disarticulates female breasts from a more holistic concept of the female body.

The breasted bodies of sports bra–clad women in popular imagery exemplified a shift in feminine ideas, one that is, as M. Ann Hall describes, "slim, strong, sinuous, athletic and healthy." Based on these images, it would also seem that the normative ideal of feminine beauty is raced, aged, and classed. Sports-bra representations are nearly devoid of any women of color. Advertisements frequently promise that the right sports bra will combat the stretch and sag of women's breasts, both of which connote age. Additionally, the Nike Inner Actives bra Chastain wore in the World Cup retailed between forty and fifty dollars. The average sports bra costs around thirty dollars, while the time and money required to discipline one's body to work toward what Leslie Heywood calls the "hot fitness body" are substantial.[57]

Journalists related this new paragon of gendered embodiment to Chastain. In an article titled "The 'Babe Factor' in Women's Soccer," *Business Week*'s Mark Hyman argued she represented a shift toward "the thewy look—mutedly but undeniably muscular" that "appears to be replacing the traditional dewy paradigm."[58] With this "athletic aesthetic" came increased sexualization, objectification, and commodification of athletic women's bodies at the turn of the twenty-first century. As Alisa Solomon maintained in the *Village Voice*, "The increasing acceptance of powerful women's bodies has been matched by a frantic attempt at containment. Yes, buff is beautiful—but only as long as its function is to be gawked at by guys."[59]

Images of women in their sports bras provided the public with additional gawk-worthy fodder. In spontaneous interactions and highly orchestrated television commercials, Chastain was plagued by men inquiring, "What's up with the shirt?" with hopes that she might flash them a glimpse of her sports bra–clad physique.[60] Across the nation, high school officials have disqualified athletes in track and cross country for appearing in their sports bras without covering shirts, judging the look too revealing (never mind the briefs or "bun huggers" worn by track and volleyball athletes, or swimmers' bathing suits, or gymnasts' leotards). These examples of bra-revealing encouragement and discouragement demonstrate that a woman in her bra—even a sports bra—is considered in dishabille and therefore erotic. Regardless of her intent, she exposes her body and draws attention to her breasts, "the most visible sign of a woman's femininity, the signal of her sexuality," according to philosopher Iris Marion Young.[61] Although the compression-oriented technology of sports bras seem to counter the prominently bosomed norm (a 1985 Jogbra advertisement, as one example, avowed that the "minimized profile is critical"), recent campaigns indicate a growing number of garments designed to approximate the socially and sexually desirable bust line.

Beware the Uniboob

Marketing undergarments, according to media scholar Dee Amy-Chinn, poses problems for advertisers because "the public circulation of images of women in various states of undress is *always* liable to offend the sensibilities of some sections of the population." Nike, which admits that many of its ads are "intended to be provocative," met this issue head-on (boob-on?) in a controversial 1999 campaign that, spread across two pages, exposed a naked woman's headless torso. Superimposed across her bare chest is the question, "After years of exercise, what kind of shape will your breasts be in?" (see figure 6.2). In smaller script below, the ad continues, "All the exercise you do to keep in shape can have the opposite effect on your breasts. That's because breasts are held up by non-elastic Cooper's ligaments. And once they stretch, they don't snap back." For this reason, breasts needed Nike's Inner Actives bra, which will work without "smashing you down."[62]

Couched in medico-scientific discourse, this promotion took on the role of an educational campaign, instructing women that engaging in fitness-related activities, while good for their bodies, would damage their breasts. This reasserted the notion of the divisibility of women's breasts from their bodies, a point emphasized by the decapitated imagery. The advertisement also revived anxiety concerning women's participation in physical culture, namely, that athleticism is detrimental to femininity. Concern for a woman's breasts became a new variation on an old theme, one that previously warned that sports participation would damage her reproductive system, or strain her face in an unfeminine grimace, or swell her muscles to unladylike proportions, thereby ringing the death knell for her appropriately gendered subjectivity.

Another source of bosomed anxiety used to sell the sports bra involves the "uniboob"—the simultaneous flattening down and smashing together of one's breasts into an undifferentiated, compacted, tubular mound. Although compressing and distributing the mass of one's breasts across one's rib cage may facilitate physical activity, such configuration stands in stark contrast to what are socially considered the "best" breasts, namely, those that are full, round, and prominent.[63] An ad for Champion's "New Shape 2000 Bra," promoted as "The bra that's changing the world," broached the subject by employing the mandate "Get In Shape," typically associated with the pursuit of physical fitness, to address the presentation of one's breasts (see figure 6.3). The ad heralds the bra's "unique cup design that eliminates 'uniboob' by delivering comfortable support with the most natural shape and definition possible." The soccer-playing, black bra–wearing model (a nod to Chastain) attests to this claim; her gravity-defying breasts remain spherical and separate from one another as she performs a "bicycle kick" maneuver that positions her in the air with her chest pointed skyward. The ad concludes, "Now you can keep in shape while getting in shape," using the pretense of physical fitness to sell the ability to put forth a bifurcated bosom as an empowering act.[64]

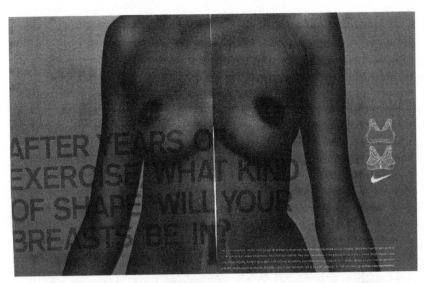

Figure 6.2: Nike, "After Years of Exercise, What Kind of Shape Will Your Breasts Be In?" *Women's Sports & Fitness,* September–October 1999, 96–97.

Champion's ad does not acknowledge the inherent contradiction between "natural" and "definition," though natural (breast) shape is that which exists in the absence of (bra) definition. Young writes that "unbound breasts show their fluid and changing shape.... The bra normalizes the breast, lifting and curving the breasts to approximate the one and only breast ideal."[65] That is the selling point emphasized in this ad—that even in the context of sport, women's breasted bodies can and should conform to a gendered and sexualized standard. A 1999 Jogbra advertisement similarly and unproblematically promotes the paradox of the organic but disciplined breast by declaring, "Only abs should be flat.... Now, a sports bra that respects and defines your natural shape" (see figure 6.4). The text concludes with a parenthetical addendum, written in the vein of one woman sharing a secret with another: "Oh, one more thing ... if you really want to flatten your abs, look for the In Shape Fit Short with tummy control panel." Here, it is not just a woman's breasts that must be molded to a normative ideal, but her stomach as well, the effects of which are achieved with the proper consumer purchase.

In addition to their consideration of uniboob-combating technology and the incongruity of simultaneously "natural" and "defined" breasts, these ads rely on the solitary woman to peddle their products. Late-twentieth-century sports-bra advertisements typically focus on the individual, encouraging her to take control of her breasts, her physique, and her life through bodywork and consumer choices. Even Brandi Chastain, whose performance was just

Figure 6.3: Champion, "Get in Shape," *Women's Sports & Fitness,* September 2000, 62.

one part of her larger team, became the instant icon of women's soccer, selected by the media as the bra-wearing torchbearer of the 1999 championship squad. The focus on the individual, as opposed to the larger collective, is indicative of a postfeminist imaginary, which envisions that society has met the goals of second-wave feminism, dismantled structural barriers, and

Figure 6.4: Champion, "Only Abs Should Be Flat," *Women's Sport and Fitness*, May–June 1996, 49.

achieved sexual equality, placing the onus of success or failure on each independent woman. In this doctrine of individualism, the emphasis on agency, choice, and action obscures the larger social forces that constrain and enable women's lives.

One advertisement veers away from concentrating on the individual to present the sports bra as a totem for workout women united in their suffering of ill-fitting, inadequate, and unflattering equipment. Lucy of Portland, then an online athletic clothing company that carried a variety of brands, published a 1999 ad titled "The Uniboob Epiphany," featuring Lucy, the "quasi-patron saint of women's fitness" (see figure 6.5).[66]

> Just as she unleashed a storm on her heavy bag, one of our sisters stopped mid-jab to reshuffle the uniboob in her bra. Spotting this arranging, re-arranging, Lucy of Portland shadowboxed her way over. "I can see you're in the middle of an epic boob wrestle. It's not your breasts you should be swearing at—it's your bra. Stand up to these deadbeat boob slings . . . Come with me and I will show you Champion Action Tech and Everlast Microplex bras. You will know the power of the perfect fit." And with that she shouted so everyone could hear: "I will not rest until all the boobs in the world stand as strong and proud as the women who bear them."

The elements of sisterhood and humor and the inclusion of a racially, ethnically, and size-diversified "army of women" in this advertisement set Lucy of Portland apart from the pack. In spite of Lucy's clarion call for "boobs" that are "strong and proud," the focus of her mission is on the "perfect fit" for physical activity.[67]

Ultimately, it is an economic rather than a cultural imperative that drives this campaign and others like it, one in which values such as "'freedom,' 'independence,' and 'pleasure'" are "reduced to matters of lifestyle and consumption." Sports-bra advertising exemplifies what Goldman, Heath, and Smith term "commodity feminism" in which gender equity "is rehabilitated for the world of advertising—its primary meanings taken over by the system of fashion."[68] It is a corporatized, not a politicized, feminism, one that translates the discourse of social activism and women's sovereignty into that of consumer choice.

Toward a Sports-Bra Feminism

Feminist scholar Wendy A. Burns-Ardolino suggests that women "should wear sports bras . . . instead of wearing push-up bras" as a means of confronting "the physical oppression of restrictive gendered clothing."[69] Certainly,

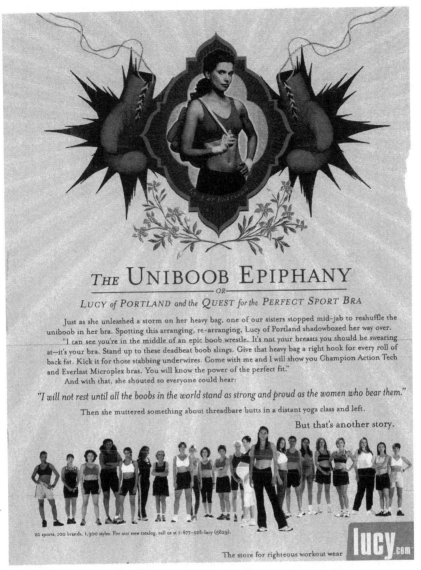

Figure 6.5: lucy.com, "The Uniboob Epiphany," *Women's Sport & Fitness*, September 2000, 52.

there are women who buy and wear sports bras as acts of resistance to repressive gender norms or without concern for their breasted appearance.[70] Then again, based on its late-twentieth-century representation in cultural industries, the sports bra is not necessarily the oppositional accoutrement that Burns-Ardolino makes it out to be. Chastain's celebration, according to *Sports Illustrated* editor William Colson, gave the world "the greatest picture of a sports bra in the history of publishing," a comment that disregards the significance of the sporting accomplishment the image represents.[71] Sexualized responses to her jubilation suggest that the promise of bodily displays made women's athletics enticing to otherwise uninterested sports fans. Women's sporting talents and performances are therefore trivialized and marginalized where they can do little to challenge the "center" of sport.[72]

Advertisements in the glossy pages of women's magazines similarly downplay sport and fetishize women's breasted bodies in ways that position the reader as both subject and object at the nexus of insecurity, consumption, and desire. The ads do not promote the sports bra as a piece of equipment that will make a woman a better athlete or help her more fully experience the physical and emotional benefits of physical activity. Rather, the dominant themes concern cup designs that eliminate the "uniboob" and getting and keeping one's breasts "in shape" by defining the "natural." The commercial media thus presents a depoliticized sports-bra feminism in which women's empowerment was packaged in the form of purchasing the right sports bra, wearing that bra in public, presenting breasts that conform to cultural ideals, and displaying the disciplined feminine body of which those breasts are a part. In the end, it's not really about sports and, to borrow from Chastain, it's not really about the bra.

7. Something to Cheer About?

I attended my first competitive cheerleading contest at the University of Maryland with only a rudimentary understanding of what to expect. It was 2010 and, seven years earlier, the Terrapins became the first collegiate program to grant the sport varsity status. I had no doubt that the women who competed on the squad were top-level athletes. The sport, I knew even from its paltry media coverage, consisted of more than synchronized chanting, clapping, leg kicks, and the occasional back handspring. There were death-defying tosses, powerful tumbling sequences, and more than a few back handsprings. Of course, this was interspersed with the synchronized chanting, clapping, and leg kicks, but athleticism was at the fore and Maryland was good. Since their inaugural season, the Terps had won three national championships (2006–8) and finished second in 2009.[1]

I will confess, with some chagrin, that for most of my life I have entertained a certain ambivalence toward cheerleading. As someone involved in varsity-level sports through college, I could not understand why anyone would want to root for others from the sidelines when they could be the ones in the game. The perfectly styled hair, expertly applied makeup, overindulgent smiles—the short skirts, perpetual suntans, and bubbly enthusiasm—it all grated on me. I think there were times, especially in high school, that I even hated the cheerleaders. But those emotions did not stem from any feminist convictions. Not entirely. In truth, more than a few of them came from envy, from wanting to be popular and desirable and confident like they seemed to be. Like I knew I never could.

This was the time-worn baggage I toted with me into Maryland's Comcast Center. Taking my seat, I scanned the program. Neither the word *cheer* nor any variation of it appeared in the document. Instead, the event was billed as an "NCSTA Meet" with no explanation as to what NCSTA was. Under the heading titled "format," the program explained, "Teams will compete in an event-based format (similar to gymnastics). Each team will compete in five events including a team routine. The other four are Partner Stunts, Tumbling, Basket Tosses and Pyramids."[2]

In fact, "cheer" did not strike me as an accurate descriptor for most of the choreographed routines that unfolded before me. To begin, gone was the cheerleader's usual costume. In place of the crotch-grazing skirts were shorts—brief and form fitting, to be sure—but similar to those worn by athletes in volleyball or track and field. There were no bared midriffs or sparkly ornamentations but rather long-sleeved compression tops with the athletes' names and identifying numbers emblazoned across the backs. These were jerseys. They were uniforms in place of the traditional "skirts and shells" one might expect. And although every member of the Terrapin squad sported either a full or half ponytail of silky, straight hair, absent were the oversized bows that typically adorn the style. As Maryland and their opponent, Fairmont State University (same type of uniforms, minus the last names, plus the hair bows), took turns on the floor, I was transfixed. Stunned. Impressed. These were glorious athletes doing extraordinary things.

The NCSTA, I later learned, stood for the National Competitive Stunts and Tumbling Association, a consortium of university teams formed in the summer of 2009 with the intent to legitimize their sport. Over the course of the following year, the nascent organization changed its name to the National Collegiate Acrobatics and Tumbling Association (NCATA), formed by six schools: Azusa Pacific University, Baylor University, Fairmont State, Maryland, the University of Oregon, and Quinnipiac University.[3] They no longer compete in competitive cheer, but have established a new sport—team acrobatics and tumbling. As of 2012, the group added teams from Alderson-Broaddus College, King College, and the University of Massachusetts, Dartmouth, but lost the Maryland squad. Sadly, the University of Maryland announced it would cut seven sports in order to overcome the athletic department's multimillion-dollar deficit. Consequently, the Terrapins no longer compete in men's cross-country, indoor track, and tennis; men's and women's swimming and diving; women's water polo; and acrobatics and tumbling.

The NCATA is clear about how it differentiates its sport from cheerleading ("whose purpose is to support a university or school") and competitive cheer ("an evolution of cheerleading into a competitive sport" with the possibility of "some crossover with the cheerleading team"). Team acrobatics and tumbling (often referred to as "Acro" or "A&T") is "an evolution of the all-female portion of competitive cheer. The purpose is to compete on behalf of a university. There is no crossover with competitive cheer or cheerleading teams." The NCATA's goal is to brand a unique identity, distinguish A&T from its cheerleading roots, and ultimately earn sanction from the NCAA.[4]

The changes came, in part, as a response to a U.S. district court ruling that found Quinnipiac in violation of Title IX for adding competitive cheer to its varsity program while simultaneously dropping women's volleyball. Five volleyball athletes and their coach, with the support of Connecticut's American Civil Liberties Union, took the case to court in a class-action suit where Judge Stefan Underhill ruled that, as it currently stood, competitive cheer was "still too underdeveloped and disorganized" to count as a varsity sport.[5] And so the word *cheer* was dropped in reference to what those in A&T do, along with many of cheerleading's signifiers that once infused the activity. "There is a stigma attached to the word cheer," commented Nancy Post, senior women's administrator at Baylor. "We do not refer to these student-athletes as cheerleaders, because they're not leading anyone. They're competing." As University of Oregon head coach Felecia Mulkey explained, the new sport "has some stunts in it that may look like cheerleading, but without any of the cheerleading stuff."[6]

So what is the problem with all the cheerleading stuff? There are a number of ways to answer that question but, at the core, is the acknowledgment that most governing bodies do not take cheerleading seriously because of its gendered and sexualized inflections. General perceptions of "cheerleading" are often conflated with those of "sideline cheerleading," which is, by and large, an auxiliary activity to other sports. Although sideline cheerleaders are decidedly athletic and may engage in their own competitions, these aspects are secondary to their primary responsibility of supporting other teams. As such, many consider cheerleading a feminized activity, despite the requisite strength, stamina, and presence of male participants, for they are supportive of, rather than central to, sport. The cheerleaders' physical and emotional labor is employed in the service of others.

Where cheerleading was once the sole purview of men, the majority of today's participants are women. These shifts have brought about an undeniable sexual aspect to the pursuit, which scholars Pamela J. Bettis and Natalie Guice Adams characterize as rife with "exotic tensions." Female cheerleaders "embody simultaneously the virtuous, 'good girls' and the sexually provocative 'bad girls.'"[7] Their abbreviated costumes and often erotically suggestive dance moves seem designed to cater to the masculine gaze.

Many of these cultural perceptions are rooted in the past and fail to acknowledge the drastic changes in cheerleading that have occurred over the past two or three decades. In particular, the advent of the "all-star" classification has significantly altered what cheerleaders do, where they do it, and for whom. At private gyms that cultivate elite-level athletes, male and female participants train solely to compete against other teams with little to no interest in animating the sidelines of other sports. In spite of their popularity, competitive cheer and its newest incarnations, like A&T, have difficulty shaking the residual perceptions of earlier and stereotypical brands of cheerleading. In this chapter, my question is whether this latest variety of sport presents another example of the persistent divide between femininity and athleticism or, alternatively, if this new manifestation gives us something to cheer about.

A Brief History of Cheerleading

Cheerleading has a long and varied history in the United States. Perhaps no other activity in the annals of physical culture has been so completely regendered, sexualized, commercialized, and sportified. In its original nineteenth-century expression, it was an activity solely for male college students. The University of Pennsylvania claimed to have organized the first cheer ensemble in 1894, though the Princeton Yell, a pep club, predated Penn by a decade.[8] Princeton alum Thomas Peebles transported the cheers to the University of Minnesota, where he formed a squad in 1898, and the activity spread quickly. Often referred to as "rooter kings" or "yell leaders," they became a fixture of college football.[9] Students soon established Gamma Sigma, a national college cheerleading fraternity that annually partnered with sports journalists to select the All-American cheer squad.

There was a good degree of prestige associated with being a "cheer leader" at the time. Faculty committees, physical education departments, and student-body groups typically selected the distinction. The *Nation* described the prominence associated with holding the position in 1911: "As a title to promotion in professional or public life, it ranks hardly second to that of having been a quarter-back."[10] For the first few decades, many football cheerleaders were the captains of other varsity sports.[11] As scholar Mary Ellen Hanson contends, "The first cheerleaders, privileged college men, were seen as heroic figures, part of the masculine world of sport and competition. Fellow warriors with players on the field, these cheerleaders exemplified leadership and athleticism."[12]

The press regularly extolled the virtues of those who roused the crowds. Calling it a "peculiarly American custom," one journalist described the typical antics of the early-twentieth-century character: yelling through a megaphone, arching his body from one side to the other while directing the crowd, shaking his fists to conduct the spectators. In 1916 *New York Tribune* contributor Robert C. Benchley selected four cheerleaders for All-American status. The

Figure 7.1: Two cheerleaders with megaphone, University of Maryland, circa 1926. Courtesy of the Special Collections, University of Maryland Libraries.

judging criteria included a preference for those who had won varsity letters in other sports, along with "agility, grace of movement, reach, proficiency in tossing the megaphone to one side at the beginning of the cheer and vocal timber."[13]

Clad in white duck trousers and V-neck sweaters (much like male tennis players of the era), cheerleaders were ubiquitous in collegiate football by the 1920s. So significant were they to the overall game-day experience that, on several occasions, fans blamed them for their teams' losses.[14] In subsequent decades, squads began to incorporate gymnastics into their repertoires, elevating the requirements for those who had to earn their spots through audition rather than by appointment. At the University of Kentucky, for instance, those wishing to try out had to first complete a six-week tumbling course.[15] By the end of the 1930s, criteria for determining the All-American team included assessments of "acrobatic ability—not only proficiency in the common cartwheels, handstands and general high jinks, but also the Ritter span [described as "a complicated back flip"] . . . Nelson Arch (a less complicated back flip) and Duos (synchronized tumbling by two or more)."[16] Together, the specialized moves and vocabulary, exclusive organizations, national recognition, and coveted station of the cheerleader characterized his standing in the chronicles of college sport.

Eventually, the appearance of girls and women along the sidelines began to alter the cheerleader's status.[17] Around the 1930s, there were scattered reports

Figure 7.2: Cheerleaders in stands, University of Maryland, circa 1931–40. Courtesy of the Special Collections, University of Maryland Libraries.

Figure 7.3: Coed cheerleaders cheering, University of Maryland, 1938. Courtesy of the Special Collections, University of Maryland Libraries.

of "dimpled-kneed coeds" at southern universities, though women were not eligible for election to the All-American squad.[18] Neither were they welcomed at many schools. The University of Pittsburgh, for example, remained stalwart until 1954 and only decided to take the "big step . . . to have girl cheer leaders" after a poll showed that 87 percent of students supported integration.[19]

As students and administrators deliberated the merits of including females, one male educator summarized the debate in 1938. "Briefly, the case *against* girl cheerleaders narrows down to several main points: non-ability to perform acrobatic Stunts, conduct unbecoming to young ladies, the development of 'hog-calleritis' [or "loud, rough, raucous voices"], and the development of overly conceited young ladies." Not only did they lack the ability to participate in cheerleading, but, as with sport, it might lead them down a path in which they would become "too masculine for their own good." On the other hand, he reasoned, the activity could be adapted to suit and cultivate preferred gender norms: "Girls are more magnetic in appearance and will become the center of attraction for the crowd and the leading of cheers will, therefore be easy." He ultimately left the decision up to school administrators who, he advised, must carefully weigh the advantages and disadvantages of cheerleading's sexual politics. Whatever the outcome, the author made it clear that distaff cheerleaders should be of a different stripe than their more virile brethren.[20]

Scholars often cite the Second World War as the gendered turning point for cheer. For various reasons, boys and men vacated the activity during this time, and girls and women filled the void. Several schools tried to ban female cheerleaders once the war ended, but these efforts apparently did little to disrupt the established pattern. Contributing to the female influx, argues scholar Molly Engelhardt, was that many states eliminated girls high school sports programs during this time and cheerleading became the only available physically active extracurricular outlet. The result was a "restructuring of the activity to comply with a social hierarchy that understood boys' activities as being more institutionally significant than girls."[21] By the 1950s, "cheerleading came to be regarded as primarily a feminized activity."[22] Feminization was not just about the sex of the participants or their gendered performances, but an issue of power.

In 1956 journalist Arturo Gonzales described his opinion of the "coeds": "Pretty young things in vestigial skirts, amply-filled sweaters and wearing baby shakos [military-style hats with visors and plumes], they've burbled and twirled to the intense enjoyment of those fans easily distracted from the male carnage at the midfield by a few well-placed curves." He cited rumors that "girls are on their way back to the spectators' seats," but any attempts to revert back to primarily male squads were short-lived; the activity had

Figure 7.4: Cheerleader in the middle of a cheer, University of Maryland, 1964. Courtesy of the Special Collections, University of Maryland Libraries.

been tainted by the effeminate. Gonzales's characterization of the "pretty young things" points to the increased sexualization of the cheerleader in the postwar era, a trend Michael Oriard attributes to the "proliferation of bowl games."[23] There, cheerleaders were among the pantheon of desirable women who augmented the sporting spectacle.

The inrush of ponytailed bobby-soxers extracted much of the athleticism once required for cheerleading, converting a physical activity into a primarily social activity. As one author described, "Cheerleading in the sixties consisted of pom-poms, cutesy chants, big smiles, and revealing uniforms. There were no gymnastic tumbling runs. No complicated Stunting. Never any injuries. About the most athletic things sixties cheerleaders did was a cartwheel followed by the splits." Over the course of a few decades, cheerleading had transformed from a prestigious, masculine domain to what sport sociologist Laurel Davis terms a "feminine preserve," where girls and women could cultivate and perform a culturally sanctioned femininity.[24]

The same gendered patterns appeared in historically and majority black high schools and colleges. At predominantly white institutions, those who determined the constitution of cheerleading squads frequently failed to include girls and women of color. In 1972 Lawrence Herkimer, one of cheerleading's grand patriarchs, charged that school "desegregation has drastically reduced the number of black cheerleaders, who were often among the very best."[25] Student bodies frequently voted in candidates for the squads, signifying the popularity of those elected and rejecting those deemed unsuitable for the position in ways that reflected racial bias. "Shutting black women out of this highly charged arena," remarks historian Pamela Grundy, "could thus symbolize rejection not just of their performance but also of themselves."[26] In response, student groups began to demand African American and Latina representation on their high school and collegiate squads during the late 1960s and early 1970s.[27]

By the mid-1970s, an estimated 95 percent of all cheerleaders were female.[28] Two developments again changed the topography of the contemporary cheerscape. In the first instance, Tex Schramm, then president and general manager of the Dallas Cowboys, established the Dallas Cowboys Cheerleaders (DCC). The professional franchise had long incorporated spirit squads (though the Baltimore Colts cheerleaders boasted the first in 1954), but the DCC were decidedly different. They exuded a wholesome sexuality as they *danced* (not cheered) their way through their inaugural 1972–73 season in hot shorts, knee-high boots, and tight-fitting, midriff-exposing, cleavage-revealing, star-spangled tops. Television made them national celebrities, and "America's sweethearts" became the model for most NFL teams. Soon sidelines and halftime shows were graced by the likes of the Chicago Honey Bears, San Diego Chargerettes, New Orleans Angels, and the Washington Redskinettes. Basketball also benefited from using women cheerleaders as part of the sportainment experience.

The second pivotal moment, the passage of Title IX, took place the same year that the DCC began to high-kick their way into American libidos. As part of the initial Title IX regulations, Peter V. Holmes, then director of HEW's Office of Civil Rights, was the first official to affirm that cheerleading did not meet the requirements of a sport, asserting, "Drill teams, cheerleaders, and the like . . . are covered [by the law] more generally as extracurricular activities."[29] This quashed concerns that school administrators might designate cheer a sport in order to show compliance with the law and, as a consequence, provide few new legitimate opportunities for athletic participation.

Before legal and cultural shifts provided greater opportunities for girls and women, cheerleading was one of the few sanctioned outlets for those who craved a modicum of physical activity. It also provided occasions to develop leadership and social skills, as well as to travel with the teams they supported. But as new sporting venues became available, the number of cheerleading participants declined.[30] And so, gradually, officials adapted the activity to accommodate those who wanted greater physicality. As *Washington Post* journalist Amy Argetsinger put it, "Cheerleading might have vanished. Instead, it harnessed the spirit of the times, evolving into a melange of highflying acrobatics and show-biz flair that required more athleticism than before."[31] Leaders of the emerging "spirit industry" re-athleticized cheer, a move that proved profitable, for they could offer training, camps, and clinics at which to teach these new skill sets as well as contests at which competitors could test their mettle.

Among the leaders of this burgeoning trade was Lawrence Herkimer. "Herkie," a former Southern Methodist University cheerleader, began conducting clinics and camps in the late 1940s. He went on to found the National Cheerleaders Association (NCA), a company that diversified to sell uniforms, pom-poms, and other equipment. His protégé, Jeffrey Webb, left the NCA to found the rival Universal Cheerleaders Association (UCA) in 1975, and developed strategies to incorporate more stunts and gymnastics into what had stagnated into a relatively undemanding activity. Today there are more than seventy-five organizations that currently regulate cheerleading in the United States, although the NCA and UCA remain the largest and most influential. And while the two retain their separate identities and competitions, both currently belong to the same parent company, Varsity Brands, Inc., a billion-dollar business for which Webb serves as chief executive officer (CEO).[32]

Beyond the Cheers

This new competitive type of cheerleading became wildly popular at both the high school and the collegiate levels. CBS televised the first high school cheerleading competition in 1978. ESPN followed suit in 1983 and, the next year, broadcast the national collegiate competition.[33] That same year, Herkimer opened the first "cheer gym" (Cheerobics Center, Inc.) singularly devoted to cheerleader instruction. This sparked a wave of private, for-profit "all-star" gyms where girls and boys train arduously and year-round for the chance to compete against other squads at local, regional, national, and now international levels. Movies like *Bring It On* (2000) and competitions broadcast by ESPN International have begun to globalize the sport. The International Federation of Cheerleaders, a nonprofit group, recently petitioned the IOC for recognition as an Olympic sport. Not to be outdone, Varsity Brands established its International Cheerleading Union and started to assert its dominance over other worldwide organizations. Cheerleading is no longer a "peculiarly American custom."

Many of the all-star gyms originally served as gymnastic training centers—their transformation a corollary of gymnastics' steady and unfortunate decline since the 1970s. The high cost of gymnastic equipment and insurance needed to sponsor a team, rumors of corrupt and abusive coaches, as well as an unexplained reduction in those who express interest in the sport have left few scholastically based programs in the United States. One result of this trend, argues journalist Kate Torgovnick, is that a "large number of homeless gymnasts channeled their energy into cheerleading."[34] Those who might otherwise direct their talents toward gymnastics have found an outlet in competitive cheer, raising the bar for all competitors and converting the sport into a new hybridized form.

Thus, by 2009, as one researcher acknowledged, "Cheerleading is a gymnastic activity, and why it is still called *cheerleading* is not quite clear. It is a competitive contact sport that involves all types of gymnastic stunts, pyramids, and partner stunts as well as throwing flyers high in the air and catching them (we hope)."[35] A related consequence of the heightened prowess and intrepidity of all-stars has been the soaring number of those hurt during practices and contests. Between 1979 and 1989, the federal government's Consumer Product Safety Commission found that the injury rate in cheerleading jumped 133 percent.[36] Between 1990 and 2002, the number of cheerleading-related hospital emergency room visits more than doubled.[37] Data from the National Center for Catastrophic Sports Injury Research determined that, in 2010, females in high school and collegiate cheerleading accounted for 64.5 and 71.4 percent, respectively, of all catastrophic injuries reported for girls and women.[38]

Those who hope to see their sport promoted to varsity status cite these alarming statistics to justify their cause. The sporting ethos, the undergirding logic suggests, is premised on the potential to do damage to one's body. Recognizing cheer as a sport would also help reduce the number of injuries by mandating specialized certifications for coaches and ensuring the athletes have safe and equal access to training facilities and equipment.[39] It would provide support from athletic departments that applies to all sports, including funding, travel, insurance, medical assistance, academic support, strength and conditioning coaching, and, in the case of some colleges and universities, the potential for scholarship money. Although this seems like a sound proposal, many members of the cheer community are reluctant to move toward sport status.

In its official position statement, the American Association of Cheerleading Coaches and Administrators (AACCA) determined that "cheerleading is in a new, developing category called 'athletic activity'" and not a sport. It explains that classifying cheerleading as a sport brings a host of unwelcome restrictions that would take away from their mission: "The primary purpose is not competition, but that of raising school unity through leading the crowd at athletic functions." The classification would also require regulations that many are loath to adopt, including limitations placed on recruiting, eligibility, training, and season duration. The organization would, however, like to see cheerleaders recognized as "student athletes," which would provide "opportunities for academic honors and even coverage under the athletic catastrophic insurance policy carried by the school or state athletics or activities association."[40] Instead of creating a new sport, the AACCA hopes to create a new category for recognizing the standing of cheerleaders.

There is a corporate imperative that the AACCA does not acknowledge. A nonprofit organization designed to promote safety education at all levels of cheerleading, the AACCA is a subsidiary of the very-much-for-profit Varsity Brands, and the promotion of cheer to a varsity sport would take money away from the powerful conglomerate. Scholastic programs could opt out of the camps, clinics, and competitions, as well as the membership, training, and sanctioning agendas that Varsity Brands provides. Athletes might buy their uniforms and accessories elsewhere. It would mean contestation for the monopolistic stranglehold that Varsity Brands currently has over cheerleading, and so there is a financial incentive to resist recognizing it as a sport. In fact, Varsity Brands CEO Jeff Webb testified in the Quinnipiac trial that cheerleading was not a sport, which hurt the school's case. But larger cultural and economic currents seem to inevitably navigate toward sportification, and, not to be left behind, USA Cheer, also an affiliate of Varsity Brands, recently created a new category of competition it calls "Stunt" (USA Cheer likes to write it in all capital letters: STUNT, though it does not appear to be an acronym).

In September 2010, USA Cheer announced its "NCAA Emerging Sport Initiative"—a plan that serves as a precursor to full-fledged championship-level, NCAA-sanctioned sporthood.[41] Stunt, the sport's website describes, "removes the crowd-leading element and focuses on the technical and athletic components of cheer."[42] Competitions, called "games," are made up of four quarters: partner stunts, jumps and group tumbling, tosses and pyramids, and a two-and-a-half-minute team routine (the traditional routine of competitive cheerleading; see table 7.1 for a clarification of the rules of Stunt, A&T, and competitive cheer). In 2011 twenty-two teams competed in USA Cheer's first national tournament, staged at the annual NCA championship in Daytona, Florida. As of 2012, Stunt hosts national championships for Division I and Division II institutions and is developing programs for high schools.

Like USA Cheer, the NCATA is up front about its mission to achieve NCAA emerging-sport and, eventually, championship-sport status. Part of this process has been a deliberate divorce from the corporatized vice grip of Varsity Brands. In a bold move, the NCATA eschewed the prestigious NCA national tournament in 2011 and instead held its own championship on the same weekend. Each participating school recognizes A&T as a varsity-level sport, and the student athletes are subject to the same perks and restrictions as members of any other athletic team. A&T athletes may not participate on spirit or sideline cheerleading squads, a stipulation the NCATA requires to remain within Title IX compliance and "protect" sideline cheer, as opposed to threatening its existence. In September 2010, the organization announced its partnership with USA Gymnastics, which sanctions their events and provides insurance policies for athletes, coaches, and officials.

There is an obvious struggle for power over competitive cheer's newest derivations. At one point, USA Cheer and the NCATA discussed the possibility of joining forces, yet USA Cheer advertised its sponsorship of Stunt just one week after the NCATA disclosed its partnership with USA Gymnastics, clearly meaning to challenge the NCATA's control. USA Cheer offered irresistible incentives for many teams and solicited both sideline and competitive squads to compete in Stunt events. The organization provided teams with free uniforms (designed suspiciously like those worn in A&T), travel and hotel accommodations to Stunt events across the country, and paid their registration fees for Stunt's national competition. In all, Oregon A&T coach Felecia Mulkey "guestimates," as she put it, that USA Cheer/Varsity Brands shelled out somewhere in the neighborhood of two million dollars to create the appearance of a well-established sport.[43]

Table 7.1. Differences between Acrobatics, Tumbling and Stunt, and Competitive Cheer

	Competitive cheer (Collegiate Level)	Acrobatics & tumbling	Stunt
Competition limits	16–20, depending on sponsoring organization	35–40 on roster; game-day roster of 28. 3 positions: base (main & secondary), back base, flyer	Minimum 20 for game play; maximum 30 on roster. 3 positions: bases, tops, and backspots
Season	Year-round	Spring sport beginning in February	Spring sport beginning in February
Minimum number of contests	N/A	6	8
Competition format	Each team performs one two-and-a-half-minute routine	2–4 teams compete at meets composed of 6 events (compulsory, stunts, pyramids, basket tosses, tumbling, team routine)	Head-to-head games with four quarters (Stunts, jumps & tumbling, tosses & pyramids, team performance)
Projected competition length	Dependent on the number of competing teams, though each team's performance is limited to two and-a-half minutes	2 hours (for 2 teams)	1 hour, 15 minutes (for 2 teams)
Scoring	Judges assign points for various skills, execution, difficulty, and team aesthetics	Preassigned difficulty values; deductions taken for mistakes; each event has a number of potential points all of which add up to a maximum of 300	As part of a set routine, skill sequences are judged on difficulty, technical execution, and synchronization. Quarter scores dependent on the number of teams; in a 2-team game, winner of a quarter receives 2 points; loser gets 1 point; final score is cumulative of all quarters

Figure 7.5: University of Oregon Acrobatics and Tumbling Team, 2012. Courtesy of the University of Oregon Athletics and Zach Ancell Photography.

Those who agreed to participate in Stunt were banned from competing in any NCATA event. USA Cheer justifies the prohibition by explaining that A&T has "no formal association with cheerleading." This is a proposition with which John Blake, executive director of the NCATA, does not entirely disagree: "It's not gymnastics and it's not competitive cheerleading, but truly a new sport. . . . It's a chance for a very popular skill set that combines a variety of activities and sports to be recognized and easily integrated into an athletic program."[44] Betwixt and between, advanced and embryonic, only time will tell who or what will win out.[45]

It seems imminent that one group or another will succeed and the NCAA will officially recognize some hybridized progeny of cheerleading and gymnastics in the future. The Women's Sports Foundation and the American Association of University Women have both expressed provisional support for NCAA recognition, so long as the version in question meets the qualifications of legitimate sport. In addition, there are so many girls who currently participate in some derivative of competitive cheer that there will inevitably be a demand for formal organization at the collegiate level. The 2010–11 data from the National Federation of State High School Associations determined that competitive cheerleading was the ninth most popular sport among girls and that popularity grows exponentially each year (see table 7.2).[46] This vastly underestimates the number of participants because it considers only those

Table 7.2.   Ten Most Popular Girls' Sports, National Federation of State High School Associations, 2010–11, Athletics Participation Summary

Schools	Number	Participants	Number
Basketball	17,767	Track & field—outdoor	475,265
Track & field—outdoor	16,030	Basketball	438,933
Volleyball	15,497	Volleyball	409,332
Softball—fast pitch	15,338	Softball—fast pitch	373,535
Cross-country	13,839	Soccer	361,556
Soccer	11,047	Cross-country	204,653
Tennis	10,181	Tennis	182,074
Golf	9,609	Swimming and diving	160,881
Swimming and diving	7,164	Competitive spirit squads	96,718
Competitive spirit squads	4,266	Lacrosse	74,927

states that recognize competitive cheer as a varsity sport and discounts the legions of those who compete for private gyms.

At the same time, the nature of competitive cheer brings issues associated with race and social class that continue to plague girls' and women's sports. As the NCATA website advertises, 89 percent of participants in A&T come from cheer gyms, indicating an undeniable class bias. One journalist broke down the cost of participation as it stood in 2010: cheer gym membership ($2,000 to $3,000 per year), cheer camps ($200 to $300 for a week of training), uniforms ($50), customized warm-ups ($45), poms ($15), and hair ribbons ($4).[47] This is just the tip of the iceberg, but the point is that the financial burden associated with competitive cheer may place the sport outside the reach of many families.

An attendant concern is the lack of racial diversity within all manifestations of cheerleading. As Adams and Bettis assess, "No official statistics are kept on the racial composition of cheerleaders in the United States. Yet, a visit to almost any cheerleading camp, a glance through *American Cheerleader*, cheerleading brochures promoting camps and competitions, any catalog selling cheerleading products, or a look at the nationally televised cheerleading championships reveals that cheerleading squads throughout the country are primarily white." Efforts to recognize competitive cheer (in any format) as an NCAA sport may increase athletic opportunities for white, middle-class girls and women but continue to disadvantage those of color. This has been an unfortunate pattern in the history of Title IX. Scholars determine that "interscholastic athletic access and participation opportunities for females are unevenly distributed along racial lines."[48] The newest and fastest-growing sports, such as rowing and soccer, are sports predominantly populated by white females, which further restricts athletic scholarship opportunities—and, therefore, access to higher education—for racial and ethnic minority females. More important, fewer athletic opportunities for girls and women of color denies them the health and social benefits of sports participation. Promoting competitive cheer to varsity status contributes to this problem.

Nothing to Cheer but Cheer Itself

Consider cheer's multiple points of change: from an enclave that once promoted the "big man on campus" to an athletically masculine pursuit, a feminized social activity, a sexualized aspect of the postmodern sports spectacle, a highly commercialized athletic activity, and, ultimately, a sport form divorced from its sideline roots, each one of cheerleading's descendants normalizes a particular gendered subjectivity. In competitive or all-star cheerleading, for example, there are certain pedagogies in place that instruct girls and women about appropriate femininity in the context of competition. Their presentations, in turn, influence cultural perceptions about the athletes.

This femininity is decidedly not "apologetic," as the 1970s theory suggested. Girls and women are not compensating for their participation in a masculine sporting domain because cheerleading has been so thoroughly feminized over the course of the past sixty years that certain gendered performances are not only commonplace but required. The engendering process is not hypodermic, but if one looks at the All-Star scoring sheet used at the NCA nationals, there are certain elements for which the judges look. "Crowd Appeal," described as "Facial Expression, Eye Contact, Energy," for example, counts for 10 percent of a teams' final score. There is also a category titled "Overall Impression" worth another 20 percent. The magazine *Girls' Life* instructs cheerleaders that part of "doin' it right" includes looking "like you're having a blast. . . . [I]t can be tough to look like you're genuinely stoked. So rehearse your game face in the mirror before brushing your teeth. Your smile will be bigger, and you'll perfect that 'tude-filled head toss. Wink!" In this context, smiling is not "a spontaneous emotional response," argue Adams and Bettis; "rather smiling is part of disciplining the body."[49] Cheerleaders' emotional labor constitutes a significant part of what they do.

Makeup, hairstyles, glitter, and costumes also contribute to the hyperfeminine personae of competitive female cheerleaders. The embellishments help them play to the crowd and enhance their uniformity in the eyes of the judges. At the same time, it is important to remember that a number of Varsity Brands' subsidiaries saturate the culture with this merchandise so that athletes are inculcated with the imperatives of consumerism. Cheerleading competitions, magazines, camps, clinics, magazines, and catalogs create integrated spaces of consumption that promote ways of behavior and modes of appearance as normal and natural in the sport, all of which require the purchase of commercial products.

Critics often note the bubbly aesthetic ingrained in competitive cheer in their rationale for discounting it as serious sport. This explains why NCATA and USA Cheer officials have worked hard to rid their sports of the conventional femininity so prevalent in cheerleading—markers that color cultural perceptions about what the athletes do. Stunt and A&T competitors wear uniforms distinct from those of their predecessors, and NCATA rules prohibit skirts and bare midriffs. "Teams are not judged on looks, choreography and uniforms, but instead on how well they execute their athletic discipline," reads the answer to an "FAQ" on the organization's website. Former Maryland head coach Jarnell Bonds insisted on purging her squad of laboriously styled "pageant hair." The heavy stage makeup was out too, as were the glitter and pom-poms. "We want them to pay attention to what we're doing, not how we look," she explained. One accoutrement proved especially difficult for Bonds to convince her athletes to abandon: "Hair bows. They love those hair bows. That's how they grew up with the sport."[50]

Here is an interesting twist. In the past, women athletes have employed strategies to assert their femininity in the context of sport in order to gain acceptance. At least, that has been integral to my argument throughout this book. Historically, athletic women, encouraged by various arbiters of gender normativity, have perpetuated conventional performances of femininity in ways that tempered any radical reformations of our perceptions of athleticism and womanhood. In the case of A&T, however, women must forsake the accessories of emphasized femininity in order to be taken seriously as athletes. Does this newest sport form expand our definition of athleticism? Of femininity? Or have the participants found a way to negotiate the persistent tension between the two categories? Better yet, does that tension even exist for them and, by extension, for other women athletes in contemporary U.S. sport?

My assessment is not entirely sanguine. Perhaps that is because immediately following the 2010 meet between the University of Maryland and Fairmont State, the Comcast Center played host to a second event: the Maryland Spirit Championship, an All-Star competition.[51] As competitors as young as five began to file in and fill the stands, my initial enthusiasm faded. I am an admitted outsider to cheer culture, but I was stunned at the sight of little girls clad in cropped uniform tops that ended just below their prepubescent bust lines, while the cut of their short skirts exposed their midriffs and the crests of their pelvic bones. Gargantuan bows overpowered their diminutive heads. Many appeared prepared to compete in a children's beauty pageant; some wore tiaras perched atop teased and curled hair; there were eyelids crusted in glitter, lips painted a cartoon red, cheeks rouged to Technicolor rosiness—caricatures of some imagined feminine ideal. Would the sight of the collegiate athletes, I wondered, provide alternative role models for these girls? Would they see the differences between their appearance and that of the varsity women before them, judge their own activity frivolous, and demand access to this exciting though inchoate sport?

Maybe I was asking the wrong questions. In her study of a girls' all-star squad, Amy Moritz found that, for participants, "cheerleading provides a place where they do not have to choose between femininity and athleticism— they can be both simultaneously and in a fluid moving context."[52] Other scholars contend that critics of the sport fail to understand that times have changed and that femininity no longer connotes weakness and oppression but rather conveys a range of gendered options from which contemporary girls now have the freedom to choose. In their extensive research on cheerleading, for instance, Adams and Bettis determined that "cheerleading offers a critical space for certain girls to take risks, to try on different identities, to delight in the physicality of their bodies, and to control and revel in their own power and desire. In this sense cheerleading does not have to be read as a debilitating discourse of victimization and exploitation, as typically interpreted by feminists."[53] These are arguments that have come to characterize third-wave feminism. That is, that girls and women have control over the making and shaping of their self-presentations. That there is power and pleasure in the feminine, and to admit as much does not require some kind of consciousness raising on the part of the "girlies," but for those so quick to condemn their performativity.[54]

I do not mean to conflate all-star with A&T and Stunt, but my concern is that the former feeds into the latter. More specifically, my concern is that by participating in competitive cheer during their formative years, by the time they become varsity athletes these women will have been inundated with particular messages about how they should look and behave with regard to femininity—messages that will be hard to shake. Then again, I am cognizant of those who may find this critique misguided. Perhaps femininity no longer signifies vulnerability or passivity but rather signals strength and power. Individuals might "do gender" with a sense of playfulness and fluidity, creating performances specific to certain contexts in ways that signify agency and empowerment.

In *Sports in America*, James Michener denounced the activity of cheerleading as he assessed it in the mid-1970s. "I cannot comprehend why parents, and particularly mothers, prefer their daughters to be cheerleaders and pompon girls rather than athletes. This relatively recent development is a perversion of the human instinct for play and makes of a young girl a blatant sex object rather than a human being in her own right." He continued with his hopes for what sport might offer in the future: "I want our society to produce real women concerned with their own activities rather than giddy cheerleaders whose lives revolve around what the boys do in football. But I fear that in this contest the cheerleaders are bound to win, and the other night I found myself arguing, 'Well, twenty years from now, when we have a new society and a new type of girl, they'll be interested in their health and their physical fitness rather than cute miniskirts.'"[55] We are now almost forty years away from Michener's original observations. Cheerleading is no longer performed exclusively for others; participants are concerned with their own activities. And there is a new type of girl who may be simultaneously interested in health, physical fitness *and* cute miniskirts. For her, the choices may not be contradictory or mutually exclusive. Perhaps, in the end, this does give us something to cheer about, though let us do so with reserve and, if possible, without the hair bows.

Epilogue

Cheering with Reserve

The summer of 2012 was one of remarkable consequence. June 23 marked the fortieth anniversary of Title IX. It was an occasion for retrospective, introspective, and prospective analyses, a time to marvel at the tremendous growth of women's sport, a reminder to keep vigilant about persistent inequities, and an opportunity to consider how to address those issues in the future. The opening ceremonies of the XXX Olympiad began just over one month later in London. It would quickly become, as multiple journalists deemed, the "Women's Games." As the two-week festival unfolded, the world watched female athletes represent their countries in record numbers and with astonishing talents. Billie Jean King was one of many who felt American women's success was "a reflection of the growth and impact of Title IX."[1] Still, amid all the revelry, problems remain. In this epilogue, I consider the status of women's sports in 2012, the various points of change that brought us there, and reassert the need to cheer with reserve.

Title IX Turns Forty

During the 1970s "revolution," proponents lobbied that sports would increase "female physical autonomy," break down "sex-role restrictions," and offer girls and women a "sense of mastery and accomplishment" that would profoundly affect the rest of their lives.[2] We have seen the fruits of their labors and, more than four decades later, the benefits of sports for girls and boys, men and women, are legion. Studies find that girls who participate in athletics earn better grades, perform better on standardized tests, are more likely to graduate high school, and are less likely to engage in risky behavior than their nonathletic peers. Overall, girls who play sports have higher levels of psychological well-being, better self-esteem, and lower rates of depression and anxiety than those who do not. They learn cooperation, how to handle setbacks and success, the value of hard work, and determination.[3]

In the United States and abroad, sport relates to issues of basic human rights and dignity. Martha Brady of the Population Council, an international nonprofit research group, writes, "The emergence of new sports opportunities for girls in the developing world represents a mold-breaking departure from traditional definitions of femininity." They develop social skills such as leadership, assertiveness, and camaraderie that oppressive gender ideologies often stamp out. "Well-designed and carefully implemented programs for girls can challenge traditional roles for them and break down gender stereotypes; increase girls' visible, active presence in the public sphere; and transform the ways girls think about themselves, and the ways their families and communities view them."[4]

In India, for instance, the burgeoning success of female athletes has begun to challenge conventions and provide role models for a new generation of girls. It may even abate the shocking rates of female feticide, girls' mortality, and "honor killings." The introduction of compulsory sports for all schoolchildren in the northern state of Harayana, along with the prominence of several female sports heroes, correlated with a decrease in the number of these crimes. Ritu Jagnal, a Haryana-based social activist, found that citizens' "attitude to women is changing and that is reflected in the rise of its women athletes. . . . It will still take time—social shifts cannot happen overnight—but it is happening." This is not an issue of Title IX, but it does demonstrate the tremendous influence that sport involvement can have. In fact, in August 2012, the United Nations Entity for Gender Equality and the Empowerment of Women partnered with the IOC to "promote women's empowerment through sports"—another indication of the potential of athletics.[5]

Then there are the health benefits associated with physical activity. Epidemiological research shows that childhood athletic opportunities have long-term effects and may be linked to lower rates of certain types of cancer, heart disease, and osteoporosis.[6] Economists Robert Kaestner and Xin Xu connect these benefits directly to Title IX, calling it "the most important school-based intervention to increase physical activity." They found that girls who participated in sports between the ages of fourteen and seventeen tended to have lower rates of obesity and increased levels of physical activity into adulthood.[7]

So we know that participation in sport provides incalcuable advantages, but we also know that those advantages do not reach all girls and women living in the United States (much less around the world). More than three-quarters of all Caucasian girls play sports, but less than two-thirds of African American and Latina girls and fewer than half of all girls from immigrant families do. More than 80 percent of American girls living in urban areas report having no physical education classes during the eleventh and twelfth grades; the same is true for nearly 70 percent of girls in rural areas. Teens with highly educated parents are more likely to participate in high school sports than their classmates whose parents completed less schooling. There are few school-sponsored opportunities for students with physical challenges and special needs.[8] What points of change are needed to level the playing field?

The National Federation of State High School Associations determined that in 2011–12, the number of girls participating in scholastic sports increased again for the twenty-third consecutive year. The number of women playing college sports grew as well. Yet boys and men still outpace girls and women in terms of participation. High school boys enjoy 1.3 million more participation opportunities than girls. Girls are twice as likely to be inactive as boys. By age fourteen, girls drop out of sports at twice the rate of boys. Evidence shows that schools, on average, spend more money on boys' programs.

Of the more than 3.1 million high school girls in scholastic sport in 2012, only 191,000 went on to play for NCAA teams, where they constituted 43 percent of all collegiate athletes.[9] Nearly three-quarters of those women were Caucasian. At NCAA schools with "big-time" Division I sports (what they call FBS, or Football Bowl Subdivision, schools), administrators spend two and a half times more money on men's sports. And although Title IX has become the scapegoat for administrations that drop men's programs (particularly wrestling, gymnastics, swimming, and baseball), the number of total men in college sports actually *increased* by 38,482 between 2002 and 2011; the number of women increased by 32,662.[10] In other words, in the past decade, more opportunities have been added for men than women, despite propaganda to the contrary.

Even as the number of women athletes seems to rise, their representation in administrative ranks has dwindled from the pre–Title IX era. In addition, Michael Messner and Cheryl Cooky found that there has been a "precipitous decline" in the amount of television coverage devoted to women's sports over the past several years. In 2009 women's sports garnered just 1.6 percent of network sports news and 1.4 percent of ESPN's *SportsCenter*.[11] For a brief window in July 2012, however, those numbers temporarily increased as the world tuned into the "Women's Games."

The "Women's Games" of 2012

Of the approximately 10,500 athletes who competed in the XXX Olympiad, 44 percent were female. I do not want to gloss over how much progress this represents. In 1960 women made up just over 11 percent of the total number of athletes. At the Barcelona Games of 1992, women accounted for one-quarter of all athletes. Twenty years later and for the first time, Team USA boasted more female than male athletes (269 to 261). So did Team Russia, Team Canada, and Team China. In fact, there were thirty-four countries that sent more female than male athletes to compete.

Women didn't just participate; they won. An oft-used phrase throughout the Games was "If women were their own country," as in, if women were their own country they would have won the medal count; if the U.S. women were their own country, they would have finished third in total gold medals and fifth in all medals combined. Indeed, "Team Title IX" earned nearly 60 percent of all U.S. medals (104) and two-thirds of America's golds (46). China came in second in the total medal count with 87; Chinese women won 49 of those. Russia was third with 82 medals, thanks to their women's 43.

Women won those medals competing in thirty fewer events than men, even though 2012 marked the first Games that each of the twenty-six Summer Olympic male sports had a female analogue. Women's boxing speaks to this discrepancy. Debuting for the first time in London, it equalized the number of sports for the sexes, but female pugilists competed in three weight divisions with twelve fighters in each class. Males competed in ten weight divisions with thirty-two fighters in each. Part of this incongruity may be due to the strong, continued, and worldwide unease about two women going toe to toe in the squared circle, which limits the growth of the sport and the number of women encouraged to pursue it.

The 2012 Paralympics also showed disparity. Hailed as an event that "allowed for greater gender equity and a fair chance for anyone to compete in Paralympic Sport at the most elite level," women made up 36 percent of the 4,200 total athletes. Although male athletes were clearly in the majority, female Paralympians made incredible strides; their 2012 representation was double what it was twenty years ago. Yet most Americans might have missed the Paralympic Games altogether. To watch the events live, they had to seek them out online. NBC, which devoted so much airtime to the Olympics, allowed just five and a half total hours of coverage to the eleven-day festival. This included a ninety-minute recap—scheduled to broadcast a week after the closing ceremonies—and four sixty-minute highlight programs on the NBC Sports Network.[12]

Americans performed well at the Paralympic Games, but nowhere near as well as they did at the 2012 Olympic Games, which took place a fortnight earlier. There, girls and women earned an impressive number of individual medals in judo, boxing, skeet shooting, gymnastics, tennis, swimming, and track and field for the United States. There were also team titles in beach volleyball, doubles tennis, gymnastics, and water polo and in relays in swimming and athletics. The U.S. women's basketball team earned its fifth straight gold medal by winning its forty-first consecutive Olympic contest. The sport's viewership was up 73 percent from the previous Games of 2008, and there are hopes that the players' success and superlative skills will infuse the struggling WNBA with enthusiasm, new fans, and better television coverage. Never mind that, on average, NBA players outearn those in the women's league by a ratio of two hundred to one.[13]

The U.S. women's Olympic soccer team also secured the gold medal, edging out Canada and Japan in thrilling contests. "A bunch of women played soccer," read an article in the online magazine *Slate;* "they did it with passion and skill and aggression and joy, they were good sports and bad, their performances were evaluated on their own terms, and a lot of people watched." In fact, 4.35 million viewers tuned in for the gold-medal game against Japan, a rematch of the 2011 World Cup final, when a worldwide audience of 13 million saw Japan emerge the victor. But will American audiences continue to watch these same athletes play professionally? Maybe a more important question is will NBC broadcast a women's soccer league's games, as it did the Olympics? Probably not. "We're nuts about Abby Wambach when she's wearing the uniform of the USA," writes Christine Brennan of *USA Today.* "When she's in a Washington Freedom jersey, not so much. For the masses, it's all about nationalism."[14]

In the past, the sport has had difficulty finding an audience, part of which is due to networks' reluctance to air their contests. On the heels of the 1999 World Cup victory, the Women's United Soccer Association (WUSA) seemed like it might prove successful. Turner Television's TNT and CNN/SI aired the contests the first year. Viewers had to go to PAX TV if they wanted to see the WUSA play after that. The league folded after three seasons. Several years later, organizers tried again with the Women's Professional Soccer league. A few months before the opening ceremonies of the London Olympics, they suspended play for the 2012 and 2013 seasons. The National Women's Soccer League began in 2013, but many remain skeptical about its viability. In the meantime, top American players—many who became celebrities during the Games—wind up playing overseas, where they join their volleyball-playing sistren, who also lack a professional league on U.S. soil.

At the same time, those women who play for Team USA fared far better than those from many other countries. Before the start of the Games, IOC president Jacques Rogge announced with pride that, "for the first time in Olympic history, all the participating teams will have female athletes." But not really. The teams from Barbados, Nauru, and the Federation of Saint Kitts and Nevis did not include any girls or women (though, to be fair, Chad and Bhutan sent teams devoid of male athletes). Thirty-four of the so-called integrated teams had just one female representative. In addition, few women hold power within national and international sports structures. The IOC established a 20 percent threshold for National Governing Bodies and International Federations—meaning that by 2005, one-fifth of all leadership positions in these organizations must belong to women. Currently, as Maureen Smith and Alison Wrynn determined, just 22 of the 106 IOC members meet that criteria.[15]

This "major boost for gender equality," as Rogge put it, came after Saudi Arabia, Qatar, and Brunei finally agreed to dispatch female athletes. Saudi Arabia was especially resistant, standing stalwart against pressure from the IOC and human rights organizations until the eleventh hour and adding two women to its roster only in the face of a possible ban from the Games. Some saw this as a potential point of change. Others called it nothing more than a "sham" and an issue of "tokenism" designed to placate the IOC. The symbolic inclusion of these women may obscure the status of women in Saudi Arabia, according to Jocelyne Cesari, director of the Islam in the West Program at Harvard University: "Saudi women in general are denied the right to practice sports. Saudi Arabia is the only country in the world that prevents girls from taking part in sports in government schools. Physical education is allowed only in private schools. Women are not allowed to play in official sports clubs or even watch matches in stadiums. Girls' football, volleyball and basketball games in private schools and colleges are held secretly."[16] Critics argue that sport is just one facet of an entire slate of opportunies denied to Saudi women.

The country's two female delegates continued to face obstacles at the Games. Their national Olympic committee directed that they must be accompanied by male guardians at all times, could not mix with male athletes, and had to follow Islamic dress codes. This last item proved especially problematic. Citing safety concerns, the International Judo Federation initially ruled that Wodjan Ali Seraj Abdulrahim could not wear her head scarf in competition. The organization, the IOC, and the Saudi Olympic committee eventually found a compromise that would keep her head covered, but this is not the first time the hijab has been a source of controversy. In 2007 FIFA banned it in soccer, saying it violated principles of safety and the prohibition against making religious statements in the context of the sport. As a result, the Iranian team had to forfeit its Olympic qualifying matches. Muslim sportswomen around the world have faced repeated issues related to religious doctrine that requires they cover their heads and bodies. Perhaps the advent of a "sports hijab" will provide a new point of change.[17]

Because of those countries with "religious and cultural requirements," explained spokesman Richard Baker, the International Volleyball Federation announced that the beach version of the game would no longer require women to wear bikinis. As an alternative, women are allowed to don "shorts of a maximum length of three centimeters (1.18 inches) above the knee, and sleeved or sleeveless tops."[18] Although some wondered if the change would affect the sport's television ratings, the majority of athletes maintained their commitment to revealing bathing suits. Even in the cool English weather, women simply (strangely) put on the bikini over pants and T-shirts or wore long-sleeve tops with their bikini briefs. The audience was denied the spectacle of the flesh (the fleshtacle?) but the integrity of the two-piece remained intact.

Women's beach volleyball, added to the Olympic program in 1996, quickly became one of the most popular spectator sports. In 2012 tickets for the women's event were among the most expensive and best selling. Without question, the competitions are exciting and the athletes incredible, but part of the game's success may be attributed to the sexualized emphasis on the body. If this is the case, according to a study from the University of Minnesota's Tucker Center for Research on Girls and Women in Sport, it does a disservice to the sport, for the "'sex sells' approach" is misguided. Simply put, "Sex sells sex, not women's sports."[19] All the same, television producers make sure to amp up the sex angle when broadcasting the game, regardless of the product they truly aim to put on the market.

Researchers found that during the 2004 Olympics, NBC devoted more airtime to women's beach volleyball than to women's soccer, softball, and volleyball combined.[20] During these broadcasts, another study determined that 20 percent of all camera shots were "tight shots" of the players' chests. Another 17 percent of these shots focused on their backsides.[21] Indeed, as *Slate*'s Justin Peters points out, the "beach volleyball ass shot has become so common that it is now used as generic clip art to illustrate any story involving balls and sand." It's a fairly accurate assessment. Although players argue that their bikini is tied to the game's "beach culture" and provides certain advantages (e.g., it is more comfortable, it keeps the sand out of their uniforms to avoid irritation), it is not terribly groundbreaking to acknowledge that the two-piece bathing suit is part of what makes the sport an audience favorite. In his weekly column for the *Telegraph,* London mayor Boris Johnson listed

"20 jolly good reasons to feel cheerful about the Games." At number nineteen he saluted the "semi-naked women playing beach volleyball" who were "glistening like wet otters."[22] Ugh.

Other sports have seized upon the misguided belief that revealing or feminine clothing makes women's sport more palatable to a general audience. The International Boxing Association (AIBA) has repeatedly tried to mandate skirts for female pugilists. AIBA president Ching-Kuo Wu maintained that the organization was not trying to feminize or sexualize the athletes. Instead, his rationale was that the skirt would help differentiate the sexes: "I have heard many times, people say, 'We can't tell the difference between the men and the women,' especially on TV, since they're in the same uniforms and are wearing headgear." The Badminton World Federation (the sport's governing body composed of twenty-three men and two women) also attempted to require skirts in order "to ensure attractive presentation."[23] In both sports, it seems the idea is to play up the femininity angle to make the athletes more attractive to potential viewers, suggesting that athleticism alone is not enough to sell the products.

Women Olympians who seem to violate the expectations of feminine appearance and performance pay a price. American weight lifter Sarah Robles explained her difficulty securing financial assistance to train for the Games: "You can get that sponsorship if you're a super-built guy or a girl who looks good in a bikini. But not if you're a girl who's built like a guy."[24] When China's sixteen-year-old swimmer Ye Shiwen swam the penultimate lap in the 400-meter individual relay, she did it faster than Ryan Lochte, winner of the corresponding men's event. Allegations of doping and genetic modification were immediate and widespread. It was simply "unbelievable," as one sportscaster put it, that a girl could swim that fast. Gabrielle Douglas was incredulous following her gold-medal performances in the individual all-around and team gymnastics: "I just made history, and people are focused on my hair?" (A few weeks later, a celebrity stylist gave her a makeover. The media made sure we knew.) Caster Semenya's return to prominence and her silver-medal finish in the 800-meter race were overshadowed by the unrelenting commentary over her "gender controversy." There were even speculations that she threw the race—deliberately losing in order to deflect suspicions that she benefited from some unfair advantage, as if subpar performance signified true womanhood.

On the other end of the spectrum were those athletes who emphasized their femininity and heterosexuality to varied reactions. There may never be a better time to be an American woman athlete, but it ain't easy. Just ask hurdler

Lolo Jones. As she prepared to race in London, *New York Times* sportswriter Jeré Longman condemned the disproportionate amount of publicity Jones received over her peers. "This was based not on achievement but on her exotic beauty and on a sad and cynical marketing campaign. Essentially, Jones has decided she will be whatever anyone wants her to be—vixen, virgin, victim—to draw attention to herself and the many products she endorses." Longman noted Jones's public discussions about her devout Christianity, chastity, and "dissolute childhood," as well as her provocative photo spreads that play "into the persistent, demeaning notion that women are worthy as athletes only if they have sex appeal." It is a point that feminist scholars have made for decades, but many took his critique to be an unfair attack on the athlete. Jones found the piece "heartbreaking," particularly her comparison to Anna Kournikova, the onetime glamour girl of tennis who never won a singles title: "I have the American record," she told the *Today Show*. "I am the American-record holder indoors. I have two world indoor titles." The problem is that more people know about Jones's scantily clad cover for *Outside* magazine than they do her athletic accomplishments.

Her defenders pointed out that male athletes appear in similar fashion. They called attention to shirtless images of quarterback Tim Tebow and swimmer Michael Phelps. "Major League Baseball pitcher Jim Palmer, whose nickname is 'cakes,' posed in his underwear for Jockey in the 1970s and Michael Jordan, a National Basketball Association star, posed with Jockey in the eighties. Current soccer star David Beckham is seen today with more clothes off than on." No he's not, and that's an important point. For all the half-dressed images of Beckham (or Tebow, or Phelps, or Palmer, or Jordan), there are exponentially more images circulating of him playing soccer. He is a sports star who happens to be good looking. For female athletes to get attention, the inverse must be true: they must be good-looking women who happen to play sports. It may not be fair, but it is the lay of the land, as *Sports Illustrated*'s Sarah Kwak points out. "The foundation upon which recent criticism of [Lolo] Jones is based is valid. It isn't fair that [Dawn] Harper and [Sharmaine] Pearson, or every Olympian for that matter, doesn't get the same attention that Jones does—whether that's because Jones is photogenic, media savvy or apt at PR. But is it any more fair to dismiss her for the very same reasons?"[25] Throughout history, it has been the most conventionally attractive women athletes, not the best athletic performers, who get the most attention. It was as true for Gorgeous Gussie Moran as it is for Anna Kournikova and Lolo Jones. In spite of intervening points of change, this is one aspect of women's sport that remains constant.

The New Banal

Although the points of change discussed in this manuscript have not always signified progress, there has been undeniable improvement in the lot
of the athletic woman. She is no longer a "freak" or a "social anomaly," as
Jan Felshin characterized in 1973.[26] We might even go so far as to claim that,
in the United States, athletic girls and women are themselves banal. There is
nothing particularly unusual about their participation in sport, and although
pockets of resistance persist, today's girl rarely faces the same barriers to participation that she did in the past. No longer restricted to the sidelines, girls
and women can choose from a range of athletic options, which includes the
possibility that the sidelines are precisely where they want to be. They may
even opt out of sport altogether and, in so doing, find a range of physical
culture opportunities available to them. A sweating, straining, strengthening
woman is no longer anathema to dominant society. That, in itself, is progress.

   For this reason, I disagree with communications scholar Patricia Clasen
who, in 2001, claimed the term *female athlete* is a paradox: "one cannot be
both a female and an athlete because being one negates the other."[27] Although
there are still tensions between femininity and athleticism, I am not convinced that the two terms are antithetical to one another. The contemporary
American sportscape allows for both concepts to coexist, overlap, and, at
times, even integrate.

   Take, for example, a recent tampon advertising campaign featuring Serena
Williams, one of the many American women to win gold in London—in both
the singles tennis event and, alongside her older sister, Venus, in doubles as
well. Never one to shy away from controversy, she also became a spokesperson for Tampax, breaking ranks with the WTA that shunned an earlier
invitation to partner with the company. In a 2009 campaign titled "Outsmart
Mother Nature," Williams appeared in a series of print ads with taglines reading "Serena Shuts Out Mother Nature's Monthly Gift," "Mother Nature Has
Met Her Match," and "Game Over, Mother Nature." Proctor & Gamble, now
the parent company of Tampax, also produced an online commercial. The
spot begins with a press conference to hype Williams's upcoming competition against "Mother Nature," who has been anthropomorphized as a small
woman wearing a tweed suit bearing a package wrapped in red paper.

   The lighthearted ad confronts many of the standard reservations associated
with menstruation and menstrual products. Cracking jokes about "Aunt Flo,"
Mother Nature tries to deliver her "monthly gift." "Bad blood?" she responds
to a reporter's question, "Well, there is plenty of blood, but none of it's bad."
At one point, the tennis star flexes her impressive bicep to emphasize that
her opponent does not stand a chance. She is neither the demure nor white

sportswoman of the 1930s and 1940s but a strong competitor not to be trifled with. The press conference is interspersed with scenes from a tennis match where Williams fires shots at her cowering opponent. There is no denying that tampon advertisements have come a long, long way since 1936, although the physicality and the dress of the sportswoman continue to provide attractive selling points for the product.

In each of the Tampax promotions, Serena Williams appears wearing a traditional short, white tennis dress, either to affirm her confidence in the product or to keep in line with the sport's conventions. It was something of a departure from her usual repertoire of attention-grabbing costumes, the likes of which would have probably stupefied the tennis shorts–wearing advocate Helen Jacobs, who in 1934 could not imagine "what further change could possibly be made to tennis attire. One might suggest bathing suits!" (One wonders what she would have made of beach volleyball uniforms.) She could have hardly conceived of Williams's 2001 "catsuit," or Venus Williams's 2010 "lacy, red-trimmed, black outfit with a corset-like top and a tutu skirt that gave the illusion of being see-through," or Ann White's 1985 "unitard."[28] Tennis fashions have continued to evolve in the postmodern era in ways that have been influenced by professionalism, corporate sponsorship, technologies in fabric and construction, media forms, and the progressive strength and athleticism of female athletes.

Yet in more than a century of change in women's tennis, much remains the same: fashion can liberate women's bodies, just as it can constrain them through gender-, race-, class-, and sexuality-based ideals of propriety. Distinguishing fashion often captures media attention and elevates an athlete's public profile, though that type of consideration may do little to improve her position as an athlete or the overall prominence of women's sport. Instead, it may trivialize her accomplishments and obscure more significant issues. Approximating the sport's sanctioned version of sartorial respectability may facilitate the participation of those traditionally ostracized from the courts without radically contesting the intractable elitism and exclusivity that, to this day, characterize tennis.

Like Helen Jacobs, participants in the National Institutes on Girls' Sports also tried to hazard a guess at what women's sport might look like in the future, for many realized they stood on the threshold of change. In the late 1950s and 1960s, physical educators could no longer uphold their foremothers' suppression of highly competitive athletics for girls and women. Many of them did not want to, and so they set out to alter the course of their organizations and the history of sport. Phebe Scott was one of those visionaries and, at the second institute in 1965, she asked attendees to imagine themselves in 1980: "If we are correct in our assumption that sports for women will continue to expand we need to concern ourselves with ways and means of making these experiences educationally sound, emotionally satisfying, and personally rewarding." She called on participants to "ensure the kind of future for women in sports that we all envision and toward which we are dedicated," to remain committed to their educational mission, and to promote the positive attributes of physical culture, in all its forms. "Let us be sure our contributions are worthwhile," she concluded.[29] They were, though perhaps not completely in line with the ways the physical educators intended.

The veritable explosion of participation opportunities in the subsequent decades attests to the value of their efforts. The institutes did not cause a revolution in women's sports, but they facilitated its progress and spoke to broader social processes already set in motion. Those kernels of reservation that many women physical educators had—that endorsing highly competitive athletics would lead to the loss of women's governance and the disregard for the "sport-for-all" philosophy—were in the minority. Unfortunately, those fears have come to pass. Part of this is due to the backlash against women's sports in the 1980s. In many ways, this backlash persists. We see it in the perseverance of the beauty myth. We see it in the doggedness of sex testing. We see it in the sexualized reactions to women in their sports bras. And we see it in all the ways that women's sport remains relegated to second-class status in the United States: the quantity and quality of media coverage, the lack of women in decision-making positions, the prevailing heterosexism and "lesbian apologetic," and the emphasis on the "hot fitness body" that may be inimical to health and sport performance and divert public attention from important athletic accomplishment.

We may even see it in the reactions to competitive cheerleading, for it does seem that some of the opposition to calling it a "sport" stems from residual ideas about who a cheerleader is and what it is she does. Those ideas are tainted by the emphasized femininity female cheerleaders have performed since they began to dominate the activity in the mid-1900s. This was implicit in another setback the NCATA suffered in August 2012, when the Second U.S. Circuit Court of Appeals affirmed Judge Underhill's 2010 decision that found Quinnipiac University in violation of Title IX: "Like the district court, we acknowledge record evidence showing that competitive cheerleading can be physically challenging, requiring competitors to possess 'strength, agility, and grace.' . . . Similarly, we do not foreclose the possibility that the activity, with better organization and defined rules, might someday warrant recognition as a varsity sport. But, like the district court, we conclude that the record evidence shows that 'that time has not yet arrived.'"[30] The court seemed to disregard the NCATA's efforts to develop Acrobatics and Tumbling and instead based its decision on older ideas about competitive cheer. It remains to be seen what impact that will have on the developing organization, though its members hope that the partnership with USA Gymnastics will help, particularly following the Olympic team's gold-medal performances in London.

The summer of 2012 held additional points of change.[31] Nike hosted its first LGBT (lesbian, gay, bisexual, transgender) Sports Summit, an encouraging sign. Augusta National Golf Club, home of the Masters Tournament and, until August 2012, a male-only private club, finally admitted two women (former U.S. Secretary of State Condoleezza Rice and business executive Darla Moore) for the first time in its eighty-year existence. But, like Saudi women in the Olympic Games, Augusta's newest members may be merely "tokens." As we cheer their inclusion, we should also wonder why it took so long, but let us hope for another historical turning point.

During this same time, softball great Michele Smith became the first woman analyst for a nationally televised Major League Baseball game. It was a critical milestone, but, overall, most reactions to Smith were "positively Archie Bunkerian," as *Deadspin* described them.[32] The sexist backlash against a woman's voice as one of authority in men's sport demonstrates that we still have a long way to go.

The summer of 2012 was also my first summer as a mother. I watched the Games of the XXX Olympiad with my daughter and imagined that the performances of the strong, talented, accomplished women would somehow etch themselves onto her impressionable seven-month-old psyche. In spite of all the problems that persist, all the progress we need to make, and the points of change that need to happen, I'll be honest: I hope she plays sports.[33]

Notes

Introduction

1. This is certainly not meant to deny the presence or politics of the ponytail in men's sports, nor is it meant to gloss over cultural differences that render the ponytail more or less acceptable for either men or women. For more on the politics of hair, see Diane Simon, *Hair: Public, Political, and Extremely Personal;* and Rose Weitz, *Rapunzel's Daughters: What Women's Hair Tells Us about Women's Lives.*

2. Victoria Sherrow continues to note that the "sun-streaked, dark-blond ponytail" of tennis champion Chris Evert was "often adorned with colorful ribbons. Many other athletes, including world-class gymnasts and figure skaters, have chosen to wear ponytails." Sherrow, *The Encyclopedia of Hair: A Cultural History,* 311.

3. Mike Lopresti, "Behold the Women of Connecticut," *USA Today,* April 7, 2009, C3; "Topic of the Times: The Ponytailed Place-Kicker," *New York Times,* September 2, 2001, 14; Welch Suggs, "Counting Ponytails," *Inside Higher Ed,* July 29, 2007, http://www.insidehighered.com/views/2007/07/19/suggs. Critiquing Suggs's phrase, legal scholar Erin Bezuvis objects to the "deployment of 'ponytail' as a metonym for women and girls. Not only is it underinclusive of women and girls who do not wear ponytails, it is overinclusive of the men and boys who do." "Stop Counting 'Ponytails," *Title IX Blog,* July 21, 2007, http://title-ix.blogspot.com/2007/07/stop-counting-ponytails.html.

4. Helen Anders, "Olympian Gymnasts Set Gold Standard for Ponytails," *Houston Chronicle,* August 15, 2008, http://www.chron.com/disp/story.mpl/life/main/5944694.html. See also Diane Pucin, who writes of the 1996 Olympic women's gymnastics team: "The girls were young, 14 or 15, tiny and perky. Viewers loved their smiles and ponytails, loved how they could role into miniature balls, twirling faster, leaping higher, tumbling ever quicker because they were so small." "Age Rule Changes the Shape of a Sport," *Los Angeles Times,* August 21, 2000, 1.

5. For a critique of "cuteness" in connection to women's gymnastics, see Ann Chisolm, "Acrobats, Contortionists, and Cute Children: The Promise and Perversity of U.S. Women's Gymnastics."

6. D. Stanley Eitzen and Maxine Baca Zinn, "The De-athleticization of Women: The Naming and Gender Marking of Collegiate Sport Teams," 132.

7. Jeré Longman, "For All the Wrong Reasons, Women's Soccer Is Noticed," *New York Times*, November 11, 2009, B15.

8. Kathleen Deveny, "Who You Callin' a Lady?," 24; Jeré Longman, "Women's Sports Push Back at Stereotypes," *New York Times*, March 21, 2010, B1.

9. Jeré Longman, "Those Soccer Plays, in Context," *New York Times*, November 17, 2009.

10. Quoted in Michael A. Messner, Margaret Carlisle Duncan, and Cheryl Cooky, "Silence, Sports Bras, and Wrestling Porn," 42. The phrase was also used in 1979 to describe then sixteen-year-old tennis phenom Tracy Austin in "Ponytail Express."

11. Jeré Longman, "Women's World Cup: Pride in Their Play, and in Their Bodies," *New York Times*, July 8, 1999; Helene A. Shugart, "She Shoots, She Scores: Mediated Constructions of Contemporary Female Athletes in Coverage of the 1999 US Women's Soccer Team," 8.

12. Mark Starr, Martha Brant, and Sam Register, "It Went Down to the Wire . . . and Thrilled Us All"; U.S. Women's National Soccer Team, "Ponytail Posse," http://www.ponytailposse.com/.

13. See Vikki Krane, "We Can Be Athletic and Feminine, but Do We Want To?"

14. Pat Griffin, *Strong Women, Deep Closets: Lesbians and Homophobia in Sport*, 68.

15. Annemarie Jutel, review of ibid. and *Life Outside: The Signorile Report on Gay Men; Sex, Drugs, Muscles, and the Passages of Life*, by Michelangelo Signorile, *Journal of Sport History* 21 (1999): 71. See also Laura Robinson, *Black Tights: Women, Sport, and Sexuality*, 60–61. Halberstam quoted in "The Olympics: Ponytails, Performance, and the Ultimate Propaganda Machine."

16. Jan Felshin, "The Triple Options . . . for Women in Sport." See also Emily Wughalter, "Ruffles and Flounces: The Apologetic in Women's Sports"; and Mary Jo Festle, *Playing Nice: Politics and Apologies in Women's Sports*. For critiques of the female apologetic, see Don Sabo, "Psychosocial Impacts of Athletic Participation on American Women: Facts and Fables"; and K. L. Broad, "The Gendered Unapologetic: Queer Resistance in Women's Sport."

17. See P. Griffin, *Strong Women, Deep Closets*.

18. Rapinoe quoted in Jerry Portwood, "Fever Pitch."

19. Barry Petchesky, "'I'm Gay,' Says Megan Rapinoe. 'That's Nice,' Says Everyone."

20. Pat Griffin, "Soccer Star Megan Rapinoe to the World: I'm Gay." On the phrase "No bow? Lesbo," see also Seth Soffian, "Undercurrent of Homophobia Still Shapes Women's Sports," *Marco Island Sun Times*, July 10, 2012, http://www.marcoislandflorida.com/article/20120710/SPORTS/307100002/Sports-exclusive-Undercurrent-homophobia-still-shapes-women-s-sports.

21. Donna Lopiano, "Sex May Sell, but Sexism Sells Women Short."

22. See Cheryl Cooky et al., "It's Not about the Game: Don Imus, Race, Class, Gender, and Sexuality in Contemporary Media"; and Kristine E. Newhall and Erin E. Buzuvis, "(E)Racing Jennifer Harris: Sexuality and Race, Law and Discourse in *Harris v. Portland*."

23. Lauren McEwen, "Gabby Douglas and Her Ponytail: What's All the Fuss About?," *Washington Post*, August 2, 2012, http://www.washingtonpost.com/blogs/therootdc/post/

gabby-douglas-and-her-ponytail-whats-all-the-fuss-about/2012/08/02/gJQAZiFZRX_
blog.html; "Really? Gabby Douglas Wins a Gold Medal and People Are Criticizing Her
Hair?"; "Gabby Douglas' Hair Sparks Debate, Outrage," *USA Today,* August 3, 2012, http://
content.usatoday.com/communities/entertainment/post/2012/08/gabby-douglas-hair
-sparks-twitter-debate-outrage/1#.UBwHoURsuHk.

24. T. F. Charlton, "The Media's Gabby Douglas Problem."

25. Collins conducted these interviews as part of her master's thesis research and was
gracious enough to share her transcripts. See Jennifer E. Collins, "Beyond the Beauty
Salon: Sport, Women of Color, and Their Hair."

26. "Dermatologic Barriers to Exercise in Black Women." See also Anahad O'Connor,
"Surgeon General Sees Hair Care as Exercise Barrier for Women," *New York Times,* August
26, 2011, A16.

27. Collins interviews.

28. Gerda Lerner, "U.S. Women's History: Past, Present, and Future," 25 (emphasis
added).

29. See Alexandra Shepard and Garthine Walker, "Gender, Change, and Periodisation"; Judith M. Bennett, *History Matters: Patriarchy and the Challenge of Feminism;* and
Ludmilla Jordanova, *History in Practice.*

30. Anne Hollander, *Sex and Suits: The Evolution of Modern Dress,* 4.

31. Karen Houppert, *The Curse: Confronting the Last Unmentionable Taboo, Menstruation,* 14.

32. Naomi Wolf, *The Beauty Myth: How Images of Beauty Are Used against Women.*

33. Natalie Zemon Davis, "'Women's History' in Transition: The European Case," 90.
See also Roberta J. Park, "Sport, Gender, and Society in a Transatlantic Perspective," 59;
Catriona M. Parratt, "From the History of Women in Sport to Women's Sport History:
A Research Agenda"; and Patricia Vertinsky, "Gender Relations, Women's History, and
Sport History: A Decade of Changing Enquiry, 1983–1993."

34. Jack Berryman, "Preface," 5; Steven A. Riess, "The New Sport History," 321; Judith
M. Bennett, "Feminism and History"; Kathleen Canning, *Gender History in Practice:
Historical Perspectives on Bodies, Class, and Citizenship.*

35. Parratt, "From the History of Women in Sport to Women's Sport History."

36. See, as examples, Evelyn Brooks Higginbotham, "Beyond the Sound of Silence:
Afro-American Women's History"; Bonnie Thornton Dill, "Race, Class, and Gender:
Prospects for an All-Inclusive Sisterhood"; Ellen Carol DuBoise and Vicky L. Ruiz, eds.,
Unequal Sisters: A Multicultural Reader in U.S. Women's History; Gerda Lerner, "Recon-
ceptualizing Differences among Women"; Linda Gordon, "On Difference"; and Cheshire
Calhoun, "The Gender Closet: Lesbian Disappearance under the Sign 'Women.'"

37. Honor R. Sachs, "Reconstructing a Life: The Archival Challenges of Women's History."

Chapter 1. What Shall We Wear for Tennis?

1. M. H., "Place Aux Dames," 521; "Major Wingfield on Lawn Tennis Costumes," 630.

2. A Lady Tennis Player, "Tennis Dress," 403.

3. Patricia Campbell Warner, *When the Girls Came Out to Play: The Birth of American
Sportswear,* 6–7.

4. Beginning in the 1960s, television coverage and the subsequent "open era" inspired a widespread "transformation in tennis clothing" and what we might consider the postmodern tennis age. Angela Lumpkin, *Women's Tennis: A Historical Documentary of the Players and Their Game,* 101.

5. Patricia Campbell Warner, "Clothing as Barrier: American Women in the Olympics, 1900–1920," 64; Hollander, *Sex and Suits,* 4.

6. See Sally Sims, "The Bicycle, the Bloomer, and Dress Reform in the 1890s"; and Catherine Horwood, "'Girls Who Arouse Dangerous Passions': Women and Bathing, 1900–39."

7. Allen Guttmann, *Women's Sports: A History,* 124; John R. Tunis, "Pour le Sport: How Tennis Helped the Modern Diana," 113; Toby Miller, *Sportsex,* 122 (emphasis in original); Billie Jean King with Cynthia Starr, *We Have Come a Long Way: The Story of Women's Tennis,* 28.

8. Barbara Burman, "Racing Bodies: Dress and Pioneer Women Aviators and Racing Drivers," 301; Hollander, *Sex and Suits,* 4.

9. Foster Rhea Dulles, *A History of Recreation: America Learns to Play,* 192–93.

10. Ibid., 240.

11. Alfred B. Starey, "Lawn-Tennis in America," 467. See also Donald J. Mrozek, *Sport and American Mentality, 1880–1910,* 137.

12. Elizabeth C. Barney, "The American Sportswoman," 71.

13. Virginia Wade with Jean Rafferty, *Ladies of the Court: A Century of Women at Wimbledon,* 17; United States Lawn Tennis Association, *Official Encyclopedia of Tennis,* 76–77 (emphasis in original); Diane Élisabeth Poirer, *Tennis Fashion,* 10; Warner, *When the Girls Came Out to Play,* 52.

14. Teddy Tinling, as told to Robert Oxby, *White Ladies,* 27; Ted Tinling, "Fashion: A Special Article," *Wimbledon: The Official Centenary Magazine, 1877–1977,* Folder "Research: Fashion," International Tennis Hall of Fame and Museum.

15. Wade with Rafferty, *Ladies of the Court,* 23.

16. Lumpkin, *Women's Tennis,* 8.

17. Dod quoted in Heiner Gillmeister, *Tennis: A Cultural History,* 204. See also Robert J. Lake, "Gender and Etiquette in British Lawn Tennis, 1870–1939: A Case Study of 'Mixed Doubles.'"

18. Henry W. Slocum, "Lawn Tennis as a Game for Women."

19. Lois W. Banner, *American Beauty,* 146.

20. Julia Christie-Robin, Belinda T. Orzada, and Dilia López-Gydosh, "From Bustles to Bloomers: Exploring the Bicycle's Influence on American Women's Fashion, 1800–1914," 323; Diane Crane, "Clothing Behavior as Non-Verbal Resistance: Marginal Women and Alternative Dress in the Nineteenth Century," 256.

21. "New York Fashions," 523; tennis player Marie Wagner quoted in United States Lawn Tennis Association, *Official Encyclopedia of Tennis,* 26.

22. Jeane Hoffman, "The Sutton Sisters," 74; Poirer, *Tennis Fashion,* 7.

23. Nancy G. Rosoff, "'Every Muscle Is Absolutely Free': Advertising and Advice about Clothing for Athletic American Women, 1880–1920," 25. See also Warner, "Clothing as Barrier," 55.

24. "Are Athletics 'Mannifying' the American Girl?," *Chicago Daily Tribune,* May 12, 1912, F3.

25. "The Lady Players at Wimbledon," *Lawn Tennis*, July 3, 1901 (emphasis in original), Folder "Tennis Costume: Women's," International Tennis Hall of Fame and Museum; Lumpkin, *Women's Tennis*, 14, 22.

26. Morrow Krum, "Tennis, Not Style, Counted When May Sutton Was Star," *Chicago Daily Tribune*, March 21, 1926, A2; Sutton quoted in "Miss Sutton as a Tennis Exponent," 26; Krum, "Tennis, Not Style, Counted," A2.

27. "Sport: Women's Tennis"; "Summer Girls Live the Strenuous Life," *Chicago Daily Tribune*, August 13, 1904, D2.

28. May G. Sutton, "Women and Dress," 327.

29. Anngel Delaney, "How We Got Rid of the Bloody Corsets and Other Tales of Women's Sports," 34. As early as 1837, though, Madam George had introduced a "Calisthenic Corset" that was "totally devoid of bone," to avoid such injuries during exercise. Alison Carter, *Underwear: The Fashion History*, 36.

30. Ted Tinling, *The Story of Women's Tennis Fashion*, 7.

31. "A Girl Tennis Champion," *New York Times*, July 10, 1898, 12; J. Parmly Paret, "Good Form in Women's Tennis," 344.

32. Editor's commentary to "Women's Apparel for the Court," *American Lawn Tennis*, May 15, 1915, 70–71.

33. Mrs. Marshall McLean and Miss Edna Wildey, "Women's Apparel for the Court," 70–71.

34. Molla Bjurstedt and Samueal Crowther, *Tennis for Women*, 151–54; Dorothea Lambert Chambers, *Lawn Tennis for Ladies*, 64–65.

35. James Laver, *Costume and Fashion: A Concise History*, 230.

36. Teddy Tinling, *Tingling: Sixty Years in Tennis*, 25.

37. Jennifer Hargreaves, *Sporting Females: Critical Issues in the History and Sociology of Women's Sports*, 116. David Gilbert provides an interesting critique of the characterizations of Lenglen and Chambers in "The Vicar's Daughter and the Goddess of Tennis: Cultural Geographies of Sporting Femininity and Bodily Practices in Edwardian Suburbia."

38. Larry Engelmann, *The Goddess and the American Girl: The Story of Suzanne Lenglen and Helen Wills*, 18.

39. Lumpkin notes that although some private clubs required women to cover their bare arms, by 1928 few players wore sleeves. Lumpkin, *Women's Tennis*, 40.

40. Engelmann, *Goddess and the American Girl*, 24; Catherine Horwood, "Dressing Like a Champion: Women's Tennis Wear in Interwar England," 49.

41. Suzanne Lenglen, *Lawn Tennis for Girls*, 99.

42. C. Willett and Phillis Cunnington, *The History of Underclothes*, 234–35.

43. Susan L. Hannel, "The Influence of American Jazz on Fashion."

44. Warner, *When the Girls Came Out to Play*, 59; Mildred Adams, "From Bloomers to Shorts: An Epic Journey," *New York Times*, August 26, 1934, SM10.

45. Laver, *Costume and Fashion*, 242; Helen Wills, "Emancipated Legs Mean Better Sports," 33.

46. Tinling, as told to Oxby, *White Ladies*, 35; "Miss Wills Holds to Modest Attire," *New York Times*, July 8, 1928, 132; Annegret Ogden, "Queen Helen: The Voice of Helen Wills," 13.

47. "Miss Wills Holds to Modest Attire," 132.

48. "U.S. Women Tennis Stars Plan to Adopt Stockingless Mode in Play at Wimbledon," *New York Times*, May 23, 1929, 37. See also "Stockings Issue at Wimbledon Left to Players' Good Taste," *New York Times*, June 7, 1929, 26; Helen Hull Jacobs, "One Woman's Shorts Story," 18.

49. Ibid. Fashion historian James Laver writes that Mrs. Fearnley-Whittingstall was the first to play without stockings at the Forest Hills tournament in 1931. Laver, *Taste and Fashion*, 178. Edelmann contends that Suzanne Lenglen introduced the style in 1933 at Roland Garros. Engelmann, *Goddess and the American Girl*, 348.

50. Bunny Austin, *Lawn Tennis Made Easy*, 106. The U.S. women's track and field team evidently donned shorts for the 1922 First International Track Meet for Women in Paris. As one assistant coach recalled, "I guess we were the first in the U.S. to come out in shorts, rather long shorts, but at least better than those baggy bloomers." Jane P. Tuttle, "Setting the Mark: Lucile Godbold and the First International Track Meet for Women," 143.

51. Tinling, as told to Oxby, *White Ladies*, 31; Helen Wills, *Tennis*, 137–38; Adams, "From Bloomers to Shorts," SM10. See, for example, "Tennis Shorts Approved by the Duchess of York," *New York Times*, February 20, 1934, 2; and "King Gustaf Disapproves Tennis Shorts for Women," *New York Times*, February 16, 1934, 16.

52. "Miss Jacobs Plans Debut in Shorts Today; First Net Champion Ever to Adopt Attire," *New York Times*, August 15, 1933, 21; Helen Hull Jacobs, "The Psychology of Tennis Clothes," 31, 118, 120.

53. Rhea B. Seeger, "Feminine Fad of Shorts and Slacks Develops into Custom: Sportswomen Set Free from Flapping Skirts," *Chicago Daily Tribune*, March 24, 1935, D17; Jack Lippert, "Short Exposure," 24; "'Shorts' Held Certain to Replace Skirts as Women's Tennis Attire in Near Future," *New York Times*, August 12, 1933, 8.

54. "Women in Shorts Irk Net Official," *New York Times*, April 15, 1934, S4.

55. "Helen Hull Jacobs Works on 18th Tennis Book," undated clipping, Helen Hulls Jacobs Collection, Box D44, International Tennis Hall of Fame and Museum; "Senorita de Alvarez Creates a Sensation at Wimbledon, Playing in Short Trousers," *New York Times*, June 24, 1931, 30; Poirier, *Tennis Fashion*, 24.

56. "Tennis Hits Beauty High at Wimbledon," 19.

57. "Warring against Shorts: Towns Are Undecided Whether the Issue Is One of Morals or Esthetics," *New York Times*, July 26, 1936, X9.

58. See, for example, "Golf Group to Act on Adoption of Shorts by Women Contestants," *New York Times*, August 1, 1934, 20; and "Shorts for Golf? No! No! Cry Mama Officials Loudly," *Chicago Daily Tribune*, July 31, 1934, 21.

59. Virginia Gardner, "'Shorts' Win Court Decision," *Chicago Daily Tribune*, July 23, 1932, 5; "Women Now May Wear 'Shorts' in the South Parks," *Chicago Daily Tribune*, May 20, 1934, A6.

60. Grace Lichtenstein, *A Long Way, Baby: The Inside Story of the Women in Pro Tennis*, 54; Selena Roberts, *A Necessary Spectacle: Billie Jean King, Bobby Riggs, and the Tennis Match That Leveled the Game*, 56.

61. Patricia Campbell Warner, "The Americanization of Fashion: Sportswear, the Movies, and the 1930s," 79–80.

62. Tinling, as told to Oxby, *White Ladies*, 28; Tinling, *Sixty Years in Tennis*, 119.

63. "Gorgeous Gussie's Lace-Fringed Panties No. 1 Attraction on Wimbledon's Courts," *New York Times,* June 21, 1949, 33. Her name is alternatively spelled as "Gussy" in some reports.

64. Tinling, *Sixty Years in Tennis,* 123.

65. Lumpkin, *Women's Tennis,* 14, 22.

66. John M. Ross, "Good Gussy," 70, 72.

67. Bill Macklin, "Falkenburg Quits Wimbledon Mixed Doubles," *Washington Post,* June 23, 1949, 17.

68. See, for example, Gwllym S. Brown, "A Little Lace Goes a Long, Long Way."

69. Bill Macklin, "'Gussie' Moran Bows to Tiny Chinese Girl," *Washington Post,* June 25, 1949, 10.

70. Ross, "Good Gussy," 70; "Glamor-Gal [*sic*] Gussy," 36; "Gorgeous Gussie," 91–92; "Gorgeous Gussie's Lace-Fringed Panties No. 1 Attraction on Wimbledon's Courts," *New York Times,* June 21, 1949, 33; Brown, "A Little Lace Goes a Long, Long Way."

71. Tinling, as told to Oxby, *White Ladies,* 44.

72. Ross, "Good Gussy," 72.

73. Tinling, *Sixty Years in Tennis,* 131; "Gussie Moran's Designer Loses Wimbledon Job over New Panties," *New York Times,* February 23, 1950, 36. He resumed his role in 1982.

74. "Tinling's Tutus for Tennis."

75. "Gussie a Winner in Her Black or White Panties," *Chicago Daily Tribune,* March 12, 1950, A5.

76. Ross, "Good Gussy," 71.

77. "Gussie Saving Silk Panties for Doubles," *Washington Post,* August 30, 1949, 15.

78. "Staid Wimbledon Warns Women to Exhibit Tennis, Not Charms," *New York Times,* June 23, 1951, 13.

79. "People."

80. "For Top Drawer Tennis—It's Gold vs. Polka Dots," *Chicago Daily Tribune,* June 5, 1958, F1.

81. "Miss Moran Joins Pros for $75,000 Guarantee," *New York Times,* August 25, 1950, 25; Tinling, as told to Oxby, *White Ladies,* 52; Festle, *Playing Nice,* 67.

82. Edwin B. Henderson, "The Negro in Tennis," 54; Sundiata Djata, *Blacks at the Net: Black Achievement in the History of Tennis,* 3.

83. "Finance a Big Problem for Most Tennis Players," *Chicago Defender,* May 11, 1940, 22.

84. Festle, *Playing Nice,* 58.

85. "Oh, Look! Girls to Don Shorts for Grass Court Tennis Meet," *Chicago Defender,* July 16, 1932, 8.

86. Pamela Grundy, "Ora Washington: The First Black Female Athletic Star," 91; Harry Webber, "Ora Beats Flora in Tennis Feud," *Baltimore Afro-American,* August 5, 1939, 21.

87. Art Carter, "Franklyn Jackson Plays on 'Borrowed Time' in Defending Singles Title," *Baltimore Afro-American,* August 26, 1939, 23.

88. "BVD's Are Again Seen on Tennis Courts in Park," *Chicago Defender,* June 17, 1922, 8.

89. Mark S. Foster, "In the Face of 'Jim Crow': Prosperous Blacks and Vacations, Travel, and Outdoor Leisure, 1890–1945," 143; E. Franklin Frazier, *The Black Bourgeoisie* and *The Negro Family in the United States,* 322.

90. Althea Gibson, *I Always Wanted to Be Somebody,* 29; Evelyn Brooks Higginbotham, *Righteous Discontent: Women's Movement in the Black Baptist Church, 1880–1920,* 196.

91. Edgar G. Brown, "Tennis Talks: Negro Will Be World's Champ within 20 Years," *Philadelphia Tribune,* June 13, 1925, 11. In 1948 Gibson Dr. Reginald Weir was the first African American to play under USLTA sanction. Allison Danzig, "Negro to Compete for the First Time in a National Tennis Tournament," *New York Times,* March 9, 1948, 30.

92. Alice Marble, "A Vital Issue," 14.

93. Gibson also became the first African American woman to desegregate women's professional golf in 1962. See Jennifer H. Lansbury, "'The Tuskegee Flash' and 'the Slender Harlem Stroker': Black Women Athletes on the Margin"; and Bruce Schoenfeld, *The Match: Althea Gibson and Angela Buxton.*

94. Grundy, "Ora Washington," 90; Gibson, *I Always Wanted to Be Somebody,* 29.

95. Hollander, *Sex and Suits,* 24.

96. Adams, "From Bloomers to Shorts," SM10.

Chapter 2. Commercial Tampons and the Sportswoman

1. Lumpkin, *Women's Tennis,* 101; Susan Brownmiller, *Femininity,* 194.

2. Worcester quoted in George Gross, "WTA Mistaken," *Toronto Sun,* February 26, 1995; Worcester quoted in Leslie Baldacci, "We've Got a Long Way to Go, Baby," *Chicago Sun Times,* March 1, 1995; Navratilova quoted in Eve Ellis, "What Is All the Fuss? They're Just Tampons," *Newsday,* February 26, 1995, 27; Navratilova quoted in Mary Ormsby, "Women's Tennis Tour Prefers Denial to Discreet," *Toronto Star,* February 15, 1995.

3. Lopiano quoted in Ellis, "What Is All the Fuss?"; Baldacci, "We've Got a Long Way to Go." See also Grace Lichtenstein, *Long Way, Baby.*

4. Caryl Ferber Conner, "Facts and Fancies about Menstruation," 19; Maxine Davis, "Menstruation," 37.

5. In *Shaping Our Mothers' World: American Women's Magazines,* Nancy A. Walker found these publications were the most popular in the 1930s and 1940s. In surveying these magazines from 1936 to 1952, I found that most tampon advertisements depicting active women appeared in *Good Housekeeping* and *Ladies' Home Journal. Cosmopolitan, American Magazine, American Weekly,* and *Motion Picture* were other publications that carried similar promotions.

6. "Tampax Makes Life Worth Living," *Good Housekeeping,* July 1939, 180.

7. Without question, all of the early spokeswomen for tampons were white, a pattern that persisted until the 1960s when companies began to court the African American market, beginning with a series of ads in black newspapers and in *Ebony.* See Sharra L. Vostral, *Under Wraps: A History of Menstrual Hygiene Technology,* 142–47.

8. Houppert, *Curse,* 14.

9. See Patricia Vertinsky, *The Eternally Wounded Woman: Women, Doctors, and Exercise in the Late Nineteenth Century;* Martha H. Verbrugge, "Gym Periods and Monthly Periods: Concepts of Menstruation in American Physical Education, 1900–1940"; Helen Jefferson Lenskyj, *Out of Bounds: Women, Sport, and Sexuality;* Nancy Cole Dosch, "'The Sacrifice of Maidens' or Healthy Sportswomen? The Medical Debate over Women's Basketball";

Susan E. Cayleff, "She Was Rendered Incapacitated by Menstrual Difficulties: Historical Perspectives on Perceived Intellectual and Physiological Impairment among Menstruating Women."

10. Ellis, "What Is All the Fuss?," 27; Brownmiller, *Femininity,* 194.

11. G. Stanley Hall, *Adolescence: Its Psychology and Its Relations to Physiology, Anthropology, Sociology, Sex, Crime, Religion, and Education,* 480; Lara Freidenfelds, *The Modern Period: Menstruation in Twentieth-Century America,* 44.

12. See Thomas Buckley and Alma Gottlieb, eds., *Blood Magic: The Anthropology of Menstruation;* Houppert, *Curse;* Janice Delaney, Mary Jane Lupton, and Emily Toth, *The Curse: A Cultural History of Menstruation;* Vern Bullough and Martha Voight, "Women, Menstruation, and Nineteenth-Century Medicine"; Elaine Showalter and English Showalter, "Victorian Women and Menstruation"; and Penelope Shuttle and Peter Redgrove, *The Wise Wound: Menstruation and Everywoman.*

13. Vertinsky, *Eternally Wounded Woman,* 41.

14. Mary Chadwick, *Women's Periodicity,* 44.

15. Freidenfelds, *Modern Period,* 24.

16. Patricia Vertinsky, "Exercise, Physical Capability, and the Eternally Wounded Woman," 8.

17. Quoted in Barbara Ehrenreich and Deidre English, *For Her Own Good: 150 Years of the Experts' Advice to Women,* 111.

18. Edward Clarke, *Sex in Education; or, A Fair Chance for Girls,* 157; George F. Comfort and Anna M. Comfort, *Woman's Education and Women's Health: Chiefly in Reply to Dr. E. H. Clarke's "Sex in Education,"* ix. See also William Capp, *The Daughter: Her Health, Education, and Wedlock;* George Lowell Austin, *Perils of American Women: or, A Doctors Talk with Maiden, Wife, and Mother;* Julia Ward Howe, ed., *Sex and Education: A Reply to Dr. E. H. Clarke's: "Sex in Education";* and Eliza Brisbee Duffey, *No Sex in Education; or, An Equal Chance for Both Boys and Girls.*

19. Mary Putnam Jacobi, *The Question of Rest for Women during Menstruation.*

20. Ibid., 19.

21. *Lancet,* April 7, 1926, 712.

22. Georgia Merriam, "Do Women Require Mental and Bodily Rest during Menstruation, and to What Extent?"

23. Clelia Duel Mosher, *Woman's Physical Freedom;* May R. Mayers, "Abdominal Exercises."

24. Vertinsky, *Eternally Wounded Woman,* 215. See also Joan S. Hult, "The Story of Women's Athletics: Manipulating a Dream, 1890–1985," 85.

25. John M. Cooper, "A Magna Charta for the Girl and Woman in Athletics," 22.

26. Clelia Duel Mosher, "The Means to the End." See also Blanche M. Trilling, "Safeguarding Girls' Athletics"; and Henry S. Curtis, "Should Girls Play Interschool Basketball?"

27. "Extracts," 524.

28. Margaret Bell, "Answers to Practical Questions on Menstruation," 208; Sarah Addington, "The Athletic Limitations of Women," 38.

29. Stephen K. Westmann, *Sport, Physical Education, and Womanhood,* 46, 49, 52–53 (emphasis in original).

30. Martha H. Verbrugge, "Recreating the Body: Women's Physical Education and the Science of Sex Differences in America, 1900–1940" and "Gym Periods and Monthly Periods."

31. Katherine F. Wells, "Overcoming Periodic Pain," 48. See also Emil Novak, *A Woman Asks the Doctor.*

32. "Questions and Answers," 955. See also Frances A. Hellebrandt and Margaret H. Meyer, "Physiological Data Significant to Participation by Women in Physical Activity," 20.

33. Joan Jacobs Brumberg, "'Something Happens to Girls': Menarche and the Emergence of the Modern American Hygienic Imperative," 118.

34. Mollie Smart and Russell Smart, "Menstrual Education," 177.

35. Brumberg, "'Something Happens to Girls,'" 123.

36. Freidenfelds, *Modern Period*, 48.

37. Kimberly-Clark, *As One Girl to Another* (1940), 14–15, Duke University Rare Book, Manuscript, and Special Collections Library (emphases in original).

38. Smart and Smart, "Menstrual Education," 178; Ronald H. Bailey, *Small Wonder: How Tambrands Began, Prospered, and Grew* (undated Tampax corporate history booklet published by Tambrands, Inc.), 28.

39. Margot Elizabeth Kennard, "The Corporation in the Classroom: The Struggles over Meanings of Menstrual Education in Sponsored Films, 1947–1983," 125.

40. "Molly Grows Up," 1953, Photo & Sound Productions for Medical Arts Productions, Library of Congress, Motion Picture, Broadcasting, and Recorded Sound Division (Prelinger Archives).

41. Vern L. Bullough, *Sex, Society, and History*, 245; Bullough, "Female Physiology, Technology, and Women's Liberation." For a extensive account of products available in the nineteenth and early twentieth centuries, see Laura K. Kidd and Jane Farrell-Beck, "Menstrual Products Patented in the United States, 1854–1921."

42. Brumberg, "'Something Happens to Girls,'" 112; Jane Beck-Farrell and Laura Klostermann Kidd, "The Roles of Health Professionals in the Development and Dissemination of Women's Sanitary Products, 1880–1940," 332–33.

43. Robert Spector, *Shared Values: A History of Kimberly-Clark*, 59.

44. Ibid., 63; Vern L. Bullough, "Technology and Female Sexuality and Physiology: Some Implications," 68. See also Fred E. H. Schroeder, "Feminine Hygiene, Fashion, and the Emancipation of American Women." In *Under Wraps*, Vostral found prices for Kotex to be half of what Bullough cites but even then notes that they were "hardly inexpensive; five cents per pad was equivalent to a loaf of bread" (66).

45. See Roseann M. Mandziuk, "'Ending Women's Greatest Hygienic Mistake': Modernity and the Mortification of Menstruation in Kotex Advertising"; and Shelley M. Park, "From Sanitation to Liberation? The Modern and Postmodern Marketing of Menstrual Products."

46. Phil Williams, "Great War Nurses Discovered a Girl's Best Friend," *Birmingham Post*, February 8, 2002, 22.

47. See Delaney, Lupton, and Toth, *Curse*, 115.

48. See Madeline J. Thornton, "The Use of Vaginal Tampons for the Absorption of Menstrual Discharges," 260.

49. See, for example, W. H. Mays, "The Tampon in Menorrhagia"; James Stafford, "The Cylindrical Vaginal Pessary-Tampon versus Other Pessaries"; Virgil O. Hardon, "A Case of Retroflexion of the Uterus Treated by Daily Replacement and the 'Supporting Tampon.'"

50. Robert L. Dickinson, "Tampons as Menstrual Guards," 246. Dickinson's work was first published in a 1945 issue of the *Journal of the American Medical Association*.

51. Kidd and Farrell-Beck, "Menstrual Products Patented," 37; Nancy Friedman, *Everything You Must Know about Tampons*, 34.

52. According to Robert Spector, Kimberly-Clark "marketed a Kotex tampon under the name Fibs . . . but it was too big and bulky and did not sell well. Another product was developed in 1948 . . . but it was too costly to make." Spector, *Shared Values*, 67.

53. Vostral, *Under Wraps*, 76.

54. Beck-Farrell and Kidd, "Roles of Health Professionals," 342. The Wix Company was a subsidiary of Holly-Pax, Inc.; Tampax, Inc., purchased both in 1939.

55. Bailey, *Small Wonder*, 5–6.

56. Advertising in the *Journal of the American Medical Association* paved the way for later promotional campaigns claiming Tampax had been "Accepted for Advertising by the American Medical Association." The same statement appeared on company stationery and Tampax cartons. It was not analogous to an endorsement from the American Medical Association (AMA) itself, but any connection to the legitimizing organization was important.

57. Tampax, "Welcome This New Day for Womanhood," *Weekly Standard*, July 26, 1936, reprinted in Bailey, *Small Wonder*, 2.

58. Ibid., 21.

59. "Sanitary Pads and Tampons: Ratings and Comparisons of Leading Brands," 241. In addition to Tampax and Wix, other tampons marketed in the 1930s and 1940s included Fibs, Lillettes, Meds, and Pursettes, among others. "Sanitary Pads and Tampons," 157.

60. See Delaney, Lupton, and Toth, *Curse*, 117.

61. J. Milton Singleton and Herbert F. Vanorden, "Vaginal Tampons in Menstrual Hygiene," 146; Lloyd Arnold and Marie Hagele, "Vaginal Tamponage for Catamenial Sanitary Protection," 790. See also Mary Barton, "Review of the Sanitary Appliance with a Discussion on Intravaginal Packs"; Maurice O. Magid and Jacob Geiger, "The Intravaginal Tampon in Menstrual Hygiene," 316.

62. Singleton and Vanorden, "Vaginal Tampons in Menstrual Hygiene," 150–52.

63. Karl John Karnaky, "Vaginal Tampons in Menstrual Hygiene," 152, 150; Irja Elizabeth Widenius, "A Study of Commercially Manufactured Catamenial Tampons," 522; Harry S. Sackren, "Vaginal Tampons for Menstrual Absorption," 329; Thornton; "Use of Vaginal Tampons"; A. W. Diddle and L. Boulware, "Vaginal Tampons for Menstrual Hygiene."

64. Dickinson, "Tampons as Menstrual Guards," 247.

65. Freidenfelds, *Modern Period*, 30.

66. Brumberg, "'Something Happens to Girls,'" 104.

67. Heather Munro Prescott, "'Guides to Womanhood': Gynaecology and Adolescent Sexuality in the Post–Second World War Era," 210.

68. Roland Marchand, *Advertising and the American Dream: Making Way for Modernity, 1920–1940*, 22; Brumberg, "'Something Happens to Girls,'" 124.

69. Michael Kammen, *American Culture, American Tastes: Social Change and the Twentieth Century*, 198; Douglas Booth, *The Field: Truth and Fiction in Sport History*, 88; Marshall McLuhan, *Understanding Media: The Extensions of Man*, 232.

70. Gregory Kent Stanley, *The Rise and Fall of the Sportswoman: Women's Health, Fitness, and Athletics, 1860–1940*, 89; Banner, *American Beauty*, 166.

71. Benjamin G. Rader, *American Sports: From the Age of Folk Games to the Age of Televised Sports,* 210; Stanley, *Rise and Fall of the Sportswoman;* Mary A. Boutilier and Lucinda SanGiovanni, *The Sporting Woman,* 33.

72. Bailey, *Small Wonder,* 22–24.

73. "Tampax Makes Life Worth Living," 180; Tampax, "As Free as though You Were Ten Years Old," *Cosmopolitan* (1937); Fibs, "Which Tampon Is Best for You?," *Ladies' Home Journal,* December 1942, 66 (emphasis in the original); Meds, "Now! New and Improved *Internal* Sanitary Protection . . . at Only 20¢!," *Good Housekeeping,* October 1940, 208. See also Fibs, "Which Tampon Can You Trust—and When?," *Ladies' Home Journal* (1942).

74. Marchand, *Advertising and the American Dream,* xxi; Meds, "This Wise, Modern Woman," *Good Housekeeping,* June 1946, 230; Tampax, "Don't Be So Conservative!," *Ladies' Home Journal,* August 1942, 88.

75. Wix, "Be Modern!," *Good Housekeeping,* July 1938, 173.

76. Vostral, *Under Wraps,* 3; Fibs, "Can You Trust Tampons?—and When," *Ladies' Home Journal,* March 1942, 62; "Which Tampon?," *Good Housekeeping,* May 1942, 158.

77. In truth, few of these women actually appeared in the water. For the purpose of this chapter, however, I considered those who appeared in bathing suits to be active women. This is based on Alison Poe's work in which she argues, "'Active' was defined as any ad including a visual reference to physical activity, however remote; for example, if a woman was shown in a bathing suit, the ad was considered to represent swimming even though the pose may have been sedentary or even seductive." Poe, "Active Women in Ads," 187.

78. Westmann, *Sport, Physical Training, and Womanhood,* 49; Bell, "Answers to Practical Questions," 208; Grace Thwing, "Swimming during the Menstrual Period," 154.

79. Tampax, "Swim Any Day of the Month with Tampax," *Good Housekeeping,* August 1947, 216; "Tampax Makes Life Worth Living"; Tampax, "*More* Swimming Days!," *Good Housekeeping,* August 1943, 178; Meds, "Why I Switched to Meds," *Good Housekeeping,* August 1941, 146; Annemarie Jutel, "Cursed or Carefree? Menstrual Product Advertising and the Sportswoman," 220.

80. See, for example, Tampax, "Swim If You Want to (with Tampax)," *Good Housekeeping,* July 1948, 116; Tampax, "Go Swimming . . . Rely on Tampax!," *Good Housekeeping,* July 1952, 14.

81. Fibs, "Fibs Kotex Tampons Cost Less!," *Good Housekeeping,* April 1941, 73; Meds, "When Is a Tampon Right for You?," *Good Housekeeping,* July 1942, 66; Meds, "This Tampon Was Really Your Idea!," *Good Housekeeping,* December 1942, 90.

82. "Cure for Cramps," 89. See also Eleanor Percival, "Menstrual Disturbances as They May Affect Women in Industry."

83. Tampax, "Objective: Reduction of Female Absenteeism," *American Journal of Nursing* (1944): 44 (emphasis in original).

84. Bailey, *Small Wonder,* 36.

85. In the early 1980s, a leotard-clad Kathy Rigby struck gymnastic poses for Stayfree maxipads, though any association with tampons remained taboo. As I discuss in the epilogue, Serena Williams signed on as spokesperson for Tampax in 2009. It is also worth noting that in men's sport, tampons have been repeatedly employed as symbols of failed athletic prowess and masculinity. Baseball pitcher Tom Seaver told a reporter,

"One player will pay attention to another by tying up his clothes of stuffing Tampax in his locker," behavior referred to as "ragging." Coaches have performed similar stunts as perverse forms of motivation. While at Indiana University, basketball coach Bobby Knight reportedly hung tampons in athletes' lockers when they failed to perform. Catholic University's Bob Valvano drew inspiration from Knight and distributed "tampons at a team meeting to question the players' manhood." Thus, tampons have been an enabling technology for women but a technology of ignominy and debasement in the masculinist context of sport. See Aaron Latham, "Tom Seaver in the Locker Room," *New York Times,* April 15, 1974, 39; and Anthony Cotton, "Valvano Settles His Grievance with Catholic," *Washington Post,* July 9, 1992, D4.

86. Jutel disagrees with this position, writing that the ads "did not set women free, but rather crystallized social beliefs about the limiting nature of female biology." Jutel, "Cursed or Carefree?," 213.

87. Poe, "Active Women in Ads," 186.

88. Janet Phillips and Peter Phillips, "History from Below: Women's Underwear and the Rise of Women's Sport"; Christine L. Wells, *Women, Sport, and Performance: A Physiological Perspective,* 97.

89. Agnes R. Wayman, "Competition," 469.

Chapter 3. Rules, Rulers, and the "Right Kind" of Competition

1. On this line, Galloway writes that she is quoting "qualified observers and representatives of affiliated organizations." June P. Galloway to NAPECW Board of Directors, May 26, 1967, 2, NAPECW Collection, Box 8: "Representatives," 4–170: "National Institutes on Girls' Sports, 1967–1969," University of North Carolina at Greensboro Archives and Special Collections.

2. Sara Staff Jernigan, "Mirror of Time: Some Causes for More American Women in Sport Competitions," 86; Jernigan, "Preparation of Women Athletes for the Olympic Games."

3. Betty Spears, "The Emergence of Sport in Physical Education," speech presented at the AAHPERD National Convention, April 16, 1973, cited in Ellen W. Gerber, "College Sport," 50–51; Nancy Theriot, "Towards a New Sporting Ideal: The Women's Division of the National Amateur Athletic Federation," 2.

4. Nancy Theberge, "Women's Athletics and the Myth of Female Frailty"; Collette Dowling, *The Frailty Myth: Women Approaching Physical Equality.*

5. See Lynne Emery, "From Lowell Mills to the Halls of Fame: Industrial League Sport for Women"; Paula Welch, "Interscholastic Basketball: Bane of College Physical Educators"; and Joan S. Hult and Roberta J. Park, "Women as Leaders in Physical Education and School-Based Sports, 1865–1930s."

6. "Intercollegiate Sports for Women," 198–99.

7. Mabel Lee, "The Case for and against Intercollegiate Athletics for Women and the Situation as It Stands To-Day," 13.

8. Florence A. Somers, *Principles of Women's Athletics,* 37; M. Lee, "Case for and against Intercollegiate Athletics," 13; John R. Tunis, "Women and the Sports Business," 214; William Burdick, "Safeguarding the Athletic Competition of Girls and Women," 367; J. Cooper,

"Magna Charta for the Girl and Woman in Athletics," 22; Tunis, "Women and the Sports Business," 214.

9. Alice Allene Sefton, *The Women's Division, National Amateur Athletic Federation.* See also Joan S. Hult, "Women's Struggle for Governance in U.S. Amateur Athletics"; Hult and Park, "Women as Leaders." The first Executive Committee, or "the Old Guard," consisted of Lou Henry Hoover, Blanche M. Trilling, Louise French, Helen Frost, Helen McKinstry, J. Anna Norris, Ethel Perrin, and Agnes R. Wayman.

10. Sefton, *Women's Division,* 7–8.

11. Ibid., 13–14.

12. Wayman, "Competition," 469; Agnes R. Wayman, "Women's Athletics: All Uses—No Abuses," 517. See also Katherine Ley and Sara Staff Jernigan, "The Roots and the Tree."

13. For 1920s positions on competition for girls and women, see especially Ethel Perrin, "More Competitive Athletics for Girls—but the Right Kinds"; Blanche M. Trilling, "The Playtime of a Million Girls or an Olympic Victory—Which?"; Wayman, "Competition"; M. Lee, "Case for and against Intercollegiate Athletics"; "Outstanding Problems in Girls' Athletics"; "How Much Competition Is Good for Girls?"; Elizabeth Richards, "Everyday Problems in Girls' Basketball"; Harry Stewart, "Track Athletics for Women"; and Curtis, "Should Girls Play Interschool Basketball?"

14. Addington, "Athletic Limitations of Women," 38. The Fédération Sportive Féminine Internationale hosted what was originally called the Women's Olympics; however, the IOC objected to the use of the term, and organizers changed the name of the event to the Women's World Games in 1926.

15. Ethel Perrin, "A Crisis in Girls Athletics," 10; June A. Kennard, "The History of Physical Education," 841; Jennifer Hargreaves, "Olympic Women: A Struggle for Recognition," 10.

16. Trilling, "Playtime of a Million Girls," 51–52.

17. Tunis, "Women and the Sports Business," 213.

18. Ethel Perrin and Grace Turner, *Play Day: The Spirit of Sport,* 20; Lou Henry Hoover, "Forward," in ibid., 10.

19. Della Durant, interview by author, University Park, Pa., June 28, 2011; Martha Adams, interview by author, University Park, Pa., June 28, 2011; Lucille Magnusson, interview by author, University Park, Pa., June 28, 2011; Margaret M. Duncan, "The Status of Intramural Programs for Women"; M. Gladys Scott, "Competition for Women in American Colleges and Universities." Scott defined "varsity" athletics as "a selected, highly trained team, participating in a series of matches with similar teams from other schools, each representing their respective institutions" (49).

20. Esther Allen Gaw in the 1941 program "An Invitation to College Women Who Play Golf," Katherine Ley Collection, Box 15, Folder "Women," American Alliance for Health, Physical Education, Recreation, and Dance Records Collection; Mary A. Daniels, "The Historical Transition of Women's Sports at the Ohio State University, 1885–1975, and Its Impact on the National Women's Intercollegiate Setting during That Period."

21. A. W. Ellis, "The Status of Health and Physical Education for Women in Negro Colleges and Universities," 58.

22. Cindy Himes Gissendanner, "African-American Women and Competitive Sport, 1920–1960," 81; Rita Liberti, "'We Were Ladies, We Just Played Basketball Like Boys': Af-

rican American Womanhood and Competitive Basketball at Bennett College, 1928–1942";
Djata, *Blacks at the Net,* 5–8.

23. Paula D. Welch and D. Margaret Costa, "A Century of Olympic Competition," 130;
Susan K. Cahn, *Coming on Strong: Gender and Sexuality in Twentieth-Century Women's
Sport,* 118.

24. Quoted in Cindy Himes Gissendanner, "African American Women Olympians: The
Impact of Race, Gender, and Class Ideologies, 1932–1968," 173. Stokes and Pickett again
made the Olympic team in 1936; once more, officials replaced Stokes in the 400-meter relay
with a white teammate. Pickett competed in the 80-meter hurdles but was disqualified
when she struck a hurdle. Coachman began her career at Tuskegee but earned her degree
from Albany State College. Tuskegee may well have produced other Olympic champions,
but during the team's glory years the 1940 and 1944 Games were canceled due to World
War II.

25. Tracey M. Salisbury, "First to the Finish Line: The Tennessee State Tigerbelles,
1944–1994."

26. Nolan A. Thaxton, "A Documentary Analysis of Competitive Track and Field for
Women at Tuskegee Institute and Tennessee State University"; Dwight Lewis and Susan
Thomas, *A Will to Win.*

27. Ed Temple with B'Lou Carter, *Only the Pure in Heart Survive,* 29.

28. Pamela Creedon, "Women, Sport, and Media Institutions: Issues in Sports Journalism and Marketing," 95.

29. Joe Jares, "Off to Russia, without Love"; Gilbert Rogin, "Flamin' Mamie's Bouffant
Belles." It is worth noting that Ed Temple insisted that the Tigerbelles must be "ladies
first, students second, and athletes third. . . . When we travel they dress up . . . I don't
want any pictures taken of them while they are all sweaty after a race. When they have
finished they get on their sweatsuits, comb their hair, and put on some lipstick." Temple
with Carter, *Only the Pure in Heart Survive,* 50–51. See also Bob Ottum, "Dolls on the
Move to Mexico."

30. Cahn, *Coming on Strong,* 133. See also Festle, *Playing Nice,* 91–94.

31. Rogin, "Flamin' Mamie's Bouffant Belles."

32. Ellen Gerber, "The Controlled Development of Collegiate Sport for Women, 1923–1936,"
9; Joan S. Hult, "The Story of Women's Athletics: Manipulating a Dream, 1890–1985," 93.

33. Nancy B. Bouchier, "Let Us Take Care of Our Field: The National Association for
Physical Education of College Women and World War II," 72.

34. John F. Kennedy, "The Soft American"; Hans Kraus and Ruth P. Hirschland, "Muscular Fitness and Health"; Robert H. Boyle, "The Report That Shocked the President."

35. Charles E. Forsythe, "Athletics in the Space Age," 28.

36. Pat Robinson, "The Sports Grill," *Atlanta Daily World,* May 1, 1952; Bill Jauss, "U.S.
Girls Add Beauty to Olympic Games," *Washington Post,* November 11, 1956, C3.

37. Sarah K. Fields, *Female Gladiators: Gender, Law, and Contact Sport in America,* 4–5.

38. Elmon L. Vernier and Phebe M. Scott, "Secondary School Athletic Programs: Detrimental or Developmental?," 100 (emphasis in original); Susan J. Douglas, *Where the
Girls Are: Growing Up Female with the Mass Media,* 39.

39. "AMA Committee on Medical Aspects of Sports, May 2–3, 1964," 46 (emphasis in
original); "Exercise and Fitness," 436.

40. Rosemary McGee, "Comparisons of Attitudes toward Intensive Competition for High School Girls"; Bea Harres, "Attitudes of Students toward Women's Athletic Competition"; Christine White, "Extramural Competition and Physical Education Activities for College Women."

41. The document was originally published by the National Section on Women's Athletics, which later became the DGWS. *Desirable Practices in Athletics for Girls & Women,* pamphlet published by AAHPER, 1941, 1942, 1949, 1953, and 1957. In the American Alliance for Health, Physical Education, Recreation, and Dance Records Collection, Division for Girls and Women's Sports: Publications, Box 2, Folder AC3:6:1: Pubs, Desirable Practices in Sports for Girls and Women, various editions, American Alliance for Health, Physical Education, Recreation, and Dance Records Collection.

42. Jane A. Mott, "National Conference on Social Changes and Implications for Physical Education and Sports Programs," 12.

43. Sara Staff Jernigan, "Women and the Olympics," 26.

44. Maura Conlisk, "Sports Competition for College Women," 64; Madge Phillips, "Sociological Considerations of the Female Participant," 195.

45. In 1963 the U.S. Olympic Development Committee dropped the word *Advisory,* and the organization became the "Women's Board."

46. United States Olympic Association, Inc., "Digest of Exploratory Conversations Held during Initial Meeting of Women's Advisory Board of the U.S. Olympic Development Committee," August 2, 1961, AAHPERD Collection, DGWS: Liaisons, Box 5, U.S. Olympic Development Committee, 1957–1962, American Alliance for Health, Physical Education, Recreation, and Dance Records Collection.

47. Ibid.

48. Rachel Bryant letter to Mabel Lee, December 4, 1957, AAHPER Collection, Box 5, Folder AC 3:6:1: Liaison Organizations, U.S. Olympic Development Committee, 1957–1962, American Alliance for Health, Physical Education, Recreation, and Dance Records Collection; Hamilton quoted in Hope Smith, "The First National Institute on Girls Sports," 32.

49. Jernigan, "Women and the Olympics," 25–26.

50. Tom Hamilton letter to Women's Board (Janet Bachna, Thelma Bishop, Sara Staff Jernigan, Ann Paterson), August 18, 1961, AAHPERD Collection, DGWS: Liaisons, Box 5, Folder AC 3:6:1 Liaison Organizations, U.S. Olympic Development Committee, 1957–1962, American Alliance for Health, Physical Education, Recreation, and Dance Records Collection; "The U.S. Olympic Development Committee's Women's Advisory Board: Suggested Plan for Broadening the Scope & Increasing the Depth of the Women's Advisory Board," undated memo, AAHPERD Collection, DGWS: Liaisons, Box 5, Folder AC 3:6:1 Liaison Organizations, U.S. Olympic Development Committee, 1957–1962, American Alliance for Health, Physical Education, Recreation, and Dance Records Collection.

51. Sara Staff Jernigan, foreword to *Proceedings: Second National Institute on Girls Sports* (Washington, D.C.: AAHPER, 1966), 5; Phebe M. Scott, foreword to *Proceedings: Second National Institute on Girls Sports,* 6; Katherine Ley letter to Sara Staff Jernigan, October 16, 1962, AAHPERD Collection, DGWS: Liaisons, Box 5, Folder AC 3:6:1 Liaison Organizations, U.S. Olympic Development Committee, 1957–1962, American Alliance for Health, Physical Education, Recreation, and Dance Records Collection.

52. Sara Staff Jernigan, "The National Institute on Girls Sports," 8; Women's Advisory Board to the United States Olympic Development Committee, January 30–February

1, 1963, Minutes of the Meetings, DGWS: Liaisons, Box 5, U.S. Olympic Development Committee, 1963–1965, American Alliance for Health, Physical Education, Recreation, and Dance Records Collection.

53. Sara Staff Jernigan, "The Institute Challenge," in *Proceedings: First National Institute on Girls Sports* (Washington, D.C.: AAHPER, 1965), 3; Jernigan, foreword, v.

54. Rachel E. Bryant letter to Nell Jackson, March 10, 1965, AAHPERD Collection, DGWS: Liaisons, Box 5, Folder AC 3:6:1, U.S. Olympic Development Committee, 1963–1965, American Alliance for Health, Physical Education, Recreation, and Dance Records Collection.

55. H. Smith, "The First National Institute," 31–32; Thomas J. Hamilton, "Goals at Different Levels of Skill," in *Proceedings: First National Institute on Girls Sports,* 33; Phebe Scott, "Suggestions for Promoting Clinics," in *Proceedings: First National Institute on Girls Sports,* 158; Sara Staff Jernigan to Ann Paterson, February 21, 1966, AAHPERD Collection, DGWS: Liaisons, Box 5, Initiatives, National Institute on Girls' Sports.

56. Karen M. Johnson, telephone interview with author, June 24, 2011.

57. Charlotte West, telephone interview with author, June 27, 2011. Dr. Roberta Park had a similar experience, recalling that because she had been coaching basketball at the University of California at Los Angeles (UCLA) for several years, she learned little new information at the fifth institute in 1969. Telephone interview with author, August 5, 2011; Dorothy McKnight, telephone interview with author, July 6, 2011.

58. Jernigan, "The Institute Challenge," 3.

59. Catherine L. Allen, "The Human Touch," in *Proceedings: First National Institute on Girls Sports,* 4.

60. Katherine Ley, "A Philosophical Interpretation of the National Institute on Girls Sports," in *Proceedings: First National Institute on Girls Sports,* 13.

61. West interview; Carole Oglesby, telephone interview with author, July 20, 2011.

62. H. Smith, "The First National Institute," 32; McKnight interview; Sara Staff Jernigan, "Two New Institutes on Girls Sports," 40.

63. Frances Schaafsma memo to Volleyball Participants, undated, AAHPERD Collection, DGWS: Initiatives, Box 3, Folder AC 3:6:1, Folder National Institute on Girls' Sports, 1963–1965, American Alliance for Health, Physical Education, Recreation, and Dance Records Collection.

64. Phebe M. Scott, "Food for Thought for the Future," in *Proceedings: Fourth National Institute on Girls Sports* (Washington, D.C.: AAHPER, 1968), 19; Phebe Scott, "Reflections on Women in Sports," in *Proceedings: Third National Institute on Girls Sports* (Washington, D.C.: AAHPER, 1966), 13.

65. Scott, "Reflections on Women in Sports," 10.

66. "Why Can't We Beat This Girl"; Scott, "Food for Thought," 19.

67. Merrit H. Stiles, "A New Look at Olympic Sports Development," in *Proceedings: Fourth National Institute on Girls Sports,* 20; Ley, "Philosophical Interpretation of the National Institute on Girls Sports," 12.

68. Evelyn S. Gendel, "Physicians, Females, Physical Exertion, and Sports," in *Proceedings: Fourth National Institute on Girls Sports,* 12; P. Scott, "Reflections on Women in Sports," 13.

69. Franklin L. Orth, "Remarks," in *Proceedings: Fifth National Institute on Girls Sports* (Washington, D.C.: AAHPER, 1969), 8; Thomas J. Hamilton, "Goals at Different Levels of Skill," in *Proceedings: First National Institute on Girls Sports,* 34.

70. Jernigan, "Preparation of Women Athletes," 597.

71. DGWS, "Statement of Policies and Procedures for Competition in Girls and Women's Sports," 32. See Ronald A. Smith, "Women's Control of American College Sport: The Good of Those Who Played or an Exploitation by Those Who Controlled?"

72. Joan S. Hult, "NAGWS and AIAW: The Strange and Wondrous Journey to the Athletic Summit, 1950–1990."

73. DGWS, "National Intercollegiate Championships for Women," 24–25.

74. Hal A. Lawson, "Physical Education and Sport in the Black Community," 190.

Chapter 4. Women's Sport and Questionable Sex

1. Dr. Manmohan Singh, the chief physician of the Indian Olympic Association, announced that Soundarajan's "gender is not female but male." See, for instance, "Indian Runner Fails Gender Test, Loses Medal," ESPN.com, December 18, 2006, http://sports .espn.go.com. Soundarajan denies the suicide attempt.

2. Dayna B. Daniels, "Gender (Body) Verification (Building)," 373. See, for example, Anne Fausto-Sterling, *Sexing the Body: Gender, Politics, and the Construction of Sexuality*; Michele Foucault, *The History of Sexuality*; Ruth Hubbard, "Gender and Genitals: Constructs of Sex and Gender"; and Thomas Laqueur, *Making Sex: Body and Gender from Greeks to Freud*. I will refrain from putting terms like *sex* and *gender* and *woman* in quotation marks throughout this chapter, if for no other reason than because it tends to get a bit tiresome for both author and reader; however, the missing punctuation should not be construed as unproblematic or uninterrogated vocabulary. Such confusion would mean that I have failed to make a most fundamental point.

3. Bernice L. Hausman, *Changing Sex: Transsexualism, Technology, and the Idea of Gender*; Shira Tarrant, *When Sex Became Gender*, 179; Joan W. Scott, "Gender as a Useful Category of Historical Analysis," 1065. Such examinations must be conducted with caution, however, as even well-intentioned rhetoric has an "othering" effect that, though well intentioned, may treat women with disrespect and disdain.

4. Official Report Los Angeles, 1984, Volume One, Part Two, Olympic Official Report Los Angeles, 1984, Volume One, 358. See "Introducing the, Uh, Ladies," 192; Gail Vines, "Last Olympics for the Sex Test?," 41.

5. Pausanias, *Description of Greece*, quoted in Donald G. Kyle, "Fabulous Females and Ancient Olympia," 135.

6. Quoted in Ellen W. Gerber, "Olympic Competition," 137–38. As David C. Young explains, Coubertin took steps to ensure those who preceded him in reviving the Games were written out of the historical record, in *The Modern Olympic Games: A Struggle for Revival*. Yves-Pierre Boulongne counters that Pierre de Coubertin was not necessarily "opposed to women's sport, or even an unrepentant misogynist," as the "feminist leagues and radical political groups" contend. Boulongne, "Pierre de Coubertin and Women's Sport," 23.

7. Eric Dunning, "Sport as a Male Preserve"; Michael S. Kimmel, "Men's Responses to Feminism at the Turn of the Century"; Michael A. Messner, "Sports and Male Domination: The Female Athlete as Contested Ideological Terrain."

8. Karen Kenney, "The Realm of Sports and the Athletic Woman, 1850–1900," 134.

9. Frederick Rand Rogers, "Olympics for Girls?" 194; "Things Seen and Heard," 18.

10. "Effect of Athletics on Women," *New York Times*, August 23, 1922, 12; "Fast Women."

11. Tunis, "Women and the Sports Business," 213; Wythe Williams, "Americans Beaten in Four Olympic Tests," *New York Times*, August 3, 1928, 3. Anita DeFrantz notes that in the 1904 Games, two men collapsed following the 800-meter race, one of whom had to be carried to his dressing room; the other received stimulants to revive him. In spite of these maladies, the IOC made no move to suspend the race from future Games. Ann Buermann Wass and Clarita Anderson write that a male competitor in the marathon race died of heart failure, "but this race was not declared unsuitable for men." See DeFrantz, "The Olympic Games: Our Birthright to Sports," 188; and Ann Buermann Wass and Clarita Anderson, "What Did Women Wear to Run?," 177.

12. The IAAF also voted to drop the broad jump, shotput, and 200-meter race. See "Sports for Women Kept in Olympics," *New York Times*, August 8, 1928, 21.

13. Susan E. Cayleff, *Babe: The Life and Legend of Babe Didrikson Zaharias*, 18–19; Rader, *American Sports*, 216. As late as the 1960s and 1970s, surveys found that Americans felt running to be "not appropriate" for women. Shorter races, though, "may be appropriate for "Negro women . . . women of Germanic and Slavic ancestry" and "for women identified in the lower levels of socioeconomic status," according to respondents. Eleanor Metheny, "Symbolic Forms of Movement: The Feminine Image in Sports," in *Sport and the Sociocultural Process*, edited by M. Marie Hart, 283–85.

14. "Olympic Games"; Sharon Kinney Hanson, *The Life of Helen Stephens: The Fulton Flash*, 96.

15. Vanessa Heggie, "Testing Sex and Gender in Sports: Reinventing, Reimagining, and Reconstructing Histories"; "Are Girl Athletes Really Girls?," 72. In his 1941 *A Farewell to Sport*, sportswriter Paul Gallico recorded that Helen Stephens, the gold medal winner of the 1936 Olympic 100-meter race, had submitted to some form of sexual verification. Officials, it seems, had "Stephens frisked for sex and had checked her in as one hundred percent female. With no thought whatsoever for the feelings of the young lady . . . [these] feelings were triumphantly if ungallantly aired in the press." This passage is both ironic and curious. If true, it is ironic because the suspicions about Stephens's sex stemmed from the Polish press, following Poland's Stella Walsh's second-place finish in the race. It was later revealed that Walsh herself was intersex. On the other hand, Gallico's statement is curious because such testing, if applied to all participants, would have surely revealed Hermann Ratjen's ruse. Gallico, *Farewell to Sport*, 233–34.

16. Sarah Teetzel writes, "No less than ten athletes competing in the women's category were publicly accused of being men and masquerading as women in media outlets between 1932 and the introduction of standardized sex testing in the 1968 Olympic Games." Teetzel, "Equality, Equity, and Inclusion: Issues in Women and Transgendered Athletes' Participation at the Olympics," 333. Neena A. Xavier and Janet B. McGill note that in 1946 and 1948, respectively, the IAAF and IOC required female competitors to produce medical certificates confirming their sex. Xavier and McGill, "Hyperandrogenism and Intersex Controversies in Women's Olympics," 3904. See also Berit Skirstad, "Gender Verification in Competitive Sport: Turning from Research to Action," 116–17.

17. Kaye N. Ballantyne, Manfred Kayser, and J. Anton Grootegoed, "Sex and Gender Issues in Competitive Sports: Investigation of a Historical Case Leads to a New Viewpoint." In their posthumous analysis, the authors of this study "deduce that Dillema had an ovotesticular DSD [Disorder of Sexual Development]." Based on combined

genotyping and DNA quantification results, they determined "she had a 46,XX/46,XY mosaic condition with a rare origin" and speculate that she have been hyperandrogenic.

18. "Introducing the, Uh, Ladies," 191. See also Barry D. Dickinson et al., "Gender Verification of Female Olympic Athletes"; and Alison Carlson, "Chromosome Count."

19. Cahn, *Coming on Strong,* 138. See also Ian Ritchie, "Sex Tested, Gender Verified: Controlling Female Sexuality in the Age of Containment"; Jaime Schultz, "Disciplining Sex: 'Gender Verification' Policies and Women's Sport"; and Stefan Wiederkehr, "'We Shall Never Know the Exact Number of Men Who Have Competed in the Olympics Posing as Women': Sport, Gender Verification, and the Cold War."

20. "Lessons from Old Olympian."

21. "Russians Bear Down for Olympics."

22. "Sex Test Disqualifies Athlete," *New York Times,* September 16, 1967, 28. These speculations were not confined to the popular media, for sport scholars openly wondered if some of the Eastern European women were masquerading men, "female impersonators," or "pseudohermaphrodites." See Waneen Wyrick, "Physical Performance," 419; Boutilier and SanGiovanni, *The Sporting Woman,* 234; and James Riordan, "Women in Sport: Some English Observations on Russian Women Who Have to Be Trained to Smile," 17.

23. See, for instance, Terry Todd, "Anabolic Steroids: The Gremlins of Sport."

24. "Are Girl Athletes Really Girls?," 63–65; "Preserving la Difference," 72.

25. See "Are Girl Athletes Really Girls?" For discussion, see C. L. Cole, "One Chromosome Too Many." The other athletes who did not attend the event were the Soviet Union's Tatyana Schelkanova and Romania's Iolanda Balas.

26. Jay Teitel, "Faster, Higher, Stronger," *Toronto Life,* December 1983, 73; "Are Girl Athletes Really Girls?," in *Women's Sports: A History,* by Guttmann, 206.

27. Deborah Larned, "The Femininity Test: A Woman's First Olympic Hurdle," 9. See also Lucinda Franks, "See Jane Run," 97–98.

28. Mary Peters with Ian Wooldridge, *Mary P.: Autobiography,* 55–56.

29. Eduardo Hay, "Sex Determination in Putative Female Athletes."

30. "Russians Win Sex-Check Track Meet," *Washington Post,* September 16, 1967, D2; "Sex Test Disqualifies Athlete," 28.

31. "Olympics Require Sex Test," *New York Times,* June 30, 1968, 48.

32. Allan J. Ryan, "Sex and the Singles Player," 39; Keith L. Moore and Murray L. Barr, "Smears from the Oral Mucosa in the Detection of Chromosomal Sex." Haley K. Olsen-Acre argues that the IOC began both sex and drug testing in 1968 as means of screening for "unfair advantages." As such, it seems as though both tests insinuate a dimension of morality and are aimed to identify those who seek to consciously circumvent the rules of competition. Olsen-Acre, "The Use of Drug Testing to Police Sex and Gender in the Olympic Games."

33. Specifically, if more than 20 percent of the nuclei from the buccal smear possesses Barr bodies, then it is predicted that at least two X chromosomes are present. See L. J. Hipkin, "The XY Female in Sport: The Controversy Continues."

34. P. Vignetti et al., "'Sex Passport' Obligation for Female Athletes: Consideration and Criticism on 364 Subjects"; Hay, "Sex Determination"; Laura A. Wackwitz, "Sex Testing in International Women's Athletics: A History of Silence" and "Verifying the Myth: Olympic Sex Testing and the Category of 'Woman.'"

35. Albert de la Chapelle, "The Use and Misuse of Sex Chromatin Screening for 'Gender Identification' of Female Athletes," 1921.

36. Quoted in "Sex Test Disqualifies Athlete," 28. There are competing versions of Klobukowska's story, but the dominant narrative is that tests revealed a triple-X chromosome pattern that the *Los Angeles Times* referred to as "superfemale" in "Polish Sprinter Fails Sex Test, Out of Meet," September 16, 1967, 1. See also Ryan, "Sex and the Singles Player"; and Cole, "One Chromosome Too Many."

37. Dr. Clayton Thomas quoted in Larned, "Femininity Test," 9; "Records of Polish Girl Sprinter Who Flunked Sex Test Barred," *New York Times*, February 26, 1968, 50.

38. "Poles Dispute Female Test," *Washington Post*, September 17, 1967, C8.

39. See Elizabeth A. E. Ferris, "Gender Testing in Sport"; and de la Chapelle, "Use and Misuse of Sex Chromatin Screening," 1921.

40. Elaine A. Ostrander, Heather J. Hudson, and Gary K. Ostrander, "Genetics of Athletic Performance"; N. C. Craig Sharp, "The Human Genome and Sport, Including Epigenetics and Athleticogenomics: A Brief Look at a Rapidly Changing Field."

41. John S. Fox, "Gender Verification: What Purpose? What Price?," 149. See also Mary Jo Kane, "Resistance/Transformation of the Oppositional Binary: Exposing Sport as a Continuum."

42. María José Martínez-Patiño, "Personal Account: A Woman Tried and Tested," S38.

43. Vines, "Last Olympics for the Sex Test?," 41.

44. Both men and women produce testosterone, as well as estrogen. Androgen insensitivity can range from "partial" to "complete," in which case it is sometimes referred to as testicular feminization. See James E. Griffin, "Androgen Resistance: The Clinical and Molecular Spectrum"; and Malcolm A. Ferguson-Smith and Elizabeth A. Ferris, "Gender Verification in Sport: The Need for Change."

45. Alison Carlson, "When Is a Woman Not a Woman?," 29. The same is true of women with gonadal dysgenesis. See Ferris, "Gender Testing in Sport."

46. See Hipkin, "XY Female in Sport."

47. De la Chapelle, "Use and Misuse of Sex Chromatin Screening," 1922.

48. Martínez-Patiño, "Personal Account," S38.

49. Coroner quoted in "Tests Show Athlete Had 2 Chromosome Types," *New York Times*, February 12, 1981, A2; "Report Says Stella Walsh Had Male Sex Organs," *New York Times*, January 23, 1981, A18; "Women Facing More than an Athletic Struggle," *New York Times*, December 21, 1980, A1. See also Dave Langlais, "The Road Not Taken: The Secret That Didn't Really Matter." Ironically, Polish officials demanded Helen Stephens undergo a sex test after she beat Walsh by 1.8 meters for the gold medal in the 100-meter race. Following Walsh's second-place finish in the 1936 Games, the Polish press insinuated that America's gold medal–winning Helen Stephens was a man. In her biography of Stephens, Sharon Kinney Hanson writes that the athlete's response to such charges was that reporters could "check the facts with the Olympic committee physician who sex-tested all athletes prior to competition." Hanson, *Life of Helen Stephens*, 96.

50. Guttmann, *Women's Sports: A History*, 169.

51. United Press International, "Sports News," December 19, 1980.

52. "U.S. Open Unit Weighs Sex Test for Applicant," *New York Times*, August 12, 1976, 52; Robin Herman, "'No Exceptions,' and No Renee Richards," *New York Times*, August 27, 1976; Susan Birrell and C. L. Cole, "Double Fault: Renee Richards and the Construction

and Naturalization of Difference," 385–86; "Renee Richards Fails Sex Test for Rome Open," *New York Times*, May 15, 1977, 178.

53. *Richards v. USTA,* 1977, quoted in Birrell and Cole, "Double Fault," 374; Pamela B. Fastiff, "Gender Verification Testing: Balancing the Rights of Female Athletes with a Scandal-Free Olympic Games," 960.

54. Hay quoted in Louis J. Elsas et al., "Gender Verification of Female Athletes," 250; Ferguson-Smith and Ferris, "Gender Verification in Sport"; Frederick quoted in Larned, "Femininity Test," 41; Sally Quinn, "Women Pass Test, but Want Respect," *Washington Post*, July 22, 1976, E1. See also Peters with Wooldridge, *Mary P.: Autobiography*, 57.

55. Los Angeles Olympic Organization Committee, *Games of the XXIIIrd Olympiad, Los Angeles 1984, International Olympic Medical Controls Brochure*, 1980, http://www.la84foundation.org; "Sex Test Results Secret," *Washington Post*, July 29, 1984, F7.

56. White quoted in Larned, "Femininity Test," 41; Peters with Wooldridge, *Mary P.: Autobiography*, 57; Elsas et al., "Gender Verification of Female Athletes," 252. Berit Skirstad surveyed 115 female athletes (21 percent of the competitors) at the 1994 Winter Games at Lillehammer and found that "66 per cent of the women said that gender verification was necessary, and approximately the same number found the test useful in that it prevented rumours. Of those interviewed at Lillehammer, 20 per cent expressed the view that the test was humiliating." Skirstad, "Gender Verification in Competitive Sport," 118.

57. Keith Moore, "Sexual Identity of Athletes," 163.

58. Erik Strömgren et al., "A Memorandum on the Use of Sex Chromatin Investigation of Competitors in Women's Divisions of the Olympic Games," February 3, 1972, IOC files, Folder "Danish Report, "Sex Tests," 1972, International Olympic Committee Historical Archives; Ferris, "Gender Testing in Sport," 692.

59. Ferguson-Smith and Ferris, "Gender Verification in Sport"; de la Chapelle, "Use and Misuse of Sex Chromatin Screening"; Albert de la Chapelle, "Gender Verification of Female Athletes"; Joe Leigh Simpson, "Gender Testing in the Olympics," 1986; Arne Ljungqvist, Joe Leigh Simpson, and the IAAF Work Group on Gender Verification, "Medical Examination for Health of All Athletes Replacing the Need for Gender Verification in International Sports: The International Amateur Athletic Plan."

60. Ljungqvist, Simpson, and the IAAF Work Group on Gender Verification, "Medical Examination for Health of All Athletes," 851; Albert de la Chapelle, "Why Sex Chromatin Should Be Abandoned as a Screening Method for 'Gender Verification' of Female Athletes"; de la Chapelle, "Use and Misuse of Sex Chromatin Screening"; Simpson, "Gender Testing in the Olympics," 1938; Ferguson-Smith and Ferris, "Gender Verification in Sport"; Joe Leigh Simpson, Arne Ljungqvist, and Malcolm A. Ferguson-Smith, "Gender Verification in Competitive Sports."

61. Elsas et al., "Gender Verification of Female Athletes," 251; Ljungqvist, Simpson, and the IAAF Work Group on Gender Verification, "Medical Examination for Health of All Athletes," 852.

62. IAAF member Anne Foulkes quoted in Vines, "Last Olympics for the Sex Test?," 39; B. Dickinson et al., "Gender Verification of Female Olympic Athletes," 1541.

63. The IAAF Medical and Anti-Doping Commission 2006, "IAAF Policy on Gender Verification," http://www.iaaf.org/.

64. Joan Stephenson, "Female Olympians' Sex Tests Outmoded," 178. Significantly, at the helm of the Olympic medical commission were the same men who established the original tests in the 1960s.

65. "Experts Slam Olympic Gene Test," 1073. For the 1985 Universiade in Kobe, Japan, technicians screened for both the X chromatin from the buccal smear and the Y chromatin from hair roots. They determined it was "impossible" to obtain a conclusive and reliable diagnosis only by checking the X chromatin and that it was "safer" to screen for the Y. Ultimately, the physicians recommended sports organizations perform both screenings to ensure the most accurate results. Hiromi Sakamoto et al., "Femininity Control at the XXth Universiade in Kobe, Japan."

66. "French Doctor Defends Controversial Sex Tests for Olympic Athletes," *Toronto Star,* January 30, 1992, C8.

67. Vines, "Last Olympics for the Sex Test?," 41.

68. "No Sex Tests, Please . . ."; Christopher Anderson, "Olympic Row over Sex Testing."

69. Elsas et al., "Gender Verification of Female Athletes," 250–51.

70. Anna Kessel, "Semenya Runs into History Books amid Gender Controversy," *Guardian,* August 20, 2009.

71. Jaime Schultz, "Caster Semenya and the 'Question of Too': Sex Testing in Elite Women's Sport and the Issue of Advantage." See also Dee Amy-Chinn, "Doing Epistemic (In)justice to Semenya"; Cheryl Cooky, Ranissa Dycus, and Shari L. Dworkin, "'What Makes a Woman a Woman?' versus 'Our First Lady of Sport': A Comparative Analysis of the United States and the South African Media Coverage of Caster Semenya"; Neville Hoad, "Run, Caster Semenya, Run! Nativism and the Translations of Gender Variance"; Mandy Merck, "The Question of Caster Semenya"; Brenna Munro, "Caster Semenya: Gods and Monsters"; Tavia Nyong'o, "The Unforgivable Transgression of Being Caster Semenya"; Jaime Schultz, "The Accidental Celebritisation of Caster Semenya"; and John M. Sloop, "'This Is Not Natural': Caster Semenya's Gender Threats."

72. IAAF, "Caster Semenya May Compete," July 6, 2010, http://iaaf.org.

73. "IAAF Adopts Eligibility Rules for Hormone Cases," *USA Today,* April 12, 2011, http://www.usatoday.com/sports/olympics/2011–04–12-iaaf—eligibility-rules-hormone -cases_N.htm; "IAAF Regulations Governing Eligibility of Females with Hyperandrogenism to Compete in Women's Competition," http://www.iaaf.org/medical/policy/.

74. Stéphane Bermon et al., "Are the New Policies on Hyperandrogenism in Elite Female Athletes Really Out of Bounds? Response to 'Out of Bounds? A Critique of the New Policies on Hyperandrogenism in Elite Female Athletes,'" 64.

75. Xavier and McGill, "Hyperandrogenism and Intersex Controversies," 3905.

76. Bermon et al., "New Policies on Hyperandrogenism."

77. Katrina Karkazis et al., "Out of Bounds? A Critique of the New Policies on Hyperandrogenism in Elite Female Athletes," 6. See also Jaime Schultz, "New Standards, Same Refrain: The IAAF's Regulations on Hyperandrogenism."

78. Dr. Eric Vilain quoted in Juliet Macur, "I.O.C. Adopts Policy for Deciding Whether an Athlete Can Compete as a Woman," *New York Times,* June 23, 2012, http://www.nytimes .com/2012/06/24/sports/olympics/ioc-adopts-policy-for-deciding-whether-athletes-can -compete-as-women.html.

79. It is not yet known how the policy on hyperandrogenism will affect transathletes who, under the IOC's 2004 "Stockholm Consensus," may be eligible to compete as their reassigned sex. See Shelia L. Cavanagh and Heather Sykes, "Transsexual Bodies at the Olympics: The International Olympic Committee's Policy on Transsexual Athletes at the 2004 Athens Summer Games"; Heather Sykes, "Transsexual and Transgender Policies in Sport"; and Jill Pilgrim, David Martin, and Will Binder, "Far from the Finish Line: Transsexualism and Athletic Competition."

80. Macur, "I.O.C. Adopts Policy."

81. "IOC Regulations on Female Hyperandrogenism," http://www.olympic.org.

82. On the closing of the muscle gap, see Precilla Y. L. Choi, *Femininity and the Physically Active Woman;* and Mariah Burton-Nelson, *Are We Winning Yet? How Women Are Changing Sports and Sports Are Changing Women.*

83. Judith Butler, "Athletic Genders: Hyperbolic Instance and/or the Overcoming of Sexual Binarism," 111.

Chapter 5. From "Women in Sports" to the "New Ideal of Beauty"

1. Between the publication's 1923 advent and 1987, researchers found that women appeared on only 482 (14 percent) of the weekly's 3,386 covers. During this period, editors promoted sportswomen on just 17 (0.5 percent) occasions. Sammye Johnson and William G. Christ, "Women Through Time: Who Gets Covered?"

2. Janet S. Fink and Linda Jean Kensicki, "An Imperceptible Difference: Visual and Textual Constructions of Femininity in *Sports Illustrated* and *Sports Illustrated for Women.*"

3. "Comes the Revolution."

4. Richard Corlis, "The New Ideal of Beauty."

5. Sammye Johnson and William G. Christ, "The Representation of Women: The News Magazine Cover as an International Cultural Artifact," 218; Naomi Wolf, *The Beauty Myth: How Images of Beauty Are Used against Women,* 10.

6. I use the term *public culture* as defined by Meaghan Morris as a "mixture of rituals, beliefs, customs, practices, and images of policy and pleasure created by all those institutions, great and small, state and private, sacred and secular." Morris, *Too Soon Too Late: History in Popular Culture,* 9.

7. Susan Faludi, *Backlash: The Undeclared War against American Women,* xix–xx, xxi–xxii.

8. Gary Wills, *Reagan's America: Innocents at Home,* 1; Sylvia Bashevkin, "Facing a Renewed Right: American Feminism and the Reagan/Bush Challenge," 672.

9. Boutilier and SanGiovanni, *The Sporting Woman,* 36; Festle, *Playing Nice,* 225; Lesley Visser, "Is the Revolution Over? Bright Picture of the 1970s Becomes Bleak," *Chicago Tribune,* November 15, 1987, 15.

10. Bil Gilbert and Nancy Williamson, "Sport Is Unfair to Women." See also Gilbert and Williamson, "Women in Sport: A Progress Report" and "Programmed to Be Losers."

11. Margaret Dunkle quoted in Nadine Brozan, "Girls on the Athletic Field: Small Gains, Long Way to the Goal," *New York Times,* January 12, 1976, 46; "A Woman's Place Is at Home Plate," *Washington Post,* August 11, 1977, A26.

12. Festle, *Playing Nice,* 178.

13. Lucille Magnusson, "The What and Why of AIAW," 71.

14. Margaret Roach, "Issue and Debate: Is Title IX Scoring Many Points in Field of Women's School Sports?," *New York Times*, September 27, 1977, 65.

15. Festle, *Playing Nice*, 178.

16. American College of Sports Medicine, "Opinion Statement on the Participation of the Female Athlete in Long-Distance Running," ix.

17. Anne Ingram and Jennifer Nupp, "Political Backlash and Implications to the Women's Civil Rights Movement Focusing on Sport and Athletic Opportunities for Women."

18. Boutilier and SanGiovanni, *The Sporting Woman*, 39; Marianne Taylor, "Women's Sports Come of Age," *Chicago Tribune*, March 1, 1981, J1, 4; Lichtenstein, *Long Way, Baby*, 26.

19. King with Starr, *We Have Come a Long Way*, 146.

20. Roberts, *Necessary Spectacle*, 93. In 1973 editor and publisher Marlene Jensen debuted the *Sportswoman*.

21. Lynn Zinser, "35 Years of Equity: NHL's Decision to Allow Women to Join Locker-Room Interviews Started Change," *Winston-Salem (N.C.) Journal*, January 25, 2010, http://www2.journalnow.com/sports/2010/jan/25/35-years-of-equity-nhls-decision-to-allow-women-to-ar-179269/.

22. Gary Deeb, "Get Used to It . . . Women Sportscasters to Stay," *Chicago Tribune*, August 12, 1975, C1. Throughout the 1970s and into present-day sports coverage, women journalists continue to face debilitating sex discrimination. See Marie Hardin and Stacie Shain, "Strength in Numbers? The Experiences and Attitudes of Women in Sports Media Careers"; and Pamela Creedon, ed., *Women, Media, and Sport: Challenging Gender Values*.

23. Jan Felshin, "The Social Anomaly of Women in Sports," 124.

24. U.S. Commission on Civil Rights, "More Hurdles to Clear: Women and Girls in Competitive Athletics," 2, 11.

25. Taylor, "Women's Sports Come of Age," J1, 4; "This Is What You Thought about . . . Women and Sports," 33.

26. Joanna Bunker Rohrbaugh, "Femininity on the Line." See also Mary Duquin, "The Importance of Sport in Building Women's Potential."

27. Ann Crittenden Scott, "Closing the Muscle Gap," 89; Marilynn Preston, "Women in Sports: A 'Fad' Gains Big Yardage," *Chicago Tribune*, January 27, 1975, C5, 8.

28. Visser, "Is the Revolution Over?," 15; Susan Jeffords, *Hard Bodies: Hollywood Masculinity in the Reagan Era*, 5.

29. Fred C. Davison, "Intercollegiate Athletics and Title IX: Equal Opportunity or Federal Incursion," *USA Today*, July 1979, 37.

30. Fields, *Female Gladiators*, 14; George Vecsey, "Help on Way for Title IX," *New York Times*, April 22, 1984, S3.

31. Welch Suggs, *A Place on the Team: The Triumph and Tragedy of Title IX*, 76–77.

32. Davison, "Intercollegiate Athletics," 37; Jerrold K. Footlick, "Of Sports, Sex, and Money," 98; John Underwood, "An Odd Way to Even Things Up."

33. Hugh Davis Graham, "The Storm over Grove City College: Civil Rights Regulation, Higher Education, and the Reagan Administration"; Sheryl Sklorman, "Girl Athletes, Citizen Activists, Title IX: The Three Point Play," 330; Candace Lyle Hogan, "Revolutionizing School and Sports: 10 Years of Title IX," 26.

34. Candace Lyle Hogan, "Sports Opinion: Time to Enforce Anti–Sex Bias Law," *Chicago Tribune,* November 4, 1979, C8.

35. Graham, "Storm over Grove City College," 418.

36. Festle, *Playing Nice,* 130; Ingram and Nupp, "Political Backlash," 7.

37. See Ying Wushanley, *Playing Nice and Losing: The Struggle for Control of Women's Intercollegiate Athletics, 1960–2000.*

38. One year earlier, the NCAA voted to hold women's Division II and III national championships in basketball, field hockey, swimming, tennis, and volleyball.

39. R. Vivian Acosta and Linda Jean Carpenter, "Women in Intercollegiate Sport: A Longitudinal, National Study, Twenty-Seven Year Update, 1977–2004"; G. Ann Uhlir, "Athletics and the University: The Post-woman's Era."

40. Sarah Ballard, "The Most Powerful Woman in Sports"; G. Ann Uhlir, "Women's Sports Education Today," 35; Festle, *Playing Nice,* 199–227; Visser, "Is the Revolution Over?," 15; Ingram and Nupp, "Political Backlash," 1.

41. Faludi, *Backlash,* 205.

42. Philip H. Dougherty, "Defining 'a Charlie' for Revlon," *New York Times,* November 28, 1986, D7.

43. Gil Troy, *Morning in America: How Ronald Reagan Invented the 1980s,* 3.

44. Lin Fassnacht quoted in Judith Zimmer, "Toy Makers Putting Muscle behind Kids' Fitness."

45. An interesting counterpart to "Get in Shape, Girl!" is the Hulkamania Workout Set that debuted in 1985. Marketed as a "complete exercise program for boys" who wanted to "get muscles" like their favorite professional wrestlers, the kit came with wrist- and headbands, a hand-gripper, two 2.5-pound dumbbells, a "Workout Chart" poster, and a cassette tape on which wrestler Hulk Hogan guided listeners through a forty-minute routine. The set had striking similarities to "Get in Shape, Girl!" but when Hogan asked the pint-sized Hulkamaniacs, "Are you in shape yet?" the meaning was decidedly different.

46. Fassnacht quoted in Zimmer, "Toy Makers Putting Muscle behind Kids' Fitness."

47. King, "Publisher's Letter," *womenSports,* June 1974, 4; Wright quoted in Jay Searcy, "Magazine Venture Is a Risky Game for Mrs. King," *New York Times,* September 8, 1974, 248.

48. Editor's letter, *Women's Sports,* December 1979, 4.

49. Boutilier and SanGiovanni, *The Sporting Woman,* 216–17.

50. Margaret Carlisle Duncan, "The Politics of Women's Body Images and Practices: Foucault, the Panopticon, and *Shape* Magazine"; Mary E. Duquin, "Fashion and Fitness: Images in Women's Magazine Ads"; Tina B. Eskes, Margaret Carlisle Duncan, and Eleanor M. Miller, "The Discourse of Empowerment: Foucault, Marcuse, and Women's Fitness Texts"; Joseph Maguire and Louise Mansfield, "'No-Body's Perfect': Women, Aerobics, and the Body Beautiful"; Pirkko Markula, "Firm but Shapely, Fit but Sexy, Strong but Thin: The Postmodern Aerobicizing Female Bodies" and "Beyond the Perfect Body: Women's Body Image Distortion in Fitness Magazine Discourse."

51. Virginia M. Leath and Angela Lumpkin, "An Analysis of Sportswomen on the Covers and in the Feature Articles of *Women's Sports and Fitness* Magazine, 1975–1989," 124. See also Barbara L. Endel, "Working Out: The Dialectic of Strength and Sexuality in

Women's Sport & Fitness Magazine"; and Janis Karen Bateman, "Billie Jean King's Publishing Adventure: A Documentary on the Evolution of *womenSports* Magazine from March 1973 through May 1975."

52. In 1998 Condé Nast, publisher of *Vogue* and *Architectural Digest,* acquired *Women's Sport & Fitness,* melding it with their previous publication *Condé Nast Sports for Women.* For financial reasons, the magazine folded in 2000.

53. Bill Mandel, "She's Got a Ticket to Ride," 29; Paddy Calistro, "Exercising Moderation No-Pain, No-Gain Workouts Aren't Winning the War on Fat," *Los Angeles Times,* January 18, 1987, 26; J. D. Reed, "America Shapes Up"; Nicolaus Mills, ed., *Culture in an Age of Money: The Legacy of the 1980s in America,* 23.

54. Jeffords, *Hard Bodies,* 24.

55. Margaret Morse, "Artemis Aging: Exercise and the Female Body on Video," 23; Fawn Vrazo, "Kicking Up Their Heels for Fitness," *Philadelphia Inquirer,* September 26, 1982; Diana Benzaia, "The Fitness Game," 116.

56. Stephanie L. Twin, *Out of the Bleachers: Writings on Women and Sport,* xxxvi, xxxix; Elaine Louie, "Working Out," *New York Times,* August 30, 1981, 298.

57. Paddy Calistro, "Exercising Moderation," 26; John Gorman, "Health Craze Helping Keep Industry Fit," *Chicago Tribune,* September 20, 1985, B1–2.

58. Allan Parachini, "New Aerobics Guidelines Announced by Women's Health Care Specialists," *Los Angeles Times,* May 6, 1986.

59. Lenskyj, *Out of Bounds;* Moya Lloyd, "Feminism Aerobics, and the Politics of the Body"; Maguire and Mansfield, "'No-Body's Perfect.'"

60. Hargreaves, *Sporting Females,* 160.

61. Kaori O'Connor, "The Body and the Brand: How Lycra Shaped America," 223. See also Tara Brabazon, "Fitness Is a Feminist Issue."

62. Markula, "Firm but Shapely"; Leslea Haravon Collins, "Working Out the Contradictions: Feminism and Aerobics."

63. Morse, "Artemis Aging," 83; Elaine Louie, "Working Out," *New York Times,* August 30, 1981, 298; Barry Glassner, "Fitness and the Postmodern Self," 186.

64. See, for example, "Perfecting Your Body"; "Why Aren't These Bodies Perfect?"; and Deborah Jamail, "How to Look and Feel Like a Winner."

65. Susan Bordo, *Unbearable Weight: Feminism, Western Culture, and the Body,* 195; Morse, "Artemis Aging," 88.

66. Kenneth H. Cooper, *Aerobics,* 39, 43.

67. Jacki Sorensen with Bill Bruns, *Aerobic Dancing,* 10.

68. Elizabeth Kagan and Margaret Morse, "The Body Electronic: Aerobic Exercise on Video; Women's Search for Empowerment and Self-Transformation," 165.

69. Susan Willis, "Work(ing) Out," 5.

70. Kagan and Morse, "Body Electronic," 165.

71. Gail Buchalter, "Richard Simmons, Diana Ross, and Jane Fonda Help Aerobic Dance LPs Boogie Up the Charts," 76.

72. Janet Jones, "Women in Motion," in *Our Bodies, Ourselves: A Book by and for Women,* by the Boston Women's Health Book Collective, 43.

73. Corlis, "New Ideal of Beauty"; J. Jones, "Women in Motion," 43; Jack McCallum, "Everybody's Doin' It," 76.

74. McCallum, "Everybody's Doin' It," 76.

75. O'Connor, "Body and the Brand," 225.

76. Judy Klemesrud, "Gym Clothes: Exercises in Style," *New York Times,* March 2, 1983, C1, C10.

77. Blair Sabol, *The Body of America,* 72; Deborah Hofman, "The Fashion of Getting Fit," *New York Times,* November 5, 1989, 78.

78. Gene Siskel, "Jamie Lee and the Curse of Overcoming a 'Perfect' Body," *Chicago Tribune,* June 2, 1985, 7; Siskel, "As an Exercise in Commentary, 'Perfect' Doesn't Live Up to Its Name," *Chicago Tribune,* June 7, 1985, A.

79. Julie Salamon, "Deep Thought's a Bad Source for Aerobic Editor," *Wall Street Journal,* June 6, 1985, 1.

80. Chris Jordan, "Gender and Class Mobility in *Saturday Night Fever* and *Flashdance,*" 121; Laurie Jane Schulze, "'Getting Physical': Text/Context/Reading and the Made-for-Television Movie," 44; Nancy Theberge, "Sport and Women's Empowerment," 389; Lenskyj, *Out of Bounds,* 129.

81. Kathryn Lance and Maria Agardy, "Sexual Fitness"; Jack Hofer, "Mixing Fitness with Pleasure," 40–41.

82. Helen Burggraf, "Bonnie August Shapes Up Sales with Fashion-Charged Bodywear," *Crain's New York Business,* August 14, 1986; Denise K. Moss, "Aerobics That Emphasize Safety Fitness Centers Join the Trend toward 'Lite,'" *Los Angeles Times,* December 10, 1985; Lee A. Rothenberger, June I. Chang, and Thomas A. Cable, "Prevalence and Types of Injuries in Aerobic Dancers."

83. Calistro, "Exercising Moderation," 26.

84. Elaine Tarantin, "Aerobics Competition Yesterday, Tomorrow, and Today," 49; Doug Smith, "Aerobic 'Athletes' Flex, Leap among Shoppers," *Los Angeles Times,* June 3, 1985, 6.

85. Mandel, "She's Got a Ticket to Ride," 29; Sandra Lee Bartky, "Foucault, Femininity, and the Modernization of Patriarchal Power," 64; Morse, "Artemis Aging," 24.

86. Fields, *Female Gladiators,* 13.

87. Suggs, *Place on the Team,* 94.

88. See David Owen, "Title IX Babies."

89. "Winter Wonders"; "To Be the Best"; "Gym Dandy"; "What a Kick!"

Chapter 6. A Cultural History of the Sports Bra

1. "What a Kick!"

2. Brandi Chastain with Gloria Averbuch, *It's Not about the Bra,* xvi–xvii.

3. Tim Crothers, "Spectacular Takeoff." See also Michael A. Messner, Margaret Carlisle Duncan, and Cheryl Cooky, "Silence, Sports Bras, and Wrestling Porn."

4. Dowling, *The Frailty Myth;* "Women in the Water," *New York Times,* July 7, 1895, 21; Alexander Wolff and Christian Stone, "She Said, He Said," 16. That breasts should somehow hinder women's athletic performance has been connected with multiple sports. As Dr. Frederick Rand Rogers argued in 1929, "The female torso" is "poorly adapted to running. No matter how well developed are the limbs, naturally developed hips and bust always provide handicaps and positive impediments to the rapid forward motion necessary for victory." Rogers, "Olympics for Girls?," 192. In 1967 *Today's Health* advised against sports

because "the female breasts and other organs can be injured seriously by a sudden blow." Rose Higdon and Hal Higdon, "What Sports for Girls?," 21.

5. Cathy Starr et al., "Biomechanical Analysis of a Prototype Sports Bra," 2; Gale Gehlsen and Lela June Stoner, "The Female Breast in Sport and Exercise," 20. See also C. E. Haycock, "Breast Support and Protection in the Female Athlete," 1:50–53.

6. Marilyn Yalom, *A History of the Breast,* 23.

7. Miranda Seymour, *Bugatti Queen: In Search of a French Racing Legend,* 26; "Pour le Sport."

8. J. Phillips and P. Phillips, "History from Below."

9. Hugh M. Lee, "Athletics and the Bikini Girls from Piazza Armerina," 62.

10. Phillis E. Cunnington and Alan Mansfield, *English Costume for Sports and Outdoor Recreation: From the Sixteenth to Nineteenth Centuries,* 361.

11. Carter, *Underwear: The Fashion History;* Stanley, *Rise and Fall of the Sportswoman,* 93. See also J. Phillips and P. Phillips, "History from Below," 138; and Elizabeth Ewing, *Underwear: A History* and *Dress and Undress: A History of Women's Underwear.*

12. Jane Farrell-Beck and Colleen Gau, *Uplift: The Bra in America,* 25, 39. They found that the first U.S. patent for a brassiere was filed in 1863.

13. Willett and Cunnington, *The History of Underclothes,* 242; Farrell-Beck and Gau, *Uplift,* 31.

14. Sophie C. Eliott-Lynn, *Athletics for Women and Girls: How to Be an Athlete and Why,* 23. Frederick Annesley Michael Webster also emphasized the importance of breast support for female athletes in *Athletics of To-Day for Women,* 261.

15. "How Two Women Changed Boston Marathon History," April 9, 2012, http://boston.cbslocal.com/2012/04/09/how-two-women-changed-boston-marathon-history/.

16. David Sharp, "The Women Who Took the Jounce Out of Jogging," 25.

17. Mary Barr, "Women Runners Full of Praise for Sports Bra," *Cleveland Plain Dealer,* November 11, 1997.

18. Diana Nyad and Candace Lyle Hogan, "Women: Empowered by the Evolution of Sports Technology," 49.

19. C. Starr et al., "Biomechanical Analysis of a Prototype Sports Bra," 2.

20. Gloria Averbuch, *The Woman Runner: Free to Be the Complete Athlete,* 163, 90; Signy Peck, "The Bra: Brandi's Public Peeldown Turned the Spotlight on the Humble Sports Bra," *Sports for Women,* 1999, http://www.sportsforwomen.com/features/year/1999/feat_bra1.html; Ann Gerhart, "Cashing in on World Cups," *Washington Post,* July 14, 1999, C1.

21. Sandra Dolbow, "Champion Sports Bra: Not for Jocks," 9.

22. Jeré Longman, "How the Women Won," 25.

23. Flip Bondy, "Women's Sports Have Arrived . . . So Deal with It," *New York Daily News,* March 23, 1997, 81; Sarah Banet-Weiser, "Hoop Dreams: Professional Basketball and the Politics of Race and Gender."

24. See Mary McDonald, "The Marketing of the Women's National Basketball Association and the Making of Postfeminism."

25. Donna de Verona, "Women's Standard Is Lifted to New Level by World Cup," *USA Today,* August 5, 1999, E3.

26. Harvey Araton, "The New Rules of the Game," 62.

27. R. Vivian Acosta and Linda Jean Carpenter, *Women in Intercollegiate Sport: A Longitudinal Study* (2000), ERIC database.

28. On women's sports in the 1990s, see Nancy E. Spencer and Lisa R. McClung, "Women and Sport in the 1990s: Reflections on 'Embracing Stars, Ignoring Players'"; and Festle, *Playing Nice*, 265–82.

29. Welch Suggs, "Left Behind."

30. In 1972 colleges and universities offered an average of just two athletic teams for women. By 1978, the year of mandatory compliance with Title IX, that number reached 5.61 teams per school. As the twentieth century drew to a close, the number of collegiate sports teams for women reached an all-time high of 8.14, marking phenomenal growth in a relatively short period of time. Acosta and Carpenter, "Women in Intercollegiate Sport."

31. See "The Women's Sports Foundation Report: Addressing the Needs of Female Professional and Amateur Athletes," 1999, http://www.womenssportsfoundation.org/Content/Research-Reports/The-Womens-Sports-Foundation-Report-Addressing-the-Needs-of-Female-Professional-and-Amateur-Athletes.aspx.

32. M. Starr, Brant, and Register, "It Went Down to the Wire," 46.

33. Stephen A. Smith, "Peace Plan," *Philadelphia Inquirer,* January 8, 1999, D1; Ken Wright, "ABL [American Basketball League] Demise Expands Talent, Reduces Jobs," *Washington Times,* February 8, 1999, B7.

34. Between 1991 and 1995, the LPGA's event winnings went from $496,000 to $642,105. In 1995 there were ten LPGA events broadcast on network television, compared to the PGA's thirty and the seniors' twenty. Leonard Shapiro, "LPGA Tries to Wedge into Market," *Washington Post,* May 24, 1995, B1; Shapiro, "Golf Analyst Denies Making Sexist Remarks," *Washington Post,* May 13, 1995, A1.

35. Michael A. Messner, *Taking the Field: Women, Men, and Sports,* 95 (emphasis in original).

36. See, for example, Susan Tyler Eastman and Andrew C. Billings, "Gender Parity in the Olympics: Hyping Women Athletes, Favoring Men Athletes"; Ray Jones, Audrey J. Murrell, and Jennifer Jackson, "Pretty versus Powerful in the Sports Pages"; Mary Jo Kane and Susan L. Greendorfer, "The Media's Role in Accommodating and Resisting Stereotyped Images of Women in Sport"; Nathalie Koivula, "Gender Stereotyping in Televised Media Sport Coverage"; Mary Schmitt, "The State of Women in Sports Media"; C. A. Tuggle and Anne Owen, "A Descriptive Analysis of NBC's Coverage of the Centennial Olympics: The 'Games of the Women'?"; Susan Birrell and Nancy Theberge, "Ideological Control of Women in Sport"; Gina Daddario, "Chilly Scenes of the 1992 Winter Games: The Mass Media and the Marginalization of Female Athletes"; Margaret Carlisle Duncan, "Sports Photographs and Sexual Difference: Images of Women and Men in the 1984 and 1988 Olympic Games"; Janet S. Fink, "Female Athletes and the Media: Strides and Stalemates"; James R. Hallmark and Richard N. Armstrong, "Gender Equity in Televised Sports: A Comparative Analysis of Men's and Women's NCAA Division I Basketball Championships Broadcasts, 1991–1995"; Catriona T. Higgs and Karen H. Weiller, "Gender Bias and the 1992 Summer Olympic Games: An Analysis of Television Coverage"; Katherine N. Kinnick, "Gender Bias in Newspaper Profiles of 1996 Olympic Athletes: A Content Analysis of Five Major Dailies"; and Daniel L. Wann et al., "The Inequitable Newspaper Coverage of Men's and Women's Athletics at Small, Medium, and Large Universities."

37. Jon Wertheim, *Venus Envy: A Sensational Season Inside the Women's Tennis Tour.*

38. "Women in Uniform," 39; Marcus Christenson and Paul Kelso, "Soccer Chief's Play to Boost Women's Game? Hotpants," *Guardian,* January 16, 2004, http://www.guardian.co.uk/uk/2004/jan/16/football.gender.

39. Mark Soltau, "Giving Women's Golf a Makeover," *San Francisco Examiner,* June 5, 1994, D1, D9. See also Todd W. Crosset, *Outsiders in the Clubhouse: The World of Women's Professional Golf.*

40. Leonard Shapiro, "LPGA Tries to Wedge into Market," *Washington Post,* May 24, 1995, B1. Pat Griffin similarly notes that the 1996 gold medal–winning U.S. softball team received makeovers before appearing on the *Oprah Winfrey Show.* Griffin, *Strong Women,* 71.

41. T. Miller, *Sportsex,* 13.

42. Jack McCallum, "Unflagging."

43. Kelley Anderson, "The Other Side of Jenny," 120–21 (emphasis in original); Joanna Cagan, "Objects of the Game," *Village Voice,* August 29, 2000, http://www.villagevoice.com.

44. Photos appeared in the June and October 1999 issues of *Gear.*

45. Jeré Longman, *The Girls of Summer: The U.S. Women's Soccer Team and How It Changed the World,* 224.

46. Laurie Schulze, "On the Muscle."

47. See Jaime Schultz, "Discipline and Push-Up: Female Bodies, Femininity and Sexuality in Popular Representations of Sports Bras."

48. Ann Gerhart, "Cashing in on World Cups," *Washington Post,* July 14, 1999, C1.

49. Robin Givhan, "Winner Takes (Off) All," *Washington Post,* July 13, 2001, C2.

50. Melanie Wells and Ann Oldenburg, "Sports Bra's Flash Could Cash In," *USA Today,* July 13, 1999, A1.

51. Rebecca Mead, "The Talk of the Town," 25.

52. Randy Harvey, "With So Much Exposure, Brandi Can Bare Her Soul," *Los Angeles Times,* December 2, 1999, D2; Steve Hummer, "Soccer's Fairy-Tale Story Has Silver End," *Atlanta Journal and Constitution,* September 29, 2000, E8; Paige Smoron, "A Nice Hamm," *Chicago Sun-Times,* July 25, 1999; Peck, "The Bra"; Nicole Brodeur, "World Cup Bra Incident Uplifts Girls," *Seattle Times,* August 26, 1999; Elise Ackerman, "She Kicks. She Scores. She Sells," *U.S. News & World Report,* July 26, 1999, 42; Mike Penner, "Moment's Over: Now U.S. Soccer Hero Chastain Can Get Back to Game," *Los Angeles Times,* September 12, 2000, D1; Alex Tresniowski, "Soccer's Happiest Feat," 56.

53. Michael Hiestand, "Moment Spurs a Movement," *USA Today,* October 28, 1999, C3; Joey Bartolomeo, "Sports Style: Underwear Busts Out," 42 (emphasis in original).

54. Willis, "Work(ing) Out."

55. Ibid., 7; Robert Goldman, Deborah Heath, and Sharon L. Smith, "Commodity Feminism," 338. See also Bordo, *Unbearable Weight.*

56. Dennis Hall, "Spears' Space: The Play of Innocence and Experience in the Bare-Midriff Fashion."

57. M. Ann Hall, *Feminism and Sporting Bodies,* 60; Leslie Heywood, *Bodymakers: A Cultural Anatomy of Women's Body Building,* 55.

58. Mark Hyman, "The 'Babe Factor' in Women's Soccer," 118. See also Rebecca Sullivan, "Goodbye Heroin Chic. Now It's Sexy to Be Strong," 62.

59. Holly Brubach, "The Athletic Aesthetic"; Alisa Solomon, "Our Bodies, Ourselves," *Village Voice*, April 19–25, 2000, http://www.villagevoice.com.

60. Shortly after the 1999 Women's World Cup, a commercial appeared on ESPN depicting Chastain playing foosball with three men, including professional basketball player Kevin Garnett. When Chastain scores, the men turn to her and wait. Finally, Garnett breaks the silence, asking "What's up with the shirt?" In another incident before a San Francisco '49ers game, a man asked Chastain, "Are you going to take off your shirt?" Chastain obliged by lifting up her sweatshirt to reveal a '49ers jersey. Harvey, "With So Much Exposure," D2; Brandi Chastain, "A Whole New Ball Game," 76. Even as the U.S. team took the field during the 2000 Olympics in Sydney, Australia, spectators held up signs reading, "Show us your sports bra," in "More Brandi, Please," *San Diego Union-Tribune*, September 30, 2000, 2.

61. Iris Marion Young, "Breasted Experience: The Look and the Feeling," 126.

62. Dee Amy-Chinn, "This Is Just for Me(n): How the Regulation of Post-Feminist Lingerie Advertising Perpetuates Woman as Object," 156 (emphasis in original); Robert Goldman and Stephen Papson, *Nike Culture: The Sign of the Swoosh*, 135; Nike, "After Years of Exercise," *Women's Sports & Fitness* (September–October 1999): 96–97.

63. Iris Marion Young, *Throwing Like a Girl, and Other Essays in Feminist Philosophy and Social Theory*, 190.

64. Champion, "Get In Shape," *Women's Sport & Fitness* (September 2000): 62.

65. I. Young, "Breasted Experience," 129.

66. Emily Scardino, "Women's Activewear Concept Stores Grow," 15.

67. Lucy, "The Uniboob Epiphany," *Women's Sport & Fitness* (September 2000): 52.

68. Myra MacDonald, *Representing Women: Myths of Femininity in the Popular Media*, 92; Goldman, Heath, and Smith, "Commodity Feminism," 336. See also C. L. Cole and Amy Hribar, "Celebrity Feminism: Nike Style, Post-Fordism, Transcendence, and Consumer Power."

69. Wendy A. Burns-Ardolino, "Reading Woman: Displacing the Foundations of Femininity," 54.

70. By that same token, it is important to acknowledge that some men, including those with gynocomastia, also wear similar versions of breast support.

71. Quoted in Hyman, "'Babe Factor' in Women's Soccer," 118.

72. Messner, *Taking the Field*.

Chapter 7. Something to Cheer About?

1. Maryland won these titles at the National Cheerleaders Association (NCA) tournament, held each year in Daytona, Florida. They won again in 2010. Beginning in 2011, Maryland and the other NCATA squads competed in their own NCATA national championships. The University of Oregon won the national titles in 2011, 2012, and 2013.

2. "NCSTA Meet," February 12, 2010. The program's date was incorrect. It should have indicated February 13. There are currently six events in an NCATA meet. See table 1 for clarification.

3. Oregon coach Felecia Mulkey explained that the name change was, in part, a suggestion of USA Gymnastics, which sanctions the NCATA meets. The predominant use

of the word *stunts* is a cheerleading term, whereas *acrobatics* refers to a specific style of gymnastics. Phone interview with author, June 24, 2011.

4. NCATA, "FAQ-Media," accessed September 17, 2011, http://www.thencata.org/faq-2 .html.

5. "Go Team!" See also Erin E. Bezuvis, "The Feminist Case for the NCAA's Recognition of Competitive Cheer as an Emerging Sport for Women."

6. Paul Steinbach, "Stunted Growth."

7. Pamela J. Bettis and Natalie Guice Adams, "Short Skirts and Breast Juts: Cheerleading, Eroticism, and Schools," 122–23.

8. "Leading Penn's Cheers," *Washington Post*, March 5, 1909, IB9.

9. Charles Thomas Hatton and Robert W. Hatton, "The Sideline Show."

10. "Organized Cheering," 5–6; Mary Ellen Hanson, *Go! Fight! Win! Cheerleading in American Culture*, 13.

11. Arturo F. Gonzales, "The First College Cheer," 103.

12. Hanson, *Go! Fight! Win!*, 121.

13. "The College Cheerleader," *Washington Post*, March 22, 1907, R19; "Picking the All-American Cheer Leaders," *Washington Post*, December 10, 1916, MT4.

14. See, for example, Ruby Smith, "Howard Fans Cheer Bisons to Victory over Lincoln," *Afro-American*, December 6, 1947, 11; "Indifferent Cheer Leaders Blamed for Harvard Defeats," *New York Times*, December 10, 1924, 29.

15. "Learned Cheer Leaders," *New York Times*, March 11, 1934.

16. "Sport: All-America."

17. Hanson, *Go! Fight! Win!*, 15; Marisa Walker, "Great Dates in Cheer," 42. Historically, as Vern Bullough notes in *The Subordinate Sex*, as women have entered particular professions, such as clerical work, elementary school teaching, and nursing, men have vacated those vocations for more powerful positions within those fields (employer, principal, physician).

18. "Sport: All-America."

19. "Girl Cheer Leaders for Pitt," *New York Times*, April 18, 1954, S7.

20. John J. Gach, "The Case for and against Girl Cheerleaders," 301–2.

21. Molly Engelhardt, "'Airheads, Amazons, and Bitches': Cheerleaders and Second-Wave Feminists in the Popular Press," 58.

22. Natalie Guice Adams and Pamela J. Bettis, *Cheerleader: An American Icon*, 29.

23. Gonzales, "The First College Cheer," 104; Michael Oriard, *King Football: Sport and Spectacle in the Golden Age of Radio and Newsreels, Movies and Magazines, the Weekly and the Daily Press*, 180–81.

24. James McElroy, *We've Got Spirit: The Life and Times of America's Greatest Cheerleading Team*, 58; Laurel R. Davis, "Male Cheerleading and the Naturalization of Gender," 153.

25. "Owner of 3 Companies Is Leading in Cheers," *New York Times*, October 28, 1972, 39, 45.

26. Pamela Grundy, *Learning to Win: Sports, Education, and Social Change in Twentieth-Century North Carolina*, 285–87.

27. See, for example, "White Pupils End Boycott of School in Madison, Ill.," *New York Times*, November 30, 1967, 36. In 1969 students at a high school in Crystal City, Texas—with a student population that was 85 percent Latino—staged a monthlong walkout to the lack of Mexican American representation on the squad.

28. Randy Neil, *The Encyclopedia of Cheerleading*, 75; Hatton and Hatton, "The Sideline Show," 27; L. Davis, "Male Cheerleading and the Naturalization of Gender."

29. Suggs, *Place on the Team*, 73.

30. Judy Klemesrud, "Still the Rah-Rah, but Some Aren't Cheering," *New York Times*, October 11, 1971, 44.

31. Amy Argetsinger, "When Cheerleaders Are the Main Event," *Washington Post*, July 10, 1999.

32. Adams and Bettis, *Cheerleader: An American Icon*, 111.

33. Laura Grindstaff, "Hold That (Gender) Line! Cheerleading on ESPN."

34. Kate Torgovnick, *Cheer! Inside the Secret World of College Cheerleaders*, xvii.

35. Frederick O. Mueller, "Cheerleading Injuries and Safety," 565.

36. Sonja Steptoe, "The Pom-Pom Chronicles."

37. Brenda J. Shields and Gary A. Smith, "Cheerleading-Related Injuries to Children 5 to 18 Years of Age: United States, 1990–2002." In a subsequent study, Shields and Smith determined that the rate of injury in cheerleading may be overreported and sensationalized. Shields and Smith, "Cheerleading-Related Injuries in the United States: A Prospective Surveillance Study."

38. Frederick O. Mueller and Robert C. Cantu, "Catastrophic Sports Injury Research: Twenty-Eighth Annual Report, Fall 1982–Spring 2010," http://www.unc.edu/depts/nccsi.

39. See Council on Sports Medicine and Fitness, "Cheerleading Injuries: Epidemiology and Recommendations for Prevention."

40. American Association of Cheerleading Coaches and Administrators, "Position Paper: Addressing the Issue of Cheerleading as a Sport," http://aacca.org/content.aspx?item=Resources/Test.xml.

41. For more on NCAA Emerging Sports, see NCAA, "Emerging Sports for Women," http://www.ncaa.org/wps/portal/ncaahome?WCM_GLOBAL_CONTEXT=/ncaa/NCAA/About+The+NCAA/Diversity+and+Inclusion/Gender+Equity+and+Title+IX/New+Emerging+Sports+for+Women.

42. College Stunt Association, http://www.collegeStunt.org/index.php.

43. Mulkey interview.

44. "NCA College Nationals Eligibility FAQ's," http://nca.varsity.com/college_nationals.aspx; "Two Cheers."

45. The NCAA recently recommended that the two organizations work together to promote one version of their sport, but USA Gymnastics will not work with a division of Varsity Brands, while Varsity Brands is loath to acquiesce control over its cheer dominion. The coming months, perhaps years, will undoubtedly bring even more controversy.

46. National Federation of State High School Associations 2010–2011 Athletics Participation Summary, http://www.nfhs.org/content.aspx?id=3282.

47. NCATA official website, http://www.thencata.org/index.html; Alissa Figueroa, "Cheerleading May Not Be a Sport, but It Is an Industry," *Christian Science Monitor*, July 22, 2010, http://www.csmonitor.com/Business/new-economy/2010/0722/Cheerleading-may-not-be-a-sport-but-it-is-an-industry.

48. Adams and Bettis, *Cheerleader: An American Icon*, 92; Moneque Walker Pickett, Marvin P. Dawkins, and Jomills Henry Braddock II, "The Effect of Title IX on Participation of Black and White Females in High School Sports: Evidence from National Longitudinal Surveys," 88; Sarah K. Fields, "Title IX and African-American Female Athletes."

49. Katie Abbondanza, "Bring It On"; Natalie Guice Adams and Pamela J. Bettis, "Alpha Girls and Cheerleading: Negotiating New Discourses with Old Practices," 159.

50. "FAQ," NCATA official website, http://thencata.org/home-2/faq/; Jarnell Bonds, interview with the author, March 9, 2010, College Park, Md.

51. The event was organized by Spirit Unlimited, an East Coast cheerleading and dance company.

52. Amy Moritz, "Cheerleading: Not Just for the Sidelines Anymore," 668. See also Molly Quinn, "Getting Thrown Around."

53. Adams and Bettis, "Alpha Girls and Cheerleading," 161.

54. See, for example, Leslie Heywood and Jennifer Drake, *Third Wave Agenda: Being Feminist, Doing Feminism;* Jennifer Baumgardner and Amy Richards, *Manifesta: Young Women, Feminism, and the Future;* and Leslie Heywood and Shari L. Dworkin, *Built to Win: The Female Athlete as Cultural Icon.*

55. James A. Michener, *Sports in America,* 141–42.

Epilogue

1. Paul Haven, "Olympics 2012: Year of the Woman." For a critique of this, see Rachael Larimore, "Why Are American Women Winning So Many Medals? It's Not Just Because of Title IX."

2. Twin, *Out of the Bleachers,* xxxvi, xxxix; Rohrbaugh, "Femininity on the Line."

3. Ellen J. Staurowsky et al., *Her Life Depends on It II: Sport, Physical Activity, and the Health and Well-Being of American Girls and Women;* Marilie D. Gammon, Julie A. Britton, and Susan L. Teitelbaum, "Does Physical Activity Reduce the Risk of Breast Cancer?"; James Jaccard and Tonya Dodge, "Participation in Athletics and Female Sexual Risk Behavior: The Evaluation of Four Causal Structures"; Deborah A. Cohen et al., "Availability of High School Extracurricular Sports Programs and High Risk Behaviors."

4. Martha Brady, "Olympics Remind Us That Sports Can Empower Women in Developing Countries," *Newsday,* August 10, 2012, http://www.newsday.com/opinion/oped/brady-olympics-remind-us-that-sports-can-empower-women-in-developing-countries-1.3895855.

5. Nilanjana Bhowmick, "India's Golden Girls: How Sport and the Olympics Can Uplift Women"; UN Women, "UN Women Signs Partnership Agreement with the International Olympic Committee to Advance Gender Equity," August 23, 2012, http://www.unwomen.org/2012/08/un-women-signs-partnership-agreement-with-the-international-olympic-committee-to-advance-gender-equality/.

6. Robert Kaestner and Xin Xu, "Effects of Title IX and Sports Participation on Girls' Physical Activity and Weight."

7. Robert Kaestner and Xin Xu, "Title IX, Girls' Sports Participation, and Adult Female Physical Activity and Weight." See also Michael W. Beets and Kenneth H. Pitetti, "Contribution of Physical Education and Sport to Health-Related Fitness in High School Students."

8. National Coalition for Women and Girls in Education, *Title IX at 40: Working to Ensure Gender Equity in Education,* 14; Don Sabo and Phil Veliz, "Go Out and Play: Youth Sports in America"; Child Trends Databank, "Participation in School Athletics: Indicators on Children and Youth"; Matthew Taylor and Greg M. Turek, "If Only She Would Play?

The Impact of Sports Participation on Self-Esteem, School Adjustment, and Substance Use among Rural and Urban African American Girls."

9. Amy Wilson, *The Status of Women in Intercollegiate Athletics.*

10. See Kate Fagan and Luke Cyphers, "Five Myths about Title IX."

11. Michael A. Messner and Cheryl Cooky, "Gender in Televised Sports: News and Highlights Shows, 1989–2009."

12. "Record Number of Females to Take Part in London 2012"; "Paralympics Receiving Minimal Coverage in U.S."

13. David Woods, "Equal Pay? Not on the Basketball Court," *USA Today,* May 19, 2012, http://www.usatoday.com/sports/basketball/story/2012-05-19/nba-wnba-basketball-salary-disparity/55079608/1.

14. Stefan Fatsis, "That Was Amazing! Now What?"; Christine Brennan, "American Women Rule the London Olympics—Now What?," *USA Today,* August 12, 2012, http://www.usatoday.com/sports/olympics/london/story/2012-08-12/London-Olympics-womens-sports-Christine-Brennan-Title-IX/57016306/1.

15. Jeré Longman, "A Giant Leap for Women, but Hurdles Remain," *New York Times,* July 29, 2012, http://www.nytimes.com/2012/07/30/sports/olympics/despite-gains-for-female-athletes-fight-for-true-equality-remains.html; Maureen Smith and Alison Wrynn, *Women in the 2012 Olympic and Paralympic Games: An Analysis of Participation and Leadership Opportunities,* 7.

16. M. Smith and Wrynn, *Women in the 2012 Olympic and Paralympic Games,* 7; Jocelyne Cesari, "Saudi Women Going to Games Is a Sham."

17. Homa Khaleeli, "Sports Hijabs Help Muslim Women to Olympic Success," *Guardian,* July 23, 2012, http://www.guardian.co.uk/sport/the-womens-blog-with-jane-martinson/2012/jul/23/sports-hijabs-muslim-women-olympics.

18. "London 2012 Olympics: Female Beach Volleyball Players Permitted to Wear Less Revealing Uniforms," *Telegraph* (London), March 27, 2012, http://www.telegraph.co.uk/sport/olympics/volleyball/9169429/London-2012-Olympics-female-beach-volleyball-players-permitted-to-wear-less-revealing-uniforms.html.

19. Mary Jo Kane, "Sex Sells Sex, Not Women's Sports."

20. C. A. Tuggle, Suzanne Huffman, and Dana Rosengard, "A Descriptive Analysis of NBC's Coverage of the 2004 Summer Olympics," 67.

21. Kimberly L. Bissell and Andrea M. Duke, "Bump, Set, Spike: An Analysis of Commentary and Camera Angles of Women's Beach Volleyball during the 2004 Summer Olympics."

22. Justin Peters, "While You Were Staring at Their Butts, Misty May-Treanor and Kerri Walsh Jennings Just Won Their Gold Medal"; Boris Johnson, "London Olympics 2012: Here's 20 Jolly Good Reasons to Feel Cheerful about the Games," *Telegraph* (London), July 30, 2010, http://www.telegraph.co.uk/comment/columnists/borisjohnson/9437495/London-Olympics-2012-heres-20-jolly-good-reasons-to-feel-cheerful-about-the-Games.html.

23. Lyndsie Bourgon, "Why Women Boxers Shouldn't Have to Wear Skirts"; Erin Skarda, "Top 10 Sports-Fashion Controversies."

24. Robles spoke with Jessica Testa in "The Strongest Women in America Lives in Poverty," *Buzzfeed.com,* n.d., http://www.buzzfeed.com/jtes/the-strongest-woman-in-america-lives-in-poverty.

25. John Zaccaro, "40 Years Later, the Larger Meaning of Title IX"; Sarah Kwak, "Lolo Jones' Openness with Personal Life Has Sparked Undue Criticism."

26. Felshin, "Social Anomaly of Women in Sports."

27. Patricia R. W. Clasen, "The Female Athlete: Dualisms and Paradox in Practice," 36, 37.

28. Jacobs, "Psychology of Tennis Clothes," 120; Mary-Jayne McKay, "Venus Williams' French Open Outfit: Is She Naked?" See also Jaime Schultz, "Reading the Catsuit: Serena Williams and the Production of Blackness at the 2002 U.S. Open."

29. Phebe M. Scott, "Women's Sports in 1980," *Proceedings: Second National Institute on Girls Sports,* 142–48 (see chap. 3, n. 51).

30. Quoted in Matt Eisenberg, "Title IX Ruling Upheld, Competitive Cheerleading Not a Sport," *Quinnipiac Chronicle,* August 10, 2012, http://www.quchronicle.com/2012/08/title-ix-ruling-upheld-competitive-cheerleading-not-a-sport/.

31. Not all of them were good. For instance, it was the season that saw the guilty verdict against a former Penn State football coach for multiple counts of child sex abuse. His access to the school's facilities and administrators' complicity and cover-up in the scandal brought swift and severe sanctions from the NCAA and reminded us not only of the "dark side" of sport, but the nefarious, unfathomable, and horrifying aspects of it as well.

32. Timothy Burke, "Michele Smith Became the First Female Analyst for a National Baseball Broadcast Yesterday. Here's How Viewers Reacted."

33. But it's okay if she doesn't.

Bibliography

Archival Collections

American Alliance for Health, Physical Education, Recreation, and Dance Records Collection. Springfield College Archives, Springfield, Mass.

Brundage, Avery. Collection. University of Illinois Archives, Urbana.

International Olympic Committee Historical Archives. Lausanne, Switzerland.

International Tennis Hall of Fame and Museum, Newport, R.I.

National Association of Physical Education for College Women Collection. University of North Carolina at Greensboro Special Collections and Archives.

Other Sources

Abbondanza, Katie. "Bring It On." *Girls' Life* 14 (April–May 2008): 70–72.

Ackerman, Elise. "She Kicks. She Scores. She Sells." *U.S. News & World Report,* July 26, 1999, 42.

Acosta, R. Vivian, and Linda Jean Carpenter. "Women in Intercollegiate Sport: A Longitudinal, National Study, Twenty-Seven Year Update, 1977–2004." *Women in Sport and Physical Activity Journal* 13 (2004): 62–89.

Adams, Natalie Guice, and Pamela J. Bettis. "Alpha Girls and Cheerleading: Negotiating New Discourses with Old Practices." *Girlhood Studies* 2 (2009): 148–66.

———. *Cheerleader: An American Icon.* New York: Palgrave Macmillan, 2003.

Addington, Sarah. "The Athletic Limitations of Women." *Ladies' Home Journal,* June 1923, 38.

Adrian, Marlene J. *Sports Women: Medicine & Sport Science.* Basel: Karger, 1987.

Agnew, Vijay, ed. *Interrogating Race and Racism.* Toronto: University of Toronto Press, 2007.

"AMA Committee on Medical Aspects of Sports, May 2–3, 1964." *Journal of Health, Physical Education, Recreation* (November–December 1964): 46.

American Alliance for Health, Physical Education, and Recreation, Sport, Health, Fitness, and Dance. AAHPER Research Consortium Symposium Papers. Washington, D.C.: AAHPER, 1978.

American College of Sports Medicine. "Opinion Statement on the Participation of the Female Athlete in Long-Distance Running." *Medicine and Science in Sports* 11, no. 4 (1979): ix–xi.

Amy-Chinn, Dee. "Doing Epistemic (In)justice to Semenya." *International Journal of Media and Cultural Politics* 6 (2010): 311–26.

———. "This Is Just for Me(n): How the Regulation of Post-Feminist Lingerie Advertising Perpetuates Woman as Object." *Journal of Consumer Culture* 6 (2006): 155–75.

Anderson, Christopher. "Olympic Row over Sex Testing." *Nature* 353 (1991): 784.

Anderson, Kelley. "The Other Side of Jenny." *Sports Illustrated for Women,* November–December 2000, 120–21.

Araton, Harvey. "The New Rules of the Game." *New York Times Magazine,* October 18, 1998.

"Are Girl Athletes Really Girls?" *Life,* October 7, 1966, 63–72.

Arnold, Lloyd, and Marie Hagele. "Vaginal Tamponage for Catamenial Sanitary Protection." *Journal of the American Medical Association* 110 (1938): 789–90.

Austin, Bunny. *Lawn Tennis Made Easy.* New York: Macmillan, 1935.

Austin, George Lowell. *Perils of American Women; or, A Doctors Talk with Maiden, Wife, and Mother.* Boston: Lee and Shepard, 1883.

Averbuch, Gloria. *The Woman Runner: Free to Be the Complete Athlete.* New York: Cornerstone Library, 1984.

Bailey, Ronald H. *Small Wonder: How Tambrands Began, Prospered, and Grew.* Undated Tampax corporate history booklet published by Tambrands.

Ballantyne, Kaye N., Manfred Kayser, and J. Anton Grootegoed. "Sex and Gender Issues in Competitive Sports: Investigation of a Historical Case Leads to a New Viewpoint." *British Journal of Sports Medicine* (2011): 614–17.

Ballard, Sarah. "The Most Powerful Woman in Sports." *Sports Illustrated,* September 29, 1986. http://sportsillustrated.cnn.com/vault/article/magazine/MAG1065270/index.htm#ixzz1JV5gv7S.

Banet-Weiser, Sarah. "Hoop Dreams: Professional Basketball and the Politics of Race and Gender." *Journal of Sport & Social Issues* 23 (1999): 403–20.

Banner, Lois W. *American Beauty.* Chicago: University of Chicago Press, 1983.

Barney, Elizabeth C. "The American Sportswoman." *Fortnightly Review,* August 1894, 63–77.

Bartky, Sandra Lee. "Foucault, Femininity, and the Modernization of Patriarchal Power." In *Feminism and Foucault: Reflections on Resistance,* edited by Irene Diamond and Lee Quimby, 61–86. Boston: Northeastern University Press, 1988.

Bartolomeo, Joey. "Sports Style: Underwear Busts Out." *Women's Sport & Fitness,* January–February 2000, 42.

Barton, Mary. "Review of the Sanitary Appliance with a Discussion on Intravaginal Packs." *British Medical Journal* 1 (April 1942): 524–25.

Bashevkin, Sylvia. "Facing a Renewed Right: American Feminism and the Reagan/Bush Challenge." *Canadian Journal of Political Science* 24 (1994): 669–98.

Bateman, Janis Karen. "Billie Jean King's Publishing Adventure: A Documentary on the Evolution of *womenSports* Magazine from March 1973 through May 1975." Ph.D. diss., University of Oregon, 1977.

Baumgardner, Jennifer, and Amy Richards. *Manifesta: Young Women, Feminism, and the Future.* New York: Farrar, Straus, and Giroux, 2000.

Beets, Michael W., and Kenneth H. Pitetti. "Contribution of Physical Education and Sport to Health-Related Fitness in High School Students." *Journal of School Health* 75 (2005): 25–30.

Bell, Margaret. "Answers to Practical Questions on Menstruation." *Hygeia* 20 (March 1942): 186–87, 208.

Bennett, Judith M. "Feminism and History." *Gender & History* 1 (1989): 251–72.

———. *History Matters: Patriarchy and the Challenge of Feminism.* Philadelphia: University of Pennsylvania Press, 2007.

Benzaia, Diana. "The Fitness Game." *Harper's Bazaar,* May 1980, 116.

Beran, Janice A. "Playing to the Right Drummer: Girls' Basketball in Iowa." *Research Quarterly for Exercise and Sport* (1985): 78–92.

Bermon, Stéphane, Martin Ritzén, Angelica Lindén Hirschberg, and Thomas H. Murray. "Are the New Policies on Hyperandrogenism in Elite Female Athletes Really Out of Bounds? Response to 'Out of Bounds? A Critique of the New Policies on Hyperandrogenism in Elite Female Athletes.'" *American Journal of Bioethics* 13, no. 5 (2013): 63–65.

Berryman, Jack. "Preface." *Journal of Sport History* 10 (1983): 5.

Bettis, Pamela J., and Natalie Guice Adams. "Short Skirts and Breast Juts: Cheerleading, Eroticism, and Schools." *Sex Education* 6 (2006): 121–33.

Bezuvis, Erin E. "The Feminist Case for the NCAA's Recognition of Competitive Cheer as an Emerging Sport for Women." *Boston College Law Review* 52 (2011): 439–64.

Bhowmick, Nilanjana. "India's Golden Girls: How Sport and the Olympics Can Uplift Women." *Time,* August 21, 2012. http://olympics.time.com/2012/08/21/indias-golden -girls-how-sports-and-the-olympics-can-uplift-women/#ixzz24TMCOcjB.

Birrell, Susan, and Cheryl L. Cole, eds. "Double Fault: Renee Richards and the Construction and Naturalization of Difference." In *Women, Sport, and Culture,* edited by Susan Birrell and Cheryl L. Cole, 373–97. Champaign, Ill.: Human Kinetics, 1994.

———. *Women, Sport, and Culture.* Champaign, Ill.: Human Kinetics, 1994.

Birrell, Susan, and Nancy Theberge. "Ideological Control of Women in Sport." In *Women and Sport: Interdisciplinary Perspectives,* edited by D. Margaret Costa and Sharon R. Guthrie, 341–59. Champaign, Ill.: Human Kinetics, 1994.

Bissell, Kimberly L., and Andrea M. Duke. "Bump, Set, Spike: An Analysis of Commentary and Camera Angles of Women's Beach Volleyball during the 2004 Summer Olympics." *Journal of Promotion Management* 13 (2007): 35–53.

Bjurstedt, Molla, and Samueal Crowther. *Tennis for Women.* New York: Doubleday, 1916.

Blaszczyk, Regina Lee, ed. *Producing Fashion: Commerce, Culture, and Consumers.* Philadelphia: University of Pennsylvania Press, 2008.

Booth, Douglas. *The Field: Truth and Fiction in Sport History.* London: Routledge, 2005.

Bordo, Susan. *Unbearable Weight: Feminism, Western Culture, and the Body.* Berkeley: University of California Press, 1993.

Boston Women's Health Book Collective. *Our Bodies, Ourselves: A Book by and for Women.* New York: Simon and Schuster, 1984.

Bouchier, Nancy B. "Let Us Take Care of Our Field: The National Association for Physical Education of College Women and World War II." *Journal of Sport History* 25 (1998): 64–85.

Boulongne, Yves-Pierre. "Pierre de Coubertin and Women's Sport." *Olympic Review* (February–March 2000): 23.

Bourgon, Lyndsie. "Why Women Boxers Shouldn't Have to Wear Skirts." *Slate,* January 18, 2012. http://www.slate.com/blogs/xx_factor/2012/01/18/women_s_boxing_and_the_olympics_why_boxers_shouldn_t_have_to_wear_skirts_.html.

Boutilier, Mary A., and Lucinda SanGiovanni. *The Sporting Woman.* Champaign, Ill.: Human Kinetics, 1983.

Bowers, Larry D. "Testosterone Doping: Dealing with Genetic Differences in Metabolism and Excretion." *Journal of Clinical Endocrinology & Metabolism* 93 (2008): 2469–71.

Boyle, Robert H. "The Report That Shocked the President." *Sports Illustrated,* August 15, 1955.

Brabazon, Tara. "Fitness Is a Feminist Issue." *Australian Feminist Studies* 21 (2006): 65–83.

Breward, Christopher, Becky Conekin, and Caroline Cox, eds. *The Englishness of English Dress.* London: Oxford University Press, 2002.

Broad, K. L. "The Gendered Unapologetic: Queer Resistance in Women's Sport." *Sociology of Sport Journal* 18 (2001): 181–204.

Brown, Gwllym S. "A Little Lace Goes a Long, Long Way." *Sports Illustrated,* July 7, 1969. http://sportsillustrated.cnn.com/vault/article/magazine/MAG1082586/2/index.htm.

Brownmiller, Susan. *Femininity.* New York: Linden Press, 1984.

Brubach, Holly. "The Athletic Aesthetic." *New York Times Magazine,* June 23, 1996, 48–51.

Brumberg, Joan Jacobs. "'Something Happens to Girls': Menarche and the Emergence of the Modern American Hygienic Imperative." *Journal of the History of Sexuality* 4 (1993): 99–127.

Buchalter, Gail. "Richard Simmons, Diana Ross, and Jane Fonda Help Aerobic Dance LPs Boogie Up the Charts." *People,* July 26, 1982, 76.

Buckley, Thomas, and Alma Gottlieb, eds. *Blood Magic: The Anthropology of Menstruation.* Berkeley: University of California Press, 1988.

Bullough, Vern. "Female Physiology, Technology, and Women's Liberation." In *Dynamos and Virgins Revisited: Women and Technological Change in History,* edited by Martha Moore Trescott, 236–51. Metuchen, N.J.: Scarecrow Press, 1979.

———. *Sex, Society, and History.* New York: Science History, Neale Watson, 1976.

———. *The Subordinate Sex.* Baltimore: Penguin Books, 1974.

———. "Technology and Female Sexuality and Physiology: Some Implications." *Journal of Sex Research* 16 (1980): 59–71.

Bullough, Vern, and Martha Voight. "Women, Menstruation, and Nineteenth-Century Medicine." *Bulletin of the History of Medicine* 47 (1973): 66–82.

Burdick, William. "Safeguarding the Athletic Competition of Girls and Women." *American Physical Education Review* 32 (1927): 367.

Burke, Timothy. "Michele Smith Became the First Female Analyst for a National Baseball Broadcast Yesterday. Here's How Viewers Reacted." Deadspin.com, August 20, 2012. http://deadspin.com/5936316/michele-smith-became-the-first-female-analyst

-for-a-national-baseball-broadcast-yesterday-heres-how-viewers-reacted?utm_campaign =socialflow_deadspin_facebook&utm_source=deadspin_facebook&utm_medium =socialflow.

Burman, Barbara. "Racing Bodies: Dress and Pioneer Women Aviators and Racing Drivers." *Women's History Review* 9 (2000): 299–326.

Burns-Ardolino, Wendy A. "Reading Woman: Displacing the Foundations of Femininity." *Hypatia* 18 (2003): 42–59.

Burton-Nelson, Mariah. *Are We Winning Yet? How Women Are Changing Sports and Sports Are Changing Women.* New York: Random House, 1991.

Bush, Akiko, ed. *Designs for Sports: The Cult of Performance.* New York: Princeton Architectural Press, 1998.

Butchart, Ronald E. "Outthinking and Outflanking the Owners of the World: A Historiography of the African American Struggle for Education." *History of Education Quarterly* 28 (1988): 333–66.

Butler, Judith. "Athletic Genders: Hyperbolic Instance and/or the Overcoming of Sexual Binarism." *Stanford Humanities Review* 6 (1998): 103–11.

———. *Gender Trouble: Feminism and the Subversion of Identity.* New York: Routledge, 1990.

Buzuvis, Erin E. "The Feminist Case for the NCAA's Recognition of Competitive Cheer as an Emerging Sport for Women." *Boston College Law Review* 52 (2011): 439–64.

Cahn, Susan K. *Coming on Strong: Gender and Sexuality in Twentieth-Century Women's Sport.* Cambridge, Mass.: Harvard University Press, 1994.

Calhoun, Cheshire. "The Gender Closet: Lesbian Disappearance under the Sign 'Women.'" *Feminist Studies* 21 (1995): 7–34.

Canning, Kathleen. *Gender History in Practice: Historical Perspectives on Bodies, Class, and Citizenship.* Ithaca, N.Y.: Cornell University Press, 2006.

Capp, William. *The Daughter: Her Health, Education, and Wedlock.* Philadelphia: F. A. Davis, 1891.

Carlson, Alison. "Chromosome Count." *Ms.,* October 1988, 40–44.

———. "When Is a Woman Not a Woman?" *Women's Sport & Fitness,* March 1991, 24–29.

Carrington, Ben, and Ian McDonald. *"Race," Sport, and British Society.* London: Routledge, 2001.

Carter, Alison. *Underwear: The Fashion History.* New York: Drama Book, 1992.

Cavanagh, Shelia L., and Heather Sykes. "Transsexual Bodies at the Olympics: The International Olympic Committee's Policy on Transsexual Athletes at the 2004 Athens Summer Games." *Body & Society* 12 (2006): 75–102.

Cayleff, Susan E. *Babe: The Life and Legend of Babe Didrikson Zaharias.* Urbana: University of Illinois Press, 1995.

———. "She Was Rendered Incapacitated by Menstrual Difficulties: Historical Perspectives on Perceived Intellectual and Physiological Impairment among Menstruating Women." In *Menstrual Health in Women's Lives,* edited by Alice J. Dan and Linda L. Lewis, 229–35. Urbana: University of Illinois Press, 1992.

Cesari, Jocelyne. "Saudi Women Going to Games Is a Sham." CNN, August 1, 2012. http://www.cnn.com/2012/08/01/opinion/cesari-saudi-women-sports/index.html.

Chadwick, Mary. *Women's Periodicity.* London: Noel Douglas, 1933.

Chambers, Dorothea Lambert. *Lawn Tennis for Ladies.* London: Methuen, 1910.

Charlton, T. F. "The Media's Gabby Douglas Problem." *Ebony,* August 8, 2012. http://www
.ebony.com/news-views/the-medias-gabby-douglas-problem-147.

Chastain, Brandi. "A Whole New Ball Game." *Newsweek,* October 25, 1999, 76.

Chastain, Brandi, with Gloria Averbuch. *It's Not about the Bra.* New York: HarperCollins, 2004.

Child Trends Databank. "Participation in School Athletics: Indicators on Children and
Youth." 2012. http://www.childtrendsdatabank.org/?q=node/367.

Chisolm, Ann. "Acrobats, Contortionists, and Cute Children: The Promise and Perversity
of U.S. Women's Gymnastics." *Signs* 27 (2002): 415–50.

Choi, Precilla Y. L. *Femininity and the Physically Active Woman.* London: Routledge, 2000.

Christie-Robin, Julia, Belinda T. Orzada, and Dilia López-Gydosh. "From Bustles to
Bloomers: Exploring the Bicycle's Influence on American Women's Fashion, 1800–1914."
Journal of American Culture 35, no. 4 (2012): 315–31.

Clarke, Edward. *Sex in Education; or, A Fair Chance for Girls.* Boston: J. R. Osgood, 1873.

Clasen, Patricia R. W. "The Female Athlete: Dualisms and Paradox in Practice." *Women
and Language* 24 (2001): 36–41.

Cohen, Deborah A., Stephanie L. Taylor, Michela Zonta, Katherine D. Vestal, and Mark
A. Schuster. "Availability of High School Extracurricular Sports Programs and High
Risk Behaviors." *Journal of School Health* 77 (2007): 80–86.

Cohen, Greta L. *Women in Sport: Issues and Controversies.* London: Sage, 1993.

Cole, C. L. "One Chromosome Too Many." In *The Olympics at the Millennium: Power,
Politics, and the Games,* edited by Kay Schaffer and Sidonie Smith, 128–46. New Brunswick, N.J.: Rutgers University Press, 2000.

———. "Resisting the Canon." In *Women, Sport, and Culture,* edited by Susan Birrell and
C. L. Cole, 5–29. Champaign, Ill.: Human Kinetics, 1994.

———. "Testing for Sex or Drugs." *Journal of Sport & Social Issues* 24 (2000): 331.

Cole, C. L., and Amy Hribar. "Celebrity Feminism: Nike Style, Post-Fordism, Transcendence, and Consumer Power." *Sociology of Sport Journal* 12 (1995): 347–69.

Collins, Jennifer E. "Beyond the Beauty Salon: Sport, Women of Color, and Their Hair."
Master's thesis, University of Maryland, 2011.

Collins, Leslea Haravon. "Working Out the Contradictions: Feminism and Aerobics."
Journal of Sport and Social Issues 26 (2002): 85–109.

"Comes the Revolution." *Time,* June 26, 1978, 54–60.

Comfort, George F., and Anna M. Comfort. *Woman's Education and Women's Health: Chiefly
in Reply to Dr. E. H. Clarke's "Sex in Education."* Syracuse, N.Y.: T. W. Durston, 1874.

Conlisk, Maura. "Sports Competition for College Women." *Journal of Health, Physical
Education, Recreation* 28 (1957): 64.

Conner, Caryl Ferber. "Facts and Fancies about Menstruation." *Today's Health* 28 (May
1950): 19.

Consumer Reports. *I'll Buy That! 50 Small Wonders and Big Deals That Revolutionized
the Lives of Consumers, a 50-Year Retrospective.* New York: Consumers Union of the
United States, 1986.

Cooky, Cheryl, Faye L. Wachs, Michael Messner, and Shari L. Dworkin. "It's Not about
the Game: Don Imus, Race, Class, Gender, and Sexuality in Contemporary Media."
Sociology of Sport Journal 27 (2010): 139–59.

Cooky, Cheryl, Ranissa Dycus, and Shari L. Dworkin. "'What Makes a Woman a Woman?' versus 'Our First Lady of Sport': A Comparative Analysis of the United States and the South African Media Coverage of Caster Semenya." *Journal of Sport and Social Issues* (2012): 1–26.

Cooper, John M. "A Magna Charta for the Girl and Woman in Athletics." In *Women and Athletics,* edited by the Women's Division, National Amateur Athletic Federation, 22–24. New York: A. S. Barnes, 1930.

Cooper, Kenneth H. *Aerobics.* New York: M. Evans, 1968.

Corlis, Richard. "The New Ideal of Beauty." *Time,* August 30, 1982.

Costa, D. Margaret, and Sharon R. Guthrie, eds. *Women and Sport: Interdisciplinary Perspectives.* Champaign, Ill.: Human Kinetics, 1994.

Council on Sports Medicine and Fitness. "Cheerleading Injuries: Epidemiology and Recommendations for Prevention." *Pediatrics* 130, no. 5 (2012): 966–71.

Crane, Diane. "Clothing Behavior as Non-Verbal Resistance: Marginal Women and Alternative Dress in the Nineteenth Century." *Fashion Theory* 3, no. 2 (1999): 241–68.

Creedon, Pamela, ed. *Women, Media, and Sport: Challenging Gender Values.* Thousand Oaks, Calif.: Sage, 1994.

———. "Women, Sport, and Media Institutions: Issues in Sports Journalism and Marketing." In *MediaSport,* edited by Lawrence A. Wenner, 88–99. London: Routledge, 1998.

Crosset, Todd W. *Outsiders in the Clubhouse: The World of Women's Professional Golf.* Albany: State University of New York Press, 1995.

Crothers, Tim. "Spectacular Takeoff." *Sports Illustrated,* July 3, 2000.

Cunningham, Patricia. "Swimwear in the Thirties: The B.V.D. Company in a Decade of Innovation." *Dress* 12 (1986): 11–27.

Cunnington, C. Willett, and Phillis Cunnington. *The History of Underclothes.* New York: Dover, 1992.

Cunnington, Phillis E., and Alan Mansfield. *English Costume for Sports and Outdoor Recreation: From the Sixteenth to Nineteenth Centuries.* London: Adam & Charles Black, 1969.

"Cure for Cramps." *Newsweek,* October 4, 1943, 89–90.

Curtis, Henry S. "Should Girls Play Interschool Basketball?" *Hygeia* 6 (1928): 607–8.

Daddario, Gina. "Chilly Scenes of the 1992 Winter Games: The Mass Media and the Marginalization of Female Athletes." *Sociology of Sport Journal* 11 (1994): 275–88.

Dan, Alice J., and Linda L. Lewis, eds. *Menstrual Health in Women's Lives.* Urbana: University of Illinois Press, 1992.

Daniels, Dayna B. "Gender (Body) Verification (Building)." *Play & Culture* 5 (1992): 370–77.

Daniels, Mary A. "The Historical Transition of Women's Sports at the Ohio State University, 1885–1975, and Its Impact on the National Women's Intercollegiate Setting during That Period." Ph.D. diss., Ohio State University, 1977.

Danzig, Allison, and Peter Schwed, eds. *Fireside Book of Tennis.* New York: Simon and Schuster, 1972.

Davis, Laurel R. "Male Cheerleading and the Naturalization of Gender." In *Sport, Men, and the Gender Order: Critical Feminist Perspectives,* edited by Michael A. Messner and Donald F. Sabo, 153–61. Champaign, Ill.: Human Kinetics, 1990.

Davis, Maxine. "Menstruation." *Good Housekeeping,* January 1952, 37.

Davis, Natalie Zemon. "'Women's History' in Transition: The European Case." *Feminist Studies* 3 (1976): 83–103.

DeFrantz, Anita. "The Olympic Games: Our Birthright to Sports." In *Women in Sport: Issues and Controversies,* edited by Greta L. Cohen, 185–92. London: Sage, 1993.

de la Chapelle, Albert. "Gender Verification of Female Athletes." *Lancet* 11 (1987): 1265–66.

———. "The Use and Misuse of Sex Chromatin Screening for 'Gender Identification' of Female Athletes." *Journal of the American Medical Association* 256 (1986): 1920–23.

———. "Why Sex Chromatin Should Be Abandoned as a Screening Method for 'Gender Verification' of Female Athletes." *New Studies in Athletics* 2 (1986): 49–53.

Delaney, Anngel. "How We Got Rid of the Bloody Corsets and Other Tales of Women's Sports." *On the Issues: The Progressive Women's Quarterly* 7 (1998), 34–37.

Delaney, Janice, Mary Jane Lupton, and Emily Toth. *The Curse: A Cultural History of Menstruation.* New York: Dutton, 1976.

de Lauretis, Teresa. *Technologies of Gender: Essays on Theory, Film, and Fiction.* Bloomington: Indiana University Press, 1987.

"Dermatologic Barriers to Exercise in Black Women." Wake Forest Baptist Medical Center news release, n.d. http://www.wakehealth.edu/News-Releases/2008/Dermatologic_Barriers _to_Exercise_in_Black_Women.htm?LangType=1033.

Deveny, Kathleen. "Who You Callin' a Lady?" *Newsweek,* November 30, 2009, 24.

Diamond, Irene, and Lee Quimby. *Feminism and Foucault: Reflections on Resistance.* Boston: Northeastern University Press, 1988.

Dickinson, Barry D., Myron Genel, Carolym B. Robinowitz, Patricia L. Turner, and Gary L. Woods. "Gender Verification of Female Olympic Athletes." *Medicine and Science in Sports and Exercise* 34 (2002): 1539–42.

Dickinson, Robert L. "Tampons as Menstrual Guards." *Consumer Reports,* September 1945, 246–47.

Diddle, A. W., and L. Boulware. "Vaginal Tampons for Menstrual Hygiene." *Journal of Iowa State Medical Society* 32 (June 1942): 256–57.

Dill, Bonnie Thornton. "Race, Class, and Gender: Prospects for an All-Inclusive Sisterhood." *Feminist Studies* 9 (1983): 131–50.

Division for Girls and Women's Sports. "National Intercollegiate Championships for Women." *Journal of Health, Physical Education, Recreation* 39 (February 1968).

———. "Statement of Policies and Procedures for Competition in Girls and Women's Sports." *Journal of Health, Physical Education, Recreation* 34 (September 1963).

Djata, Sundiata. *Blacks at the Net: Black Achievement in the History of Tennis.* Vol. 1. Syracuse, N.Y.: Syracuse University Press, 2006.

Dolbow, Sandra. "Champion Sports Bra: Not for Jocks." *Brandweek,* January 14, 2002, 9.

Dosch, Nancy Cole. "'The Sacrifice of Maidens' or Healthy Sportswomen? The Medical Debate over Women's Basketball." In *A Century of Women's Basketball: From Frailty to Final Four,* edited by Joan S. Hult and Marianna Trekell, 125–36. Reston, Va.: American Alliance for Health, Physical Education, Recreation, and Dance, 1991.

Douglas, Susan J. *Where the Girls Are: Growing Up Female with the Mass Media.* New York: Random House, 1994.

Dowling, Collette. *The Frailty Myth: Women Approaching Physical Equality.* New York: Random House, 2000.

DuBoise, Ellen Carol, and Vicky L. Ruiz, eds. *Unequal Sisters: A Multicultural Reader in U.S. Women's History.* New York: Routledge, 1990.

Duffey, Eliza Brisbee. *No Sex in Education; or, An Equal Chance for Both Boys and Girls.* Philadelphia: J. M. Stoddard, 1874.

Dulles, Foster Rhea. *A History of Recreation: America Learns to Play.* 2nd ed. New York: Appleton-Century-Crofts, 1965.

Duncan, Margaret Carlisle. "The Politics of Women's Body Images and Practices: Foucault, the Panopticon, and *Shape* Magazine." *Journal of Sport and Social Issues* 18 (1994): 48–65.

———. "Sports Photographs and Sexual Difference: Images of Women and Men in the 1984 and 1988 Olympic Games." *Sociology of Sport Journal* 7 (1990): 22–43.

———. "The Status of Intramural Programs for Women." *Research Quarterly* (March 1937): 75–77.

Dunning, Eric. "Sport as a Male Preserve." In *Women, Sport, and Culture,* edited by Susan Birrell and Cheryl L. Cole, 163–80. Champaign, Ill.: Human Kinetics, 1994.

Duquin, Mary E. "Fashion and Fitness: Images in Women's Magazine Ads." *Arena Review* 13 (1989): 97–109.

———. "The Importance of Sport in Building Women's Potential." *Journal of Physical Education, Recreation, and Dance* 53 (1982): 18–20, 36.

Dyreson, Mark. "Sport History and the History of Sport in North America." *Journal of Sport History* 35 (2008): 405–14.

Eastman, Susan Tyler, and Andrew C. Billings. "Gender Parity in the Olympics: Hyping Women Athletes, Favoring Men Athletes." *Journal of Sport and Social Issues* 23(1999): 140–70.

Ehrenreich, Barbara, and Deidre English. *For Her Own Good: 150 Years of the Experts' Advice to Women.* New York: Anchor Press, 1978.

Eisenberg, Matt. "Title IX Ruling Upheld, Competitive Cheerleading Not a Sport." *Quinnipiac Chronicle,* August 10, 2012. http://www.quchronicle.com/2012/08/title-ix-ruling-upheld-competitive-cheerleading-not-a-sport/.

Eitzen, D. Stanley, ed. *Sport in Contemporary Society: An Anthology.* 7th ed. Boulder, Colo.: Paradigm, 2004.

Eitzen, D. Stanley, and Maxine Baca Zinn. "The De-athleticization of Women: The Naming and Gender Marking of Collegiate Sport Teams." In *Sport in Contemporary Society: An Anthology,* edited by D. Stanley Eitzen, 129–38. 7th ed. Boulder, Colo.: Paradigm, 2004.

Eliott-Lynn, Sophie C. *Athletics for Women and Girls: How to Be an Athlete and Why.* London: Robert Scott, 1925.

Ellis, A. W. "The Status of Health and Physical Education for Women in Negro Colleges and Universities." *Journal of Negro Education* 8 (1939): 58–63.

Elsas, Louis J., et al. "Gender Verification of Female Athletes." *Genetics in Medicine* 2 (2000): 249–54.

Emery, Lynne. "From Lowell Mills to the Halls of Fame: Industrial League Sport for Women." In *Women and Sport: Interdisciplinary Perspectives,* edited by D. Margaret Costa and Sharon R. Guthrie, 107–21. Champaign, Ill.: Human Kinetics, 1994.

Endel, Barbara L. "Working Out: The Dialectic of Strength and Sexuality in *Women's Sport & Fitness* Magazine." Ph.D. diss., University of Iowa, 1991.

Engelhardt, Molly. "'Airheads, Amazons, and Bitches': Cheerleaders and Second-Wave Feminists in the Popular Press." In *Disco Divas: Women and Popular Culture in the 1970s,* edited by Sherrie A. Inness, 54–68. Philadelphia: University of Pennsylvania Press, 2003.

Engelmann, Larry. *The Goddess and the American Girl: The Story of Suzanne Lenglen and Helen Wills*. New York: Oxford University Press, 1988.

Eskes, Tina B., Margaret Carlisle Duncan, and Eleanor M. Miller. "The Discourse of Empowerment: Foucault, Marcuse, and Women's Fitness Texts." *Journal of Sport and Social Issues* 22 (1998): 317–44.

Ewing, Elizabeth. *Dress and Undress: A History of Women's Underwear*. New York: Drama Book Specialists, 1978.

———. *Underwear: A History*. New York: Theatre Arts Books, 1972.

"Exercise and Fitness." *Journal of the American Medical Association* 188 (1964): 433–36.

"Exercise for Lovemaking." *Mademoiselle*, Fall 1981, 142–44.

"Experts Slam Olympic Gene Test." *Science* 255 (1992).

"Extracts." *American Physical Education Review* (1925).

Fagan, Kate, and Luke Cyphers. "Five Myths about Title IX." espnW, April 30, 2012. http://espn.go.com/espnw/title-ix/7729603/five-myths-title-ix.

Faludi, Susan. *Backlash: The Undeclared War against American Women*. New York: Doubleday, 1991.

Farrell-Beck, Jane, and Colleen Gau. *Uplift: The Bra in America*. Philadelphia: University of Pennsylvania Press, 2002.

Farrell-Beck, Jane, and Laura Klosterman Kidd. "The Roles of Health Professionals in the Development and Dissemination of Women's Sanitary Products, 1880–1940." *Journal of the History of Medicine and Allied Sciences* 51 (1996): 325–52.

Fastiff, Pamela B. "Gender Verification Testing: Balancing the Rights of Female Athletes with a Scandal-Free Olympic Games." *Hasting Constitutional Law Quarterly* 19 (1992): 937–61.

"Fast Women." *Time*, February 13, 1928. http://www.time.com/time/magazine/article/0,9171,731567,00.html.

Fatsis, Stefan. "That Was Amazing! Now What?" *Slate*, August 9, 2012. http://www.slate.com/articles/sports/fivering_circus/2012/08/u_s_women_s_soccer_2012_olympics_abby_wambach_hope_solo_and_alex_morgan_just_won_gold_but_will_they_have_a_league_to_play_in_.html.

Fausto-Sterling, Anne. *Sexing the Body: Gender, Politics, and the Construction of Sexuality*. New York: Basic Books, 2000.

Feldberg, Georgina D. *Women, Health, and Nation: Canada and the United States since 1945*. Montreal: McGill-Queen's University Press, 2003.

Felshin, Jan. "The Social Anomaly of Women in Sports." *Physical Educator* 30 (1973): 122–24.

———. "The Triple Options . . . for Women in Sport." *Quest* 21 (1974): 36–40.

Ferguson-Smith, Malcolm A. "Gender Verification and the Place of XY Females in Sport." In *Oxford Textbook of Sports Medicine*, edited by Mark Harries, Clyde Williams, William D. Stanish, and Lyle J. Micheli, 355–56. 2nd ed. New York: Oxford University Press, 1998.

Ferguson-Smith, Malcolm A., and Elizabeth A. Ferris. "Gender Verification in Sport: The Need for Change?" *British Journal of Sports Medicine* 25 (1991): 17–20.

Ferris, Elizabeth A. E. "Gender Testing in Sport." *British Medical Bulletin* 48 (1992): 683–97.

Festle, Mary Jo. *Playing Nice: Politics and Apologies in Women's Sports*. New York: Columbia University Press, 1996.

Fields, Sarah K. *Female Gladiators: Gender, Law, and Contact Sport in America*. Urbana: University of Illinois Press, 2005.

———. "Title IX and African-American Female Athletes." In *Sport and the Racial Divide: African-American and Latino Experiences in an Era of Change,* edited by Michael E. Lomax, 126–45. Jackson: University Press of Mississippi, 2008.

Fink, Janet S. "Female Athletes and the Media: Strides and Stalemates." *Journal of Physical Education* 69 (1998): 37–40.

Fink, Janet S., and Linda Jean Kensicki. "An Imperceptible Difference: Visual and Textual Constructions of Femininity in *Sports Illustrated* and *Sports Illustrated for Women.*" *Mass Communication & Society* 5 (2002): 317–39.

Footlick, Jerrold K. "Of Sports, Sex, and Money." *Newsweek,* March 16, 1981, 98.

Forsythe, Charles E. "Athletics in the Space Age." *Journal of Health, Physical Education, Recreation* 29 (September 1958): 28–30.

Foster, Mark S. "In the Face of 'Jim Crow': Prosperous Blacks and Vacations, Travel, and Outdoor Leisure, 1890–1945." *Journal of Negro History* 84 (1999): 130–49.

Foucault, Michel. *The History of Sexuality.* Translated by Robert Hurley. Vo1. 1. New York: Pantheon Books, 1978.

Fox, John S. "Gender Verification: What Purpose? What Price?" *British Journal of Sport Medicine* 27 (1993).

Franks, Lucinda. "See Jane Run." In *Out of the Bleachers: Writings on Women and Sport,* edited by Stephanie L. Twin, 94–103. Old Westbury, N.Y.: Feminist Press, 1979.

Frazier, E. Franklin. *The Black Bourgeoisie.* New York: Free Press, 1957.

———. *The Negro Family in the United States.* Rev. ed. Chicago: University of Chicago Press, 1966.

Freidenfelds, Lara. *The Modern Period: Menstruation in Twentieth-Century America.* Baltimore: Johns Hopkins University Press, 2009.

Friedman, Nancy. *Everything You Must Know about Tampons.* New York: Berkley Books, 1981.

Gach, John J. "The Case for and against Girl Cheerleaders." *School Activities* 9 (1938): 301–2.

Gaines, Jane M., ed. *Fabrications: Costume and the Female Body.* New York: Routledge, 1990.

Gallico, Paul. *Farewell to Sport.* New York: Alfred A. Knopf, 1941.

Gammon, Marilie D., Julie A. Britton, and Susan L. Teitelbaum. "Does Physical Activity Reduce the Risk of Breast Cancer?" *Menopause* 3 (1996): 172–80.

Gehlsen, Gale, and Lela June Stoner. "The Female Breast in Sport and Exercise." In *Sports Women: Medicine and Sport Science,* edited by Marlene J. Adrian, 13–22. Basel: Karger, 1987.

Gerber, Ellen W. "College Sport." In *The American Woman in Sport,* edited by Ellen W. Gerber, Jan Felsin, Pearl Berlin, and Waneen Wyrick, 48–85. Reading, Mass.: Addison-Wesley, 1974.

———. "The Controlled Development of Collegiate Sport for Women, 1923–1936." *Journal of Sport History* 2 (1975): 1–28.

———. "Olympic Competition." In *The American Woman in Sport,* edited by Ellen W. Gerber, Jan Felshin, Pearl Berlin, and Waneen Wyrick. Reading, Mass.: Addison-Wesley.

Gerber, Ellen W., Jan Felshin, Pearl Berlin, and Waneen Wyrick. *The American Woman in Sport.* Reading, Mass.: Addison-Wesley, 1974.

Gibson, Althea. *I Always Wanted to Be Somebody.* Edited by Ed Fitzgerald. New York: Harper and Brothers, 1958.

Gilbert, Bil, and Nancy Williamson. "Programmed to Be Losers." *Sports Illustrated,* June 1, 1973, 60–73.

———. "Sport Is Unfair to Women." *Sports Illustrated,* May 28, 1973. http://sportsillustrated .cnn.com/vault/article/magazine/MAG1087396/index.htm.

———. "Women in Sport: A Progress Report." *Sports Illustrated,* July 29, 1974. http:// sportsillustrated.cnn.com/vault/article/magazine/MAG1088817/index.htm.

Gilbert, David. "The Vicar's Daughter and the Goddess of Tennis: Cultural Geographies of Sporting Femininity and Bodily Practices in Edwardian Suburbia." *Cultural Geographies* 18 (2011): 187–207.

Gillmeister, Heiner. *Tennis: A Cultural History.* London: Leicester University Press, 1997.

Gissendanner, Cindy Himes. "African-American Women and Competitive Sport, 1920–1960." In *Women, Sport, and Culture,* edited by Susan Birrell and Cheryl L. Cole, 81–92. Champaign, Ill.: Human Kinetics, 1994.

———. "African American Women Olympians: The Impact of Race, Gender, and Class Ideologies, 1932–1968." *Research Quarterly for Exercise and Sport* 67 (1996): 172–82.

"Glamor-Gal [*sic*] Gussy." *Senior Scholastic,* May 10, 1948, 36.

Glassner, Barry. "Fitness and the Postmodern Self." *Journal of Health and Social Behavior* 30 (1989): 180–91.

Goldman, Robert, Deborah Heath, and Sharon L. Smith. "Commodity Feminism." *Critical Studies in Mass Communication* 8 (1991): 333–51.

Goldman, Robert, and Stephen Papson. *Nike Culture: The Sign of the Swoosh.* Thousand Oaks, Calif.: Sage, 1999.

Gonzales, Arturo F. "The First College Cheer." *American Mercury* (November 1956): 101–4.

Gordon, Linda. "On Difference." *Genders* 10 (1991): 91–111.

"Gorgeous Gussie." *Life,* April 25, 1949, 91–92.

"Go Team!" *Economist* (July 31, 2010).

Graham, Hugh Davis. "The Storm over Grove City College: Civil Rights Regulation, Higher Education, and the Reagan Administration." *History of Education Quarterly* 38 (1998): 407–29.

Griffin, James E. "Androgen Resistance: The Clinical and Molecular Spectrum." *New England Journal of Medicine* 326 (1992): 611–18.

Griffin, Pat. "Soccer Star Megan Rapinoe to the World: I'm Gay." *It Takes a Team* Blog, July 3, 2012. http://ittakesateam.blogspot.com/.

———. *Strong Women, Deep Closets: Lesbians and Homophobia in Sport.* Champaign, Ill.: Human Kinetics, 1998.

Grindstaff, Laura. "Hold That (Gender) Line! Cheerleading on ESPN." *Contexts* (Summer 2005): 71–73.

Grundy, Pamela. *Learning to Win: Sports, Education, and Social Change in Twentieth-Century North Carolina.* Chapel Hill: University of North Carolina Press, 2001.

———. "Ora Washington: The First Black Female Athletic Star." In *Out of the Shadows: A Biographical History of African American Athletes,* edited by David K. Wiggins, 79–92. Fayetteville: University of Arkansas Press, 2006.

Guttmann, Allen. *Women's Sports: A History.* New York: Columbia University Press, 1991.

"Gym Dandy." *Time,* July 27, 1992.

Hall, Dennis. "Spears' Space: The Play of Innocence and Experience in the Bare-Midriff Fashion." *Journal of Popular Culture* 39 (2006): 1025–34.

Hall, G. Stanley. *Adolescence: Its Psychology and Its Relations to Physiology, Anthropology, Sociology, Sex, Crime, Religion, and Education.* New York: Appleton, 1907.

Hall, M. Ann. *Feminism and Sporting Bodies.* Champaign, Ill.: Human Kinetics, 1996.

Hallmark, James R., and Richard N. Armstrong. "Gender Equity in Televised Sports: A Comparative Analysis of Men's and Women's NCAA Division I Basketball Championships Broadcasts, 1991–1995." *Journal of Broadcasting and Electronic Media* 43 (1999): 222–35.

Hannel, Susan L. "The Influence of American Jazz on Fashion." In *Twentieth-Century American Fashion,* edited by Linda Welters and Patricia A. Cunningham, 57–77. New York: Berg, 2004.

Hanson, Mary Ellen. *Go! Fight! Win! Cheerleading in American Culture.* Bowling Green, Ohio: Bowling Green State University Popular Press, 1995.

Hanson, Sharon Kinney. *The Life of Helen Stephens: The Fulton Flash.* Carbondale: Southern Illinois University Press, 2004.

Hardin, Marie, and Stacie Shain. "Strength in Numbers? The Experiences and Attitudes of Women in Sports Media Careers." *Journalism and Mass Communication Quarterly* 82 (2005): 804–19.

Hardon, Virgil O. "A Case of Retroflexion of the Uterus Treated by Daily Replacement and the 'Supporting Tampon.'" *Atlanta Medical and Surgical Journal* 2 (February 1886): 737–40.

Hargreaves, Jennifer. "Olympic Women: A Struggle for Recognition." In *Women and Sports in the United States: A Documentary Reader,* edited by Jean O'Reilly and Susan K. Cahn, 3–14. Boston: Northeastern University Press, 2007.

———. *Sporting Females: Critical Issues in the History and Sociology of Women's Sports.* London: Routledge, 1994.

Harres, Bea. "Attitudes of Students toward Women's Athletic Competition." *Research Quarterly* 39 (1968): 279–84.

Hart, M. Marie, ed. *Sport and the Socio-cultural Process.* Dubuque, Iowa: Wm. C. Brown, 1972.

Hatton, Charles Thomas, and Robert W. Hatton. "The Sideline Show." *Journal of the National Association of Women Deans, Administrators, and Counselors* 41 (1978): 23–28.

Hausman, Bernice L. *Changing Sex: Transsexualism, Technology, and the Idea of Gender.* Durham, N.C.: Duke University Press, 1995.

Haven, Paul. "Olympics 2012: Year of the Woman." Yahoo Sports, July 26, 2012. http://sports.yahoo.com/news/olympics-2012-woman-152723371—oly.html.

Hay, Eduardo. "Sex Determination in Putative Female Athletes." *Journal of the American Medical Association* 4 (1972): 39–41.

Haycock, C. E. "Breast Support and Protection in the Female Athlete." In *American Alliance for Health, Physical Recreation, and Dance Research Consortium: Symposium Papers, Sport, Health Fitness, and Dance.* Washington, D.C.: AAPHERD, 1978.

Heggie, Vanessa. "Testing Sex and Gender in Sports: Reinventing, Reimagining, and Reconstructing Histories." *Endeavour* 34 (2010): 157–63.

Hellebrandt, Frances A., and Margaret H. Meyer. "Physiological Data Significant to Participation by Women in Physical Activity." *Research Quarterly of the American Association
for Health, Physical Education, and Recreation* 10 (1939): 10–23.

Henderson, Edwin B. "The Negro in Tennis." *Negro History Bulletin* 15 (December 1951): 54.

Heywood, Leslie. *Bodymakers: A Cultural Anatomy of Women's Body Building.* New Brunswick, N.J.: Rutgers University Press, 1998.

Heywood, Leslie, and Jennifer Drake. *Third Wave Agenda: Being Feminist, Doing Feminism.*
Minneapolis: University of Minnesota Press, 1997.

Heywood, Leslie, and Shari L. Dworkin. *Built to Win: The Female Athlete as Cultural Icon.*
Minneapolis: University of Minnesota Press, 2003.

Higdon, Rose, and Hal Higdon. "What Sports for Girls?" *Today's Health* (October 1967): 21.

Higginbotham, Evelyn Brooks. "Beyond the Sound of Silence: Afro-American Women's
History." *Gender & History* 1 (1989): 50–67.

———. *Righteous Discontent: Women's Movement in the Black Baptist Church, 1880–1920.*
Cambridge, Mass.: Harvard University Press, 1994.

Higgs, Catriona T., and Karen H. Weiller. "Gender Bias and the 1992 Summer Olympic Games: An Analysis of Television Coverage." *Journal of Sport and Social Issues* 18
(1994): 234–46.

Hipkin, L. J. "The XY Female in Sport: The Controversy Continues." *British Journal of
Sports Medicine* 27 (1993): 150–56.

Hoad, Neville. "Run, Caster Semenya, Run! Nativism and the Translations of Gender Variance." *Safundi: The Journal of South African and American Studies* 11 (2010): 397–405.

Hofer, Jack. "Mixing Fitness with Pleasure." *Today's Health,* June 1980.

Hoffman, Jeane. "The Sutton Sisters." In *Fireside Book of Tennis,* edited by Allison Danzig
and Peter Schwed, 74. New York: Simon and Schuster, 1972.

Hogan, Candace Lyle. "Revolutionizing School and Sports: 10 Years of Title IX." *Ms.,*
May 1982, 25–29.

Hollander, Anne. *Sex and Suits: The Evolution of Modern Dress.* New York: Kodansha
International, 1994.

Horwood, Catherine. "Dressing Like a Champion: Women's Tennis Wear in Interwar
England." In *The Englishness of English Dress,* edited by Christopher Breward, Becky
Conekin, and Caroline Cox, 45–60. London: Oxford University Press, 2002.

———. "'Girls Who Arouse Dangerous Passions': Women and Bathing, 1900–39." *Women's
History Review* 9 (2000): 653–73.

Houppert, Karen. *The Curse: Confronting the Last Unmentionable Taboo, Menstruation.*
New York: Farrar, Straus, and Giroux, 1999.

Howe, Julia Ward, ed. *Sex and Education: A Reply to Dr. E. H. Clarke's: "Sex in Education."*
Boston: Roberts Brothers, 1874.

Howell, Reet. *Her Story in Sport: A Historical Anthology of Women in Sports.* West Point,
N.Y.: Leisure Press, 1982.

"How Much Competition Is Good for Girls?" *Literary Digest* (April 17, 1926): 76.

Hubbard, Ruth. "Gender and Genitals: Constructs of Sex and Gender." *Social Text* 46–47
(1996): 157–65.

———. "The Story of Women's Athletics: Manipulating a Dream, 1890–1985." In *Women
and Sport: Interdisciplinary Perspectives,* edited by D. Margaret Costa and Sharon R.
Guthrie, 83–106. Champaign, Ill.: Human Kinetics, 1994.

Hult, Joan S. "NAGWS and AIAW: The Strange and Wondrous Journey to the Athletic Summit, 1950–1990." *Journal of Health, Physical Education, Recreation* 70 (1999): 24–31.

———. "Women's Struggle for Governance in U.S. Amateur Athletics." *International Review for the Sociology of Sport* 24 (1980): 249–61.

Hult, Joan S., and Roberta J. Park. "Women as Leaders in Physical Education and School-Based Sports, 1865–1930s." *Journal of Physical Education, Recreation, and Dance* 64 (1993): 35–40.

Hult, Joan S., and Marianna Trekell. *A Century of Women's Basketball: From Frailty to Final Four.* Reston, Va.: American Alliance for Health, Physical Education, Recreation, and Dance, 1991.

Hylton, Kevin. *"Race" and Sport: Critical Race Theory.* London: Routledge, 2009.

Hyman, Mark. "The 'Babe Factor' in Women's Soccer." *Business Week,* July 26, 1996, 118.

IAAF. "IAAF Regulations Governing Eligibility of Females with Hyperandrogenism to Compete in Women's Competitions." 2011. http://www.iaaf.org/mm/Document/AboutIAAF/Publications/05/98/78/20110430054216_httppostedfile_HARegulations(Final)-Appendices-AMG-30.04.2011_24299.pdf.

Ingram, Anne, and Jennifer Nupp. "Political Backlash and Implications to the Women's Civil Rights Movement Focusing on Sport and Athletic Opportunities for Women." Paper presented at the World Congress of Sociology, Mexico City, Mexico, August 16–21, 1982.

Inness, Sherrie A., ed. *Disco Divas: Women and Popular Culture in the 1970s.* Philadelphia: University of Pennsylvania Press, 2003.

"Intercollegiate Sports for Women." *American Physical Education Review* 29 (1924): 198–99.

"Introducing the, Uh, Ladies." *Journal of Health, Physical Education, Recreation* 198 (1966): 191–92.

Jaccard, James, and Tonya Dodge. "Participation in Athletics and Female Sexual Risk Behavior: The Evaluation of Four Causal Structures." *Journal of Adolescent Research* 17 (2002): 42–67.

Jackson, Steven J., and David L. Andrews, eds. *Sport, Culture, and Advertising: Identities, Commodities, and the Politics of Representation.* London: Routledge, 2005.

Jacobi, Mary Putnam. *The Question of Rest for Women during Menstruation.* New York: Putnam, 1877.

Jacobs, Helen Hull. "One Woman's Shorts Story." *World Tennis,* August 1984, 18.

———. "The Psychology of Tennis Clothes." *Ladies' Home Journal,* June 1934, 31, 118, 120.

Jamail, Deborah. "How to Look and Feel Like a Winner." *Harper's Bazaar,* May 1982, 130.

Jares, Joe. "Off to Russia, without Love." *Sports Illustrated,* July 12, 1965. http://sportsillustrated.cnn.com/vault/article/magazine/MAG1077414/index.htm.

Jeffords, Susan. *Hard Bodies: Hollywood Masculinity in the Reagan Era.* New Brunswick, N.J.: Rutgers University Press, 1994.

Jernigan, Sara Staff. "Mirror of Time: Some Causes for More American Women in Sport Competitions." *Quest* 22 (1974): 82–87.

———. "The National Institute on Girls Sports." *Journal of Health, Physical Education, Recreation* 34 (June 1963): 8.

———. "The Preparation of Women Athletes for the Olympic Games." *Olympic Review* 38–39 (November–December, 1970): 588–608.

———. "Two New Institutes on Girls Sports." *Journal of Health, Physical Education, Recreation* 36 (1965): 40.

———. "Women and the Olympics." *Journal of Health, Physical Education, Recreation* 33 (1962): 25–26.

Johnson, Sammye, and William G. Christ. "The Representation of Women: The News Magazine Cover as an International Cultural Artifact." In *Silent Voices*, edited by Doug A. Newsom and Bob J. Carrell, 215–35. Lanham, Md.: University Press of America, 1995.

———. "Women Through Time: Who Gets Covered?" *Journalism Quarterly* 65 (1988): 889–97.

Jones, Ray, Audrey J. Murrell, and Jennifer Jackson. "Pretty versus Powerful in the Sports Pages." *Journal of Sport and Social Issues* 23 (1999): 183–92.

Jordan, Chris. "Gender and Class Mobility in *Saturday Night Fever* and *Flashdance*." *Journal of Popular Film and Television* 23 (1996): 116–22.

Jordanova, Ludmilla. *History in Practice*. London: Arnold, 2000.

Jutel, Annemarie. "Cursed or Carefree? Menstrual Product Advertising and the Sportswoman." In *Sport, Culture, and Advertising: Identities, Commodities, and the Politics of Representation*, edited by Steven J. Jackson and David L. Andrews, 214–25. London: Routledge, 2005.

Kaestner, Robert, and Xin Xu. "Effects of Title IX and Sports Participation on Girls' Physical Activity and Weight." *Advances in Health Economics and Health Services Research* 17 (2006): 79–111.

———. "Title IX, Girls' Sports Participation, and Adult Female Physical Activity and Weight." *Evaluation Review* 34 (2010): 52–78.

Kagan, Elizabeth, and Margaret Morse. "The Body Electronic: Aerobic Exercise on Video; Women's Search for Empowerment and Self-Transformation." *Drama Review* 32 (1988): 164–80.

Kammen, Michael. *American Culture, American Tastes: Social Change and the Twentieth Century*. New York: Basic Books, 2000.

Kane, Mary Jo. "Resistance/Transformation of the Oppositional Binary: Exposing Sport as a Continuum." *Journal of Sport and Social Issues* 19 (1995): 191–218.

———. "Sex Sells Sex, Not Women's Sports." *Nation*, August 15–22, 2011. http://www.thenation.com/article/162390/sex-sells-sex-not-womens-sports.

Kane, Mary Jo, and Susan L. Greendorfer. "The Media's Role in Accommodating and Resisting Stereotyped Images of Women in Sport." In *Women, Media, and Sport: Challenging Gender Values*, edited by Pamela J. Creedon, 28–44. London: Sage, 1994.

Karkazis, Katrina, Rebecca Jordan-Young, Georgiann Davis, and Silva Comporesi. "Out of Bounds? A Critique of the New Policies on Hyperandrogenism in Elite Female Athletes." *American Journal of Bioethics* 12 (2012): 3–16.

Karnaky, Karl John. "Vaginal Tampons in Menstrual Hygiene." *Western Journal of Surgery, Obstetrics, and Gynecology* 51 (1943): 150–52.

Kelly-Gadol, Joan. "The Social Relations of the Sexes: Methodological Implications of Women's History." *Signs: Journal of Women in Culture and Society* 1 (1976): 810–12.

Kennard, June A. "The History of Physical Education." *Signs* 2 (1977): 835–42.

Kennard, Margot Elizabeth. "The Corporation in the Classroom: The Struggles over Meanings of Menstrual Education in Sponsored Films, 1947–1983." Ph.D. diss., University of Wisconsin, Madison, 1989.

Kennedy, John F. "The Soft American." *Sports Illustrated*, December 26, 1960. http://sportsillustrated.cnn.com/vault/article/magazine/MAG1134750/index.htm.

Kenney, Karen. "The Realm of Sports and the Athletic Woman, 1850–1900." In *Her Story in Sport: A Historical Anthology of Women in Sports,* edited by Reet Howell, 107–40. West Point, N.Y.: Leisure Press, 1982.

Kidd, Laura K., and Jane Farrell-Beck. "Menstrual Products Patented in the United States, 1854–1921." *Dress* 24 (1997): 27–43.

Kimmel, Michael S. "Men's Responses to Feminism at the Turn of the Century." *Gender and Society* 1 (1987): 261–83.

King, Billie Jean, with Cynthia Starr. *We Have Come a Long Way: The Story of Women's Tennis.* New York: McGraw-Hill, 1988.

Kinnick, Katherine N. "Gender Bias in Newspaper Profiles of 1996 Olympic Athletes: A Content Analysis of Five Major Dailies." *Women's Studies in Communication* 21 (1998): 212–37.

Koivula, Nathalie. "Gender Stereotyping in Televised Media Sport Coverage." *Sex Roles* 41 (1999): 589–603.

Krane, Vikki. "We Can Be Athletic and Feminine, but Do We Want To?" *Quest* 53 (2001): 115–33.

Kraus, Hans, and Ruth P. Hirschland. "Muscular Fitness and Health." *Journal of Health, Physical Education, Recreation* 24 (1953): 17–19.

Kwak, Sarah. "Lolo Jones' Openness with Personal Life Has Sparked Undue Criticism." *Sports Illustrated,* August 6, 2012. http://sportsillustrated.cnn.com/2012/olympics/2012/writers/sarah_kwak/08/06/lolo-jones-perception/index.html#ixzz23AvVW3yv.

Kyle, Donald G. "Fabulous Females and Ancient Olympia." In *Onward to the Olympics: Historical Perspectives on the Olympic Games,* edited by Gerald P. Schaus and Stephen Wenn, 131–52. Waterloo, Ontario: Wilfrid Laurier University Press, 2007.

A Lady Tennis Player. "Tennis Dress." *Godey's Lady's Book and Magazine,* November 1887, 403.

Lake, Robert J. "Gender and Etiquette in British Lawn Tennis, 1870–1939: A Case Study of 'Mixed Doubles.'" *International Journal of the History of Sport* 29, no. 5 (2012): 691–710.

Lance, Kathryn, and Maria Agardy. "Sexual Fitness." *McCall's,* August 1981, 89–90, 120.

Langlais, Dave. "The Road Not Taken: The Secret That Didn't Really Matter." *Running Times,* October 1988, 21–22.

Lansbury, Jennifer H. "'The Tuskegee Flash' and 'the Slender Harlem Stroker': Black Women Athletes on the Margin." *Journal of Sport History* 28 (2001): 233–52.

Laqueur, Thomas. *Making Sex: Body and Gender from Greeks to Freud.* Cambridge, Mass.: Harvard University Press, 1990.

Larimore, Rachael. "Why Are American Women Winning So Many Medals? It's Not Just Because of Title IX." *Slate,* August 10, 2012, http://www.slate.com/blogs/five_ring_circus/2012/08/10/olympics_and_title_ix_the_equal_rights_legislation_is_not_a_one_size_fits_all_answer_to_why_american_women_are_winning_so_many_medals_.html.

Larned, Deborah. "The Femininity Test: A Woman's First Olympic Hurdle." *womenSports,* July 1976, 9.

Laver, James. *Costume and Fashion: A Concise History.* 4th ed. London: Thames and Hudson, 2002.

———. *Taste and Fashion.* London: George G. Harrap, 1946.

Lawson, Hal A. "Physical Education and Sport in the Black Community." *Journal of Negro Education* 48 (1979): 187–95.

Lay, Mary M., Laura J. Gurak, Clare Gravon, and Cynthia Myntti, eds. *Body Talk: Rhetoric, Technology, Reproduction*. Madison: University of Wisconsin Press, 2000.

Leath, Virginia M., and Angela Lumpkin. "An Analysis of Sportswomen on the Covers and in the Feature Articles of *Women's Sports & Fitness* Magazine, 1975–1989." *Journal of Sport and Social Issues* 16 (1992): 121–26.

Lee, Hugh M. "Athletics and the Bikini Girls from Piazza Armerina." *Stadion* 10 (1984): 45–76.

Lee, Mabel. "The Case for and against Intercollegiate Athletics for Women and the Situation as It Stands To-Day." *American Physical Education Review* 29 (January 1924): 13–19.

Lenglen, Suzanne. *Lawn Tennis for Girls*. Edited by Eustace E. White. New York: American Sports, 1920.

Lenskyj, Helen Jefferson. *Out of Bounds: Women, Sport, and Sexuality*. Toronto: Women's Press, 1986.

Lenskyj, Helen Jefferson, and Stephen Wagg, eds. *A Handbook of Olympic Studies*. New York: Palgrave Macmillan.

Lerman, Nina E., Ruth Oldenziel, and Arwen P. Mohun, eds. *Gender and Technology: A Reader*. Baltimore: Johns Hopkins University Press, 2003.

Lerner, Gerda. "Reconceptualizing Differences among Women." *Journal of Women's History* 1 (1990): 106–22.

———. "U.S. Women's History: Past, Present, and Future." *Journal of Women's History* 16 (2004): 10–27.

"Lessons from Old Olympian." *Life*, March 19, 1956, 113–14.

Lewis, Dwight, and Susan Thomas. *A Will to Win*. Mount Juliet, Tenn.: Cumberland Press, 1983.

Ley, Katherine, and Sara Staff Jernigan. "The Roots and the Tree." *Journal of Health, Physical Education, Recreation* 33 (1962): 24–26, 57.

Li, Peter S. "Contradictions of 'Racial' Discourse." In *Interrogating Race and Racism*, edited by Vijay Agnew, 37–54. Toronto: University of Toronto Press, 2007.

Liberti, Rita. "'We Were Ladies, We Just Played Basketball Like Boys': African American Womanhood and Competitive Basketball at Bennett College, 1928–1942." *Journal of Sport History* 26 (1999): 567–84.

Lichtenstein, Grace. *A Long Way, Baby: The Inside Story of the Women in Pro Tennis*. Greenwich, Conn.: Fawcett, 1974.

Lippert, Jack. "Short Exposure." *Scholastic*, April 18, 1936, 24–25.

Ljungqvist, Arne, Luis Horta, and Gary Wadler. "Doping: World Agency Sets Standards to Promote Fair Play." *Nature* 455 (2008): 1176.

Ljungqvist, Arne, Joe Leigh Simpson, and the IAAF Work Group on Gender Verification. "Medical Examination for Health of All Athletes Replacing the Need for Gender Verification in International Sports: The International Amateur Athletic Plan." *Journal of the American Medical Association* 267, no. 6 (1992): 850–52.

Lloyd, Moya. "Feminism, Aerobics, and the Politics of the Body." *Body and Society* 2 (1996): 79–98.

Lomax, Michael E., ed. *Sport and the Racial Divide: African-American and Latino Experiences in an Era of Change*. Jackson: University Press of Mississippi, 2008.

Longman, Jeré. *The Girls of Summer: The U.S. Women's Soccer Team and How It Changed the World.* New York: HarperCollins, 2000.

———. "How the Women Won." *New York Times Magazine,* June 23, 1996, 25.

Lopiano, Donna. "Sex May Sell, but Sexism Sells Women Short." *Street and Smith's Sportsbusiness Journal* (February 4–10, 2002): 31.

Lumpkin, Angela. *Women's Tennis: A Historical Documentary of the Players and Their Game.* Troy, N.Y.: Whitson, 1981.

M. H. "Place Aux Dames." *Lippincott's Magazine of Popular Literature and Science.* November 1881, 521.

MacDonald, Myra. *Representing Women: Myths of Femininity in the Popular Media.* London: Edward Arnold, 1995.

Magid, Maurice O., and Jacob Geiger. "The Intravaginal Tampon in Menstrual Hygiene." *Medical Record* 155 (1942): 316–20.

Magnusson, Lucille. "The What and Why of AIAW." *Journal of Health, Physical Education, Recreation* (March 1972): 71–72.

Maguire, Joseph, and Louise Mansfield. "'No-Body's Perfect': Women, Aerobics, and the Body Beautiful." *Sociology of Sport Journal* 15 (1998): 109–37.

"Major Wingfield on Lawn Tennis Costumes." *Harper's Bazaar,* October 1, 1881, 630.

Mandel, Bill. "She's Got a Ticket to Ride." *Women's Sports and Fitness,* December 1984, 29.

Mandziuk, Roseann M. "'Ending Women's Greatest Hygenic Mistake': Modernity and the Mortification of Menstruation in Kotex Advertising." *Women's Studies Quarterly* 38 (2010): 42–62.

Mangan, J. A., and Roberta J. Park, eds. *From "Fair Sex to Feminism": Sport and the Socialization of Women in the Industrial and Post-industrial Eras.* London: Frank Cass, 1987.

Marble, Alice. "A Vital Issue." *American Lawn Tennis,* July 1950, 14.

Marchand, Roland. *Advertising and the American Dream: Making Way for Modernity, 1920–1940.* Berkeley: University of California Press, 1985.

Markula, Pirkko. "Beyond the Perfect Body: Women's Body Image Distortion in Fitness Magazine Discourse." *Journal of Sport and Social Issues* 25 (2001): 158–79.

———. "Firm but Shapely, Fit but Sexy, Strong but Thin: The Post-Modern Aerobicizing Female Bodies." *Sociology of Sport Journal* 12 (1995): 424–53.

Martínez-Patiño, María José. "Personal Account: A Woman Tried and Tested." *Lancet* 366 (2005): S38.

Mayers, May R. "Abdominal Exercises." *American Journal of Nursing* 28 (April 1928): 363–64.

Mays, W. H. "The Tampon in Menorrhagia." *Pacific Medical Journal* 34 (March 1891): 151–56.

McCallum, Jack "Everybody's Doin' It." *Sports Illustrated,* December 3, 1984, 76.

———. "Unflagging." *Sports Illustrated,* August 14, 2000. http://sportsillustrated.cnn.com/vault/article/magazine/MAG1019901/index.htm.

McDonald, Mary. "The Marketing of the Women's National Basketball Association and the Making of Postfeminism." *International Review for the Sociology of Sport* 35 (2000): 35–47.

McElroy, James. *We've Got Spirit: The Life and Times of America's Greatest Cheerleading Team.* New York: Simon and Schuster, 1999.

McGaw, Judith. "Why Feminine Technologies Matter." In *Gender and Technology: A Reader,* edited by Nina E. Lerman, Ruth Oldenziel, and Arwen P. Mohun, 13–36. Baltimore: Johns Hopkins University Press, 2003.

McGee, Rosemary. "Comparisons of Attitudes toward Intensive Competition for High School Girls." *Research Quarterly* 27 (1957): 60–73.

McKay, Mary-Jayne. "Venus Williams' French Open Outfit: Is She Naked?" CBS News. http://www.cbsnews.com/8301-31749_162-20005718-10391698.html.

McKinnon, Catharine A. *Feminism Unmodified: Discourses on Life and Law.* Cambridge, Mass.: Harvard University Press, 1987.

McLean, Mrs. Marshall, and Miss Edna Wildey. "Women's Apparel for the Court." *American Lawn Tennis,* May 15, 1915, 70–71.

McLuhan, Marshall. *Understanding Media: The Extensions of Man.* New York: McGraw-Hill, 1964.

McManus, Marjorie. *Magazine Publishing Management.* New Canaan, Conn.: Folio, 1976.

Mead, Rebecca. "The Talk of the Town." *New Yorker,* July 26, 1999, 25.

Merck, Mandy. "The Question of Caster Semenya." *Radical Philosophy* 160 (2010): 2–7.

Merriam, Georgia. "Do Women Require Mental and Bodily Rest during Menstruation, and to What Extent?" *Columbus Medical Journal* 13 (1894): 294–301.

Messner, Michael A. "Sports and Male Domination: The Female Athlete as Contested Ideological Terrain." In *Women, Sport, and Culture,* edited by Susan Birrell and Cheryl L. Cole, 65–80. Champaign, Ill.: Human Kinetics, 1994.

———. *Taking the Field: Women, Men, and Sports.* Minneapolis: University of Minnesota Press, 2002.

Messner, Michael A., and Cheryl Cooky. "Gender in Televised Sports: News and Highlights Shows, 1989–2009." Center for Feminist Research, University of Southern California, 2010. http://dornsife.usc.edu/cfr/gender-in-televised-sports/.

Messner, Michael A., Margaret Carlisle Duncan, and Cheryl Cooky. "Silence, Sports Bras, and Wrestling Porn." *Journal of Sport and Social Issues* 27 (2003): 38–51.

Messner, Michael A., and Donald F. Sabo, eds. *Sport, Men, and the Gender Order: Critical Feminist Perspectives.* Champaign, Ill.: Human Kinetics, 1990.

Metheny, Eleanor. *Connotations of Movement in Sports and Dance.* Dubuque, Iowa: Wm. C. Brown, 1965.

———. "Symbolic Forms of Movement: The Feminine Image in Sports." In *Sport and the Socio-Cultural Process,* edited by M. Marie Hart, 277–90. Dubuque, Iowa: Wm. C. Brown, 1972.

Michener, James A. *Sports in America.* New York: Random House, 1976.

Miller, Toby. *Sportsex.* Philadelphia: Temple University Press, 2001.

Mills, Nicolaus, ed. *Culture in an Age of Money: The Legacy of the 1980s in America.* Chicago: Ivan R. Dee, 1990.

"Miss Sutton as a Tennis Exponent." *Town and Country,* June 2, 1906, 26.

Moore, Keith L. "Sexual Identity of Athletes." *Journal of the American Medical Association* 205 (1968).

Moore, Keith L., and Murray L. Barr. "Smears from the Oral Mucosa in the Detection of Chromosomal Sex." *Lancet* 2 (1955): 57–58.

Moritz, Amy. "Cheerleading: Not Just for the Sidelines Anymore." *Sport and Society* 14 (2001): 660–69.

Morris, Meaghan. *Too Soon Too Late: History in Popular Culture.* Bloomington: Indiana University Press, 1998.

Morse, Margaret. "Artemis Aging: Exercise and the Female Body on Video." *Discourse* 10 (1987–88): 19–52.

Mosher, Clelia Duel. "The Means to the End." *American Physical Education Review* 30 (1925): 535–40.

———. *Woman's Physical Freedom.* New York: Woman's Press, 1923.

Mott, Jane A. "National Conference on Social Changes and Implications for Physical Education and Sports Programs." *Journal of Health, Physical Education, Recreation* 29, no. 7 (1958): 12–13, 63.

Mrozek, Donald J. *Sport and American Mentality, 1880–1910.* Knoxville: University of Tennessee Press, 1983.

Mueller, Frederick O. "Cheerleading Injuries and Safety." *Journal of Athletic Training* 44 (2009): 565–66.

Mueller, Frederick O., and Robert C. Cantu. "Catastrophic Sports Injury Research: Twenty-Eighth Annual Report, Fall 1982–Spring 2010." http://www.unc.edu/depts/nccsi.

Munro, Brenna. "Caster Semenya: Gods and Monsters." *Safundi: The Journal of South African and American Studies* 11 (2010): 383–96.

National Coalition for Women and Girls in Education. *Title IX at 40: Working to Ensure Gender Equity in Education.* Washington, D.C.: National Coalition for Women and Girls in Education, 2012.

Neil, Randy. *The Encyclopedia of Cheerleading.* Shawnee Mission, Kans.: International Cheerleading Foundation, 1975.

Newhall, Kristine E., and Erin E. Buzuvis. "(E)Racing Jennifer Harris: Sexuality and Race, Law, and Discourse in *Harris v. Portland.*" *Journal of Sport and Social Issues* 32 (2008): 345–68.

Newsom, Doug A., and Bob J. Carrell, eds. *Silent Voices.* Lanham, Md.: University Press of America, 1995.

"New York Fashions." *Harper's Bazaar,* June 20, 1896, 523.

"No Sex Tests, Please . . ." *Maclean's,* July 27, 1992, 10.

Novak, Emil. *A Woman Asks the Doctor.* Baltimore: Williams and Wilkins, 1935.

Nyad, Diana, and Candace Lyle Hogan. "Women: Empowered by the Evolution of Sports Technology." In *Designs for Sports: The Cult of Performance,* edited by Akiko Bush. New York: Princeton Architectural Press, 1998.

Nyong'o, Tavia. "The Unforgivable Transgression of Being Caster Semenya." *Women and Performance: A Journal of Feminist Theory* 20 (2012): 95–100.

O'Connor, Kaori. "The Body and the Brand: How Lycra Shaped America." In *Producing Fashion: Commerce, Culture, and Consumers,* edited by Regina Lee Blaszczyk, 207–30. Philadelphia: University of Pennsylvania Press, 2008.

Ogden, Annegret. "Queen Helen: The Voice of Helen Wills." *Californians,* January–February 1989, 12–13, 57.

Olsen-Acre, Haley K. "The Use of Drug Testing to Police Sex and Gender in the Olympic Games." *Michigan Journal of Gender and Law* 13 (2007): 207–36.

"Olympic Games." *Time,* August 10, 1936.

"The Olympics: Ponytails, Performance, and the Ultimate Propaganda Machine." *Chronicle of Higher Education* 47 (September 15, 2000): B4.

"Organized Cheering." *Nation,* January 5, 1911, 5–6.

Oriard, Michael. *King Football: Sport and Spectacle in the Golden Age of Radio and News-reels, Movies and Magazines, the Weekly and the Daily Press.* Chapel Hill: University of North Carolina Press, 2001.

Ostrander, Elaine A., Heather J. Hudson, and Gary K. Ostrander. "Genetics of Athletic Performance." *Annual Review of Genomics and Human Genetics* 10 (2009): 407–29.

Ottum, Bob. "Dolls on the Move to Mexico." *Sports Illustrated,* September 2, 1968. http://sportsillustrated.cnn.com/vault/article/magazine/MAG1081548/index.htm.

"Outstanding Problems in Girls' Athletics." *American Physical Education Review* 31 (May 1926): 846.

Owen, David. "Title IX Babies." *New Yorker,* May 15, 2006, 44–49.

Palmer, Bill. *Girls in Ponytails Chasing a Ball: The Rise of Women's Intercollegiate Soccer, 1972–2006.* Charleston, S.C.: BookSurge, 2008.

"Paralympics Receiving Minimal Coverage in U.S." *Sports Illustrated,* August 23, 2012. http://sportsillustrated.cnn.com/more/news/20120823/paralympics-broadcasting/#ixzz25svQvj4r.

Paret, J. Parmly. "Good Form in Women's Tennis." *Harper's Bazaar,* June 9, 1900, 341–44.

Park, Roberta J. "Sport, Gender, and Society in a Transatlantic Perspective." In *From "Fair Sex to Feminism": Sport and the Socialization of Women in the Industrial and Post-Industrial Eras,* edited by J. A. Mangan and Roberta J. Park, 58–93. London: Frank Cass, 1987.

Park, Shelley M. "From Sanitation to Liberation? The Modern and Postmodern Marketing of Menstrual Products." *Journal of Popular Culture* 30 (1996): 149–68.

Parratt, Catriona M. "From the History of Women in Sport to Women's Sport History: A Research Agenda." In *Women and Sport: Interdisciplinary Perspectives,* edited by D. Margaret Costa and Sharon R. Guthrie, 5–14. Champaign, Ill.: Human Kinetics, 1994.

"People." *Time,* November 2, 1962. http://www.time.com/time/magazine/article/0,9171,874598-2,00.html.

Percival, Eleanor. "Menstrual Disturbances as They May Affect Women in Industry." *Canadian Nurse* 39 (1943): 335–37.

"Perfecting Your Body." *Mademoiselle,* October 1981, 120–23.

Perrin, Ethel. "A Crisis in Girls Athletics." *Sportsmanship* (December 1928): 10.

———. "More Competitive Athletics for Girls—but the Right Kinds." *American Physical Education Review* (October 1929): 474.

Perrin, Ethel, and Grace Turner. *Play Day: The Spirit of Sport.* New York: American Child Health Association, 1929.

Petchesky, Barry. "'I'm Gay,' Says Megan Rapinoe. 'That's Nice,' Says Everyone." Deadspin.com, July 3, 2012. http://deadspin.com/5923161/im-gay-says-megan-rapinoe-thats-nice-says-everyone.

Peters, Justin. "While You Were Staring at Their Butts, Misty May-Treanor and Kerri Walsh Jennings Just Won Their Gold Medal." *Slate,* August 8, 2012. http://www.slate.com/blogs/five_ring_circus/2012/08/08/misty_may_treanor_kerri_walsh_jennings_2012_olympics_while_you_were_staring_at_their_butts_they_just_won_another_gold_medal_.html.

Peters, Mary, with Ian Wooldridge. *Mary P.: Autobiography.* London: Paul, 1974.

Phillips, Janet, and Peter Phillips. "History from Below: Women's Underwear and the Rise of Women's Sport." *Journal of Popular Culture* 27 (1993): 129–48.

Phillips, Madge. "Sociological Considerations of the Female Participant." In *Women and Sport: A National Research Conference,* edited by Dorothy V. Harris, 185–202. University Park: Pennsylvania State University, 1971.

Pickett, Moneque Walker, Marvin P. Dawkins, and Jomills Henry Braddock II. "The Effect of Title IX on Participation of Black and White Females in High School Sports: Evidence from National Longitudinal Surveys." *Journal of Race and Policy* 5 (2009): 79–90.

Pilgrim, Jill, David Martin, and Will Binder. "Far from the Finish Line: Transsexualism and Athletic Competition." *Fordham Intellectual Property, Media, and Entertainment Law Journal* 13 (2003).

Poe, Alison. "Active Women in Ads." *Journal of Communication* 26 (1976): 185–92.

Poirer, Diane Élisabeth. *Tennis Fashion.* New York: Assouline, 2003.

"Ponytail Express." *Sports Illustrated,* September 17, 1979.

Portwood, Jerry. "Fever Pitch." *Out,* July 2, 2012. http://www.out.com/entertainment/sports/2012/07/02/megan-rapinoe-womens-soccer-lesbian-girlfriend.

"Pour le Sport." *Time,* March 18, 1929. http://www.time.com/time/magazine/article/0,9171,737570,00.html.

Prescott, Heather Munro. "'Guides to Womanhood': Gynaecology and Adolescent Sexuality in the Post–Second World War Era." In *Women, Health, and Nation: Canada and the United States since 1945,* edited by Georgina D. Feldberg, 199–222. Montreal: McGill-Queen's University Press, 2003.

"Preserving la Difference." *Time,* September 16, 1966, 72.

"Questions and Answers." *Hygeia* 23 (December 1945).

Quinn, Molly. "Getting Thrown Around." *Taboo* 7 (Fall–Winter 2003): 7–24.

Rader, Benjamin G. *American Sports: From the Age of Folk Games to the Age of Televised Sports.* 4th ed. Upper Saddle River, N.J.: Prentice Hall, 1999.

"Really? Gabby Douglas Wins a Gold Medal and People Are Criticizing Her Hair?" *Clutch,* August 1, 2012. http://www.clutchmagonline.com/2012/08/really-gabby-douglas-wins-a-gold-medal-and-people-are-criticizing-her-hair/.

"Record Number of Females to Take Part in London 2012." August 16, 2012. http://www.paralympic.org/news/record-number-females-take-part-london-2012.

Reed, J. D. "America Shapes Up." *Time,* November 2, 1981. http://www.time.com/time/magazine/article/0,9171,950613,00.html.

Richards, Elizabeth. "Everyday Problems in Girls' Basketball." *American Physical Education Review* 25 (December 1910): 91.

Riess, Steven A. "The New Sport History." *Reviews in American History* 18 (1990): 311–25.

Riordan, James. "Women in Sport: Some English Observations on Russian Women Who Have to Be Trained to Smile." *Bulletin of Physical Education* 16 (1980): 17–24.

Ritchie, Ian. "Sex Tested, Gender Verified: Controlling Female Sexuality in the Age of Containment." *Sport History Review* 34 (2003): 80–98.

Roberts, Selena. *A Necessary Spectacle: Billie Jean King, Bobby Riggs, and the Tennis Match That Leveled the Game.* New York: Crown, 2005.

Robinson, Laura. *Black Tights: Women, Sport, and Sexuality.* Toronto: HarperCollins, 2002.

Rogers, Frederick Rand. "Olympics for Girls?" *School and Society* 30 (1929): 190–94.

Rogin, Gilbert. "Flamin' Mamie's Bouffant Belles." *Sports Illustrated*, April 20, 1964. http://sportsillustrated.cnn.com/vault/article/magazine/MAG1075866/index.htm.

Rohrbaugh, Joanna Bunker. "Femininity on the Line." *Psychology Today*, August 1979, 30–42.

Rosoff, Nancy G. "'Every Muscle Is Absolutely Free': Advertising and Advice about Clothing for Athletic American Women, 1880–1920." *Journal of American and Comparative Cultures* 25 (2002): 25–51.

Ross, John M. "Good Gussy." *Colliers*, September 3, 1949, 70–72.

Rothenberger, Lee A., June I. Chang, and Thomas A. Cable. "Prevalence and Types of Injuries in Aerobic Dancers." *American Journal of Sports Medicine* 16 (1988): 403–7.

"Russians Bear Down for Olympics." *Life*, August 6, 1956, 91–96.

Ryan, Allan J. "Sex and the Singles Player." *Physician and Sports Medicine* 4 (1976): 39–41.

Sabo, Don. "Psychosocial Impacts of Athletic Participation on American Women: Facts and Fables." In *Sport in Contemporary Society: An Anthology*, edited by D. Stanley Eitzen, 374–87. New York: St. Martin's Press, 1993.

Sabo, Don, and Phil Veliz. "Go Out and Play: Youth Sports in America." Women's Sports Foundation research report. 2008. http://www.womenssportsfoundation.org/.

Sabol, Blair. *The Body of America*. New York: Arbor House, 1986.

Sachs, Honor R. "Reconstructing a Life: The Archival Challenges of Women's History." *Library Trends* 56 (2008): 650–66.

Sackren, Harry S. "Vaginal Tampons for Menstrual Absorption." *Clinical Medicine and Surgery* 46 (1949): 329.

Sakamoto, Hiromi, et al. "Femininity Control at the XXth Universiade in Kobe, Japan." *International Journal of Sports Medicine* 9 (1988): 193–95.

Salisbury, Tracey M. "First to the Finish Line: The Tennessee State Tigerbelles, 1944–1994." Ph.D. diss., University of North Carolina at Greensboro, 2009.

"Sanitary Pads and Tampons: Ratings and Comparisons of Leading Brands." *Consumer Reports*, September 1945, 240–42.

Scardino, Emily. "Women's Activewear Concept Stores Grow." *DSN Retailing Today*, August 4, 2003, 15.

Schaffer, Kay, and Sidonie Smith. *The Olympics at the Millennium: Power, Politics, and the Games*. New Brunswick, N.J.: Rutgers University Press, 2000.

Schaus, Gerald P., and Stephen Wenn, eds. *Onward to the Olympics: Historical Perspectives on the Olympic Games*. Waterloo, Ontario: Wilfrid Laurier University Press, 2007.

Schiebinger, Londa. *Feminism and the Body*. New York: Oxford University Press, 2000.

Schmitt, Mary. "The State of Women in Sports Media." In *Sport in Society: Equal Opportunity or Business as Usual?*, edited by Richard E. Lapchick, 234–36. London: Sage, 1996.

Schoenfeld, Bruce. *The Match: Althea Gibson and Angela Buxton*. New York: HarperCollins, 2004.

Schroeder, Fred E. H. "Feminine Hygiene, Fashion, and the Emancipation of American Women." *American Studies* 17 (1976): 101–10.

Schultz, Jaime. "The Accidental Celebritisation of Caster Semenya." *Celebrity Studies* 3 (2012): 283–96.

———. "Caster Semenya and the 'Question of Too': Sex Testing in Elite Women's Sport and the Issue of Advantage." *Quest* 63 (2011): 228–43.

———. "Discipline and Push-Up: Female Bodies, Femininity, and Sexuality in Popular Representations of Sports Bras." *Sociology of Sport Journal* 21 (2004): 185–205.

———. "Disciplining Sex: 'Gender Verification' Policies and Women's Sport." In *A Handbook of Olympic Studies,* edited by Helen Lenskyj and Stephen Wagg, 443–60. New York: Palgrave Macmillan.

———. "New Standards, Same Refrain: The IAAF's Regulations on Hyperandrogenism." *American Journal of Bioethics* 12 (2012): 32–33.

———. "Reading the Catsuit: Serena Williams and the Production of Blackness at the 2002 U.S. Open." *Journal of Sport and Social Issues* 29 (2005): 338–57.

Schulze, Laurie Jane. "'Getting Physical': Text/Context/Reading and the Made-for-Television Movie." *Cinema Journal* 25 (1986): 35–50.

———. "On the Muscle." In *Fabrications: Costume and the Female Body,* edited by Jane M. Gaines, 59–78. New York: Routledge, 1990.

Scott, Ann Crittenden. "Closing the Muscle Gap." *Ms.,* September 1973, 89.

Scott, Joan W. "Gender as a Useful Category of Historical Analysis." *American Historical Review* 91 (1986): 1053–75.

Scott, M. Gladys. "Competition for Women in American Colleges and Universities." *Research Quarterly* 16 (March 1945): 49–71.

Sefton, Alice Allene. *The Women's Division, National Amateur Athletic Federation.* Stanford, Calif.: Stanford University Press, 1941.

"Semenya Withdraws from Event amid Firestorm of Anger." *Sports Illustrated,* September 11, 2009. http://sportsillustrated.cnn.com.

Seymour, Miranda. *Bugatti Queen: In Search of a French Racing Legend.* New York: Random House, 2004.

Sharp, David. "The Women Who Took the Jounce Out of Jogging." *Health,* September 1994, 25.

Sharp, N. C. Craig. "The Human Genome and Sport, Including Epigenetics and Athleticogenomics: A Brief Look at a Rapidly Changing Field." *Journal of Sports Science* 10 (2008): 1–7.

Shepard, Alexandra, and Garthine Walker. "Gender, Change, and Periodisation." Special issue, *Gender and History* 20, no. 3 (2008).

Sherrow, Victoria. *The Encyclopedia of Hair: A Cultural History.* Westport, Conn.: Greenwood Press, 2006.

Shields, Brenda J., and Gary A. Smith. "Cheerleading-Related Injuries in the United States: A Prospective Surveillance Study." *Journal of Athletic Training* 44 (2009): 567–77.

———. "Cheerleading-Related Injuries to Children 5 to 18 Years of Age: United States, 1990–2002." *Pediatrics* 17 (2006): 122–29.

Showalter, Elaine, and English Showalter. "Victorian Women and Menstruation." *Victorian Studies* 14 (1970): 83–91.

Shugart, Helene A. "She Shoots, She Scores: Mediated Constructions of Contemporary Female Athletes in Coverage of the 1999 US Women's Soccer Team." *Western Journal of Communication* 67 (2003): 1–31.

Shuttle, Penelope, and Peter Redgrove. *The Wise Wound: Menstruation and Everywoman.* New York: Richard Marek, 1978.

Simon, Diane. *Hair: Public, Political, and Extremely Personal.* New York: St. Martin's Press, 2000.

Simpson, Joe Leigh. "Gender Testing in the Olympics." *Journal of the American Medical Association* 236 (1986).

Simpson, Joe Leigh, Arne Ljunqvist, and Malcolm A. Ferguson-Smith. "Gender Verification in Competitive Sports." *Sports Medicine* 16 (1993): 305–15.

Sims, Sally. "The Bicycle, the Bloomer, and Dress Reform in the 1890s." In *Dress and Popular Culture,* edited by Patricia A. Cunningham and Susan Voso Lab, 125–45. Bowling Green, Ohio: Bowling Green State University Popular Press, 1991.

Singleton, J. Milton, and Herbert F. Vanorden. "Cheerleading-Related Injuries in the United State: A Prospective Surveillance Study." *Journal of Athletic Training* 44 (2009): 567–77.

———. "Vaginal Tampons in Menstrual Hygiene." *Western Journal of Surgery, Obstetrics, and Gynecology* 51 (1943): 146–52.

Skarda, Erin. "Top 10 Sports-Fashion Controversies." *Time,* September 1, 2011. http://www .time.com/time/specials/packages/article/0,28804,2091186_2091153_2091164,00.html.

Skirstad, Berit. "Gender Verification in Competitive Sport: Turning from Research to Action." In *Values in Sport: Elitism, Nationalism, Gender Equality, and the Scientific Manufacture of Winners,* edited by Torbjörn Tännsjö and Claudio Tamburrini, 116–22. London: E and FN Spon, 2000.

Sklorman, Sheryl. "Girl Athletes, Citizen Activists, Title IX: The Three Point Play." *High School Journal* 64 (1981): 326–30.

Slocum, Henry W. "Lawn Tennis as a Game for Women." *Outing,* July 1889, 289–300.

Sloop, John M. "'This Is Not Natural': Caster Semenya's Gender Threats." *Critical Studies in Media Communication* 29 (2012): 81–96.

Smart, Mollie, and Russell Smart. "Menstrual Education." *Marriage and Family Living* 21 (May 1959): 177–79.

Smith, Hope. "The First National Institute on Girls Sports." *Journal of Health, Physical Education, Recreation* 35 (1964): 32.

Smith, Maureen, and Alison Wrynn. *Women in the 2012 Olympic and Paralympic Games: An Analysis of Participation and Leadership Opportunities.* Ann Arbor, Mich.: SHARP Center for Women and Girls, 2013.

Smith, Robert A. *A Social History of the Bicycle.* New York: American Heritage Press, 1972.

Smith, Ronald A. "Women's Control of American College Sport: The Good of Those Who Played or an Exploitation by Those Who Controlled?" *Sport History Review* 29 (1998): 103–20.

Somers, Florence A. *Principles of Women's Athletics.* New York: A. S. Barnes, 1939.

Sorensen, Jacki, with Bill Bruns. *Aerobic Dancing.* New York: Rawson, Wade, 1979.

Spector, Robert. *Shared Values: A History of Kimberly-Clark.* Lyme, Conn.: Greenwich, 1997.

Spencer, Nancy E., and Lisa R. McClung. "Women and Sport in the 1990s: Reflections on 'Embracing Stars, Ignoring Players.'" *Journal of Sport Management* 15 (2001): 318–49.

"Sport: All-America." *Time,* December 11, 1939. http://www.time.com/time/magazine/article/0,9171,763027,00.html.

"Sport: Women's Tennis." *Time,* August 31, 1925. http://www.time.com/time/magazine/article/0,9171,720931,00.html#ixzz1UCRZREpk.

Stafford, James. "The Cylindrical Vaginal Pessary-Tampon versus Other Pessaries." *Medical Record* 41 (April 1892): 482–84.

Stanley, Gregory Kent. *The Rise and Fall of the Sportswoman: Women's Health, Fitness, and Athletics, 1860–1940.* New York: Peter Lang, 1996.

Starey, Alfred B. "Lawn-Tennis in America." *Outing,* September 1883, 463–68.

Starr, Cathy, Donna Branson, Randa Shehab, Cheryl Farr, Shiretta Ownbey, and Jane Swinney. "Biomechanical Analysis of a Prototype Sports Bra." *Journal of Textile and Apparel, Technology and Management* 4 (2005): 1–14.

Starr, Mark, Martha Brant, and Sam Register. "It Went Down to the Wire . . . and Thrilled Us All." *Newsweek,* July 19, 1999, 46.

Staurowsky, Ellen J., Mary Jane DeSousa, Gaele Ducher, Noah Genter, Kathleen E. Miller, Sohalia Shakib, Nancy Theberge, and Nancy Williams. *Her Life Depends on It II: Sport, Physical Activity, and the Health and Well-Being of American Girls and Women.* East Meadow, N.Y.: Women's Sports Foundation, 2009.

Steinbach, Paul. "Stunted Growth." *Athletic Business,* November 2009. http://athleticbusiness.com/articles/article.aspx?articleid=2817andzoneid=8.

Stephenson, Joan. "Female Olympians' Sex Tests Outmoded." *Journal of the American Medical Association* 276 (1996).

Steptoe, Sonja "The Pom-Pom Chronicles." *Sports Illustrated,* January 6, 1992, 40–46.

Stewart, Harry. "Track Athletics for Women." *American Physical Education Review* 27 (May 1922): 207.

Suggs, Welch. "Left Behind." *Chronicle of Higher Education,* November 30, 2001.

———. *A Place on the Team: The Triumph and Tragedy of Title IX.* Princeton, N.J.: Princeton University Press, 2005.

Sullivan, Rebecca. "Goodbye Heroin Chic. Now It's Sexy to Be Strong." *Time,* July 19, 1999, 62.

Sutton, May G. "Women and Dress." *Harper's Bazaar,* May 1910, 327.

Sykes, Heather. "Transsexual and Transgender Policies in Sport." *Women in Sport and Physical Activity Journal* 15 (2006): 3–13.

Tarantin, Elaine. "Aerobics Competition Yesterday, Tomorrow, and Today." *IDEA Today* (July–August 1992): 49.

Tarrant, Shira. *When Sex Became Gender.* London: Routledge, 2006.

Taylor, Matthew, and Greg M. Turek. "If Only She Would Play? The Impact of Sports Participation on Self-Esteem, School Adjustment, and Substance Use among Rural and Urban African American Girls." *Journal of Sport Behavior* 33, no. 3 (2010): 315–36.

Teetzel, Sarah. "Equality, Equity, and Inclusion: Issues in Women and Transgendered Athletes' Participation at the Olympics." In *Cultural Imperialism in Action: Critiques in the Global Olympic Trust; Eighth International Symposium for Olympic Research,* edited by Kevin B. Wamsley and Gordon H. MacDonald, 331–38. London, Ontario: International Centre for Olympic Studies, 2006.

Temple, Ed, with B'Lou Carter. *Only the Pure in Heart Survive.* Nashville: Broadman Press, 1980.

"Tennis Hits Beauty High at Wimbledon." *Life,* July 24, 1929.

Thaxton, Nolan A. "A Documentary Analysis of Competitive Track and Field for Women at Tuskegee Institute and Tennessee State University." Ph.D. diss., Springfield College, 1970.

Theberge, Nancy. "Sport and Women's Empowerment." *Women's Studies International Forum* 14 (1987): 387–93.

———. "Women's Athletics and the Myth of Female Frailty." In *Women: A Feminist Perspective,* edited by Jo Freeman, 389–402. Mountain View, Calif.: Mayfield, 1989.

Theriot, Nancy. "Towards a New Sporting Ideal: The Women's Division of the National Amateur Athletic Federation." *Frontiers* 3 (1978): 1–7.

"Things Seen and Heard." *Sportsman* 20 (October 1936): 18.

"This Is What You Thought about . . . Women and Sports." *Glamour,* May 1980, 33.

Thornton, Madeline J. "The Use of Vaginal Tampons for the Absorption of Menstrual Discharges." *American Journal of Obstetrics and Gynecology* 46 (1943): 510–22.

Thwing, Grace. "Swimming during the Menstrual Period." *Journal of Health and Physical Education* 14 (1943): 154.

Tinling, Teddy. *The Story of Women's Tennis Fashion.* London: Wimbledon Lawn Tennis Museum, 1977.

———. *Tingling: Sixty Years in Tennis.* London: Sidgwich and Jackson, 1983.

Tinling, Teddy, as told to Robert Oxby. *White Ladies.* London: Stanley Paul, 1963.

"Tinling's Tutus for Tennis." *Sports Illustrated,* July 11, 1955. http://sportsillustrated.cnn.com/vault/article/magazine/MAG1129924/index.htm.

"To Be the Best." *Time,* September 19, 1988.

Todd, Terry. "Anabolic Steroids: The Gremlins of Sport." *Journal of Sport History* 14 (1987): 87–107.

Torbjörn Tännsjö, and Claudio Tamburrini, eds. *Values in Sport: Elitism, Nationalism, Gender Equality, and the Scientific Manufacture of Winners.* London: E and FN Spon, 2000.

Torgovnick, Kate. *Cheer! Inside the Secret World of College Cheerleaders.* New York: Touchstone, 2008.

Tortora, Phyllis G., and Keith Eubank. *Survey of Historic Costume.* 3rd ed. New York: Fairchild, 1998.

Trescott, Martha Moore, ed. *Dynamos and Virgins Revisited: Women and Technological Change in History.* Metuchen, N.J.: Scarecrow Press, 1979.

Tresniowski, Alex. "Soccer's Happiest Feat." *People,* July 26, 1999, 56.

Trilling, Blanche M. "The Playtime of a Million Girls or an Olympic Victory—Which?" *Nation's Schools* (August 1929): 51–54.

———. "Safeguarding Girls' Athletics." In *Women and Athletics,* edited by the Women's Division, National Amateur Athletic Federation, 11–12. New York: A. S. Barnes, 1930.

Troy, Gil. *Morning in America: How Ronald Reagan Invented the 1980s.* Princeton, N.J.: Princeton University Press, 2005.

Tuggle, C. A., and Anne Owen. "A Descriptive Analysis of NBC's Coverage of the Centennial Olympics: The 'Games of the Women'?" *Journal of Sport and Social Issues* 23 (1999): 171–82.

Tuggle, C. A., Suzanne Huffman, and Dana Rosengard. "A Descriptive Analysis of NBC's Coverage of the 2004 Summer Olympics." *Journal of Sports Media* 2 (2007): 53–75.

Tunis, John R. "Pour le Sport: How Tennis Helped the Modern Diana." *Harper's Bazaar,* July 1929, 113.

———. "Women and the Sports Business." *Harper's Monthly Magazine,* July 1929, 211–21.

Tuttle, Jane P. "Setting the Mark: Lucile Godbold and the First International Track Meet for Women." *South Carolina Historical Magazine* 102 (2001): 135–52.

Twin, Stephanie L. *Out of the Bleachers: Writings on Women and Sport.* Old Westbury, N.Y.: Feminist Press, 1979.

"Two Cheers." *Athletic Management,* June–July 2001. http://www.athleticmanagement.com/ 2011/05/26/two_cheers/index.php.

Uhlir, G. Ann. "Athletics and the University: The Post-Woman's Era." *Academe* 73 (1987): 25–29.

———. "Women's Sports Education Today." *Educational Digest* (April 1983): 32–35.

Underwood, John. "An Odd Way to Even Things Up." *Sports Illustrated,* February 5, 1979. http://sportsillustrated.cnn.com/vault/article/magazine/MAG1094580/index.htm.

United States Lawn Tennis Association. *Official Encyclopedia of Tennis.* New York: Harper and Row, 1972.

UN Women. "UN Women Signs Partnership Agreement with the International Olympic Committee to Advance Gender Equity." August 23, 2012. http://www.unwomen .org/2012/08/un-women-signs-partnership-agreement-with-the-international-olympic -committee-to-advance-gender-equality/.

U.S. Commission on Civil Rights. "More Hurdles to Clear: Women and Girls in Competitive Athletics." *Clearinghouse Publication,* no. 63 (July 1980).

Verbrugge, Martha H. "Gym Periods and Monthly Periods: Concepts of Menstruation in American Physical Education, 1900–1940." In *Body Talk: Rhetoric, Technology, Reproduction,* edited by Mary M. Lay, Laura J. Gurak, Clare Gravon, and Cynthia Myntti, 67–97. Madison: University of Wisconsin Press, 2000.

———. "Recreating the Body: Women's Physical Education and the Science of Sex Differences in America, 1900–1940." *Bulletin of the History of Medicine* 71 (1997): 273–304.

Vernier, Elmon L., and Phebe M. Scott. "Secondary School Athletic Programs: Detrimental or Developmental?" *Theory into Practice* 3 (1964): 98–104.

Vertinsky, Patricia. *The Eternally Wounded Woman: Women, Doctors, and Exercise in the Late Nineteenth Century.* Urbana: University of Illinois Press, 1994.

———. "Exercise, Physical Capability, and the Eternally Wounded Woman." *Journal of Sport History* 14 (1987): 7–27.

———. "Gender Relations, Women's History, and Sport History: A Decade of Changing Enquiry, 1983–1993." *Journal of Sport History* 21 (1994): 1–24.

Vignetti, P., A. Rizzuit, L. Bruni, M. C. Tozzie, P. Martcozzi, and L. Tarani. "'Sex Passport' Obligation for Female Athletes: Consideration and Criticism on 364 Subjects." *International Journal of Sports Medicine* 17 (1996): 239–40.

Vines, Gail. "Last Olympics for the Sex Test?" *New Scientist* 135 (1992): 39–41.

Vostral, Sharra L. *Under Wraps: A History of Menstrual Hygiene Technology.* Lanham, Md.: Rowman and Littlefield, 2008.

Wackwitz, Laura A. "Sex Testing in International Women's Athletics: A History of Silence." *Women in Sport and Physical Activity Journal* 5 (1996): 51–68.

———. "Verifying the Myth: Olympic Sex Testing and the Category of 'Woman.'" *Women's Studies International Forum* 26 (2009): 553–60.

Wade, Virginia, with Jean Rafferty. *Ladies of the Court: A Century of Women at Wimbledon.* New York: Atheneum, 1984.

Wakefield, Wanda Ellen. "Out in the Cold: Sliding Sports and the Amateur Sports Act of 1978." *International Journal of the History of Sport* 6 (2007): 776–95.

Walker, Marisa. "Great Dates in Cheer." *American Cheerleader,* February 2005, 42.

Walker, Nancy A. *Shaping Our Mothers' World: American Women's Magazines.* Jackson: University Press of Mississippi, 2000.

Wann, Daniel L., Michael P. Schrader, Julie A. Allison, and Kimberly K. McGeorge. "The Inequitable Newspaper Coverage of Men's and Women's Athletics at Small, Medium, and Large Universities." *Journal of Sport and Social Issues* 22 (1998): 79–87.

Warner, Patricia Campbell. "The Americanization of Fashion: Sportswear, the Movies, and the 1930s." In *Twentieth-Century American Fashion,* edited by Linda Welters and Patricia A. Cunningham, 79–98. New York: Berg, 2004.

———. "Clothing as Barrier: American Women in the Olympics, 1900–1920." *Dress* 24 (1997): 55–68.

———. *When the Girls Came Out to Play: The Birth of American Sportswear.* Amherst: University of Massachusetts Press, 2006.

Wass, Ann Buermann, and Clarita Anderson. "What Did Women Wear to Run?" *Dress* 17 (1990): 169–84.

Wayman, Agnes R. "Competition." *American Physical Education Review* 34 (1929): 469.

———. "Women's Athletics—All Uses—No Abuses." *American Physical Education Review* 29 (1924): 517–19.

Webster, Frederick Annesley Michael. *Athletics of To-Day for Women.* London: Frederick Warne, 1930.

Weitz, Rose. *Rapunzel's Daughters: What Women's Hair Tells Us about Women's Lives.* New York: Farrar, Straus, and Giroux, 2004.

Welch, Paula D. *History of American Physical Education and Sport.* Springfield, Ill.: Charles C. Thomas, 1981.

———. "Interscholastic Basketball: Bane of College Physical Educators." In *Her Story in Sport: A Historical Anthology of Women in Sports,* edited by Reet Howell, 424–31. West Point, N.Y.: Leisure Press, 1982.

Welch, Paula D., and D. Margaret Costa. "A Century of Olympic Competition." In *Women and Sport: Interdisciplinary Perspectives,* edited by D. Margaret Costa and Sharon R. Guthrie, 123–38. Champaign, Ill.: Human Kinetics, 1994.

Wells, Christine L. *Women, Sport, and Performance: A Physiological Perspective.* Champaign, Ill.: Human Kinetics, 1985.

Wells, Katherine F. "Overcoming Periodic Pain." *Parents* (February 1939): 26, 48, 52.

Wenner, Lawrence A., ed. *MediaSport.* London: Routledge, 1998.

Wertheim, Jon. *Venus Envy: A Sensational Season Inside the Women's Tennis Tour.* New York: HarperCollins, 2001.

Westmann, Stephen K. *Sport, Physical Education, and Womanhood.* Baltimore: Williams and Wilkins, 1939.

"What a Kick!" *Time,* July 19, 1999.

White, Christine. "Extramural Competition and Physical Education Activities for College Women." *Research Quarterly for Exercise and Sport* 25 (1954): 244–63.

"Why Aren't These Bodies Perfect?" *Mademoiselle,* August 1984, 218–21.

"Why Can't We Beat This Girl." *Sports Illustrated,* September 30, 1963. http://sports illustrated.cnn.com/vault/article/magazine/MAG1075207/index.htm.

Widenius, Irja Elizabeth. "A Study of Commercially Manufactured Catamenial Tampons." *American Journal of Obstetrics and Gynecology* 48 (1944): 510–22.

Wiederkehr, Stefan. "'We Shall Never Know the Exact Number of Men Who Have Competed in the Olympics Posing as Women': Sport, Gender Verification, and the Cold War." *International Journal of the History of Sport* 26 (2009): 556–72.

Wiggins, David K., ed. *Out of the Shadows: A Biographical History of African American Athletes.* Fayetteville: University of Arkansas Press, 2006.

Willett, C., and Phillis Cunnington. *The History of Underclothes.* New York: Dover, 1992.

Williams, Phil. "Great War Nurses Discovered a Girl's Best Friend." *Birmingham Post,* February 8, 2002, 22.

Willis, Susan. "Work(ing) Out." *Cultural Studies* 4 (1990): 1–18.

Wills, Gary. *Reagan's America: Innocents at Home.* New York: Doubleday, 1987.

Wills, Helen. "Emancipated Legs Mean Better Sports." *Ladies' Home Journal,* April 1927, 33.

——. *Tennis.* New York: Charles Scribner's Sons, 1928.

Wilson, Amy. *The Status of Women in Intercollegiate Athletics.* NCAA, 2012. http://ncaa-publications.com/.

"Winter Wonders." *Time,* February 15, 1988.

Wolf, Naomi. *The Beauty Myth: How Images of Beauty Are Used against Women.* New York: Doubleday, 1991.

Wolff, Alexander, and Christian Stone. "She Said, He Said." *Sports Illustrated,* May 22, 1995, 16.

"Women in Uniform." *Time,* November 23, 1998, 39.

Women's Division, National Amateur Athletic Federation. *Women and Athletics.* New York: A. S. Barnes, 1930.

Wughalter, Emily. "Ruffles and Flounces: The Apologetic in Women's Sports." *Frontiers: A Journal of Women Studies* 3 (1978): 11–13.

Wushanley, Ying. *Playing Nice and Losing: The Struggle for Control of Women's Intercollegiate Athletics, 1960–2000.* Syracuse, N.Y.: Syracuse University Press, 2004.

Wyrick, Waneen. "Physical Performance." In *The American Woman in Sport,* edited by Ellen W. Gerber, Jan Felshin, Pearl Berlin, and Waneen Wyric, 403–84. Reading, Mass.: Addison-Wesley, 1974.

Xavier, Neena A., and Janet B. McGill. "Hyperandrogenism and Intersex Controversies in Women's Olympics." *Journal of Clinical Endocrinology and Metabolism* 97, no. 11 (2012): 3902–7.

Yalom, Marilyn. *A History of the Breast.* New York: Random House, 1997.

Young, David C. *The Modern Olympic Games: A Struggle for Revival.* Baltimore: Johns Hopkins University Press, 1996.

Young, Iris Marion. "Breasted Experience: The Look and the Feeling." In *The Politics of Women's Bodies,* edited by Rose Weitz, 125–36. New York: Oxford University Press, 1998.
———. *Throwing Like a Girl, and Other Essays in Feminist Philosophy and Social Theory.* Bloomington: Indiana University Press, 1990.
Zaccaro, John. "40 Years Later, the Larger Meaning of Title IX." Fox News, June 23, 2012. http://www.foxnews.com/opinion/2012/06/23/40-years-later-larger-meaning-title-ix/#ixzz23AyyWeXY.
Zeveloff, Julie. "Hair over Health: For Many Black Women, Style Trumps Exercise." Columbia News Service, April 1, 2008. http://jscms.jrn.columbia.edu/cns/2008-04-01/zeveloff-obesityhairdo.html.
Zimmer, Judith. "Toy Makers Putting Muscle behind Kids' Fitness." *Adweek,* April 14, 1986.

Index

JAIME SCHULTZ is an assistant professor of kinesiolgy and women's studies at Penn State University.

Sport and Society

The University of Illinois Press
is a founding member of the
Association of American University Presses.

University of Illinois Press
1325 South Oak Street
Champaign, IL 61820-6903
www.press.uillinois.edu